PENGUIN BOOKS

COME TO THINK OF IT

Daniel Schorr is the last of Edward R. Murrow's legendary CBS team still fully active in journalism. He has won three Emmys, decorations from European heads of state, a Peabody Award for "a lifetime of uncompromising reporting of the highest integrity," awards from civil liberties groups, and the Alfred I. DuPont–Columbia University Golden Baton for "exceptional contributions to radio and television reporting and commentary," the most prestigious award in broadcasting. He is now a senior news analyst for National Public Radio. He lives in Washington, D.C.

DANIEL SCHORR

Come to Think of It

—⟨⟨⟨⟩⟩⟩—

Commentaries from National
Public Radio's Senior News Analyst

PENGUIN BOOKS

To my colleagues and friends at NPR, some of them a third my age, whose welcome established the climate that made this career possible.

I wish to acknowledge Janaya Williams, my NPR producer, without whose tireless efforts this book would not have come to be.

PENGUIN BOOKS
Published by the Penguin Group
Penguin Group (USA) Inc., 375 Hudson Street, New York, New York 10014, U.S.A.
Penguin Group (Canada), 90 Eglinton Avenue East, Suite 700, Toronto, Ontario, Canada M4P 2Y3
(a division of Pearson Penguin Canada Inc.) • Penguin Books Ltd, 80 Strand, London WC2R 0RL,
England • Penguin Ireland, 25 St Stephen's Green, Dublin 2, Ireland (a division of Penguin Books
Ltd) • Penguin Group (Australia), 250 Camberwell Road, Camberwell, Victoria 3124, Australia
(a division of Pearson Australia Group Pty Ltd) • Penguin Books India Pvt Ltd, 11 Community
Centre, Panchsheel Park, New Delhi – 110 017, India • Penguin Group (NZ), 67 Apollo Drive,
Rosedale, North Shore 0632, New Zealand (a division of Pearson New Zealand Ltd) • Penguin
Books (South Africa) (Pty) Ltd, 24 Sturdee Avenue, Rosebank, Johannesburg 2196, South Africa

Penguin Books Ltd, Registered Offices: 80 Strand, London WC2R 0RL, England

First published in the United States of America by Viking Penguin,
a member of Penguin Group (USA) Inc. 2007
Published in Penguin Books 2008

10 9 8 7 6 5 4 3 2 1

THE LIBRARY OF CONGRESS HAS CATALOGED THE HARDCOVER EDITION AS FOLLOWS:
Schorr, Daniel, 1916–
Come to think of it : notes on the end of the millennium / Daniel Schorr.
p.   cm.
Includes index.
ISBN 978-0-670-01873-4 (hc.) • ISBN 978-0-14-311447-5 (pbk.)
1. United States—Politics and government—1989–
2. United States—Foreign relations—1989–   I. Title.
E839.5.S336 2008   973.928—dc22   2007038082

Printed in the United States of America
Designed by Carla Bolte • Set in Granjon

Contents

Introduction

Let me explain how this book came to be in the twilight of a journalistic career stretching over some seventy years. Or perhaps I should say "careers," as I learned to adapt myself to one medium after another.

In the beginning was the newspaper. In the years after World War II, I reported from Europe for the *Christian Science Monitor,* the *New York Times,* and the London *Daily Mail.*

In the 1930s radio began to purvey news, something that was resisted at first by the newspapers, fearing competition. Eventually the Associated Press, owned by America's newspapers, agreed to furnish radio stations with five-minute newscasts in return for their agreement not to develop their own news-gathering organizations.

That could not last, and as war approached, it didn't. I did my first radio broadcast on ABC in 1948, reporting from Amsterdam on the first meeting of European notables after the war. I can still remember trying to make myself heard over a squawky shortwave signal. Winston Churchill delivered a historic speech about uniting the wartime enemies in a European council. Hard to remember, but there was no tape recording.

Television was in its infancy. I had seen the first demonstration of this experimental medium at the 1939 New York World's Fair. I had no inkling of how this interesting toy would come to dominate the news business.

And I hardly knew what Edward R. Murrow had in mind when he offered me a job with CBS News, reporting from Washington, at first for radio, but soon for television.

I had joined CBS just in time to become involved in coverage of the hearings of the red-baiting senator Joe McCarthy. But it began to become clear that a reporter's words were peripheral to the drama of the live event. ABC found that the hearings attracted more viewers than its afternoon soap operas.

In 1973, television came to dominate the hearings of the Senate Watergate Committee. From outside the hearing room, I did commentary on what was happening inside. But nothing I said could match the drama of former White House counsel John Dean telling how he had warned President Nixon of a "cancer on the presidency." Not even my discovery, while I was on the air, that my name appeared on a list of White House "enemies."

Each new development in communications technology seemed to accentuate the drama of the medium and diminish the role of purveyor of information. During the five years I worked for CNN, having been Ted Turner's first editorial employee, I learned how the camera had come to take precedence over the reporter. The key word in cable television has become the word "live."

That does not mean that we are starved for verbal information. Indeed, we are deluged with information, served up to us in myriad new ways. In this era of the Internet, everyone can be a reporter, an editor, a publisher. Every blogger seems to have an audience. I found it amazing when Internet rumormonger Matt Drudge served up some gossip about President Clinton's having an affair with a White House intern, and pretty soon the president was on the road to impeachment.

On myriad Web sites, people can post comments and upload pictures. Jeffrey Cole, director of the Center for the Digital Future at the University of Southern California, says, "Traditional media informed people but didn't empower them."

New media phenomena like Google and Yahoo provide amazingly swift means of acquiring information. The Gannett newspapers are experimenting with something called citizen journalism, permitting readers to discuss stories online with reporters. In current events classes, a survey indicates, there is a growing tendency to use Internet-based news rather than print or television news.

In some cases the mobile phone has begun to replace the computer as a means of communication. A Pew Research Center poll indicates that one-third of bloggers consider themselves as engaged in some form of journalism. A national survey by the Joan Shorenstein Center on the Press, Politics and Public Policy, at Harvard's John F. Kennedy School of Government, found Americans estranged from the daily newspaper and relying more heavily on television. Twenty-eight percent of teens pay almost no attention to daily news. (Full disclosure—I am an advisory board member of the Shorenstein Center.)

So why this book? Stay tuned. This has to do with my sense that we threaten to be overwhelmed with information, and we frequently do not have the ability to understand what it means.

Until 1985 I had been mainly a dispenser of news in one or another medium. When I parted company with CNN and had no wish to retire, I decided that, in my next job, I would do less reporting and more analyzing—more thoughtful and less strenuous.

Providentially National Public Radio provided the answer. Robert Siegel, at the time the news director, offered me a position that would be called senior news analyst. This was the department of "What does it all mean?" Having traversed the world from Jakarta to Little Rock, I could now bring my experience to bear on trying to make tangled events understandable. My quest was for meaning.

It did not occur to me that my analyses might have some enduring value. For that I must thank the folks at Viking Penguin, who came up with the idea of assembling some of the transcripts into a book.

Apprehensively I looked at some of the scripts at random. Some I might write differently today; I'll let you decide which. I have also authorized the editors to deal with any errors of grammar and diction they may find. I see no point in perpetuating errors. Where time has proved one or another analysis to be wrong, that stays.

In retrospect, it appears to me that the seventeen years charted in those day-to-day and week-to-week essays also serve to chart the passage to a new era of history. The old era was dominated by the cold war, two great systems, capitalist and Communist, represented in two great countries, the United States and the Soviet Union, locked in what was called a nuclear stalemate. With the collapse of the Soviet system, the early years of a new millennium were shaped by a new kind of conflict with a radical Islam that defied national borders.

A short numerical expression—9/11—denoted a lethal assault on America. And 9/11 began the era of the suicide bomber, whose depredations left much of the Western world gasping. This was a new age of anxiety, whose frustration was measured in phrases like "weapons of mass destruction" and "homeland security."

But let me say in all candor that anxiety can be a news analyst's friend. I found people more ready to pause for reflection and seek some meaning in the jumble of events.

For me, a microphone and a typewriter (yes, a typewriter) became the tools of a new career. Radio liberated me from having to don makeup, read a teleprompter, and go out and stand in front of a camera. I could spend more time on content and less time on the mechanics of communicating. A computer. A telephone. C-SPAN and CNN kept me in touch with the world.

My longest trip of the day is a few hundred yards to a studio (one of them bears my name as a gift from NPR on my ninetieth birthday). In bad weather I can record from a microphone in my study at home.

NPR has afforded me a kind of journalism long on thinking and short on running around—for the senior citizen now called senior analyst.

Journalism has been called a first rough draft of history. I hope you have as much pleasure looking at the past this way as I had telling it to people on the radio.

1991

The Mideast Is a Mess and There Is No New World Order

A Look Back at 1990

DECEMBER 31, 1990

More improbable than what the imagination can conceive is what actually happened this year, and so let's change format from future shock to past shock and review some of the events of a wildly implausible 1990.

Millie's Book, reportedly dictated by a dog to the first lady of the land, tops the bestseller list way ahead of Nancy's book and Ronnie's book. President Reagan's public enemy number one, President Daniel Ortega, ends up not saying uncle to the Contras but embracing Violeta Chamorro, the upset winner in Nicaragua's free election, and saying to her, "You know I respect and love you."

David Souter, the mystery judge, is probed in a massive investigation of his background, which unearths the facts that he reads a lot and likes cottage cheese, but he is easily confirmed to the Supreme Court anyway. Strongman Manuel Noriega, whom the United States invaded Panama to bring to justice, a year later is running a telephone talkathon from his Miami jail cell, center of a First Amendment contest and nowhere near being tried.

The leader of the free world says that his mother made him eat broccoli and, being president of the United States now, he doesn't have to eat it anymore. A Northwest Airlines plane is forced down by a leaky toilet, and a space shuttle flight is almost aborted because of a malfunctioning urine-disposal system. The flag-burning controversy behind us, the hot issue for patriots is Roseanne Barr screeching "The Star Spangled Banner" on a baseball field and making unladylike gestures to her

I

detractors. An exhibition of Mapplethorpe photos that ties up Congress for a week and produces an obscenity trial in Cincinnati is still there when the shooting stops, except that the pictures have tripled in value and attracted some Japanese buyers.

And finally, President Bush, having let Saddam Hussein know that the United States has no interest in his territorial dispute with Kuwait, five months later is massing a force of a half million to tell him otherwise. Inconceivable—all inconceivable. And we haven't even gotten around yet to Gorbachev threatening to resign but staying, and Margaret Thatcher threatening to stay but resigning, or President Bush flip-flopping on taxes—"Read my lips"—and Milli Vanilli saying, "Read our lip sync." Historic probability no longer applies when the forces it copes with are reduced to theater of the absurd. Maybe the scientists in Pasadena had it right when they reported that the spacecraft *Galileo* orbiting our planet detected evidence of life, but not of intelligent life.

Bush Should Address Domestic Issues, Too

JANUARY 29, 1991

In another time of war, the State of the Union address might have stimulated a guns-versus-butter debate. But this time, the debate was over before it started. There was no war on poverty to be cut back, no substantial new domestic initiatives to be put on hold. There are mainly new ways of allocating existing funds, the rhetoric of empowerment of the poor, and reliance on private compassion called A Thousand Points of Light. Indeed, even the old phrases like "guns versus butter" and "belt-tightening" have a faintly archaic ring when we're talking about those often beltless as well as butterless. The buzzwords today are "underclass" and "homelessness." Once these were called home-front problems, important to address in time of war along with crime, drugs, crumbling bridges, and decaying cities. But the concept of wartime home front seems to be gone.

The Texas entrepreneur H. Ross Perot says, "We lunge at international problems, and we have stopped trying to resolve domestic issues. And yet," he says, "if you want to see rape, plunder, and pillage, you don't have to go to Kuwait, you can find them in New York, Detroit, and Chicago." In this neglected war, there may not be body bags, but there are body counts. Living under the government poverty line, which is less than $13,000 a year for a family of four, are some 31.5 million Americans, and the number is rising, and assistance is shrinking.

In a *New York Times* poll, 72 percent of those interviewed said the poverty problem is worse than it was ten years ago. Seventy-seven percent said President Bush's attempts to address the problem were negligible. The chances are they would have remained negligible even without a war. When asked before the war what is the Bush domestic agenda, Chief of Staff John Sununu said, "Not that much."

And so the war has probably not changed very much in terms of domestic agenda, but at least it gives us something else to talk about, and we don't have to debate the peace dividend anymore.

A New Can-Do Spirit Is Ready to Be Harnessed

MARCH 4, 1991

A current joke around Washington goes this way: The good news is that Saddam Hussein is captured and faces war crimes prosecution. The bad news is that jurisdiction is being given to the Senate Ethics Committee. That's a way of saying we don't get the glorious outcomes on the home front that the military delivers in the desert. But like it or not, the neglected domestic agenda now comes blinking into the sunlight as though emerging from an air-raid shelter.

President Bush, who says he has not yet quite tasted the euphoria of victory, will not be able to savor it very long. Democrats have an obvious interest in changing the subject from a triumphant war leader to an uncertain domestic leader, but in Republican councils, too, there is talk of outflanking the Democrats and using the president's immense popularity to launch an administration war against unresolved problems of poverty, environment, and infrastructure.

Indiana senator Richard Lugar says that his constituents think differently about the country than they did before the war, that there is a new can-do spirit waiting to be harnessed. One Republican leader close to President Bush who asked not to be quoted said that he could conceive of the president breaking through the budget deficit ceiling to propose a program of health insurance for 30 million needy Americans and new programs to repair roads and bridges.

This spirited America seeing itself anew may not last very long. Some conflicts are already emerging in their traditional partisan forms. Organized labor is ready to fight against an administration proposal for a North American Free Trade Agreement. Congressional liberals are ready to reopen the battle against the president's version of an anti-discrimination bill. But in these heady first days after victory, there does seem to be a new breeze blowing. An immensely popular president can use his prestige for almost anything he wants to do—a new world order, a new American order, whatever.

Israel May Disagree with Bush on Peace

MARCH 7, 1991

As important as the words President Bush used to sketch out his framework for Middle East peace were the words that never crossed his lips.

"Democracy"—the big D word—not mentioned once, and for good reason. The Middle East is not Eastern Europe, where supporting democracy means backing the good guys, like Lech Walesa and Václav Havel, against the Communist bad guys. In the Middle East, democracy can mean giving voice to Islamic fundamentalists, rocking the pillars of state, and, to reformers, challenging the feudal regimes, which are America's allies. In Kuwait, a democratic opposition leader has been shot and paralyzed, and the opposition charges that Sabah family loyalists are using violence and intimidation to crush a movement for democracy. So no D word in the president's speech last night.

"Soviet Union," missing in action from a speech that praised almost everybody associated with the great victory. Wasn't it only the other day the president was saying that post–cold war cooperation had made the United Nations coalition possible? And wasn't a Soviet-American partnership sealed in Malta and Helsinki supposed to undergird the new world order? Ah, yes, but that was before Gorbachev's freelance efforts to arrange a cease-fire for Saddam Hussein and other evidence that the Soviet Union has its own fish to fry in the Middle East, so "Soviet Union" gets dropped from the credits.

"Conference," as in international Middle East peace conference, the one President Bush said he would talk about once there was no longer linkage with Kuwait, sank from his speech without a trace. For one reason, see above, because the president is no longer so wild about giving the Soviets a role in Middle East diplomacy. For another reason, because more promising than a conference, to which Israel remains adamantly opposed, is the new two-track policy that Secretary of State James Baker is pushing on his trip in the region. This would involve synchronizing Israeli talks with its neighboring Arab states, which the Shamir government wants, and Israeli direct talks with the Palestinians, about which Yitzhak Shamir is less enthusiastic. International conference went thataway.

Interesting what a president doesn't say in the big victory speech and how much it tells us.

The Mideast Is a Mess and There Is No New World Order

MARCH 13, 1991

Standing militarily astride a region from the Gulf to the Mediterranean, America finds that in the wake of victory, old obstacles to a durable peace remain intractable and new ones have emerged. Suddenly democracy is a problem. The Bush administration, having fulfilled its pledge to restore the legitimate government of Kuwait, stands silent as that legitimacy is challenged by democratic forces. They are survivors of an occupation ordeal that the Sabah family did not share.

In Iraq, American troops look on from still-provisional cease-fire lines while Saddam Hussein's army proceeds to crush Shiite and Kurdish rebels whom an American president might once have hailed as freedom fighters. Learned debates go on inside the Bush administration about whether democracy for Iraq is really a good idea. It could mean upsetting the stability of rule by the minority Sunni Muslims and the military class on which Saddam Hussein's regime has rested.

On the Palestinian issue, Secretary Baker has made no perceptible progress in setting the stage for a two-track process. On one track, Israel would talk peace with Arab states, and on the other, self-determination with the Palestinians. Complicating the process is the fact that Jordan and the Palestine Liberation Organization, which were benched for backing the wrong side in the war, nevertheless want to get quickly back into the game. And perverse though Baker may find it, the West Bank

Palestinians are sticking with Yasser Arafat's leadership, and that makes it easier for the Shamir government to keep its heels dug in against concessions.

Things might have been worse in the Middle East without a war, but not much seems to be better. Smart ideas seem harder to come by than smart bombs. There is great frustration for a superpower, the superpower, in being able to win wars but not make peace in the Middle East.

Ethnic Tensions Worldwide

MAY 22, 1991

The question is not about the survival of democracy in India but about the survival of India.

Other countries have known waves of violence and assassination, including our own in the sixties. India's political institutions, though younger and less durable than ours, can probably weather the storm, bringing to an unexpectedly abrupt end the Nehru-Gandhi dynasty that was passing into history anyway. It is not India's government but India's society that is in crisis. India is threatened by an aggravated form of the ethnic, religious, caste conflicts that are sweeping large parts of the world from Iraq to Yugoslavia, from South Africa to Azerbaijan. These conflicts sometimes threatening to undermine the foundations of the nation-state in a reversion to primitive tribalism may take on different forms, but mostly they have one thing in common: passions that feed on privation and hatreds that are fueled by poverty. India is a country about ten times as crowded as America. As Barbara Crossette of the *New York Times* has observed, it is the world's largest producer of illiterates and child laborers. People without jobs, families, or futures become easy recruits for separatists, secessionists, and various hate movements. This is not the way things were supposed to be in what the founding fathers of Indian independence conceived as a model for the Third World of a progressive secular state.

I remember covering the visit of President Dwight Eisenhower to India in 1959.

With what pride Prime Minister Jawaharlal Nehru and his daughter Indira Gandhi told him of how India would overcome caste taboos and religious conflicts as it raised economic and educational standards. But in the stormy twilight of the Nehru-Gandhi era, a Hindu fundamentalist party has emerged for the first time, feeding on rage against minority religions, starting with Islam. Unable to control its population explosion, unable to distract its desperate people from reverting to religious and caste conflict, India can probably pull itself together to complete its tenth national election, but then what?

Winning the War in the Mideast Isn't Equal to Peace

JUNE 10, 1991

President Bush is reliably reported to be considering a move in the Middle East as bold in its way as war with Iraq and less likely to be celebrated with any early victory parade. It is to force the issue of a Palestinian peace conference by simply issuing invitations to Israel and the Arab states to meet face-to-face under his aegis, possibly joined by President Mikhail Gorbachev, in an effort to jump-start the peace process.

Sources say the president hinted at such a possibility in his recent letters to Israeli prime minister Shamir and to Arab leaders. He said that if agreement on procedure for a conference remained deadlocked, the alternative to letting the peace initiative die would be to take some unilateral action by assembling "a forum to break the taboos."

The replies from Shamir and the Arab leaders presenting apparently irreconcilable conflicts on the role of the United Nations, on the number of conference sessions, and the makeup of a Palestinian delegation have tended to confirm the administration's impression that advance agreement on procedure is impossible. And so attention is turning to the so-called unilateral invitation idea, which has been under study for several weeks.

In varying versions, it would be a Bush invitation to come to Washington or a Bush-Gorbachev invitation for a meeting in Cairo. September is being talked about as a possible date. Secretary of State Baker might return to the Middle East to prepare the parties for the public invitations.

It should be emphasized that President Bush has not decided whether to proceed with this high-risk venture, and the chances that he will are rated at no better than fifty-fifty.

On the one hand, he is keenly aware that winning a war in the Middle East is not the same as bringing peace to the Middle East and that he has not been able to deliver on his March 6 statement to Congress that the time has come to put an end to the Arab-Israeli conflict.

On the other hand, hard though it may be for Israeli and Arab leaders to reject a straight-out invitation from the president, he has no assurance at this point that they will all come and that if they do, the conference will not turn into a well-publicized fiasco.

And so the president is weighing the risks of making this leap into the unknown against the risks of giving up on peace in the Middle East. All that's known about the president's thinking at this point is that he's recognized the time has come to make that decision.

Yugoslav Tribal Hatred Threatens Europe

AUGUST 5, 1991

Patched together from the ruins of empires after World War I, Yugoslavia came apart in World War II. Serbs and Croats, divided by a common language and uncommon hostility, murdered each other by the thousands. Glued back together by Communist ideology and the force of Marshal Tito's personality, the federation now is breaking apart again in a paroxysm of ethnic passion. The most charismatic personality in Yugoslavia today is not a uniter, like Tito; he is a divider, the fiery Slobodan Milosevic, regional chief of the Serbian Communist Party. He rides a tiger of tribal hatred that he can probably no longer get off. That hatred, which has ancient and modern origins, has been fanned most recently by the decline of communism and a move toward a free market. Croatia and Slovenia, the most advanced republics, tried to jump off the sinking ship into Western Europe. The Serbs, with long-standing grievances about being exploited and left behind, exploded.

Now they demand control of 40 percent of Croatia where Serbs live, and a place in the sun on the Adriatic. Inward-looking, they reject pacification by the European Community. Ready to fight it out, they count on the support of the largely Serbian federal army. This is a prescription for disaster. Svieto Job, a seasoned Yugoslav diplomat who has just arrived here from Belgrade, calls it total irrationality.

The impending catastrophe of dismemberment frightens Europe:

first, with the prospect of a tide of refugees from civil war; then, with the possibility that neighboring countries linked to minorities in Yugoslavia may be drawn into the carving-up process; and finally, with the worry about what example may be set for other separatists elsewhere, from the Baltic states of the Soviet Union to the Basques of Spain.

If the breakup of multinational states is a phenomenon of the post–cold war world, it is one to which the outside world has yet to devise an answer other than good offices, appeals for sanity, and hand-wringing.

CIA Intelligence Should Be Unbiased

OCTOBER 1, 1991

When policy drives intelligence, the chances are that both will suffer.

Catering to the client—the president and his entourage—is not a new phenomenon in the CIA. The agency told Presidents Eisenhower and Kennedy what they wanted to hear about Cuba, ready to rise up against Castro, and the result was the 1961 Bay of Pigs fiasco. George Bush, as President Ford's CIA director, named an outside Team B of right-wingers to write a scarier assessment of the Soviet military potential than the intelligence analysts were willing to provide, and the result was more billions voted during the Carter and Reagan administrations to make some of the weapons that the Bush administration is now trying to dispose of.

But the harnessing of analysis to political and ideological design reached its peak during the Reagan administration. In William Casey, who shared the Reagan view of the Soviet Union as the source of all evil, the president had a man interested in action, not assessment, concerned with outcome, not process. And in Robert Gates, a protégé rapidly advanced over the heads of more senior professionals, Casey had a perfect instrument for reaching desired outcomes, the more perfect because Gates needed no instruction in hard-line anticommunism.

The advent of Gorbachev promised change in the Soviet Union, but there wasn't the slightest hint of that in the 1986 speech by Gates to the Commonwealth Club of California. In that speech, he described the battle lines drawn in a historic struggle against Soviet tyranny, and he said that might require covert operations and sometimes overt military forces. It would be interesting to see the more recent speech by Gates that Secretary of State Baker had suppressed.

It's unfortunate, in a way, for Gates that his confirmation hearings coincide with President Bush's initiative to dismantle the relics of the cold war, because his accusers are painting him in public hearings as one of those relics.

Mideast Peace Conference in Madrid

OCTOBER 21, 1991

Nine days to Madrid and counting. And the countdown to the Arab-Israeli peace conference is not likely to be tranquil. Israel is trading blows with guerrillas in Lebanon, and a meeting in Tehran of Islamic radicals opposed to the peace conference is making threats on the lives of Palestinians who plan to attend. A lot of people are crossing their fingers and holding their breath until October 30, when Presidents Bush and Gorbachev are scheduled to open a historic conclave of Arabs and Israelis that many thought would never happen. But then what? All indications point to a tunnel at the end of the light. The participants are coming to the table kicking, if not yet screaming, dragged there by Mr. Bush, the president of the world after the collapse of the Soviet Union and the president of the Middle East since the war with Iraq.

The atmosphere is totally unlike 1978, when the electrifying trip of Egyptian president Anwar Sadat to Jerusalem generated a surge of popular support on both sides for reconciliation, which was then sealed in the Camp David agreement. Now people on both sides look suspiciously at a conference cooked up by their leaders in long secret sessions, and governments emphasize and reemphasize the rigidity of their positions. Prime Minister Shamir says he'll go to Madrid because he sees no better alternative, and that kind of resignation seems to typify the mood before the meeting.

You can hear many variations on the theme of deadlock and walk-out. "Breakthrough to a dead end" is the way Tom Friedman of the *New York Times* describes the appearance of things. But perhaps it is a good thing that expectations are so low. Whatever pressures made the parties come will probably make them stay for a while rather than bear the onus of collapse and the wrath of America.

Secretary Baker presumably has some cards to play when the time comes for him to turn from presider to mediator. For now, it's enough to reflect that if the next nine days are successfully ridden out and the great conclave in Madrid actually happens, it will be a miracle. Peace in the Middle East would be a later and greater miracle.

American Voters Are in an Angry Mood

NOVEMBER 4, 1991

Perhaps Americans have seen too many photo opportunities and too few economic opportunities. Perhaps they perceive their officials as concentrating too much on perks and too little on work. A former Moscow correspondent is reminded of the Soviet Union years ago, where people habitually referred to the governing class as "they" in expressions like "They lie, and they will always lie." The government was "they," not "we."

The mood of the American voters—those who are still voters—appears to be apprehensive about personal and family futures and angry about the elected leaders they hold responsible for their anxiety. That anger may spill out in emotional ways. Polls indicate that three-quarters of the voters favor limiting the terms of state and federal officeholders. And that current is running strong in tomorrow's election in Washington State, even though it could mean retiring the popular House Speaker, Tom Foley, who's in a position to do much for his state. Connecticut and New Jersey are up in arms against their tax-raising governors, Lowell Weicker and Jim Florio, who aren't even running. David Duke and Senator Harris Wofford, who have in common only that they challenge the establishment, are fighting close races in Louisiana and Pennsylvania in campaigns of unbridled harshness. In Mississippi, businessman Kirk Fordice is gaining on incumbent Democratic governor Ray Mabus with criticism of deficit spending and what Fordice calls an "inordinate emphasis on education."

The *Washington Post,* which has done some nationwide, in-depth polling and interviewing, reports a tide of pessimism and crisis of confidence in government, only a third of Americans saying they trust their government to do what is right most of the time. American anger seems to work retroactively. On the day of the dedication of the Reagan

Library, the great communicator, the winner of landslides, was found to have been an average or below-average president by almost three-quarters of those polled by the *Los Angeles Times*. Asked with which ex-president they'd like to spend time, the largest number, 35 percent, said Jimmy Carter. Maybe Americans have come to understand about malaise.

The Soviet Union in Disarray

NOVEMBER 13, 1991

The boiling cauldron once called the USSR has taken on the surreal quality of a bad dream.

President Gorbachev's reported threat to resign—not again!—if he can't unite the republics in a treaty raises the question of what's left for him to resign from. Russian president Boris Yeltsin, the hero of the August 19 coup, is now criticized by Gorbachev for wanting to use force to rein in the Chechen-Ingush region, as Gorbachev tried to do in the Baltic states when he was in charge. And Gorbachev, the author of several false starts on economic reform, inferentially criticizes Yeltsin for encouraging hoarding by too-early talk of decontrolling prices.

This doesn't help to create coherence in policy, but it may help to sell books, which shows that Gorbachev has learned something about the free market, and so may his disclosures of how he brushed off President Bush's warning last June of a coup to unseat him. Now it's Gorbachev who's first off the mark with a warning of another coup attempt if economic conditions get worse. And they are getting worse, worse than a month ago, when Soviet representatives reported to the financial leaders of the West in Bangkok that Soviet GNP was running at minus 13 percent and retail prices were up 96 percent.

Now, as it gets colder, the shortages are greater and the lines are longer. And the latest opinion survey in the Soviet Union recalls the despair of a people who expect, by more than a two-thirds majority, conditions to get yet worse and, by a 55 percent majority, new outbreaks of ethnic strife. And there's no confidence in leadership to take them out of this abyss. The goodwill and the sense of fresh start generated by the aborted coup three months ago have been frittered away. Yeltsin, like Gorbachev before him, seems unable to settle on a cabinet or a policy, torn between reformers and get-tough advocates. Nor does it help that at this critical juncture, a postelection American Congress seems to be taking a harder look at aid to the Soviet Union and foreign aid generally.

When Gorbachev stumbled, there was Yeltsin, the popular hero. But already the question is being asked, "Now, after Yeltsin, who—or what?" And to that question nobody seems to have an answer.

Bush's Indecision Has an International Effect

NOVEMBER 25, 1991

After his undoubtedly worst week in office, President Bush is out in the country, bashing back at Congress and talking up domestic problems. He may, in time, recover politically from the disastrous series of snafus, from credit cards to civil rights. He may get his act and his actors together on dealing with the recession and health care. He has ordained that there'll be no more improvised remarks on the economy, whoever does the improvising. From now on, all statements with economic impact must be cleared with economic advisers—a radical innovation.

But the appearance of disarray that has columnists joking about a Soviet-style coup in the White House has its consequences. A price is paid at home and abroad when a president is perceived as irresolute, reactive, and worried about reelection.

Under these conditions, congressional Democrats seem a little more inclined to test whether the president, in spite of his threats, will really take the political risk of vetoing a death penalty anticrime bill or letting it be blocked by a Republican filibuster.

In the Middle East, Israel and the Arabs, speculating that the president cannot afford now the collapse of his peace initiative, are emboldened to delay replying to his RSVP on the next round of talks in Washington, and they probe the reaction to their new conditions.

The victorious war against Iraq, which was to be the reelection block-buster, has turned problematic. Shivering, homeless Kurds are back on television. Saddam Hussein lets children die while he stonewalls against UN-supervised relief. Saddam Hussein becomes a promising issue for Democrats. On television yesterday, Governor Mario Cuomo taunted Mr. Bush about the Iraqi dictator still in power, being photographed reviewing his troops. So now the *Washington Post* reports—and the

White House denies—that Mr. Bush has an interagency committee reviewing ideas for a more aggressive campaign to oust the Iraqi dictator. But no one denies that Saddam Hussein is a political problem for the administration as it nears 1992.

A weakened incumbent may be the Democrats' delight. But dangers to the country lie in what others may do to test that weakness and what the president may do to display his strength.

The Politics of Japan's Pearl Harbor Apology

DECEMBER 4, 1991

"Love," in the words of novelist Erich Segal, "means never having to say you're sorry." Since Japan and America don't love each other, a lot of energy is being expended on the question of who is sorry. Japan, its government has finally decided to say, is sorry about Pearl Harbor. America, says President Bush, the navy pilot who was shot down by the Japanese, is not sorry about Hiroshima, so there. Maybe it's just as well the president isn't going to Japan until after the Pearl Harbor anniversary, but this ritual of remembrance, with its "so sorry's" and "not so sorry's" may serve a purpose, helping to exorcise old grudges and put current competition into less angry perspective.

For, like it or not, America and Japan seem doomed to live with each other as joint leaders of a world being remade. American strategic interests are oriented to Japan, and Japanese interests are, well, occidented toward America. America depends on Japan to maintain the balance of power in Asia as Japan relies on America to maintain stability in Europe and the Middle East. Japan paid one-third of the costs of the Gulf War, and soon its military force, the fourth largest in the world, will be legally able to aid in United Nations peacekeeping efforts abroad.

Despite sharp trade disputes, the two countries, producing together 40 percent of the world's goods, need each other for markets and, in the case of America, for capital. There remains the unsolved cultural problem of the inscrutable East and the inscrutable West. But the Japanese nationalist Shintaro Ishihara, the author of the defiant bestseller *The Japan That Can Say No,* argues in the *Economist* under the headline "Forget Pearl Harbor," "Sounding a call for accommodation by blending Eastern and Western values, the two countries will lead the new global order." A companion article by Clyde Prestowitz, president of the Economic Strategic Institute, strikes a similar note, concluding that Japan and America "will have to recognize and live with their systemic differences."

Speaking of Pearl Harbor, President Bush says, "I'm over that." And I think most Americans are or should be over that; should be and maybe in time will be.

The State of Peace on Earth in 1991

DECEMBER 22, 1991

"This being Christmas season, why don't you write about how peace on Earth has been doing?" said the guy who runs this program, and I escaped before he thought to ask about "goodwill toward men."

Well, how has peace on Earth fared in 1991? You look at the year-end issue of *Life* magazine, page after page of wrenching pictures called "The Face of War": Desert Storm, the Yugoslav civil war. You're almost at the middle of the magazine before you reach "The Bright Side of 1991," portraits of Jodie Foster, but also of General Norman Schwarzkopf. And then "America's Cauldron of Anger," conflicts over money, sex, race, politics, and about Americans suffering from something called compassion fatigue.

But going beyond the picture magazine, you think about where there is more peace and where there is less peace than a year ago, and these are not always easy calls.

Central America—surely more peace. Sporadic fighting in Nicaragua, some Contras who laid down their arms say they didn't get land that was promised them, but as things go in today's world, mark that peace. Same with El Salvador, where UN secretary-general Javier Pérez de Cuéllar is spending the last ten days of his term trying to patch together an accord between the government and the FMLN rebels.

Cambodia—the great national reconciliation is having a rough going. Some survivors of genocide aren't quite ready to welcome back the Khmer Rouge leaders, but the fragile truce is holding. Mark Cambodia peace—in pencil.

Afghanistan—the proxy war between America and the Soviet Union is over; the civil war, not yet. Now a Russian vice president is trying to broker peace among rival mujahideen leaders. Peace is a maybe, no better than that.

Korea—that seemed to be heading for the peace side of the ledger when North and South reached a nonaggression pact, but North Korea balks at halting its nuclear weapons program or allowing inspection, although all American nuclear weapons have been pulled out of South Korea. Not war, but how can you say peace?

South Africa—communal warfare halted, black-white strife halted, and a national convention looks toward ending apartheid and the birth of an interracial democracy. One holds one's breath at what could be one of the brighter pages in peacemaking in a not-very-peaceful world.

The Middle East—where those words about peace originated—Iraq beaten back, but not down, and what may be peace for Kuwait is not peace for Iraq's Kurds and Shiites. And the Arab-Israeli peace conference? Chalk one up for peace at their meeting and wonder if they'll still be talking to each other this time next year.

Europe? In Yugoslavia, where thousands have been killed, some in grisly massacres, there is no prospect for peace although Cyrus Vance for the United Nations and Lord Carrington for the European Community keep trying.

And finally, the onetime USSR, now the Commonwealth of Independent States. No longer a global threat, but still a threat—and perhaps a nuclear threat—to itself. Call the Soviet collapse for now a step toward peace, and keep your fingers crossed.

Suddenly it strikes you that peace on Earth and goodwill toward men are indivisible. Without the latter, you're never really sure of the former.

The New Iron Curtain Democracies Are Not Like Ours

DECEMBER 30, 1991

Two years ago this time, the Berlin Wall had tumbled down, freedom was breaking out all over Eastern Europe, and at year's end, we celebrated the advance of democracy, our system. Two years later, although the evil empire itself lies in ruins, and elected leaders replace autocrats, we find ourselves more apprehensive than triumphant. At year's end, disconcertingly, the march of democracy creates less euphoria than dysphoria.

Russia's elected president, Yeltsin, has trouble finding common ground with Ukraine's elected Leonid Kravchuk and others in this patched-together commonwealth, all driven by nationalist imperatives. They cling to arms, mainly for protection against each other. They set up roadblocks and cling to scarce food and other resources. They feel that Yeltsin's plan to decontrol prices in Russia this week will suck in the produce from the other republics.

In Georgia, the elected president, Zviad Gamsakhurdia, who used democracy to introduce his own brand of tyranny, fights to hold on to power in a ruined parliament building. Sovereign Azerbaijan is on the march against the Armenians in Ngooro-Karabakh, and there is no longer any Soviet army to intervene.

In the former Yugoslavia, the elected Serbian president, Slobodan Milosevic, wars against Croatia. And in Algeria, the Arab world's first free election is bringing to power a party seeking to create an Iranian-style Islamic republic. The lesson of this year seems to be that democracy is not nirvana, and that democracy works only when it is accompanied by a sense of community. Too easily we assumed that since America's Founding Fathers left us with a "more perfect union," this would automatically happen wherever democracy was tried.

Perhaps the American experience left us insufficiently prepared for what happens when the breakup of autocracy releases long-festering ethnic hostilities, fueled by economic deprivation, manipulated by demagogues. Democracy doesn't flourish on insecurity and hatred. Perhaps there's a lesson there even for a democracy that has worked, all things considered, for a couple of hundred years.

1992

Enter Bill Clinton

Bush Campaigns in New Hampshire and Faces the Voters

JANUARY 15, 1992

In this winter of discontent, President Bush has the problem of redefining himself to a state which is painfully redefining itself.

Since the last presidential campaign, New Hampshire has gone from economically secure to insecure, from confident to scared. Its population has begun shrinking while its rolls of jobless, welfare, food stamps, and bankruptcies have been swelling. Five of its seven biggest banks, emblems of solidity, have closed.

New Hampshire—rugged, self-reliant—is not accustomed to privation. Some of its jitteriness spills over into anger, and some of that anger is directed at President Bush. Today Mr. Bush brought the message that he knows he has big problems but that he identifies with the people's concerns. However, voters in New Hampshire have trouble identifying with him. They're seeing their third Candidate Bush, and each one has been different.

In 1980, he played Republican moderate to Ronald Reagan's archconservative. He scoffed at voodoo economics and supported the *Roe v. Wade* decision legalizing abortion. The 1988 Bush played Reagan heir apparent to Robert Dole's pretender to the throne. The vice president favored banning abortion, he supported Reagan economics, and he promised no new taxes. That promise, as Patrick Buchanan delights to point out, President Bush broke.

And who is the 1992 Bush? He would've liked to present himself as the global leader, triumphant in cold war over the Communists and hot war over Saddam Hussein and ready to arm-wrestle Japan in the war for economic primacy.

But even if all these were more definitive triumphs than they have yet turned out to be, world leadership is not uppermost on New Hampshirites' minds. They are less concerned about America's global condition than with their own condition. And having seen two earlier George Bushes, they are skeptical of the blurry image of George III who attends orchestrated events and expresses what sounds like orchestrated empathy. New Hampshirites know who they are and they know the trouble they're in. They're not sure they know who George Bush really is, and some suspect that he may have no real core at all.

Clinton Handles Accusations—Can the United States?

JANUARY 27, 1992

Governor Clinton is trying to change the subject from adultery to adulthood, the maturity of Americans, and the responsibility of their news media.

Inferentially acknowledging some past infidelity that his marriage has dealt with and overcome, Clinton challenges voters to say whether he must expose his private life to public scrutiny or be disqualified from seeking the presidency. That's a tough question for a society that has inherited an element of puritanism in its public morality, not always reflected in private morality. Americans become retrospectively aware of extramarital affairs of past presidents, but they seem unwilling to accept, as Europeans generally do, that political leaders are offered and sometimes succumb to many temptations. Henry Kissinger has said, "Power is the ultimate aphrodisiac."

The voters' decision comes easily when character and judgment are also involved. One didn't have to invoke morality four years ago in order to condemn Gary Hart, a candidate who was conducting current escapades, lying about them, and betraying not only his family but the supporters who believed in him. That raised doubts about whether he was stable enough to be trusted with power.

There would also have been a problem with at least one infidelity of President Kennedy, had it been known at the time. He conducted an affair, at times in the White House, with a woman whom he shared with

Sam Giancana, a Chicago Mafia don, in the face of FBI warnings that he was opening himself to possible blackmail.

But what about some past involvement over and done with, not denied, having no known implication for ability to fulfill public responsibilities? Does Bill Clinton fairly ask whether the press should be playing the game of gotcha? And does Hillary Clinton fairly say that families in public life are still entitled to a zone of privacy? Or is the process of choosing leaders to be at the mercy of the relentless cycle of media exploitation working its way up from disreputable tabloid to the most reputable journal, stimulating curiosity, gossip, and titillation? The real question's about the maturity of American society.

The Gulf War May Be a Liability for the Bush Administration

MARCH 22, 1992

Coming out of a cabinet meeting last Thursday, President Bush was asked by reporters what he planned to do about Iraq. "Here is the Iraq man right here," he said, pointing to Secretary of Defense Dick Cheney, who shrugged and said nothing. A year ago, when Mr. Bush was celebrating victory in the Gulf War, he wouldn't have referred Iraq to anybody. That simple gesture with his thumb told volumes about what's happened in a year, how the triumph that was supposed to grease the way to a landslide reelection has turned into a puzzlement, a stalemate, and perhaps a political liability.

In the wake of military victory, leading an unprecedented coalition, America stood astride the Middle East as the only dominant force. Before Congress, on March 6, the president called for the creation of a new regional security structure for limits on the Middle East arms race and, at long last, resolving the Arab-Israeli conflict. A year later, the arms race is proceeding at full speed; Iran and Syria are arming to the teeth; efforts to bring the Gulf states, Syria, and Turkey into a regional security organization have collapsed; and Saudi Arabia is balking at the prepositioning of American weapons. Arab-Israeli peace talks are stalemated. Our relations with Israel are at a new low, and worst of all, defeated Iraq refuses to act defeated.

The colossal Reagan-Bush miscalculation that led to the American buildup of Iraq has become a continuing source of embarrassment with new revelations almost daily. The latest: a *New York Times* report that the Bush administration, in its ardent courtship of Saddam Hussein, hindered the Justice Department from investigating Iraq's role in a multibillion-dollar bank fraud scheme in Atlanta. And if the past is an embarrassment, the future is a menace.

After a war that was supposed to have removed any offensive threat, it's become clear that apart from chemical and biological weapons, Iraq has been conducting a nuclear weapons program on the order of the Manhattan Project, with some fifteen thousand atomic scientists and technicians still there. The covert operation against Saddam Hussein that President Bush was supposed to have authorized in November has obviously not worked yet. The talk of deadlines and early military action to knock out nuclear installations is being soft-pedaled. The White House is supposedly running into resistance to an air strike from General Colin Powell, the chairman of the Joint Chiefs of Staff. In the days when the president was sure of what he wanted to do, General Powell's reservations did not seem to matter so much.

For a president running for reelection with a lot of domestic negatives, nothing is potentially as positive as putting on the old hat of commander in chief, but nothing is potentially as negative as a military operation that fails. That was the lesson of Desert One, President Carter's abortive effort to rescue the hostages in the embassy in Tehran, and that is a lesson that Mr. Bush may be recalling when he jerks his thumb, points to Dick Cheney, and says, "Here is the Iraq man right here."

The Federal Government Is a Mess, but What Else Is New?

MARCH 30, 1992

The sky is falling; whence cometh our salvation? The House, chasing its tail, and maybe its Speaker, is in a state of wild confusion. The Senate is going into a state of wild confession. The respected Warren Rudman, bowing out amid much general wailing, says the legislators have lied. Well, maybe not lied but not told the whole truth about the awful deficit and what it will take to fix it—namely, limit entitlement programs.

The equally respected John Danforth, not bowing out, says, "We have bankrupted America and given our children a legacy of bankruptcy. We have defrauded the country to get ourselves elected." Strong stuff, and it's apparently no better in the executive branch of the government, which seems to be decomposing before our eyes.

A Republican who has served ten years at a subcabinet level in the Reagan and Bush administrations writes in the *New York Times,* anonymously for fear of reprisal, that the federal structure is a sham led by "the recreation president." The tormented mole lets it all hang out about the risk-averse, in-box mentality in government, the somnolent agencies displaying posters, exhorting to total equality. The sabotaging of statutory mandates, the sense that nothing is to be accomplished except the creation of good feelings and the illusion of action, with no federal agency moving except when political reaction makes it necessary.

"And in today's Washington," this bureaucrat says, "matters affecting the current and future well-being of Americans are seen only as nettlesome disruptions that must be calmed, not problems that must be solved or responsibilities that must be faced."

So what else is new? That about describes the way Americans have increasingly been seeing their government. New only is this belated display of remorse and self-flagellation. But what do Americans do about public servants who seem to be saying "Stop me before I kill again"? This may be a good time to remember that government paralysis and dismantlement seemed a good idea at one time. Americans seemed happy to support candidates from Jimmy Carter on, and especially Ronald Reagan, who ran on platforms of contempt for government. So if the government turns out contemptible, who should be surprised?

A Comparison of the King and Denny Beating Videos

MAY 13, 1992

Welcome back to *Crime and Punishment in Videoland.* In our last exciting episode, a jury refused to believe what it saw on videotape of four policemen beating Rodney King. In our coming episode, a jury will be asked to believe what it sees on videotape of four gang members beating truck driver Reginald Denny.

"Ah, but this is different," says FBI special agent Charlie Parsons. "This is not a matter of interpretation."

Well, neither did the other seem to be until the defense got going with slow motion and frozen frames.

There is a sense of surrealistic parody between the episodes. Officer Theodore Briseno was seen with his foot on Rodney King. Gang member Kiki Watson is seen with his foot on Reginald Denny, who, to add to the surrealism, bears the name of a Hollywood actor of the thirties. Police Chief Daryl Gates is so sure that video has it right this time that he has already pronounced his verdict: "These are very, very vicious criminals." Gates blows hot and cold on television. He criticized TV for focusing too much on the intersection of Florence and Normandie streets, where field commanders ordered what in wartime would be called desertion under fire. But Gates invited television to witness him playing street cop in bulletproof jacket personally arresting one of the suspects backed up by two hundred police.

Television, a pain in the neck for the police in the Rodney King affair, now is being found to have its prosecutorial uses. To help identify rioters, citizens are being asked to turn in their home video, and subpoenas are being issued to TV stations for their videotape whether broadcast or not. News directors are resisting, reluctant to be turned into instruments of law enforcement and fearing reprisals against their reporters and camera operators.

Police and prosecutors often complain about the trouble that video causes them. It isn't video they're worried about—just video they can't control.

Nationalistic Movements Spread to Europe

JUNE 1, 1992

From Kabul to Croatia, in a vast belt where the Communist grip has been broken, the first wave of liberation and self-determination is being followed by a dangerous second wave of nationalist conflict and ethnic fragmentation.

The challenge to newly established entities and borders is most immediately threatening to stability in Europe. But as we learn from two world wars, America cannot long avoid becoming embroiled. Ukraine is free from Russia, now Crimea wants to be free from Ukraine, after which northern Crimea may want to secede from Crimea. Parts of Siberia want sovereignty from Russia. Part of Moldova from Moldova. Armenia is consolidating its hold on Nagorno-Karabakh, an enclave inside Azerbaijan, and one of these days, Azerbaijan will surely try to fight its way back. In Afghanistan, where the acting president survived an attempt to shoot down his plane, warlords carve out their own fiefdoms. The capital is in a state of anarchy, without army, without police. Contending factions agree only on imposing Islamic law. In Yugoslavia, Serbian troops and militia on the march against Bosnia-Herzegovina seek to reduce ancient Sarajevo to rubble trying to seize two-thirds of that new state in the name of the one-third Serbian population. And as though on a rampage against history, the Serbs have renewed their bombardment of the ancient Croatian port of Dubrovnik. And now the ethnic rage released by the collapse of communism threatens to turn inward in Serbia.

The manic president, Slobodan Milosevic, tends to respond to pressures by opening new fighting fronts. And so now, facing United Nations sanctions and mass protests in Belgrade against his rule, he may turn on the Albanian-populated Serbian province of Kosovo as he has long threatened to do. From there, the fighting could spread to Macedonia. Greece, Bulgaria, and Albania could be drawn into the resulting conflict. The history of Europe's efforts to find borders that would satisfy nationalist aspirations gave us the word "irredentism," the struggle for unredeemed territory. From Danzig to Trieste, irredentism became the slogan for conquest. Now the post-Communist borders are proving unstable, challenging the international community to find ways of imposing stability or facing us with enough irredentisms to last a century.

Watergate's Twentieth Anniversary

JUNE 14, 1992

Liane Hansen, host: This Wednesday marks the twentieth anniversary of the botched break-in at the Watergate headquarters of the Democratic National Committee. The ensuing cover-up and the tapes that recorded it were finally

*exposed over a summer of televised congressional hearings that jarred the
nation's faith in the presidency and ultimately forced the resignation of Richard Nixon. Aspiring to be an elder statesman, Nixon is making his comeback
with numerous public appearances and books. But senior news analyst Daniel Schorr suspects there's at least one former Nixon supporter who isn't
welcoming him with open arms.*

Of the many things to be said during the Watergate anniversary week,
let's start with the long-strained Nixon-Bush relationship. It didn't surprise me when the former president spent two hours the other day
briefing Mr. Bush's opponent Ross Perot or when Nixon warned that
the incumbent was missing the boat on aid to Russia, for one of the ill-
kept secrets of Washington going back to Watergate and before is how
little regard Richard Nixon has had for George Bush even while using
him and advancing his career.

In 1968, Congressman Bush was on a speculative list of possible Nixon
running mates, but was never seriously considered. Instead, he was
backed by the Nixon White House in a losing campaign for senator
against Lloyd Bentsen in 1970. In a postelection critique written by
counsel Charles Colson for the president, Bush was criticized for having been too liberal and for refusing to use "some very derogatory
information about Bentsen." In other words, in Nixonian terms, Bush
was a softy. But softies have their uses. In 1971, Colson recommended
Bush for speaking assignments, saying, "He takes our line beautifully."
As United Nations ambassador in 1972, Bush was criticized in a White
House memo for allowing himself to look subdued and troubled
over a feud between President Nixon and UN secretary-general Kurt
Waldheim.

Nothing showed President Nixon's low regard for Bush better than
what happened after the 1972 election, which Nixon won in a landslide
despite Watergate. Treasury Secretary George Shultz, who was to be
promoted to a supercabinet level in a restructuring of the executive
branch, offered Bush the job of his deputy, in effect, treasury secretary.
Bush wanted it badly, but Nixon had another assignment in mind for
him, the thankless position of Republican national chairman in the post-
Watergate period, replacing Senator Robert Dole, who had proved to
be too independent.

Swallowing his disappointment, Bush agreed, after being promised that he could sit at the cabinet table. It was Bush then who, during the unraveling of Watergate, had to make all those bland statements about Nixon's innocence. In his memoirs, Nixon makes only two references to Bush as Republican chairman. When the Senate fired up its investigative hearings in the spring of 1973, Bush was recorded as pleading for "some action that would get us off the defensive." In June 1974, with impeachment looming, Bush called Nixon and asked to appear at a fund-raising telethon, an idea that Nixon apparently regarded as goofy.

But then Bush did what was in Nixonian terms the unforgivable thing. On August 7, he wrote him on behalf of the Republicans, urging him to resign for the good of the country. By then, Nixon was already considering resigning and Chief of Staff Alexander Haig was discussing the conditions with Vice President Gerald Ford. But to Nixon, Bush's effort to get out of the cataclysm was a stab in the back.

So Nixon spent the next ten years working at his rehabilitation as elder statesman and, the first chance he had, took a shot at Bush. In a 1983 appearance on CNN's *Crossfire* with Patrick Buchanan, Nixon suggested that Vice President Bush be dumped from the 1984 Reagan reelection ticket. Nixon said that Bush was not as good on the attack as he, Nixon, had been for Dwight Eisenhower in '52 and '56, as Spiro Agnew had been for him in 1968. Nixon said that Reagan needed someone stronger as his number two.

In 1988, Nixon circulated a memorandum calling Bush "a weak individual on television" and Senator Dole "strong and courageous." And now in 1992, while giving lip-service support to President Bush, Nixon has said that he sees Perot as a "formidable candidate" who "is not going to flame out." Want to know why Nixon is not likely to be invited to address the Republican convention in Houston? Because having carried water at Watergate, Bush is Nixon's softy no longer.

Relief Planes Are Landing Slowly in Sarajevo

JULY 1, 1992

The Balkan quagmire beckons and America, straining as it will to stay out, is being sucked into a mess much the worse for having been so long ignored.

Having delegated responsibility to Europe, Secretary of State Baker now denounces Europe for finding reasons not to act. A year ago, Europe and America chose to believe Serbian president Milosevic when he promised to respect self-determination for the other republics. As fighting got under way, making a mockery of these assurances, European plans for intervention foundered on squabbling among France, Germany, and Britain. Twenty thousand corpses and millions of refugees later, the West focuses on the siege of Sarajevo as the challenge that it cannot duck.

France steps out ahead, undeterred by memories of disaster in Dien Bien Phu and Algeria, while Germany is deterred by memories of Hitlerite aggression, and America by more recent memories of peacekeeping marines blown up in Beirut. The Bush administration is alternately contemptuous of President François Mitterrand for his grandstanding flight into Sarajevo and grateful to the French for taking the lead in securing Sarajevo airport and bringing in the first relief supplies.

The American military shrinks from this conflict, which is not a definable war to plan and win like Grenada, Panama, or even the Persian Gulf. Unlike the Gulf, says Defense Secretary Cheney, this is an internal civil war, forgetting that Serbia has invaded states that we recognize as sovereign. President Bush has apparently now decided that history, if not the voter, will not forgive him if he stands by while people are killed and starved out. And so America edges toward the quagmire first with sanitary air power.

The American role is defined as relief, not peacemaking. But as was learned from trying to feed the Kurds in northern Iraq, relief from the air doesn't work without some peace on the ground. Who knows what missile it may be that is launched against an American plane? The reasons to stay out would make a long catalog. And there's perhaps only one reason to get embroiled: America is the superpower, and the whole world is watching.

Anne Frank's Capture by Nazis Fifty Years Ago

JULY 8, 1992

Linda Wertheimer, host: Fifty years ago this week, a Jewish girl named Anne Frank took refuge with seven other people in the attic of a house on

Amsterdam's Prince's Canal. They were found by Nazi police in August of 1944 and taken to concentration camps. Only Anne's father survived. Anne Frank left behind a diary that was published. It sold more than 20 million copies. To mark the anniversary, the World Jewish Congress is holding an international conference on anti-Semitism in Brussels. News analyst Daniel Schorr was a correspondent in the Netherlands in the early postwar years. He visited the house several times.

The house at Prinsengracht 363 has a second-floor bookcase in the hall that swings open to reveal a narrow staircase up to a hidden attic. I visited in 1963 with Anne's father, Otto Frank, onetime Frankfurt businessman. On the walls were pictures cut out of magazines pasted up by Anne and stripes on the wallpaper marking how Anne and her sister Margot grew during their two years in hiding and a map with red and blue pins marking the advance of the Allies who did not advance far enough, soon enough.

Frank recalled August 4, 1944, when the Nazi police broke in, having been tipped off by somebody: "First they looked for arms and then the one in charge asked, 'Where are your jewels?'" The jewels they stuffed into a briefcase emptied of its contents, which included Anne's diary, left strewn on the floor. Papers didn't interest them.

Frank was at first reluctant to see the diary published—too intimate, too personal. But a Jewish historian, Dr. Louis de Jong, persuaded him that it belonged to history. It was published, first in Dutch in 1947, then in almost every known language. It became a source of controversy, a target for neo-Nazis seeking to deny Anne Frank's existence along with the Holocaust.

And so to authenticate it, Nazi hunter Simon Wiesenthal undertook to find the Nazi officer who arrested her. In 1963, with the help of the Netherlands Institute for War Documentation, he tracked down Karl Silberbauer, an Austrian now back on the Vienna police force. Working on a CBS documentary, I was led by Wiesenthal to Inspector Silberbauer's home.

"Yes," says Silberbauer, "I arrested Anne Frank. I was just doing my duty. I didn't know the people we were rounding up would go to extermination camps. If Anne Frank hadn't left that diary behind, I wouldn't be having this trouble."

Anne Frank remains a powerful symbol for those who deny and for those who believe. One visit to the Anne Frank house I made in the early fifties with violinist Isaac Stern. He had just married a German refugee in Israel and had read the diary on his way to concerts in Amsterdam. He asked me to take him to the house and was profoundly moved by what he saw. That night, in his dressing room in the Amsterdam Concertgebouw, warming up to play the Beethoven Concerto, he looked at his open violin case. Pinned up in it I saw pictures of his wife and of Anne Frank. I heard him say softly, "This one tonight is for you, too."

Anne Frank wrote in her diary that despite the Nazis, she believed in the goodness of all men. Her father, back from the death camps, said that was childish idealism, that he himself could not forgive the murderers.

Aid Without Intervention Is Not Working

JULY 29, 1992

Taunted by Governor Clinton about the survival of Saddam Hussein, President Bush snapped, "Whose son do you want to go to Baghdad to find him?" When Clinton said that air strikes may be needed to protect relief supplies in Bosnia, White House spokesman Marlin Fitzwater called that reckless, although Defense Secretary Cheney was suggesting much the same thing. Rarely does an election campaign provide an uplifting dialogue about international problems, and this one is proving to be no exception. That's a pity, because a serious dilemma has arisen that requires some careful and unpolemical thinking.

That dilemma is that from Sarajevo to Somalia, the comfortable policy of furnishing humanitarian assistance but avoiding military intervention is not working. It is not working because in the post–cold war era, it has come up against genocidal passions among warring clans in Somalia, Serbian ethnic purifiers in Bosnia, and Saddam Hussein's legions in Iraq out to destroy Kurds and Shiites. The line between aid and intervention is becoming blurred. In Bosnia, Canadian troops escorting United Nations relief convoys have started shooting back at snipers. Before long, American naval and air support for relief efforts and for sanctions may be a fact. And if any Americans are lost or captured, there will be further hard decisions to make.

For Somalia, UN secretary-general Boutros Boutros-Ghali wants a force of four thousand, which may have to shoot its way into areas of mass starvation. In Iraq, the Bush administration now seems ready to ally itself with the opposition Kurds and Shiites that it had shunned so long, planning now for an Afghan-like insurrection. Anarchy and ethnic strife, features of the new world disorder, leave America without the luxury of being able to bestow aid while avoiding risk. The specter of the quagmire inspires dread during an election campaign, but misery and carnage are no respecters of political schedules. America has some tough decisions ahead, and they will be tougher if they become embroiled in partisan strife.

The End of the Cold War Leads to Ethnic Strife

SEPTEMBER 6, 1992

This isn't the way it was supposed to be. Three years ago, minus two months, when the Berlin Wall came down and the whole Communist structure behind it, the Western world celebrated a rebirth of freedom, an almost biblical second coming. President Bush heralded a new world order, defined in one of many speeches as characterized by the rule of law rather than resort to force, the cooperative settlement of disputes rather than anarchy and bloodshed, and an unstinting belief in human rights.

True, the fear of superpower confrontation and nuclear Armageddon has receded because the other superpower has receded. Mr. Bush says American children will no longer have nightmares about nuclear annihilation, although I don't know any children who were having such nightmares. What the president and most of us did not foresee was that the thawing of the cold war glacier would confront us with conflict and misery more horrible than the theoretical visions of superpower collision.

The danger now is not bombs but people, people in rage against each other and people fleeing from the rage. And as people flee, they generate a second wave of rage among peoples unwilling to cope with a tide of refugees. As in France, where North African immigration has served as a rallying cry for right-wing extremists, so now in Germany refugees in Rostock are terrorized by bands reviving Nazi Sieg Heil slogans. And the quaking government of Chancellor Helmut Kohl is backing away from the traditionally liberal German policy on immigrants.

In Germany it used to be—until recently—that a Yugoslav or a Bulgarian or a Pole who reached the border posts would be admitted if he/she pronounced the magic word *Asyl,* "asylum." That brought temporary entry pending investigation of the refugee's status, by which time the refugee would usually have melted into the population. No longer will that be true. Refugees face deportation to the thousand points of blight from which they fled. The German government fears the combustible mix of rising unemployment, especially in former East Germany, an influx of refugees, and reawakened xenophobia.

After World War II, one spoke of DPs, displaced persons, uprooted by war. And now, without any general war, but with several regional wars, we witness the phenomenon of displaced peoples, whole nationalities in flight from that dirty process called ethnic cleansing. And it may get worse before it gets better. All through Eastern Europe and into the former Soviet Union, people are arming themselves in fear of becoming the next Bosnians. Speak of swords into plowshares. The order of the day in large parts of Eastern Europe is plowshares into swords. Only in Czechoslovakia, where the Velvet Revolution is being succeeded by a velvet divorce, does ethnic conflict appear so far to be peaceful.

Forty years of cold war have fine-tuned Western military and political reflexes to deal with the Communist menace. But the language of trip wires and fail-safe is totally useless to deal with a new world disorder—NATO, EC, CSCE, all stand impotent against the ethnic madness. The United Nations cautiously approaches the idea of an international peacekeeping force. Maybe someday. Maybe someday armies conceived as war-fighting forces will be converted into a real peace corps. Maybe someday. For now the horror goes on.

The Christian Coalition Wants Control of the GOP

SEPTEMBER 13, 1992

Outside the Beltway and outside the headlines it's been going on for a long time, but suddenly it's come into view, a struggle for the soul of the Republican Party.

The Christian Coalition, led by television evangelist Pat Robertson, has set its sights on achieving working control of the Republican Party by the 1996 elections. With its fundamentalist antiabortion, antigay, antiliberal, profamily precepts, the Christian Coalition would move America away from its traditional secular politics and bring it closer to the European idea of parties with Christian in their names, like Germany's Christian Democratic and Christian Social parties.

Usually when zealots lay siege to a party, the effect is to take the party out of the mainstream, where the votes are, and this can cost elections. Barry Goldwater was the darling of the Republican activists in 1964, and George McGovern of the Democratic activists in 1972; both of them won the convention and lost the election.

Although the Robertson supporters have their sights set on 1996 and are officially supporting the Bush-Quayle ticket this year, the tensions are already evident. The Republican platform adopted in Houston bears the marks of Christian Coalition pressures, but the candidates tend to put distance between themselves and the platform when they face the voters.

Thus, in Los Angeles the other day, Vice President Quayle said he disagreed with some planks of the platform—he wouldn't say which—and that he was not against single mothers or homosexuals. He also refused to endorse a complete ban on abortion, saying that this question needed more reflection, that he was looking for some middle ground. That kind of fudging will not be possible for long if the Christian Coalition succeeds in flexing its fundamentalist muscle.

Pat Robertson seemed for a while to disappear from view when he lost his own bid for nomination four years ago. What with Jerry Falwell, Jimmy Swaggart, and Jim Bakker in eclipse, it did not seem the best of times for televangelists. But as the magazine the *Nation* documented last April and the *Washington Post* more recently, Robertson began quietly organizing at a grassroots-precinct level the Christian Coalition, in effect, a successor to Falwell's Moral Majority. But the Christian Coalition introduced some interesting innovations. It classified itself as a tax-exempt, nonpartisan citizen action organization and raised more than $13 million. It didn't look for national attention; indeed, executive director Ralph Reed said, "We're flying below radar." And it has used direct mail and computerized lists most effectively.

Largely unnoticed until recently is that the sophisticated organization, flying below radar, had some three hundred delegates at the Republican convention, claims a quarter million members in forty-nine states, and controls the Republican committees in a half dozen states.

Its fund-raising letters, printed by the million, talk of a feminist agenda that encourages women to leave their husbands, kill their children, practice witchcraft, destroy capitalism, and become lesbians. That kind of language, familiar in evangelical churches, may soon be entering the lexicon of American politics. The question is whether money, sophistication, and hard work at the grass roots can win ideological control of a national party in a country that historically shuns extremes.

The Curmudgeon's Guide to Presidential Debates

OCTOBER 11, 1992

About these debates, people seem not to know what to look for, and they wait for the pundits to tell them next morning who won. So that you can rate the candidates right away, I would like to offer a curmudgeon's guide to scoring a presidential debate.

First, grammar. If a candidate says, "Who do you trust," you should immediately talk back to your TV set and say, "Not somebody who can't say whom." Anyone who can't master the English language certainly can't master the economy. That's my rule of the omnipotent whom.

Second, clichés. Count how many times each candidate uses "trust," "change," "middle class," "character," "values," "family values," "traditional values," "traditional family values." Check President Bush especially for multiple uses of "waffling" and Governor Clinton for "pathetic and desperate" and Ross Perot for "It's that simple" and "I love America."

Next, subject switching. Also known when I was young as "so's your old man" argumentation. Note if Clinton responds to President Bush on the draft by saying, "Yeah, and how about Iraq-gate?" or vice versa. And how often Perot responds to a challenge on investigating his volunteers by asking, "Yeah, and how about Watergate?" This kind of argument reminds me of the Intourist guide in Moscow, who, asked by an American tourist about the shabby apartment houses he saw, snapped back, "Yes, but in the South you have lynching."

Next, time warps. Note when a candidate doesn't seem to know what happened when and how the events may have been related to each other. Now this may require some research on your part. For example, if Vice President Quayle says again that President Bush had to go back on his "no new taxes" pledge because of the oncoming war with Iraq, note that the president reversed himself on taxes on June 26, 1990, and Iraq invaded Kuwait on August 2, 1990. Or if President Bush asks again what Clinton was doing in Moscow in 1969, a year after Czechoslovakia was crushed, note that also in 1969, President Nixon met with the Soviets and launched arms control negotiations in Helsinki.

Next, epithets. You can expect the usual flurry of epithets, "indecisive," "weak," "unwise," "inexperienced," maybe even "double-dealing." These are par for the course. But watch out for a special kind of epithet subtly appealing to antielitist feeling, used mainly by President Bush: "Harvard boutique," "Harvard trained." Suddenly, "Oxford" has become a dirty word. I don't mean the Oxford shoe or the Oxford shirt, but the Oxford University: vaguely un-American, associated with the Oxford peace movement, with Oxford debates. Mr. Bush calls Governor Clinton an Oxford debater as though all Oxford students are professional debaters and Clinton should be stripped of his amateur standing in debates.

Finally, moments. A debate usually has its moment. The gaffe: President Ford, "There is no Soviet domination of East Europe." The deft putdown: Ronald Reagan to President Carter, "There you go again." The ill-considered personal touch: President Carter telling of consulting his daughter Amy about control of nuclear weapons. And the outrageous question ill-handled: Governor Michael Dukakis's response to a hypothetical about the rape and murder of his wife with a statement of his opposition to the death penalty. I say watch for these moments of theater in the coming debates and then don't let them overshadow all the rest; rarely does a debate moment tell you much of what you really need to know. Well, that's it for a curmudgeonly view of debate watching. From here on, you're on your own.

The Pundit's Concession Speech '92

NOVEMBER 5, 1992

Organized punditry, the guardian of the nation's conventional wisdom, should also be obliged to make a concession statement in defeat. And so, as a charter member of the fraternity, here goes.

Conventional wisdom was that voters, turned off on the candidates in the process, would stay away from the polls in droves, perhaps driving the turnout down to less than 50 percent of eligible voters. Alerted by heavy registration, the pundits retreated to seeing an uptick and finally an upsurge, but we were never fully prepared for a turnout of 105 million and 55 percent.

Conventional wisdom was that taxes represented a potent issue against Clinton. But exit pollers reported that Clinton won among many of those who expect him to raise taxes.

Also wrong, the predictions that voters, as gullible as in 1988, would fall for Willie Horton issues of crime and race. They didn't. Family values: only 15 percent of those questioned in exit polls cited that as an important issue. War service: more war veterans voted for Clinton than for Bush.

Conventional wisdom was that voters would trust the incumbent on Iran-Contra more than Governor Clinton's explanations on the draft. Wrong. Fifty-two percent didn't believe Clinton; 67 percent didn't believe Bush. That also disposes of my own assessment that issues like Irangate and Iran-Contra were too complicated to have any election impact.

Conventional wisdom, to which I subscribed, was that Ross Perot shot himself in the head by withdrawing last July and then in the foot in October with conspiracy theories, and that in any event support for a third candidate fades rapidly near the end because voters don't want to waste their votes. So Perot ended up soaring to 19 percent, a humbling experience for all pundits.

As to Congress, conventional wisdom was that anti-incumbency fever would lay low dozens upon dozens of current officeholders. Wrong. Twenty-three of twenty-eight senators were returned and 93 percent of House incumbents who were seeking reelection. Even in the fourteen states that enacted term limits, 98 of 104 incumbents in the House were given new terms.

We cling fiercely to the one piece of conventional wisdom that still stands: that the pocketbook is the overriding issue, that an incumbent presiding over a troubled economy usually loses. Other than that, pundits, like Republicans, have a lot of reassessing to do.

The State of Peace on Earth in 1992

DECEMBER 20, 1992

"Do it again like last year," said the man who runs this program, "about how peace on Earth has been doing this year," and so a tradition is born.

I went back to last year's script, which started with reference to the year-end issue of *Life* magazine—page after page of wrenching pictures of Desert Storm and the Yugoslav civil war. "The Face of War," *Life* called it.

And this time, it was the former Yugoslavia again, and for Desert Storm substitute Somalia. Maybe for Somalia one has to broaden the definition of peace on Earth. Maybe skeletal children and bloated bellies are not the same as war, but certainly they are not peace. And when America's troops engage in a new kind of Desert Storm expedition, an invasion of rescue, handing out food and teaching African kids to sing "Jingle Bells," they're no longer warmakers, but peacemakers—a new kind of Peace Corps. So ring one up for peace on Earth.

Much of what I said last year about some parts of the world I could repeat today. Central America—more peace than a year ago? Yes.

Cambodia—I said the great national reconciliation is having rough going. This year, rougher going. South Africa? "One holds one's breath," I said, "at what could be one of the brighter pages in peacemaking," but in 1992 ugly communal strife slowed the movement to interracial democracy. One holds one's breath still, but South Africa does not belong on the "more peace than last year" side of the ledger.

The Middle East. Last year I said "chalk one up for peace" that Arabs and Israelis are meeting. A year later, "Play it again, Sam." The new Yitzhak Rabin government seems more serious about peace than its predecessor Shamir government; the Islamic fundamentalists try to sabotage peace. With fingers crossed, let's still call it peace.

Europe, the Balkans: a great setback for peace. Something close to genocide goes on in Bosnia, and Serbian expansionism threatens to spread into conquests of the Kosovo enclave in Serbia and nearby Macedonia, and everybody says that would draw Albania and Greece and maybe Turkey into an international war. Peace on Earth? No progress in the Balkans.

And the onetime USSR. A year ago I referred to it as the CIS, Commonwealth of Independent States. Was that only a year ago? Now there is no name for that vast region, where little shooting wars go on among people trying to split their countries into smaller and smaller pieces. And Russia, great Russia, a brooding giant, stumbling unsteadily and making the world nervous about where its weight may fall, not more peaceful than last year.

And Germany, which I didn't mention last year. But Germany must be counted less peaceful than a year ago. An outbreak of neo-Nazi violence mainly directed against foreigners, but also large-scale demonstrations for the defense of democracy. Let's leave Germany in the middle.

Back to *Life* magazine for pictures of America. The general tone— more upbeat than last year. New figures strode across our stage in 1992: Bill and Hillary Clinton, Ross Perot, and a two-page spread for Carol Moseley Braun, the new senator. And way in the back of the book, after the obits, one group picture of the Bushes and the Quayles. There is a sense that America has turned the page toward something new. Maybe looking to come to peace with one another and with ourselves. Maybe? Not even at this time of year does an unsentimental reporter surrender to optimism.

The world out there looks pretty awful in lots of places. America looks a little better, peacewise and goodwill-wise, maybe.

1993

Bosnia, Hillary, Health Care, and NAFTA

The UN's Role as Peacekeeper Is Now Dubious

JANUARY 4, 1993

At the start of 1992, some of us trend spotters were spotting a trend toward the emergence of the United Nations into its full peacemaking, peacekeeping glory. Secretary-General Pérez de Cuéllar had brokered the pullout of Soviet forces from Afghanistan. A UN transitional authority was guiding traumatized Cambodia toward elections. A Security Council big-power consensus had laid the groundwork for war with Iraq and for keeping tabs on Iraq after the war. The UN had redefined "threat to peace" to include human tragedy in countries like Yugoslavia and Somalia. And an African secretary-general, Boutros-Ghali of Egypt, was looking toward the day when an international blue-hat force free of colonial taint would be on call to douse the flames of conflict around the world.

The dawn of 1993 tempers those expectations. From Cambodia to no-man's-land in Lebanon, the UN is having difficulty exerting its influence. Today Secretary-General Boutros-Ghali was the target of a violent demonstration in Addis Ababa. Last Thursday, Boutros-Ghali was jeered in Sarajevo, where the UN is viewed as a hindrance to a military rescue. Indeed, the fear of Serbian reprisals against the peacekeeping troops makes these troops seem like hostages deterring Western action. Yesterday Boutros-Ghali was jeered again in Mogadishu, where President Bush had been cheered. Boutros-Ghali is widely believed in Somalia to have tilted toward one faction when he was Egyptian foreign minister.

The demonstrators made clear that they don't want the Americans replaced by the UN blue hats. That will undoubtedly complicate the problem of replacing the American-led force with a UN force. In a moment of odd symbolism, a U.S. marine restrained a UN security guard who was firing shots into the air to disperse a crowd of protesters around the UN compound. This is not to say that it's time to spot a reverse trend away from an international order toward American solitary leadership. Tom Hughes of the Carnegie Endowment for International Peace said in conversation today, "The United States will continue to function best by operating through international consensus rather than unilaterally."

But it may well be that the hot spots are becoming too many and too complex for any world order to surmount, and that's why 1993 seems to start on such a note of subdued expectations.

"The Hillary Problem"

JANUARY 27, 1993

"She broke more precedents than her husband, had a greater passion for the underdog and was always a little further to the left." Hillary? No, Eleanor, Eleanor Roosevelt, as described by historian William Manchester. I knew Mrs. Roosevelt, used to have tea with her from time to time. She used to have her own White House press conferences for women reporters, wrote a syndicated column and eleven books, toured slums and sharecroppers' camps, fought against discrimination and injustice, and her many conservative critics called her Eleanor or "that woman" and hated her with a passion. She became a kind of lightning rod for her husband. So Hillary Clinton—okay, Hillary Rodham Clinton—still has a way to go in stirring up outrage.

I have hitherto not talked of the problem of Mrs. Clinton, because I've had trouble identifying the problem. At most every Washington cocktail party, people ask knowingly, "So, what about Hillary?" and it comes out sounding like a Russian nobleman asking, "So, what about Rasputin?"

The problem seems to be mainly inside the Beltway. Nationwide, according to a *Washington Post*–ABC poll, 64 percent of people think it's fine that she's been named head of a task force on health care reform. Only 36 percent worry that she may have too large a role.

It is no mystery why the president named her head of the task force: to signal that he considers health reform a high-profile problem. He could have named Vice President Al Gore, but clearly he thought this would have more impact.

So, what's the problem now? That task force members will feel inhibited talking back to the first lady? Those who say that don't know Donna Shalala, Les Aspin, and Leon Panetta, task force members. That she'll be hard to fire if she strikes out? Well, she's done this kind of work before, and there is no reason to believe that as coordinator with adequate staff she will strike out. On television today, conservative commentator Ben Wattenberg worried that she might not be available to accompany the president to some summit. Oh come on, Ben! In this era of rapid social transition, people simply seem to have trouble coming to terms with the visible symbol of an unpaid partner of the chief executive. If they need some way of blowing off steam, they can go back fifty years for some epithets about "that woman in the White House."

Health Care Is a Major Issue in the Clinton Economic Plan

FEBRUARY 21, 1993

Jacki Lyden, host: Today, President Clinton travels to the West Coast to rally support for his economic program. NPR's senior news analyst Daniel Schorr says what we heard in the president's address to Congress last week was merely a preview.

That was only one big budgetary shoe that President Clinton dropped last Wednesday. The second shoe is being fashioned on the last of health reform to be dropped in May. Health has come to play an extraordinary role in the president's and the first lady's thinking about the function of government. It wasn't surprising that $50 billion in health cost controls would be part of the administration's deficit-cutting strategy. In his follow-up road tour, the president has made a big point of health costs out of control, with 1,500 separate health insurance companies, and with 14 cents of every health dollar going not for treatment but for administration.

The burden of health costs is not a new theme, but you wouldn't immediately think of child vaccination as part of a stimulus package, along with summer jobs and education. Half of our two-year-olds don't receive immunizations against deadly diseases, Mr. Clinton told Congress; our plan will provide them for every eligible child. These words mark the start of a battle that recalls the 1955 controversy over the mass vaccination of children against polio. When it developed that many children were having trouble getting the new Salk vaccine, President Eisenhower announced that no child would be denied vaccine for want of ability to pay, and he threatened to buy up the entire supply for government distribution unless the pharmaceutical industry developed a voluntary program of distribution at reasonable prices. In the end, the federal government provided grants to the states to help pay for inoculation of those who couldn't afford it, and the crippling, paralytic disease was all but wiped out.

Now, with memories of a 1990 measles epidemic, a similar confrontation shows signs of developing with the pharmaceutical industry over vaccines for several childhood diseases, including measles, diphtheria, and mumps. The administration's goal is to make sure that every child under two gets inoculated, and the president appears to be willing to threaten government controls, if necessary. The pharmaceutical industry's already getting into a defensive mode, some companies saying they'll give assurances that they'll hold future price rises to the general inflation level, and denying that industry profits are the reason for poor distribution of vaccines.

But the main battle over health and cost containment will come in May, when Hillary Rodham Clinton's task force is scheduled to produce a master plan for reform. Then, a massive attack is expected to be mounted against both the insurance and the pharmaceutical industries. The president is already warming up for that with remarks like "The pharmaceutical industry spends $1 billion more each year on lobbying and advertising than it spends on developing new and better drugs."

Task force working papers indicate that the health reform plan will also call for a second round of tax increases, $50 billion or more, to pay for insurance coverage for those who now lack it. These increases may include a tax on health benefits over a certain limit, a tax on corporations, and special taxes on products defined as "bad for your health." This innovative approach would target not only tobacco and alcohol, but pollutants and guns, which are arguably a health hazard.

As a London economist has noted, the momentum behind some kind of federal reform to America's health system now seems unstoppable, but probably not without a battle royal over who controls, and who pays.

The Horror of Ethnic Cleansing in Bosnia

MARCH 24, 1993

In this one-crisis-at-a-time capital, this is Russia week, so Bosnia never came up among the thirty-one questions put to President Clinton at his news conference yesterday—and perhaps just as well, for what was there to say about the fact that while America was dropping food and shunning quagmires, the struggle for East Bosnia may have reached a point of no return? To save the lives of people fleeing in terror from the Serbian guns, the United Nations forces had to give up protecting them in place and began evacuating them, thus joining and carrying out the population transfer that some have called "ethnic cleansing."

The food drops go on and German and Russian planes are joining in the effort, but soon there may be few Muslims left to receive the food. The United Nations Security Council dithers over enforcement of the no-fly zone, but that will hardly affect what is happening on the ground. The peace negotiations are stalled, for the Vance-Owen proposed patchwork map becomes increasingly meaningless as the Serbs, already in control of 70 percent of Bosnia, take control of one Muslim patch after another. Fait accompli, the diplomats call it, and when the fait is finally accompli and the surviving Muslims are herded into an economically unviable enclave in western Bosnia, then there will be a thirty-nation conference to express outrage and warn Serbia to stop short of Kosovo and Macedonia. But what has happened so far that should deter the drive for a Greater Serbia muscling its way onto the world stage?

When those Bosnian Muslims who survive write the history of their tragedy, there will not be many foreign heroes. There will be General Philippe Morillon of France, who tried to protect Srebrenica with his own body in what could only be called a beau geste. There will be no American names, for there is something anonymous about food from the skies. And it may be remembered that on the day that marked the beginning of the end for East Bosnia, the matter didn't even come up in the East Room of the White House.

The Connection Between Recent Terrorist Acts

MARCH 28, 1993

Before the World Trade Center bombing on February 26, the worst recent act of terrorism on American soil was the January 25 shooting fray outside CIA headquarters in Langley, Virginia, in which two agency employees were killed, three others wounded. The suspected assassin, Mir Aimal Kansi, came from a region of Pakistan near the Afghan border and reportedly returned there before dropping out of sight. In that ten-year staging area for the Afghan mujahideen guerrillas, young people of the area supported them, learned their fierce, Iranian-oriented Islamic ideas, and their guerrilla tactics.

In the Trade Center investigation, Mahmoud Abouhalima, identified as a major suspect, was arrested in Egypt and returned to New York. He had worked as a driver and personal assistant for the fundamentalist sheikh Omar Abdel-Rahman—both Egyptian-born, both dedicated to bringing down the government of Egypt. Abouhalima was also a passionate supporter of the Afghan mujahideen, helping to raise money and recruit volunteers to go to Pakistan to fight with them. What are these tenuous, terrorist connections: Afghan freedom fighters, Pakistan, Iran, Egypt, Langley, Brooklyn, Jersey City?

American intelligence is becoming dimly aware of a new face of terror. The movement has its fountainhead in fiercely fundamentalist Iran but is so loosely organized—if, indeed, organization is the word—that it's difficult to identify anything that might be called a network. One day we may hear of the bombing of the Israeli embassy in Buenos Aires, another day of the murder of an Iranian dissident leader in Rome, another day of attacks on tourists in Egypt, spurred on by the taped incitements of Sheikh Omar. It is hard to identify specific state sponsors, as in the Libyan-organized bombing of the Berlin discotheque frequented by American GIs, or the Iranian-encouraged Lebanese bombing of American marines, or the downing of Pan Am 103, probably supported by both Libya and Iran.

Now the pattern is more diffuse. From Iran, where theology and ideology merge, a wave of incitement flows through religious channels. The faithful are called upon to act on their own in fulfilling three sacred missions: to bring down secular Arab governments like Egypt's, to seek the destruction of Israel, and to strike at America, the great Satan. The zealots tend to cluster around mosques where they will hear from radical sheikhs like Omar Abdel-Rahman not specific orders, but rhetoric like "Hit hard and kill the enemies of God in every spot." The radicals assemble most easily not in Arab countries like Egypt or Syria, where tough rulers give them little elbow room, but in South and North America. The targets in Latin America are most often American, including even Kentucky Fried Chicken franchises, an unlikely symbol of the great Satan.

The State Department calls Iran the "world's most dangerous state sponsor of terrorism," but the sponsorship flows like an underground stream through organizations variously called Hezbollah, Islamic Jihad, Muslim Brotherhood, Hamas—or no name at all, just a local mosque. So the trail may take you to Cairo, or to the Afghan border, but the pattern of terrorism today is unstructured groups with a common set of beliefs, grievances, and hatreds, and some local fundamentalist cleric on hand to give them blessing.

Clinton's Bosnia Stance Is Courageous and Perilous

MAY 3, 1993

"Brinksmanship," "eyeball-to-eyeball," "quarantine the aggressor"—the slogans of past American tests of resolve come back in Bosnia.

Once again, the issue is credibility—the hope that expressed willingness to use force will obviate the need to use it. But it's a gamble, and riding on it is the risk of American involvement in a foreign war that could stymie President Clinton's plans for American renewal as Vietnam undermined President Johnson's Great Society program.

It's too early to know whether a turning point has been reached in Bosnia, whether the combined impact of tougher sanctions, belated Russian pressure, and the threat of American air strikes will finally stay the bloody hand of the Bosnian Serbs. But vital, in the days and weeks ahead, is to make the prospect of military intervention seem believable. That will not be easy. When I talked to General Colin Powell, chairman of the Joint Chiefs of Staff, over the weekend, he reacted testily to reports that he'd opposed military involvement, saying, "I advise the president, and we do what he wants done." Clearly, any suggestion of Pentagon foot-dragging at this point would be unhelpful.

The administration apparently also wants to keep the Serbs guessing about how far bombing plans have gone. In conversation, Communications Director George Stephanopoulos said the president had approved a plan, but then he asked to change that to "direction." The greatest problem for American credibility is that Mr. Clinton has said he doesn't want to act alone, but so far has little international support. The Europeans simply refuse to see the Balkan killing fields in the same stark terms that he does.

Secretary of State Warren Christopher faces the formidable task of convincing the NATO allies, familiar with the doctrine of deterrence from forty-odd years of cold war, that once again collective resolve to use force if necessary is the way to peace.

President Clinton's decision in principle to use force was dictated less by geopolitics than by conscience spurred by pictures of brutality in Bosnia and recollections of the Holocaust. For this decision, he is receiving bipartisan applause. But his bold initiative in American moral as well as political leadership has put him out on a perilous limb. There is no easy way back from a commitment of American power.

With the Soviet Union Gone, the West Is a New Target for Terrorism

MAY 16, 1993

It became known as the Reagan Doctrine, although he never called it that.

The doctrine was the principle that anti-Communist insurgencies everywhere deserved American support, and Ronald Reagan was dedicated to seeing that they got it—usually by covert operations managed by the CIA. "Support for freedom fighters is self-defense," Reagan pronounced, and that went for Jonas Savimbi's UNITA insurgency in Angola, and for Nicaragua, where Colonel Oliver North evaded congressional bans by erecting an extralegal structure of financing and support for the anti-Sandinista Contras, and most particularly, it went for Afghanistan—financing and arming the mujahideen guerrillas in an operation so huge that it became almost a joke to call it covert—but now the Soviet Union, the ultimate target of the insurgencies, is vanquished and some of the freedom fighters are coming home to roost, turning their guerrilla skills against governments that America supports and against America itself.

In Angola, Savimbi, whom President Reagan once likened to America's founding fathers, has repudiated the election that was supposed to end sixteen years of civil war, and using America-supplied weapons he has returned to civil war and ethnic cleansing. His siege of one city left fifteen thousand dead. In Nicaragua, the remnants of the Contra guerrillas are continuing a violent campaign against the government of President Violeta Chamorro, who is supported by the United States. But it is the mujahideen guerrillas who have become the most troublesome of all.

During the anti-Soviet war, the CIA, operating from the Pakistan frontier area, ladled out money, training, and arms, including Stinger shoulder-mounted antiaircraft missiles, to all twelve factions. Two of them were as virulently anti-Western as they were anti-Soviet. Some of those the CIA dealt with then are back in action against America and its friends. The core of Islamic extremists trying to drive tourists away from Egypt by terror and bring down the Mubarak government are Egyptians who fought as volunteers with the Afghan guerrillas.

Closer to home, Mir Aimal Kansi is wanted for the shooting of five CIA employees driving to work last January. Kansi came from the border area of Pakistan where the mujahideen and the CIA used to hold sway—and he is believed to have returned there before he disappeared underground, and the group claiming credit for the bombing of the World Trade Center in New York, in a letter the police believe to be authentic, calls itself the Liberation Army, Fifth Battalion, and that sounds like mujahideen language. Furthermore, Egyptian-born Mahmoud Abouhalima, chief suspect in the bombing, fought for the rebels in Afghanistan, and Egyptian sheikh Omar Abdel-Rahman raised money for the mujahideen and sent his two sons to fight with them. At least twice, the sheikh visited Peshawar, Pakistan, where the CIA and the guerrillas mingled. The CIA says it had nothing to do with the sheikh's entry into this country, despite his name being on an FBI list of suspected terrorists. Ambassador Robert Oakley, expert on terrorism, told me that the Afghan war did for militant Islam what the Spanish civil war did for the Communists. It gave the veterans an esprit de corps, it radicalized them and gave them a sense of further mission, and with the Soviets gone, the freedom fighters' mission now turns westward.

Clinton Must Make His Own Comeback

JUNE 1, 1993

President Clinton may scoff at his 36 percent approval rating in the volatile opinion polls, but he knows that he must restore public confidence in himself if he's to have a chance of winning the legislative battles ahead. He cannot often repeat last week's feat of squeezing out a narrow victory in a House which is not under much constituent pressure to support him.

The recipe for a comeback is to face up to some subjects and to change other subjects. His Vietnam memorial wall appearance was an example of a subject to be confronted, braving the jeers of combat veterans. That won him a banner headline in the normally critical *Washington Times*— "Clinton Calls for Healing at the Wall." Gays in the military is another vexing subject, eluding the hope for consensus, that he may soon have to step up to.

But then there is the problem of changing the subject from the popular perception of contradictory economic priorities, nepotism, cronyism, creeping drift to the left, and general kids' stuff. That is where his new counselor David Gergen comes in. Gergen has already rendered his first service, changing the subject on weekend talk shows from White House bumbling to himself.

Before he even had the key to his office, he was all over television, being sage and statesmanlike—a good start, but now he has to help make the president begin looking sage and statesmanlike and convincing the nation that Ross Perot is dead wrong about Mr. Clinton's being unqualified for top management.

That may require reducing the number of balls the president seems to keep in the air at one time. It may mean less time on the hustings, which he enjoys so much, and more time in the Oval Office. It may mean distancing himself from Hollywood pals who sometimes make him seem like a fellow entertainer. And it may mean less from the first lady on the politics of meaning, and more attention to the meaning of politics.

As we know from Truman, Eisenhower, and Reagan, the presidency is not a matter of formal qualification. It's a matter of gaining the confidence of the nation by giving the nation confidence in itself. Image making is a part of that, but not all. David Gergen can help, but essentially the president will have to be the architect of his own salvation.

We Must Be Consistent in How We Handle Terrorists

JUNE 28, 1993

For President Clinton's first use of offensive force, Baghdad represented a well-nigh best-case scenario—a blow against the world's most notorious bad guy, who apparently tried to kill our good guy, a chance to demonstrate to the military and the public that Mr. Clinton does not shrink from the measured use of force with unmanned missiles that risk no American lives, a chance to demonstrate the gospel according to Secretary of State Warren Christopher, that, although stymied by allies in trying to save Bosnia, America will act on its own where its vital interests are involved—maybe too weak to lead, but not too weak to act; but, once White House euphoria has worn off, it will be seen that the Baghdad strike raises problems. In the first place, in Iraq, how does one distinguish between unilateral and multilateral concerns? Is the plot against George Bush more deserving of a military response than Saddam Hussein's resistance to the removing of chemical equipment and the monitoring of missile test sites? The president last week warned Iraq of quite serious consequences. There is a danger if friend and foe perceive America as quicker on the trigger where an anti-American provocation is involved than a general threat to peace and stability. Second, what about other cases of anti-American provocation? Neither the United Nations nor the United States has yet acted beyond sanctions falling short of an oil embargo to force Libya to hand over two indicted suspects in the bombing of Pan Am 103. That explosion during the Christmas season of 1988 killed all 259 aboard. What about Libya, and, for that matter, Syria and Iran, suspected of involvement in that bombing; and what if it turns out that the Sudan and Iran are linked to the group that bombed the World Trade Center and planned further attacks on buildings and individuals?

Administration officials who say the Baghdad raid serves as a warning to all state sponsors of terrorism should be aware of the danger of empty warnings. President Reagan, during his first week in office, pledged swift and effective retribution for terrorist acts. Five years later he ordered a raid on Libya in reprisal for a bombing in Berlin that targeted American GIs; but when it came to dealing with Iran over American hostages in Lebanon, his policy looked more like ransom than reprisal. For President Clinton, the raid on Baghdad is not the last hard decision he will have to make if he's to be consistent about responding to state-supported terrorism.

The Foster Suicide Case

JULY 30, 1993

If you were president and your lawyer had drawn up a list of everything he knew that was going wrong and then he committed suicide, would you permit that document to be circulated outside your office? That question suggests the classic dilemma raised by the torn-up note left behind by deputy counsel Vincent Foster, which the White House kept to itself for thirty hours, in part, it was said, so his wife could see it. It is the dilemma of the president's need for confidentiality versus the requirements of investigators. That may sound like the familiar controversy over the doctrine of executive privilege, a doctrine with no constitutional basis but asserted by presidents back to George Washington.

President Eisenhower asserted it in 1954 to defy subpoenas for White House personnel from Senator Joseph McCarthy's red-hunting subcommittee. Mr. Eisenhower stated, "It is not in the public interest that any of the conversations or communications of executive branch personnel or any documents concerning such advice be disclosed." President Nixon tried to assert executive privilege to withhold his Oval Office tapes in 1974, but a unanimous Supreme Court ruled that he could not do that in the face of a criminal investigation. Nixon wrote in his memoirs, "I was the first President to test the principle of executive privilege in the Supreme Court, and by testing it on such weak ground . . . I probably ensured the defeat of my cause." Nixon's effort to hide the evidence of his own wrongdoing ensured that for a long time to come, assertions of executive privilege would be suspect.

The Foster investigation falls into a murky twilight zone. There is clearly a concern in the White House about the confidential information the investigators may see. Counsel Bernard Nussbaum insisted on conducting the search of Foster's office in the presence of the police, describing what he'd found but not allowing them to see the documents. The torn-up note presented a problem. It is described as "dealing with negative things that have occurred," including the White House travel office controversy. Clearly, the note bears on the inner workings of the White House. It may also bear on the motive for Foster's suicide. The suicide was not a crime, says counselor David Gergen, but it is the subject of official investigation, and so once again, the dilemma. The president's need for secrecy; the need of investigators, if not the public, to know the facts behind the suicide.

The Powerful Symbolism of the Peace Signing

SEPTEMBER 13, 1993

They strode onto the stage of history, and before they exited, a lot of taboos lay shattered on the sunny White House lawn.

Former secretary of state Henry Kissinger, who pledged to Israel two decades ago that the United States would never deal with the PLO, was on hand to see the scrapping of that pledge. A handshake between Yasser Arafat and Prime Minister Yitzhak Rabin closed three decades of what had been proclaimed as eternal enmity between the Jewish state and Arab forces dedicated to driving that state into the sea. Today was theater, and all the principals played their designated roles. The quintessential piece of business was the handshake. In 1979, President Carter brought the hands of President Anwar Sadat of Egypt and Prime Minister Menachem Begin of Israel together into a triple handshake to symbolize a Camp David agreement made in the USA.

But in the PLO-Israel agreement, negotiated more directly, Rabin and Arafat were left to decide if their hands would touch. It was carried off as though rehearsed a hundred times. Rabin, who had said he would shake hands "if necessary," hesitated a fraction of a second for Israeli consumption before accepting Arafat's proffered hand. If anyone stole the show today, it was the usually wooden Rabin, who completely upstaged Foreign Minister Shimon Peres with his emotional call of "Enough of blood and tears." Symbolism, yes, but the power of symbolism should not be underestimated. For Arafat and Rabin, after today there is no going back. They have committed their political futures to each other. They have gotten out at the end of a very long limb together. Hovering over the prayer meeting on the White House lawn were intimations of tough bargaining ahead and distant sounds of resistance and violence among those in both camps of the Middle East determined to disrupt the move toward peace. The partners in the diffident handshake of today are now partners in an open-ended battle for peace.

Why Broadcast Media Are Arenas for Revolution

OCTOBER 24, 1993

Where once the symbolic target of the mob was the Bastille or the Winter Palace, in Moscow on Sunday, October 3, it was the television headquarters called Ostankino. As the anti-Yeltsin rebels massed around the TV complex, Ilya Konstantinov, the head of the National Salvation Front, announced that television is the key to success. Much of the killing took place at Ostankino—sixty-two dead and some four hundred wounded—and when the battle of Ostankino was lost, the rebellion was lost. In Somalia, the turning point between uneasy peace and war came on June 5, when General Mohamed Aidid's forces ambushed Pakistani peacekeepers, killing twenty-four of them. The Pakistanis were on their way to silence Aidid's radio station, which had previously been bombed by American helicopters. An Italian official said, "We had a strong feeling that attacking the radio station was a mistake." In Haiti on October 11, the day American troops were prevented from landing, the armed thugs in civilian dress called "attachés" seized the radio center. Only a week before, the station had been taken back from the military junta by President Jean-Bertrand Aristide's transitional government, under diplomatic escort.

More and more, in the revolutionary situations of the past decade, television and radio became not only observers of the conflict but the arena of the conflict. In Czechoslovakia in November 1989, the turning point in the anti-Communist uprising came when television employees seized control of the facilities and started broadcasting across the country scenes of bloody suppression of demonstrations. One day, the demonstrators carried a banner reading, "Television Lies," and the next day they carried a banner saying, "Long Live TV." In Romania, the downfall of dictator Nicolae Ceausescu started when television failed to turn off in time to keep the nation from seeing him on his palace balcony, stunned by a chorus of boos and catcalls. The televison studio then became the actual headquarters of the revolutionary government as Ceausescu's security battalions fought for control against the regular army and the people. The climactic moment came when rebel leaders announced from studio four that the dictator had fled. And poet Mircea Dinescu appeared on camera shouting, "We've won, we've won!"

It would be nice to think that once the bad guys lose control of the airwaves, radio and televison become instruments of freedom. But that ain't necessarily so. Now that President Yeltsin has solidified his control of television, he's banned some of the programs that didn't toe his line, as well as suppressed some newspapers. Access to television is denied to opposition parties. In the Czech Republic, television is relatively balanced, but in Romania, it's under government control. And almost forgotten are the heady days of 1989, when an anchorman apologized to the audience for having lied for years. From outside, radio and television can leap across borders and have potent effects. Communist rule in East Germany was undermined by the ability of East Germans to see West German television. Singaporean prime minister Kuan Lee Yu said the Tiananmen massacres in Beijing happened because Chinese students had seen antiregime demonstrations in the Philippines and South Korea on Chinese television and thought they could do the same thing. But nothing has become so central to conflict as control of radio and television inside one's country. So it's no surprise to find that more often than not, the battle to dominate becomes a battle for the broadcast studios.

The Post–Cold War CIA

NOVEMBER 7, 1993

Twenty years ago, the CIA was the truly silent service, so secretive that there were no road signs on Route 123 in McLean, Virginia, to tell you where it is. No longer.

As much as it tries, the CIA can't seem to stay out of the public eye, and when it's in the public eye, that usually spells trouble for America's intelligence agency. Lately, Senator Daniel Patrick Moynihan, onetime vice chairman of the Senate Intelligence Committee, has been calling for the abolition of the CIA as a cold war anachronism. And retired lieutenant general William Odom, who once headed the National Security Agency, the even more secretive national eavesdropping agency, says the CIA should retire its flag with victory and reemerge in some new incarnation.

In its transitional state, somewhere between cold war and something else, it finds itself unusually beleaguered. Its director, James Woolsey, likes to say that having helped to slay the dragon of communism, it finds itself having to deal with a thousand snakes in a world of tribal conflict and terrorism. Under increasing pressure, Woolsey continues to defend a policy of keeping secret his agency's total budget. As known to most people who are in the know, that number is $28 billion, down a billion from last year. Woolsey tried to explain to me, again, why the budget has to be secret—the fear that once the total is known, then next thing amounts for various activities will become known, and first thing, the enemy—whoever that is—will know too much.

On Haiti, the agency has been caught between a rock and a hard place. A couple of years ago, a highly unfavorable psychological profile of exiled president Jean-Bertrand Aristide was written by Brian Latell, a career officer with a Ph.D. degree who is given to controversial opinions. He'd become a favorite of the late William Casey for a profile of Fidel Castro that others in the agency had dismissed as psycho fiction. He also wrote a lurid paper predicting revolution in Mexico. Senator Jesse Helms got hold of the Aristide profile, which concludes that the Haitian president is mentally unstable, and Helms used it to belabor the Clinton administration for its support of Aristide. Senator John Kerry said the agency, by smearing Aristide, seems to be pursuing a separate foreign policy.

Next, as part of a process of opening the agency to the daylight, Director Woolsey authorized release of a lot of old intelligence estimates. These, it turned out, show that the agency had been spectacularly wrong on some of its estimates, especially on the Soviet Union. Next, the agency was dragged into a fight over the confirmation of Morton Halperin as assistant secretary of defense for peacekeeping and democracy. Republican opponents of Halperin demanded from the CIA information about Halperin's earlier foreign contacts, of which they were suspicious. The agency said it didn't have anything on Halperin. To prod the agency, Senator John Warner blocked action on the whole intelligence authorization bill. The agency says it will look again for Halperin's files.

This is not the way things used to be for the CIA. In its forty-five years since President Truman established it, its people were generally faceless. The honor roll at CIA headquarters shows many stars with no names, agents anonymous even in death. An agency briefing for Congress used to be behind closed doors, but no longer. Maybe it's because the cold war is over that the agency no longer gets the immunity to controversy that it generally enjoyed except for the midseventies, when its mistakes and misdeeds were being investigated by Congress. These days, I imagine, Jim Woolsey would like to take down those road signs that tell you where the CIA is and go back to being the agency that people hardly dare to talk about.

The United States Spends More Money on Destruction Than Salvation

NOVEMBER 10, 1993

Robert Siegel, host: The fifteenth edition of something called World Military and Social Expenditures *was published today by a little think tank called World Priorities Inc., which is located in the Georgetown neighborhood of Washington, D.C. News analyst Daniel Schorr says it's a little report with a big message.*

For twenty years, Ruth Leger Sivard, an economist who used to work for Dun & Bradstreet and for the government, has been crunching numbers in a most unusual way. She's been comparing the resources that humanity devotes to its salvation and to its destruction. And, in her latest report, once again salvation comes in a melancholy second best. You can count it in military spending—more than $600 billion last year for arms, nearly half of that by America, despite the end of the cold war. And, since 1946, America alone has spent more than $5.5 trillion on nuclear weapons.

You can count it in wars. You can count the nuclear firepower. When all current commitments to reduce nuclear weapons are met, the five acknowledged nuclear powers will still have nine hundred times all the explosive power expended in World War II.

You can also count it in the lives of people. One adult in four world-wide can't read or write. Life expectancy at birth is twenty-one years shorter in India than in Japan. And one-fifth of the world's population goes hungry every day. Weep for the Third World, but weep also for the First World, for America. It, along with the former Soviet Union and Israel among developed countries, spends more for arms than for education. And so half the adult population is functionally illiterate, and 36 million Americans are poor—a twenty-seven-year record.

Ruth Sivard used to compare military and social spending for the Arms Control Agency, which didn't help the selling of the Pentagon budget. So the Nixon administration abolished her job. Since 1973, Mrs. Sivard has been producing her reports privately, lately with increasing foundation support. *World Military and Social Expenditures* goes under the acronym *WMSE*. For making you wonder why we seem so much more devoted to destroying our world than improving it, there's nothing like "whimsy."

NAFTA as the Defining Moment in the Clinton Presidency

NOVEMBER 17, 1993

The great debate, as it's called, has taken on the quality of a public ritual.

Members dutifully followed the prearranged scenario, hardly listening to each other as they made their little speeches about this thing called NAFTA. The real drama lay elsewhere, reflected in the news agency running straw votes that climb steadily toward, and then past, the magic number of 218. Not because of what members of Congress were hearing from each other today, but what they had already heard from a horse-trading White House and from their own constituents. Horse trading for votes played a part, but that should not be exaggerated. Over the Veterans Day weekend, members had found, some to their surprise, that the tide had shifted among their constituents. That more were now in favor than opposed, and that few were inclined to punish their representatives if they voted in favor.

What did it? Pollsters found that the Gore-Perot debate had influenced some. Polls also suggested that President Clinton's intensive sales effort had paid off. That he finally managed to make clear that he was serious about this and that made a difference. History may recall that greater than the drama of Capitol Hill was the drama of Pennsylvania Avenue. The president was perceived as having stopped waffling, stuck out his chin, faced up to some traditional allies, and said this he would fight for—win, lose, or draw. As great a cliché as "great debate" is "defining moment," but that is what NAFTA may signify. The president's expressed conviction that, more than a trade agreement, NAFTA is a matter of whether America acts from confidence or fear conveys a sense of core values like his passionate speech on crime in Memphis last weekend.

On NAFTA, it's been uphill all the way. The president, who has often shown a disposition to compromise or leave it to Congress to decide rather than lose, this time was willing to risk losing and facing the Asian powers in Seattle as a defeated man. That's what you call the defining moment.

Confrontation Looms over North Korean Nuclear Weapons

NOVEMBER 24, 1993

If the Kennedy-Khrushchev collision over Soviet missiles in Cuba in 1962 represented the first nuclear confrontation, North Korea and America may well be headed toward the second. The aging and isolated Kim Il Sung and his erratic son are harder for Western intelligence to read than Nikita Khrushchev. But the world's last Stalinist regime gives every sign of being determined to push on with the development of nuclear weapons unpersuaded by proffered carrots, and undeterred by threatened sticks.

President Clinton, thrice burned in Bosnia, Somalia, and Haiti, shows little appetite for engagement in what may become the gravest international crisis of his first year, perhaps of his presidency. In his talks with South Korean president Kim Young Sam, Mr. Clinton's emphasis was still on the benefits that North Korea would reap from agreeing to inspection. He seemed to be less inclined than the South Korean president to suggest a deadline for compliance with the inspection requirements. But there is an unavoidable deadline. The monitoring equipment of the International Atomic Energy Agency on site in North Korea needs new batteries and film. And if the North Korean government refuses to allow this minimal form of monitoring to continue, the IAEA will have no recourse but to report within the next month that it cannot give any assurance that North Korea is still a nonnuclear power. That would leave Mr. Clinton with hardly any viable options. United Nations sanctions might be vetoed by China, sensitive about its own nuclear weapons. Or, if they were applied, might lead to an invasion of South Korea. President Clinton has warned that this might bring massive retaliation. Sanctions could also lead to collapse and chaos in North Korea, already in dire economic straits. That leaves the administration watching with foreboding as the clock or calendar runs out on a formal declaration that North Korea's nonnuclear status can no longer be verified. The administration continues to hope that North Korea, urged by China, may still see reason, but that may be only whistling "Dixie." And one of these days, a weapons test explosion may signal the latest entry into the nuclear club by a dangerous and unpredictable regime.

Los Angeles Times *Names Words Its Writers Should Not Use*

DECEMBER 2, 1993

Just what we needed—a list of banned words.

As the Roman Catholic Church provided an Index Librorum Prohibitorum to tell the faithful what books not to read, so now the *Los Angeles Times* weighs in with guidelines telling its writers what words not to use, words that may offend sensitivities of particular ethnic, racial, sexual, or other groups. It's good in this era of political correctness to be able to turn to a political correctional facility for help. Some of the taboo words will not come as a surprise. "Babe," "gal," "coed," "mankind," "mailman," and "man-made," all outlawed as slighting of women. Gays are gays, but not admitted, acknowledged, or avowed gays. On the ethnic side, "Hispanic" is out; "Latino" is in. Also out—"Indians" and "New World," which may have been new to Columbus but not to the aborigines. "WASP" is considered pejorative. "Black" as a noun is discouraged in favor of "Afro-American," but then "white" is encouraged in preference to "Anglo." However, "white trash" is out. "Ghetto" is out, and so is "barrio." "Slum" is okay.

"Handicapped person" is banned, and so are "crippled," "lame," and "deaf." You have to be a scholar to understand some of these taboos. "Gyp" and "gyp joint" may be offensive to Gypsies; "welshing" on a bet may be an allusion to the Welsh people. Out also is "Dutch treat"—that is, splitting the check, the history of which I know something about as a onetime correspondent in the Netherlands. Along with "Dutch uncle," "Dutch courage," and "Dutch crossing," which is jaywalking in Britain, this expression entered the language when England was at war with the Netherlands in the seventeenth century. No Netherlander I know today is offended by "Dutch treat" or any of the other Dutch pejoratives. That's because the ancient conflicts and prejudices that brought the expressions into the language are long since gone. But our fragmenting, PC society today is adding a multitude of prickly new pejoratives. How many centuries must pass before the words are considered harmless? Until then, we gravely inscribe them in indexes of prohibitions. I would call that crazy, or deranged, except these words are also on the *L.A. Times* taboo list. So is "normal."

Daniel Schorr Restrains Himself from the Muck

DECEMBER 26, 1993

On this holiday weekend, you got a minute? I want to tell you about my problem.

I'm an old-fashioned-type journalist who doesn't like writing personal gossip and scandal. Oh, I don't mean Watergate-type political scandal or financial scandal—which, in fact, I do rather enjoy. CIA assassination conspiracies, yes, but not character assassination. But then, a news analyst has a professional obligation not to duck scandal when it involves the public interest—not just an interested public. And then deciding whether, in pleading public interest, you're being a hypocrite and just rationalizing your way into wallowing in scandal with the rest of them.

So, for example, when the Senate Intelligence Committee, in a report in 1975, made a veiled reference to President Kennedy's affair with a mistress of Mafia boss Sam Giancana, I did not pursue the lead. I guess that was a mistake. I generally stayed away from the Gary Hart womanizing story, and when I once referred to it in a commentary on NPR, he called me to say that I was buying the conventional wisdom about that episode and that the conventional wisdom was wrong. And I didn't argue with him.

Now, here are the Clintons appearing in Christmastide magazine photos as a model, happy family on top of the world. But against the background drumbeat of unseasonal and unpalatable allegations about their private lives. What do we have here? A couple of Arkansas state troopers out for a book and a buck? An Arkansas lawyer who has long been gunning for the Clintons? Eleven thousand words in an ultraconservative magazine by David Brock, who did a job on Anita Hill. Surely I don't have to deal with that.

But, as in some Greek tragedy where the protagonists seem to contrive their own doom, the Clintons themselves raised the issue from gossip and innuendo, gave the story legs, in the words of Mark Shields. It comes out that President Clinton has made telephone calls to the state troopers for reasons that are disputed, but never mind, he has made them.

So now there is a concrete presidential action. And then Hillary Rodham Clinton speaks out about the "outrageous" attack, challenging the motives behind it, and now the story's on the front page of the *New York Times,* which had tried to stay away from it. The *Washington Post* also has a story on page one, above the fold. And inside, an editorial captioned "Once more into the muck." And here is stodgy old C-SPAN doing a call-in show with some of the principals.

So, you see my problem. No way anymore that I can just say, "I don't do tabloid journalism." The line between tabloid journalism and political journalism is becoming very fuzzy. I never mentioned on the air the rumors about a George Bush affair. I didn't touch the Gennifer Flowers story until the Clintons appeared on *60 Minutes* and legitimized it for me. Maybe if they appear on *60 Minutes* again—no, I don't think so.

So you think the Clintons have problems? Just think about my problem trying to practice respectable journalism when nothing much out there looks very respectable. Maybe next year I'll get it figured out. Meanwhile, Happy New Year.

The State of Peace on Earth in 1993

DECEMBER 29, 1993

This year was more the year of the skinhead than of the egghead. In many places, voices of reason proved less persuasive than voices of unreason, appealing to nationalist, religious, and tribal hatreds. The grand illusion of 1989, when the Berlin Wall and communism came tumbling down, has yielded to the grand disillusion of 1993, when oppressors and would-be oppressors reared their heads from Haiti to Russia. Historian Arthur Schlesinger notes, "The disenchantment that four years brought exactly two centuries ago. The radiant promise of the French revolution of 1789 degenerated into the reign of terror of 1793."

In this century, President Wilson entered the First World War to make the world safe for democracy, only to have democracy threatened after that war by fascism. The Second World War vanquished fascism, only to have communism spread across Russia, Eastern Europe, China, and parts of the Third World.

So, in 1993, both communism and fascism lie prostrate, or do they? In these four years, democracy has not found the way of filling empty mouths or minds. So the former Communists, as they are called, are making something of a comeback in Italy and eastern Germany, and fascism is making a comeback among the xenophobic neo-Nazis of Germany and in the scary figure of Vladimir Zhirinovsky in Russia. And now, another threat in radical Islam, challenging the secular states of the Middle East and America, which supports them. And America, thrice burned in its peacemaking efforts in Bosnia, Somalia, and Haiti, shrinks back from global police duties, finding enough violence to police at home, thank you.

The promise of 1993 lay in old conflicts that showed signs of peaceful resolution. South Africa on its way to putting behind generations of apartheid. Israel and the Palestinians trying to turn an autonomy agreement into reality, and Northern Ireland, where only the first murmurs of possible peace were heard in an agreement between Britain and the Republic of Ireland.

But four years have taught that democracy and freedom don't automatically happen when an antidemocratic ideology collapses. People without hope hearken less to democracy than to demagogy, and the lure of messianic visions may produce new forms of authoritarianism.

1994

O.J. and Other Big News

The Clinton Administration's Foreign Policy

JANUARY 5, 1994

Linda Wertheimer, host: News analyst Daniel Schorr says the Clinton administration is trying to diffuse its most threatening foreign policy problems so that it can concentrate on domestic issues like crime, health care, and welfare.

Traditional foreign policy bipartisanship is showing signs of strain under mounting Republican criticisms of administration handling of issues ranging from NATO enlargement to North Korean nuclear weapons. Three Bush administration officials take aim at Clinton policies in today's *New York Times* and *Washington Post* alone. Former deputy chief of staff Robert Zoellick urges more NATO protection for East European states. Former national security adviser Brent Scowcroft and his former aide Richard Haass warn of a peril point approaching in a whole array of national security issues from Ukraine to North Korea.

The administration seems intent, not so much on resolving as on diffusing some of these problems. On North Korea the president is ascribed by an official as having misspoken when he said two months ago that North Korea cannot be allowed to develop a nuclear weapon. The official line now is that North Korea cannot be allowed to become a nuclear power. A pending agreement for resuming inspections disregards whether North Korea already has one or more nuclear devices.

As to the clamor of East European countries for NATO protection, Secretary of Defense Les Aspin and Joint Chiefs chairman General John

Shalikashvili made clear at a meeting with journalists today that non-binding partnership is as far as the United States is willing to go. Any more formal defense commitment, they say, would be destabilizing.

On another irksome issue, Ukraine is being offered economic assistance and a meeting with President Clinton in Moscow in return for a quick resolution of the problems of disposing of nuclear weapons on Ukrainian soil.

And Bosnia, as an issue at a NATO summit in Brussels, is being completely soft-pedaled. A French effort to revive the question of bombing Serbian artillery positions is being dismissed by the Pentagon. An official who's following the drafting of the NATO final communiqué had trouble today remembering what was being said about Bosnia beyond calling it "a tragedy."

President Clinton's first trip to Europe will not rank as the ten days that shook the world. He'll apparently be content if it leaves the world shaking a little bit less so he can get on with reinventing America.

Tracing the Roots of White House Special Investigations

JANUARY 16, 1994

Liane Hansen, host: While President Clinton was proving his foreign policy mettle, back home aides were scrambling to contain Whitewater. Last Wednesday, the White House agreed to the appointment of a special counsel. To NPR's senior news analyst Daniel Schorr, it all has a familiar ring.

Welcome, or shall I say welcome back, to the arcane world of special prosecutors, special counsel, and independent counsel. And I guess first off, you'll want to know the difference among them.

Special counsel, named by the attorney general to look into allegations too sensitive for normal Justice Department handling because they involve high officials, is an institution that goes back at least to President Grant, who had one named in 1875. And so did Presidents Theodore Roosevelt, Coolidge, and Truman.

Special prosecutor was a Watergate innovation. President Nixon's first two attorneys general, John Mitchell and Richard Kleindienst, ended up as defendants in the conspiracy themselves. To calm public opinion, the new attorney general, Elliot Richardson, went outside the department to name a fellow Bostonian, former solicitor general Archibald Cox, as a special prosecutor, with his own staff, his independence guaranteed. But when Cox proved to be too independent for Nixon's comfort, the beleaguered president ordered him fired. When Richardson and his deputy William Ruckelshaus refused to do it, the next in line, Solicitor General Robert Bork, did the deed in what came to be known as the "Saturday Night Massacre." That generated a wave of public protest, which White House chief of staff Alexander Haig called a "firestorm." And a new special prosecutor was named, Leon Jaworski of Texas, who was once again guaranteed independence and got it.

But in the wake of Watergate, President Carter concluded that total independence from the executive branch was needed for investigations involving the president and his official family. The result was the Special Prosecutor Law, which established a procedure under which, once a preliminary investigation had established there was a serious allegation, an outside prosecutor would be named by a three-judge appeals court panel, and thereafter be responsible only to those judges.

In time, the name was changed from special prosecutor to independent counsel, to avoid stigmatizing those being investigated. In the next fourteen years, special prosecutors and independent counsel conducted fourteen investigations, probing into everything from allegations of drug use by Carter chief of staff Hamilton Jordan—he was cleared—to charges involving lobbying and financial dealings against Reagan attorney general Edwin Meese and staffers Michael Deaver and Lyn Nofziger. Meese was cleared, Deaver convicted of perjury, Nofziger convicted of illegal lobbying, but reversed on appeal.

The biggest independent counsel investigation ever, of course, was Lawrence Walsh's seven-year, $40 million probe into the Iran-Contra scandal, resulting in ten convictions, the principal two of which, Admiral John Poindexter's and Colonel Oliver North's, were reversed on appeal. The release of Walsh's final report by the three judges is still pending.

Meanwhile, the Whitewater real estate deal produced a clamor for a special investigation. So now back to the old traditional special counsel, named by the attorney general, responsible to the attorney general, just as in the days of President U. S. Grant. So special counsel, special prosecutor, independent counsel. Got it straight?

Action on Bosnia Can Be Credited to Public Outrage

FEBRUARY 9, 1994

Success, they say, has a thousand fathers and failure is an orphan. But the word "success" in this case should be qualified. The Serbs pulled back their guns before, last August, when NATO made a fist and the Serbs then agreed to a demilitarized Sarajevo under United Nations control. But the guns were back on the mountaintops three weeks later, when the heat was off.

Even if this truce fails, NATO coming together with the UN's Boutros-Ghali on a threat of the first offensive action in the alliance's forty-four-year history represents a success that can best be measured by imagining what a bleak world order we would face if they'd remained in paralyzed discord. It's remarkable how fast things changed.

One day the generals were telling us how hard it is to pinpoint artillery from the air. Then they suddenly discovered advanced radar that can locate and relay the source of artillery fire. One day the Europeans were saying their peacekeeping forces would be sitting ducks for Serbian reprisal, and then the peacekeepers were told to prepare to dig in to defensive positions. One day President Clinton was saying the civil war would go on until those folks got tired of killing each other, and that America had no national interest justifying military involvement. Then the administration discovered another kind of national interest, a public sense of outrage.

The administration had allowed itself to be lulled by opinion polls into thinking that Americans had no great interest in Bosnia. There was no great reaction when the president brushed off Bosnia in the State of the Union address. But then came the Saturday-morning massacre in Sarajevo, the grisly scenes on television, and a majority of polled Americans now wanted to see the Serbian guns bombed.

Another part of the story was skillful and resolute French diplomacy. Putting aside the spitting contest with the Clinton administration that had marred the Brussels summit last month, the French got the Clinton administration to join in the two-track initiative—ultimatum and negotiation. At that point, Russian president Yeltsin, who had been prepared to oppose action, saw the handwriting of isolation on the wall, and he got busy putting pressure on his Serbian friends to back off. And that's how successes against aggression are made. First, your people get you to make a fist.

The American Melting Pot Isn't Looking for More Ingredients

APRIL 3, 1994

In German, the word is *Asyl,* and for years it worked magic. *Asyl* means "asylum," and refugees from Eastern Europe or from Asia needed only to say *"Asyl"* when they reached Germany's border. Then they were assured of entry, pending investigation, which usually had not happened before they blended into the population.

But with the immigrants increasing into the hundreds of thousands, and with the crushing burden of having to absorb East Germany after unification, Germany experienced a rash of antiforeigner outbreaks, burning of their shelters and several murders, and finally, a government proud of its constitution changed its rule. And the word *Asyl* no longer works magic.

Xenophobia, the fear of aliens, is not a very pleasant thing. And now it's being felt in another open society, America. Especially in border states like Florida, Texas, and California. You can detect the symptoms of xenophobia when politicians find pay dirt in antiforeigner rhetoric and actions.

In Florida, where Haitians continue to slip through the anti-immigration blockade, Governor Lawton Chiles makes hay by demanding that the federal government pay for all immigration, legal and illegal.

In California, Governor Pete Wilson scores points by claiming that the state is being bankrupted by the costs of services to illegal immigrants. Senator Dianne Feinstein, up for reelection next year, wants to charge a $1 toll at border crossings to pay for beefing up the border patrol.

Now the federal government is getting into the crackdown-on-immigrants act. The Immigration and Naturalization Service wants to restrict the right of asylum seekers to work, and it wants to levy $130 charges for asylum applications. How the people are supposed to pay without working is not clear.

A White House task force on welfare reform is considering cutting benefits to immigrants as one way of reducing the costs. Moves to cut aliens off health and welfare benefits do not seem to take into account, compassion aside, that more threats to public health and safety may come from sick and destitute people.

Misinformation helps to fuel the anti-immigrant anger. Senator Feinstein emphasized that 1.3 million Californians are out of work, while 1.3 million undocumented aliens are settled in the state. That ignores the fact that aliens are consumers, helping to create work.

A host of reports documents immigration as a boon rather than a bane. A new study by the nonprofit Alexis de Tocqueville Institution points out that the ten states with the fewest immigrants have on the average the highest unemployment rates. But the xenophobic mood is not interested in scientific studies. Not when Governor Wilson can make headlines calling for a constitutional amendment barring citizenship for children of illegal immigrants born in this country. We can no longer allow compassion to overrule reason, says the governor, as thousands cheer.

The Gallup poll says 65 percent of Americans favor cutting back on legal immigration. That percentage has doubled in thirty years. That's where the emotion is, and that's where the votes are, and I'll spare you the quote from Emma Lazarus on the base of the Statue of Liberty.

Justice Blackmun

APRIL 6, 1994

Harry Blackmun is a friend and so there may be a little bias here. More than any other justice, he has sought to demystify the Supreme Court and bring it closer to the people. The Court is a remote institution, he once told me. People fear the Court and it shouldn't be that way. He has ruffled judicial feathers on occasion by public lectures and interviews. More than most justices, he believes that the Supreme Court should not defer too much to the executive and Congress, because he holds the Court to be the final recourse of the people, there to protect them against arbitrary action by the other branches of government.

Baseball fan Blackmun jokes about being President Nixon's number three pick, after Judges Hainsworth and Carswell were rejected in 1970.

He's also a music fan who has brought concerts to the Supreme Court and last summer narrated Prokofiev's *Peter and the Wolf* at the Aspen Music Festival.

In Aspen, where he presides over the annual Justice in Society Seminar, one sees the true Blackmun—Harry to everybody, unpretentious, modest, almost shy. Each year the highlight of the seminar is his off-the-record briefing on the *Roe v. Wade* decision, how it came to be and how it has fared since he wrote it in 1973. Without breaking confidences, let me say that until 1992, Blackmun's briefings on the abortion decision concluded on a steadily gloomier note. Once he spoke of *Roe* almost in the past tense, as something that had helped a generation of women, even though it was going to be reversed. But in 1992, *Roe* was reaffirmed in a 5–4 decision and Blackmun noted the emergence of a new center in the Court, including Justices Kennedy, Souter, and O'Connor. His spirits visibly brightened.

Blackmun has come a long way since 1970 when he came into the Court, content to be called Justice Berger's Minnesota twin, feeling that on that august bench he was out of his depth. He is modest and humble still, but no longer unsure of his opinions. The third oldest justice in the Court's history, he postponed retiring as long as he thought his legacy in danger. Now he feels his legacy is safe. As he wrote President Clinton with characteristic modesty, one does the very best one can with such talent as one possesses.

Mandela and Arafat Face Tough Challenges of Governing

MAY 4, 1994

There are not many other places recently where we've witnessed a peaceful transfer of power. The last-minute piece of theater in that Cairo theater, with Yasser Arafat having trouble with a map, served to remind us of how much blood has been shed over maps from Kuwait to Bosnia. A pause for a moment of euphoria in South Africa and the Middle East is understandable. But then comes the hard part—the morning after, when revolutionaries must become governors. When something other than slogans of liberation must be devised to meet people's expectations of better lives, lest exaltation turn into disillusionment and diehards gather strength to challenge authority.

Compared to South Africa, Gaza and Jericho represent a micro problem. But Yasser Arafat and his lieutenants have displayed more talent for agitation than for administration. Under constant pressure, they must now deal with security, gun control, collapsing roads, sewers and water supply, and serious unemployment. They have their work cut out for them.

South Africa, which has worked well for whites but not for blacks, represents a macro challenge in governing. Half of the 30 million blacks are unemployed. Half are illiterate or semiliterate, half live below the poverty line. Nelson Mandela has set his sights on national conciliation first. But that must go hand in hand with economic improvement. And Mandela has campaign promises to meet. Two and a half million jobs and a million new houses in the next five years.

"We are rolling up our sleeves to begin tackling the problems," says Mandela. "A true beginning to complete the march of peace," says Yasser Arafat. Both look to America and international institutions for aid. Both will need a lot of aid. But in the end, it is their own journeys into self-determination they're undertaking and without much of a road map and with no way back.

Diplomacy Avoids Many Words to Dodge Involvement

JUNE 19, 1994

In the dictionary, the definition of "genocide" is quite straightforward—"the deliberate and systematic extermination of a national or racial group."

So the extermination of hundreds of thousands of people, mainly Tutsis, in Rwanda is genocide? Well, not necessarily. Or, at least, "not officially," says our State Department. Department spokeswoman Christine Shelley says, "We have reason to believe that acts of genocide may have occurred in Rwanda, but, as a legal matter, you can't apply that label to all the killings that have been going on." How many acts of genocide does it take to make genocide? "That's not a question I'm in a position to answer," says Ms. Shelley.

But why the strange tap dance? Because if what's been happening in Rwanda is genocide, then the international community is obligated to do something about it. The 1948 United Nations Genocide Convention, which the United States didn't get around to signing until 1989, says that signatories are obliged to prevent and punish acts intended to destroy ethnic groups. " 'Genocide' is a word that carries an enormous amount of responsibility," a senior official told the *New York Times*. So if you ban the word, you can duck the responsibility.

Orwell would have understood about that. Looking ahead to 1984, he invented the language of Newspeak, one of whose principles was eliminating undesirable words or stripping words of undesirable meanings. So during the Nixon administration, "disarmament" was retired in favor of "arms control" to avoid the impression that we would tear down our defenses. Later, "arms control" was retired in favor of "arms reduction" when President Reagan embraced the idea of cutting down on nuclear arms. "Aggressor" is another loaded word like "genocide" that implies that, if you name it, you should do something about it.

Until recently, President Clinton used "aggressor," but in a gingerly way, to apply to attacks by the Bosnian Serbs on the Bosnian Muslims. Thus, at a news conference on April 21, "I have always felt the Serbs were the primary aggressors, though not always not the initiators of a particular aggression." Next day, Mr. Clinton expressed anger at the "continued aggression" in the Gorazde area. But then, a day later, he said, "The government forces are also engaging in attacks, and I believe they should both stop and go back to the bargaining table." In his Annapolis speech on May 25, the president made one more reference to "Serbian aggression and ethnic cleansing," and then no more. At this point, naming an aggressor is clearly regarded as counterproductive. And so, at least for now, "aggressor" joins "genocide" as politically incorrect in the parlance of diplomacy, where the politics of meaning is sometimes replaced by the politics of meaninglessness.

Some Perspective on the Simpson Case

JULY 10, 1994

President Clinton probably would have rescheduled his European trip had he known that he'd be practically snuffed out on television by the O. J. Simpson hearings. Maybe the Wimbledon tennis matches would have been played only during weekends. As it was, NBC, which owns the American rights, felt obliged on occasion to preempt Wimbledon for that Los Angeles courtroom.

Among the few Americans who don't love murder less, but love tennis more, this caused considerable anguish. NBC tried to explain that when you get a story as big as this, well, everybody has to make sacrifices. The director of news preempts the director of sports under an arrangement originally devised to ensure that the news department could break in even on a Super Bowl in the event of World War III.

What makes this hard to understand is that somebody above the news director and sports director level could reasonably have argued that with every other network carrying the O.J. hearings, NBC could have had not only the tennis fans but everybody who didn't want to watch the courtroom drama, which for long periods was not very dramatic anyway.

There is something wrong with all television showing the same thing. Now, I have a suggestion to make—it's addressed to Governor Wilson of California. He's staggering under a budget deficit that forces him to shortchange the schools and deny services to immigrants. My suggestion is that this television gold mine called courtroom murder cases should not be given to the networks free, but should be auctioned off to one network, like the NFL or the baseball World Series. I can see billions of dollars flowing into California's treasury. If Rupert Murdoch's Fox network, say, ran off with the high bid, I can imagine some bad feelings among the other networks and a lot of talk about the First Amendment and freedom of information. I can imagine California coming back with "So, where were you when exclusive rights to sports were being auctioned off?"

Anyway, if every American who watches television is forced to look at the same thing—well, isn't that an implied restraint of trade? Meanwhile, something needs to be done to keep murder-trial addicts in touch with the world. CNN does it by occasional beeps, alerting you to words crawling across the bottom of your screen, telling you of tornadoes, stock prices, and the latest on Whitewater. I think that we in public radio have a special responsibility in that respect. My idea is that people keep their radios on while riveted to the television screen, and at intervals we will come in with just the bare bones of what you need to keep in touch with reality:

BEEP—BEEP—BEEP
Flood damage in the South, fire damage in Colorado.

BEEP—BEEP—BEEP
Haitian refugees still coming. No invasion yet. This will be updated every half hour.

BEEP—BEEP—BEEP
The judge has just ruled in the O. J. Simpson case—oh, but you knew that already. Go back to your set.

BEEP—BEEP

Advice for Future Witnesses

AUGUST 3, 1994

What do I have to show for fifty-eight hours spent watching Whitewater hearings?

All right, Senator, let me amend that testimony. Maybe I did fall asleep several times, and sometimes my mind wandered into how the banking committees might be using this time to save the sinking dollar. But in aggregate, it's been an awful lot of time spent watching hearings that produced no John Dean to jump ship and torpedo the president, and no Oliver North to instruct us on the patriotic virtues of lying and shredding.

There are, however, some useful lessons for future witnesses to learn from the current hearings. First, don't confuse a heads-up with a heads-down. Don't immediately start covering up when you hear a reporter is working on a story that may mention the president and the first lady. Don't go all out on damage control before you know what the damage may be. Most of the White House people who ran around in panic about that criminal referral didn't have the foggiest idea what the Clintons were supposed to have done.

Second, don't overprepare, overrehearse, and overproduce your testimony. As Roger Altman has discovered, hell hath no fury like a senator outwitted by skillful evasion. "Too clever by half," the British call it, a phrase that every Rhodes scholar will recognize. Don't sit around with aides and lawyers trying out various versions of what you are supposed to remember.

Third, in any remotely possible conflict of interest, recuse yourself—and fast. The lawyers and ethics people who tell you you don't have to don't have your interests at heart. No one ever got into trouble from an unnecessary recusal. Don't refuse to recuse.

Fourth, resist questions containing analogies to Watergate or any other gate. When a senator asks, "What did the president know and when did he know it?" just look blank.

Fifth, and finally, about diaries. No, I'm not going to say don't keep one. Do keep one, and make sure you don't tell it the truth. Start each page not with "Dear diary" but "Dear Senator." That's just to remind you that one day it may be read aloud with sneers by unfriendly unpeople. Think of your private life as being an open book. In short, write as they tell you to drive—defensively.

"Socialized" Medicine Could Be the Cure for America's Ills

AUGUST 10, 1994

Highly charged controversies often come down to hot-button words meant to arouse anger and fear. The fighting words of the health reform debate, dusted off from the Medicare debate of thirty years ago, are "socialized medicine."

When Senator Phil Gramm uses the expression, Hillary Rodham Clinton accuses him of ranting and raving. Senator Robert Dole, who praises the miracle of health care he received from the military after being wounded in Italy, seems to be unaware that he's talking about socialized medicine, free government care.

Opponents tend to associate the word "socialized" with socialistic. In its first dictionary meaning, to "socialize" is to make fit for society or life with others. But perhaps that points to the true underlying issue that agitates the nation and confuses Congress. Listen to talk shows and you'll hear people, asked if they are willing to pay for universal health care, almost universally respond, "Hell no."

Put that way, it sounds as though they're being asked to pay for others. It is remarkable that Americans, willing to extend health care to Rwandans, balk at extending health care to other Americans. Social insurance, like many social arrangements, does not work well on a purely voluntary basis. The young and fit need to pay more than their share now and hope to be compensated when they are old and possibly unfit.

But Senator George Mitchell, struggling for a centrist consensus, has chosen to play down the idea of a mandate, another fighting word. Mrs. Clinton's misgivings about the Mitchell plan are based on a lack of confidence that Americans will respond in sufficient numbers to a voluntary, market-incentive approach. The Clinton administration, delighted at last to have health reform on the floor in both chambers, is basing its current strategy on the hope that what it sees as an overly voluntary-centered bill can be strengthened, when reconciled in conference, with a stronger House bill.

But few supporters of health reform are bold enough to confront Americans with the fundamental issue that ultimately you can't make any community effort like health insurance work on a purely voluntary basis. Insurance pools require some system of cost sharing. In the end, if health care is to be extended to all Americans, it will have to be, well, socialized.

Haiti Action Signed, Sealed, and Ready for Delivery

SEPTEMBER 12, 1994

On October 11 a year ago, the USS *Harlan County,* with two hundred military trainers on board, was turned away from Port-au-Prince by a riot on the docks. Around the time of the anniversary, with Congress likely gone, the chances are the Americans will be back, this time with about twenty thousand troops.

If ever a die was cast, a Rubicon crossed by presidential pronouncements, this one has been. Jeane Kirkpatrick may argue, as she does in the *Washington Post,* that democracy is not an entitlement that can be imposed by force. Anthony Lewis may argue, as he does in the *New York Times,* that a military operation without congressional authority will lack legitimacy. Senators Robert Dole and John McCain may argue, as they do on television, that liberating Haiti represents no vital national interest.

These arguments have been largely overtaken. The threats and advertised preparations have gone too far to be reversed without making a mockery of the president's word. That would do serious damage to the national interest, and thus the argument for invasion now becomes self-fulfilling. One can only watch in fascination as the D-day, H-hour preparations proceed.

Joint Chiefs chairman John Shalikashvili confers with President Aristide on how to avert a bloodbath of revenge killing during and after the occupation. The National Security Council debates whether General Raoul Cedras should be hunted down as was done with Manuel Noriega in Panama, and less successfully with Mohamed Aidid in Somalia. The Voice of America gears up to replace Haitian Radio with its own broadcasts in Creole.

The working premise of the planners is that if American casualties are held to a minimum by a massive show of force, the president can carry this off without undue damage to his already weakened position at home. Few in the administration believe that a generally unpopular and uncomprehended invasion will improve his position. But barring a last-minute cave-in by the Haitian military junta, there appears to be no way back from invasion. Mr. Clinton must sometimes wonder where he got the idea he could put the world on hold and be a domestic president.

The Miscalculations of Saddam Hussein

OCTOBER 10, 1994

In October 1973, shortly after the Saturday Night Massacre that brought President Nixon's Watergate crisis to a head, he put American forces on a worldwide alert as a warning to the Soviet Union against military intervention in the Middle East. So widespread was the assumption that he was engineering a distraction that Secretary of State Kissinger called a news conference to appeal for a minimum of confidence that the administration was not playing with American lives.

It is hard to know to what extent bellicose Soviet moves were influenced by a perception of a floundering Nixon. America's antagonists have made calculations and sometimes miscalculations about the president's standing with the public and about his will and capacity to act. So when Ross Perot says President Clinton has timed the Iraq confrontation as a political diversion, or when Senate candidate Oliver North says the president doesn't have the forces needed to deal with Saddam Hussein, one wonders how this will influence Saddam Hussein's calculations.

Saddam Hussein's 1990 miscalculation, influenced by soft words from President Bush and Ambassador April Glaspie as he prepared to invade Kuwait, was that there was a political imperative in America against risking American lives. That was undoubtedly fueled by the abrupt pullout from Lebanon after the car-bomb attack on the American marines, and after the extraordinary lengths to which the Reagan administration went to try to ransom a handful of hostages in Lebanon with arms sales to Iran.

His 1994 miscalculation appeared to be that without going to war, he could apply pressure for the easing of sanctions by a threat to Kuwait that would pin down American forces, counting on early pressure to bring them home. His calculation about the lack of American staying power was undoubtedly fueled by evacuation from Somalia and Rwanda when the going got tough, and the demands for speedy withdrawal from Haiti, where the going hasn't been tough at all.

The administration has been obliged to go to unusual lengths in statements and deployments to convince the Iraqi ruler that the president has the capacity and the will to act and all the forces he needs at his command. Iraqi forces may now be withdrawing from the Kuwaiti border, but Saddam Hussein is in a position to play a cat-and-mouse game, and it remains to be seen whether, given public impatience and unsparing political opponents, President Clinton can match him in this game over the long haul.

Questioning the Purpose of the CIA in the Nineties

NOVEMBER 6, 1994

For the first time since the midseventies, the CIA is to undergo a comprehensive examination by a bipartisan presidential commission, with former defense secretary Les Aspin as chairman and former senator Warren Rudman as vice chairman. This investigation will go far beyond the Aldrich Ames scandal to question whether there are too many intelligence agencies for a world without a major antagonist and whether they come anywhere near earning their keep. Members of the commission have yet to be named, under a formula by which President Clinton gets to appoint nine and congressional leaders select eight, divided between the parties. That, says the authorizing legislation, is in order to enhance the credibility of the commission.

And that reminds me of what happened when the question of credibility was raised about the last presidential commission to investigate the CIA. This was a blue-ribbon panel named in January 1975 by President Ford. It was headed by Vice President Nelson Rockefeller, and included former governor Ronald Reagan, former NATO commander General Lyman Lemnitzer, and AFL-CIO secretary treasurer Lane Kirkland. At a White House lunch with the publisher and editors of the *New York Times,* President Ford was asked what credibility such establishment types would have in investigating the CIA. The president explained that he had to choose very carefully because the commission might run into CIA misdeeds much worse than what they thought they were investigating. "Like what?" asked A. M. Rosenthal, the irrepressible *Times* executive editor. "Like assassination," snapped the president. And then he added, "But that's off the record." Well, the *Times* agreed to keep it off the record, but I learned of the president's explosive reference to assassinations and I reported it on CBS, and that led to the investigation of assassination conspiracies against Fidel Castro and others. Apparently, no assassination plot actually succeeded.

So who knows what the Aspin-Rudman commission will find when it pokes its nose into the attics and closets of an agency living in dread of what its next scandal will be. Curiously, while awaiting the big probe, the agency has lately been surfacing stories not about recent failures, but about some of its hush-hush operations going back to the fifties and the sixties. I don't wish to appear unduly suspicious, but it is as though some clandestine expert on diversionary propaganda is trying to change the subject.

And so we learn that in the 1950s and 1960s, at the height of the cold war, the CIA funneled millions of dollars into supporting Japan's ruling Liberal Democrats as a bulwark against communism. We already knew, from the earlier investigations, that the agency had done the same thing in Italy. Further, we learned of a cloak-and-dagger operation in the sixties to destabilize the first democratically elected prime minister

in Guyana, Chedi Jagan. He was considered by the Kennedy administration to be too leftist. Add Guyana to Guatemala, Chile, and Cuba as
arenas for CIA hostile operations in the Western Hemisphere. Then
we learn that in the 1950s a major covert operation was devoted to supporting anti-Communist rebels in Indonesia, for fear that President
Sukarno was coming increasingly under Communist influence. Add
that to the earlier revelations that Sukarno was one of the persons the
CIA considered trying to assassinate. That came out in a Senate report
on assassination plots that I talked about earlier.

But that's all old stuff, however interesting historically. The question
now is not what the CIA did in the fifties and sixties, but what it did and
failed to do in the seventies and eighties, and what purpose it serves in
the nineties.

What Will Happen to U.S. Foreign Policy?

NOVEMBER 14, 1994

The old adage has it that partisan politics stops at the water's edge, but
the water's edge is fast disappearing under the Republican wave. In
Jakarta, President Clinton is reassuring Asian leaders that constitution-
ally he still has the responsibility for the conduct of foreign policy. But
Mr. Clinton—pardon the expression—is whistling "Dixie." The Republican majority, starting with Jesse Helms, the next chairman of the
Senate Foreign Relations Committee, is staking out foreign policy positions that can be disruptive to the administration's plans, and the early
articulation of these positions is already casting a menacing shadow.
Helms will be no Arthur Vandenberg, the champion of bipartisan foreign policy. The Michigan isolationist was converted to internationalism
by Pearl Harbor, then cooperated with President Truman in his principal foreign policy enterprises like the Marshall Plan and NATO.

In the breathless week since the election, Helms has asserted these
positions, among others: Opposition to joining in peacekeeping missions
of the United Nations, which he says obstructs American purposes and
costs billions of dollars. Opposition to most foreign aid, which he calls
sinking $2 trillion down foreign rat holes to countries that often oppose
us. Reservations about the Middle East peace process, especially softness

on Syria, and any plan to station American troops on the Golan Heights.

Add to this that Senator Robert Dole has called for pulling American troops out of Haiti by Thanksgiving; that Republicans are questioning the deal to provide nuclear reactors to North Korea, at a moment when China has just agreed to support that arrangement; that Republicans believe President Clinton has been too friendly to Russia; plus signs of protectionist trade sentiments among the new crop of populist congressional Republicans, and then you can understand why President Clinton finds himself facing worried questions from Asian leaders.

"I don't expect the election to have any impact on our foreign policy," the president said at his news conference in Manila. But foreign officials can read, and they know when a president has been seriously weakened. They also know what an assertive Congress with a power of the purse, the power of treaty ratification, and the power of confirmation can do to reduce a foreign policy to shambles.

The question is whether the triumphant Republicans fully realize that they are no longer the opposition sounding off, that what they say counts, that it has effects, and will lead America's friends and enemies in the world to make their own calculations about how far they can go.

On Politicians' Doctoring the Truth

DECEMBER 18, 1994

Is it only a crochety old-timer who worries about the buffeting that facts take in the political marketplace?

I'm not talking about subjective values, like truth and lying, as when Jacques Delors, favored to win the presidential election in France, suddenly bowed out, saying, "I would have felt I was lying to the French people in proposing a program that could not be implemented." Gracious! If all the politicians making promises they know they could not keep threw in the towel, we'd have an awful lot of vacant offices. No, I'm speaking of something else: about objective facts and the tendency of politicians to smooth them out, alter them, or make them up to serve some purpose.

Take Senator Jesse Helms, who recently became exercised with the news media for playing up his remark about President Clinton needing a bodyguard if he came to North Carolina. Helms said that the interview in the *Raleigh News and Observer* originally had the word "jokingly" in it, but the editor took it out. Deputy managing editor Mike Yopp said that was not accurate. The word "jokingly" was never in the story.

Or House Speaker Newt Gingrich, who sometimes seems to talk faster than he can think. There's his now famous remark about "up to a quarter of the White House staff using drugs in the four or five years before coming aboard"—a statement at best questionable. But then there is Gingrich's story about a ten-year-old boy put in detention for saying grace in a St. Louis public school cafeteria, a story denied by the principal, who said the boy was disciplined for totally unrelated reasons, or Gingrich's statement that in Washington, eight hundred babies a year were left in Dumpsters—eight hundred is a total for all abandoned babies in Washington, of whom, in well-publicized cases, only two were found in Dumpsters.

Oliver North, unsuccessful candidate for the Senate from Virginia, is, of course, a special case. He told high school students, "I didn't lie to Congress in the Iran-Contra affair," belying his own public testimony that he had. He accused his opponent, Senator Charles Robb, of favoring abortion, up to the last month of pregnancy, although Robb has never favored late-term abortions. North also had a favorite story about his own origins, about a penniless immigrant grandfather from England who became an indentured apprentice in Norfolk and worked off his ship passage, which had been paid by an English businessman, in one year, two years, three years—depending on which North speech you heard. But the enterprising Norfolk newspaper the *Virginian Pilot* dug up from immigration records that North's grandfather, also named Oliver, paid his own way to America and apparently was never indentured.

North was not the first politician to invent part of his own biography. There was Senator Joseph Biden, who had not only borrowed from a speech of British Labourite Neil Kinnock to say that he was the first member of his family to go to a university, but added that he'd graduated in the first half of his class in Syracuse Law School, when he actually ranked number seventy-six out of eighty-five. And then there was President Lyndon Johnson, who often talked of his great-great-grandfather having died at the Alamo. When challenged, he said, "No, it was actually the Battle of San Jacinto," but as biographer Doris Kearns Goodwin noted, that wasn't right, either. The ancestor was a real estate trader who died at home in bed.

Ronald Reagan, who seemed to have difficulty distinguishing facts from movie episodes, would be a chapter in himself. One of his favorite stories, about a heroic World War II tail gunner posthumously awarded the Congressional Medal of Honor, turned out after many retellings, even to the Congressional Medal of Honor Society, to be taken from a 1944 movie, *Wing and a Prayer*. It doesn't matter. Sissela Bok, who wrote a book about lying, says that such deceit cuts at the roots of what we mean by democracy, and it may help to explain why some Americans say, "Why vote? It only encourages them."

The State of Peace on Earth in 1994

DECEMBER 25, 1994

Time once again for our annual look at how peace on Earth fared in the past year. First, the relatively good news, which I fear will be a lot shorter than the bad news. The hopeful indications a year ago that three of the world's most enduring conflicts, in South Africa, the Middle East, and Northern Ireland, might be nearing resolution have generally been sustained. In South Africa under President Nelson Mandela, a multiracial society is taking shape. In Northern Ireland the guns and bombs have fallen silent and a truce shows promise of developing into formal peace negotiations.

In the Middle East the Rabin-Arafat handshake has been followed by a gradual transfer of authority in Gaza and Jericho in preparation for West Bank elections. This has been to the accompaniment of violence from extremists on both sides. But the peace process displays an amazing hardiness in the face of terrorism. A Jordan-Israel peace treaty has been added to the roster. Peace between Israel and Syria, which would be the capstone of the process, is not yet.

To that good news should be added conflicts resolved or averted: the return of President Jean-Bertrand Aristide to head a popular government in Haiti and an agreement with North Korea which, if it holds, may spare the world having to face an outlaw nuclear power that could arm other outlaws like Iran and Libya.

The rest of this report is dismal. Ruth Leger Sivard, busy with other projects, has not this year updated her unique survey of global conflict, which last year recorded twenty-nine conventional wars in progress around the world. But a new survey of global trends by American scholar Paul Kennedy records the number of wars steadily increasing and fewer ending than starting.

In Rwanda alone a half million Tutsis and Hutus have been slaughtered, and probably another half million have died of starvation and disease. Elsewhere in Africa, civil war and chaos have taken their toll in Somalia, the Sudan, and Angola.

In Bosnia, where ex-president Jimmy Carter has tried to work the magic he used in North Korea and Haiti, it is too early to speak of peace, and the three-year death toll stood at two hundred thousand. Russia found itself embroiled in hostilities with insurgents in regions on its border that it once ruled.

But peace on Earth is not just an absence of armed conflict. Around the world some 18 million people have been driven from their homelands, a refugee problem that rivals the dislocation caused by World War II. Add those displaced in their countries and you get closer to 40 million. And then, uncounted acts of brutality, including sexual violence and violence against children. Laconically, "global trend" sums it up. Torture and maltreatment are part of war. They cannot be quantified and are rarely a part of public discussion.

As a large part of the world seemed to sink into barbarism, a large part of the civilized world shrank back, feeling frustrated and impotent. From Somalia to Bosnia, international peacekeeping, the hope of a new world order after the cold war, found itself unable to cope.

In 1994, America remained at peace, in the sense, that is, of having no external enemy. But, alas, in a country ridden with violence and the fear of violence and anger against those considered intruders, and doubts about its own leaders, it takes a stretch to talk of peace.

Not a great year peacewise, goodwill-wise. Better luck next year.

1995

Violence at Home and Abroad

Some Innovations in Money Raising

FEBRUARY 12, 1995

I've been thinking of some innovations in money raising that may make a modest contribution to decreasing the deficit without new taxes. First of all, I think that business donations to members of Congress should be brought into the open by selling advertising space in the Capitol. Prime space at high rates could be sold on the rostrum of the Senate and the House. Behind the Speaker there would be a logo for Rupert Murdoch's Fox television or perhaps Coca-Cola, a Georgia-based product. In addition, members of Congress could wear neat but visible ID tags representing their commercial sponsors in lettering large enough to be picked up by C-SPAN. The presiding officer would recognize members by saying, for example, "The gentleman from Illinois and Prudential is recognized." I could see an even split in revenue between the members' campaigns and the budget to run Congress.

Second, nationalize baseball by drafting owners and players into the National Service Corps. Gate receipts and proceeds of television commercials would go into the federal treasury. The players would be put on salary, plus $5,000 for their future education at the end of two years of service, plus a certificate presented by the president. Olympic-type silver medals would be awarded to pennant winners, and gold medals to the World Series winners. I haven't figured out yet what to do with the owners, but they could probably be gainfully employed selling hot dogs and popcorn.

My most imaginative idea of all, if you'll pardon the immodesty, is selling the television rights to sensational court trials. There's no question that the O. J. Simpson trial, for example, is a multibillion-dollar asset that the state of California simply gives away to all comers. My idea is that as each trial comes up, the state auction off the television rights to the networks on an exclusive basis, like the NFL or the baseball leagues. Remember them?

One of the beauties of this idea is that the other networks could go back to normal programming, and wouldn't have to keep their audiences updated on the soap operas. And audiences would be given options, just in case there are any who don't want to spend all their time watching the big trial. The states, which would grow filthy rich, would be expected to share the proceeds with the federal government, which doesn't have much in the way of criminal trials to sell, because the juiciest crimes are usually crimes under state law. But Congress has already made a modest start on federalizing a lot more crime, and the lure of profits from television may accelerate that process. The general principle is that if the government needs money, it should follow the advice of bank robber Willie Sutton: go where the money is—sports and television.

The New World Order Becomes New World Anarchy

MARCH 19, 1995

In the bad old days of the 1950s in Moscow, one heard sardonic jokes like "We don't have much private crime, because crime is a state monopoly" and "Well, one thing you can say about a police state—it's well policed."

Now a police state no longer, Russia is in the grip of organized crime so pervasive as to menace the existence of the state. Russian Mafia groups carry out assassinations with impunity, control banks, are probably involved in smuggling nuclear materials out of Russia, and have established international connections reaching to Brooklyn and beyond. A famous television personality who wanted to break the criminal grip on advertising sales is slain, and President Boris Yeltsin displays his impotence by organizing a big funeral and firing the police chief.

Russia is not alone in the former Soviet Union. The United States Institute of Peace has just published a survey of former Soviet republics in Central Asia, saying that most people in Kazakhstan and Uzbekistan believe that corruption is rampant, particularly in government and law enforcement.

Things are not much better in the former Soviet satellites. Poland has had a rash of bombings believed to be part of gang turf battles for control of prostitution and car thefts. A newspaper investigation discovered that explosives could be purchased from the so-called antiterrorist police at the Warsaw airport, as the explosion of freedom brought freedom for explosions.

In the underdeveloped regions we used to call the Third World, in Pakistan, to which our attention was lately called by the murder of two American consular officers, President Benazir Bhutto says that Islamic holy warriors are now aligned with the narcotics trade, spreading a wave of terror. In Africa, governments are appealing for international assistance against drug trafficking that hurts their ability to attract investment. In Somalia, which the civilized world has pretty much given up, there is no functioning government at all, only marauding bands.

That may seem very far away, but in our Third World neighbor, Mexico, an investigation of assassinations reaching to the summit of the ruling party has found evidence of a scheme to collect bribes from drug traffickers in return for protecting their operations. The new world order isn't turning out to be what we hoped. The collapse of tyranny was supposed to lead to a flowering of democratic reform, not to new tyrannies of organized crime working in various unholy alliances with political and religious terrorists. In some parts of the world, it is as though the clock is being turned back a couple of thousand years to the days before the nation-state, when power was in the hands of warring tribes and clans. Now the marauders have computers and planes and limitless drug profits to undermine the state. What do we call it, the new world anarchy?

Security Measures Must Not Include Surveillance Abuses

APRIL 24, 1995

We have met the enemy and this time, to our dismay, it is us.

The demand for more internal security raises anew the question of how much freedom to yield in defense of a free society. Senator Arlen

Specter is among those quick to say that, faced with what he calls a "clear and present danger," federal intelligence agencies must have more leeway to conduct infiltration and surveillance. The current guidelines requiring a showing of probable cause before a group can be targeted date back to the midseventies, and it may be instructive to recall what brought them about. Congressional investigations exposed CIA surveillance of anti–Vietnam War groups and monitoring of mail. The FBI maintained a so-called COINTELPRO program, or rather, a series of programs that spied on student groups, left-wing organizations, the civil rights movement, and the women's liberation movement. It conducted wiretaps and break-ins, and concocted forged documents to sow dissension. An FBI memo of 1970 gave the justification: "Terrorist violence is all around us and more has been threatened. These violence-oriented, black and white savages are at war with the government and the American people." Since then, the Vietnam War, Watergate, Irangate, and a host of abuses have served to further undermine confidence that the government will use its powers judiciously rather than repressively. Contributing to a pervasive distrust of government are Hollywood and television films depicting the federal government as something between a vast conspiracy, as in *JFK,* and a vast irrelevancy, as in *Dave* and *Forrest Gump.* Contributing also has been the tendency of politicians to demonize government, a tendency that didn't start with Speaker Newt Gingrich, that goes back at least as far as Jimmy Carter's campaign for a "government as good as the people."

Now we may be at a crossroads moment when America's whole view of government and the anarchists who would bring it down would be agonizingly reconsidered, and President Clinton, who no longer has to worry about being considered irrelevant, will ask for broader powers to penetrate the potential threats. He promises that this will not be at the expense of Americans' liberties. But, remembering the investigative excesses of the past, it would wise for Congress not to allow itself to be stampeded into giving carte blanche to the feds. Nothing like having to get a court order to keep the investigators accountable. Government is in the unprecedentedly delicate situation of having to demonstrate both that it is not oppressive and that it can defend itself.

The Unabomber's Deal with the Media

APRIL 30, 1995

Liane Hansen, host: The Unabomber is back. This past week a package-bomb explosion killed a timber company executive in Sacramento, California. In all, there have been sixteen bombs nationwide since 1978. The New York Times said it received a letter from the bomber promising to stop the attacks if the paper would publish an article written by him. Publisher Arthur Sulzberger said he wouldn't allow his paper to be held hostage by those who threaten violence, but, he said, the Times would make a journalistic decision about whether or not to publish it. NPR's senior news commentator Daniel Schorr has these thoughts on the Times' dilemma.

The phenomenon of blackmailing the news media has grown with the growing importance of the media as a way for terrorists to achieve ego satisfaction. And often news managers submit, rather than face the consequences of refusal. In 1975, the German Baader-Meinhof Gang negotiated the release of five of its members in return for releasing a kidnapped politician. As part of the deal, German television showed the gang members boarding a plane and broadcast dictated propaganda statements. A German television executive later said, "We lost control of our medium."

A year later, Croatian nationalists in this country hijacked a Chicago-bound plane carrying ninety-two passengers and crew, and threatened to kill them unless the group's propaganda statement was published in American newspapers. The *New York Times*, the *Chicago Tribune*, the *Washington Post*, and the *Los Angeles Times* were induced by the American authorities to comply. The passengers were released. The hijackers eventually flew to Paris, where they surrendered in response to an ultimatum from the French authorities.

Benjamin Bradlee, the retired executive editor of the *Post*, says that today he would probably not have yielded to that threat, but back then, he could not face the possibility of a story that would say, "Umpteen American hostages were killed today because Bradlee refused to publish."

A year after that, in 1977, the New York serial killer who called himself Son of Sam demanded that Jimmy Breslin, then a *New York Daily News* columnist, publish his letters. And after talking to the police, Breslin did so. And when finally captured, the killer, David Berkowitz, said in a prison interview that seeing his letters in Breslin's column "gave him a rush." Robert Ressler, an FBI veteran, believes that seeing his prose in print probably escalated Berkowitz's murderous activities.

That points to the dilemma the *New York Times* now faces. Giving terrorists the media kicks they demand may or may not deter them from further violence. In any event, if the blackmail succeeds, it invites others to try threats of violence as a way to validate their importance. The *Times,* which has been consulting the FBI, is walking on eggshells. "We can't be held hostage," says Sulzberger, "but we'll look at the manuscript, make a journalistic decision, and whether we publish it ourselves or not, we'll do all we responsibly can to make it public." That is clearly intended to gain time, to keep the serial bomber negotiating rather than sending new bombs. But at the end, there will be a decision to make and it will be an agonizing one. To surrender to blackmail is to invite more blackmail. But then, every editor has in mind Ben Bradlee's fear of being blamed for umpteen Americans killed.

The Oklahoma City Disaster

MAY 21, 1995

Statisticians will tell you it's dangerous to make long-range projections from short-range data, but I'm a journalist, not a statistician, and accustomed to living with danger.

It seems to me that in the little more than a month since the Oklahoma City bombing, America has begun to undergo a profound mood change. People are suddenly aware that hatred of government can exact a heavy price if carried too far; people are becoming a little kinder and gentler, in the words of George H. W. Bush, but also feeling a lot more vulnerable.

After Oklahoma City, a *Wall Street Journal* reporter, Clare Ansberry, went to Butler, Pennsylvania, a town of thirty-five thousand— a thousand miles from Oklahoma City, and found something new stirring—a sense of the fragility of life. Schoolteacher Missy Frye, torn between teaching her children to love everyone and to trust no one, nurse Becky Gray, pausing a little longer in her nursing home rounds to listen to disoriented residents and stroke their hands, and Mayor Richard Chaunce, telling a group of leather-clad, tattooed motorbikers, "Government serves all the people." Government does what? That's Butler, Pennsylvania, but Butler is not alone.

The National Rifle Association must have felt a lot of heat since the resignation of life member George H. W. Bush to make it finally apologize for its fund-raising letter with the inflammatory reference to the government agents as "jackbooted thugs." NRA executive vice president Wayne LaPierre said he was sorry if anyone thought he was talking about all federal law enforcement officers. His letter sure sounded as though he was. It said that if you have a badge, you have the government's go-ahead to harass, intimidate, even murder, law-abiding citizens.

But never mind. Government bashing seems no longer chic. A new *Washington Post*–ABC nationwide poll found that since Oklahoma City, anger at government is down, satisfaction with government is up. Three out of four believe that people are too quick to criticize the federal government. Sixty-two percent do not believe that government threatens their personal rights and freedoms. Eighty-eight percent are not afraid of the federal government. Ninety percent do not think it's ever justified to take violent action against the federal government. And about half think that private militia groups threaten their personal rights and freedom.

Surprised? It should be noted the survey also indicates deep pockets of disaffection. But most Americans seem to have been shocked into an awareness that when dissatisfaction with government goes to an extreme, at the end of that continuum lies Oklahoma City. The poll quoted a typical comment from a pharmacist in Elgin, Texas: "The bombing in Oklahoma just opened our eyes to what could happen, and did happen." Would it surprise you also to know that many Americans are reconsidering their enthusiasm for antigovernment rhetoric on talk radio? In the *Post*-ABC poll, 58 percent agreed with President Clinton's charge that some talk show hosts spread hateful ideas and give the impression that violence is acceptable.

America seems different now than before April 19. I don't know how different or how long it will last. Richard Given, a lawyer in Butler, Pennsylvania, says that around his office, people are divided over how to prevent another tragedy, about gun control, about new powers for the FBI. He said, "Our hearts brought us together and now our brains are starting to split us again."

Still Many Unanswered Questions Concerning Waco

JULY 9, 1995

Because Waco has become the battle cry of the militias and Tim McVeigh, it is hardly possible to discuss in rational terms the bombing of the Branch Davidian compound.

Critics tend to speak not of a tragic mistake by the government, but a criminal conspiracy. When the House Subcommittee on Crime holds its hearings on Waco next week, it could help to illuminate what went wrong with the governmental process if it manages to insulate itself from some of the passion that surrounds the issue.

In April 1993, Attorney General Janet Reno was new to her job and unfamiliar with the principal players. She had grave doubts about the wisdom of the plan to storm the compound with tanks and a gas banned by international treaty. She lay awake at night, she later said, asking, "Oh my God. What if it blows the place up?" So how, under the influence of officials and advisers pursuing their own interests and prejudices—how did she finally decide to go ahead?

What failed was governmental process, and here are some of the questions that have not yet been satisfactorily answered. What was the role in the decision making of the FBI under Director William Sessions, himself then on the skids? Why did he advise Reno that there was child abuse going on in the compound, something never corroborated? Why did Sessions and his assistants, including Larry Potts, since promoted to deputy director, push so single-mindedly for the attack? Were they worried about their positions and about the damage of the standoff to FBI morale and prestige? A subquestion there is, What was the role of the FBI's psychological advisers? Why did the FBI seem to lean so heavily on consultants with a strong anticult bias and discount those more versed in the pathology of religious cults? Why did the FBI ignore the advice that David Koresh was looking for a way out?

What was the role of presidential advisers? President Clinton's friend Webster Hubbell was number two in the Justice Department. Also sitting in on the meetings with the FBI was White House deputy counsel Vincent Foster, who committed suicide three months after the April 19 attack. His suicide note had a cryptic line, "FBI lied in their report to the A.G.," attorney general. The subject of that report was not mentioned. Foster's widow, Lisa, told the FBI in an interview, according to the *Washington Times,* that Waco had caused her husband a great deal of stress, that he was horrified by the destruction of the compound, that he felt that everything was his fault. And that leads to the final question. What was the role of the president? Attorney General Reno said she briefed Mr. Clinton on the eve of the attack but did not ask for his approval, and she took full responsibility. But was that his sole involvement? If the president was so far removed from the decision making, then why did the president's lawyer, monitoring the planning session for the White House, feel that it was his, Foster's, fault? These are questions that go to the heart of how government agencies and the president function in a grave and delicate situation. If the House committee can illuminate some of these questions, it will have performed a service.

Federal Investigations Could Lead to More Mistrust

JULY 17, 1995

Whitewater, Waco, and coming later, Ruby Ridge. The summer festival of investigations gets under way.

The congressional committees have a fine line to walk, probing for signs of impropriety in the White House and law enforcement agencies without feeding paranoia about government as the enemy of the people. The word that flashes subliminally on the walls of the hearing rooms is "cover-up." What anxiety about Whitewater prompted White House aides, after the suicide of Vincent Foster, to spirit papers out of his files and stonewall the investigating Park Police like a threatening alien presence? In the disastrous decision to storm the Branch Davidian compound with tanks and a gas banned by international treaty, was there any pressure from the White House to hurry up and get the thing over with? Vincent Foster and Webster Hubbell attended planning sessions leading up to that decision. Did they not brief the president? In the Ruby Ridge shoot-out, how high in the FBI does responsibility go for the unusually broad authorization to shoot, and why were documents bearing that decision destroyed? What are we dealing with, jackbooted thugs or just jackrabbits burrowing their way to safety? What is this suffocating aura of irregularity that envelops the federal government? The FBI director has to demote his recently promoted deputy director. A former associate attorney general must testify more or less on his way to prison for other offenses. The body of Vincent Foster, a suicide to all but conspiracy theorists, must be figuratively exhumed again. The misbehavior in our law enforcement agencies creates a miasma of distrust at a time when there are forces ready to exploit and exaggerate that mistrust. How then to ferret out misdeeds without totally undermining law enforcement? The congressional committees have an opportunity to clear the air unless they choose for partisan reasons to add to the smog.

The O.J. Trial Touches on Journalistic Ethics

AUGUST 13, 1995

Feeling my analytical talents could be better applied elsewhere, I've been resolutely staying away from the O. J. Simpson trial, but now that the issue of journalistic sources has been raised, I can no longer desist.

Last September, Tracie Savage of Los Angeles station KNBC reported that DNA tests showed that blood on a sock was that of Simpson's slain wife. The Simpson defense tried to have Ms. Savage called and forced to reveal her source in order to demonstrate a police conspiracy. But the Savage story was wrong. The DNA tests had not been done at the time, and Judge Ito ruled that a wrong source could not have been much of a source and denied the motion to force her to testify.

But had the source been right, Ms. Savage might have faced having to reveal it or possibly going to jail for contempt of court. That's an issue that has sometimes confronted reporters and news organizations way back through the 1950s and '60s, when Marie Torre of the *New York*

Post and Myron Farber of the *New York Times* actually went to jail rather than reveal their sources.

I must acknowledge a more than casual interest in this issue. In 1976, the House Ethics Committee threatened me with a contempt of Congress citation carrying a jail term and a fine if I did not tell where I had gotten a suppressed report of the House Intelligence Committee on CIA misdeeds. In an open hearing I argued that I would not and could not betray a source I had promised to protect. Fortunately for me, the Ethics Committee voted 6–5 against proceeding with the contempt citation. I say "fortunately for me" because it was unlikely that I would find support in the courts.

The law of the land was and is the 1972 5–4 decision of the Supreme Court in the cases of Paul Branzburg of the *Louisville Courier-Journal* and Earl Caldwell of the *New York Times.* The one had reported on hashish production, the other on the Black Panthers having drugs and illegal weapons. The Court held that if the grand jury needed their evidence, they would have to give it. That means that the First Amendment offers no absolute protection of sources against the fair-trial guarantees of the Sixth Amendment. There followed a rash of subpoenas for reporters, as defense lawyers discovered a new opportunity to delay criminal proceedings. The Reporters Committee for Freedom of the Press counted more than five hundred subpoenas in a six-year period.

A novel twist in this issue came in 1991. The *Minneapolis Star Tribune*'s editor had revealed a reporter's source without asking his permission. The source, Dan Cohen, a political consultant, sued the paper for breach of contract, saying he'd been promised anonymity. The Supreme Court held, 5–4, that Cohen had a right to sue.

Now, in the O. J. trial, the latest wrinkle. What kind of source is it that gives you a bum steer? I would think that Tracie Savage doesn't owe that source anything, assuming, that is, that there was a source. Judge Ito thinks she may have just listened to elevator gossip.

Senator Packwood's Diaries May Render a Public Service

SEPTEMBER 11, 1995

What lies behind is only the first phase of the Robert Packwood scandal, mainly involving personal misconduct with women. Ahead of us, as the diaries and massive other documentation are studied, lies a deeper and more pervasive second phase involving legislative misconduct at the public expense.

Whether it was a felony, as Senator Bob Packwood speculated, for Senator Phil Gramm to siphon $100,000 in so-called soft money into his 1992 campaign is now being explored by the Senate Ethics Committee. But more important is where that kind of money comes from and what it purchases from legislators hungry for campaign funds.

The quid pro quo phenomenon is not new. The late Philip Stern described it in his book *The Best Congress Money Can Buy*. Public-interest organizations like Common Cause have inveighed against it for years. But seldom are we afforded the kind of first-person evidence that Packwood presents in his politically suicidal diaries. Take the case of superlobbyist Ronald Crawford unearthed by the *New York Times*. Crawford has been a good friend and ardent money raiser for Packwood. Packwood recalls that when Crawford needed a special tax loophole for the Shell Oil Company, Packwood said, "Ron, I still hate the oil companies, but I'll do you a favor." When Crawford needed a favor for the cable television industry, Packwood came through with support for deregulation. Packwood boasted in his diary that "much of Crawford's income is dependent on his relationship with me." Crawford brought in the big bucks, but Packwood also didn't sneeze at small bucks. Of a $3,000 contribution from a timber and paper company he wrote, "I'm glad to have anything I can get."

It is hard to know what possessed Packwood to document day by day the correlation between money received and legislative favors extended. That is something the average powerful chairman of a powerful committee prefers to gloss over. But Packwood has broken that code of silence about the hard uses of soft money. And as he resigns in dishonor, that may be one of the greatest services he has rendered.

Examining the Powell Mania

SEPTEMBER 17, 1995

In dinner conversations for months, the subject that inevitably came up was O. J. Simpson. Then, for a few days, it was Cal Ripken, and this past week it has been overwhelmingly Colin Powell. And no wonder. The publication of his memoirs has been greeted with a wave of publicity such as I've never witnessed. A wave in which he zestfully bathes. In his interviews, he runs a gamut from "Aw, shucks, just an ordinary kid from the South Bronx," to a self-confident leader who believes he has what it takes to inspire America.

"I'm tanned, rested, and ready—ha, ha," he said to one group of admirers at a *Time* magazine reception. He seems fully aware that the nation hangs on every teasing word that may betray his intentions. Will he run or won't he? And if he does, on what ticket? Tantalizingly, he suggests it could be Republican, maybe independent, perhaps even Democratic, just to be all-inclusive.

The pundits predicted that he'd avoid taking positions on issues, but perhaps preemptively, he took positions on issues—pro-choice, pro–registration of guns, pro–affirmative action, pro–death penalty. So much for the pundits who think they have Powell figured out.

If Powell hasn't proved himself as a political leader, he has certainly proved himself as a political performer. Movie lobbyist Jack Valenti, onetime Lyndon Johnson aide, told him admiringly, "If you run for president, you'll be formidable. And if you don't, you'll be rich." Well, would Valenti believe formidable and rich?

Formidable is the way the media have thrown skepticism to the winds to worship at the Powell shrine. "Powell Mania," the *Washington Post* calls it. "Can Colin Powell Save America?" trumpets the cover of *Newsweek*. "He would make a good president and it would be good for the country," says ABC's usually abrasive Sam Donaldson. Only now and then do you get questions about how Powell handled or didn't handle the My Lai massacre in Vietnam, or whether he was too quick to call off the war against Iraq. For the rest, the media are acting the way much of the American public is acting—so hungry for someone new in politics as to suspend disbelief and join a sort of national revival meeting.

No one knows better than Colin Powell how fast a balloon can be deflated. So he troops in and out of TV studios, but he doesn't inhale the adulation. He is still the military planner who wants to know where the battle will end before he commits his forces. But Powell Mania sells books, and he rides the wave like a skilled surfer.

The Unabomber's Manifesto

SEPTEMBER 19, 1995

Ben Bradlee, the retired executive editor of the *Washington Post,* recalls in his memoirs how, along with four other newspapers in 1976, he complied with the demand to publish the manifesto of Croatian nationalists, who had hijacked a TWA plane with ninety-two passengers and crew on board.

First, Bradlee arranged for an appeal from the FBI to accede in the public interest. Then, he writes, he followed instructions, meek as a lamb, and slunk home, once. "I'm not sure I'd do it twice," he says. Bradlee's description reflects the stomach-turning revulsion an editor feels at publishing under blackmail threat. Newspapers are quick to criticize the government for bargaining with terrorists, as in the Tehran hostage crisis on President Carter's watch and the Lebanon hostage crisis on President Reagan's watch, citing the incentives created for further terrorism.

But when the *Times* and *Post* publishers faced having the lives of unknown potential victims on their hands, they held their noses and acceded. Maybe, as they say, the case of the Unabomber is unique. Every case is unique. And now the publishers find themselves in a continuing relationship with the Unabomber, trying to get him to abandon threats against property as well as persons in return for printing three annual follow-up tracts. The key to the decision seems to be Sulzberger's statement that "this centers on the role of a newspaper as part of a community." Once an editor lived by the slogan "Publish and be damned." No longer. The laws of the press have become blurry in recent years of growing public resentment of what is perceived as arrogance and insensitivity. The new talk in press circles is of something called "civic journalism," which might be defined as journalism with a human face.

William Serrin, director of graduate studies of New York University's Journalism Department, says he is stunned at the violation of one of the most inviolate rules of journalism, that no one should dictate what you cover. I don't agree. The view to which I subscribe is that the newspapers acted as responsible members of a community.

Planning Peace While Waging War

SEPTEMBER 27, 1995

It used to be that first the fighting stopped and then peace was negotiated. But in Bosnia and, to some extent, in the Middle East, violence goes on even while the structure of peace is cobbled together. Remember when the normal order of events was cease-fire followed by formal truce, then a peace treaty? That went for cross-border conflicts like the two world wars and Korea, where there's a truce, but still no peace treaty.

In contemporary civil, communal, and ethnic conflicts the order may be different. In Vietnam, the fighting went on till the very end. In South Africa, the African National Congress refused officially to lay down its arms until it was sure of the transition of power. In the Middle East today, Israel and the PLO push ahead with a transfer of power knowing that it is constantly threatened by extremists on both sides.

It is Bosnia, however, where the situation is the most bizarre. Playing along with the urgings of the American brokers, Serbia, Croatia, and Bosnia are writing the constitution for a cooperative Bosnian state even while they continue killing each other to make sure that state never comes to be. The Croats ally themselves with the Muslims against the Serbs, except when the Croats are busy themselves killing Muslims. One partition map is drawn in Geneva, but another map is drawn with mortar and missile on the ground. Croatian president Franjo Tudjman has never repudiated the map he drew on a menu during an official dinner in London showing his vision of Bosnia in ten years as divided between Croatia and Serbia with no Muslim area at all.

Are people kidding themselves about a Bosnian state with democratic elections and a rotating presidency? President Clinton, deadpan, talks of another great step toward peace, but Assistant Secretary of State Richard Holbrooke, who isn't running for reelection, says if this vague outline is all we have, it will not bring peace.

That doesn't mean the exercise in constitution writing is just a charade. It does mean that until the parties can be cajoled or coerced into a cease-fire, the negotiations don't mean very much. There can be no confidence that lines will be respected and power will be shared until the fighting stops. Planning peace while waging war is not a great recipe for success.

The Simpson Trial May Produce More Than Verdicts

OCTOBER 3, 1995

President Clinton referred the other day to the circuslike atmosphere of the televised Simpson trial, but if it was a spectacle, it was one that tested America's view of itself, its prejudices, and its institutions, and the verdict is bound to have wide-ranging spillover effects. In the first place, on attitudes toward law enforcement agencies. In voting not guilty, the jury in effect condemned Mark Fuhrman as a lying racist symbol of a discredited police force. This dovetails neatly with the assault on federal law enforcement agencies arising from the Waco and Ruby Ridge episodes. It leaves confidence in the forces of law and order, starting with the LAPD, at a low ebb.

Connected with that, racial polarization. It was clear all along that white Americans were inclined to believe Simpson guilty, and black Americans that he was being framed. In the end, the jury implicitly, if not explicitly, endorsed the argument of counsel Johnnie Cochran that this was not just a murder case, but an issue of civil rights—never mind that a black who was not a superstar could not have commanded such a powerful defense. In the end, the defense managed to present Simpson as a persecuted African American. It is hard to imagine that that will have a calming influence on racial relations in America.

And finally, in the end there is politics. I would give a lot to know what General Colin Powell is thinking tonight, a black man whose soaring ratings in the opinion polls indicate that he has transcended race in the eyes of most Americans. Could he lead this country out of the wilderness of racial hatred that the Simpson trial has led us deeper into? And will he after today feel that the pressure is greater on him than before to try to bring this country together? I suspect that the trial and the verdict will have fallout that today cannot even be foreseen. But after such an experience, one senses that nothing will be the same.

The Million Man March Promotes an Atmosphere of Revival

OCTOBER 16, 1995

All advanced signs pointed to an outburst of separatist feeling with demands for land and reparations for slavery. Contributing to this surcharged atmosphere was the Republican congressional revolution against welfare and illegitimacy, simplistically associated with blacks. The O. J. Simpson verdict fortuitously two weeks before this march dramatized racial polarization, and Detective Mark Fuhrman became an emblem of unequal justice.

But the hundreds of thousands who came, came with their own agendas, many more in the mood for a festival of black togetherness than an antiwhite jihad. Many more were in the mood for an assertion of dignity and self-reliance than a demonstration of victimization. In the way that rallies sometimes have of leading their leaders, this demonstration under sunny skies developed a revivalist spirit of its own.

It's hard to know what role President Clinton's speech played in helping to set the mood of the meeting. Louis Farrakhan's deputy Akbar Muhammad called it the greatest speech of Clinton's life and credited Farrakhan with bringing it about. It was not the first time a president has spoken in words of bridging the racial gulf. Thirty years ago before a joint session of Congress, President Johnson said, "It is not just Negroes, but really it is all of us who must overcome the crippling legacy of bigotry and injustice." The Negroes have become the blacks, and the blacks have become the African Americans, and the gulf is still there. But the emphasis today on voter registration and the power of the ballot suggested that these African Americans, militant though their leaders may be, are not ready for self-isolation.

Those who feared the enhancement of Farrakhan's influence found their fears realized. The Nation of Islam leader has presided over a spectacular success. The chant of "I am somebody" from the multitudes sounded a lot more powerful than when I first heard it from the ill-fated Poor People's March in 1968. But the question is now whether success will change Louis Farrakhan and moderate his strident bigotry. If not, then today's festival is only the prelude to more divisiveness.

Welfare Reform Could Push Millions into Poverty

OCTOBER 30, 1995

On September 14, the Department of Health and Human Services completed a study indicating that under the House welfare reform bill, 2.1 million children will be pushed into poverty, and under the somewhat milder Senate version, the number would be 1.1 million. Secretary Donna Shalala took the report to the White House and handed it to President Clinton, urging him to oppose both versions of the bill that would end the federal welfare entitlement. Nevertheless, on September 17, three days later, the president said he would be willing to sign the Senate version of the bill. In another era, the secretary would have resigned. Indeed, that is precisely what HEW secretary John Gardner did in 1968 when President Johnson signed welfare restrictions over his objections. But an aide to Secretary Shalala said that is not the way she operates.

While sitting on the HHS report, White House aides decided on a strategy to combat the whole Republican budget package. That strategy was to emphasize the negative impact on children of cuts in Medicaid, food stamps, disability, and other programs, and so cabinet secretaries fanned out across the country, saying the Republican budget was bad for children, and Hillary Rodham Clinton said in a recent speech that national policies, including health care and welfare, are mirrored every day in the lives and experiences of our children. Senator Daniel Patrick Moynihan, charging the administration with an "obscene act of social regression," accused it of covering up the HHS report. Finally, the White House admitted the existence of a preliminary report and said a more complete one was being drawn up. If anybody in the White House saw a contradiction between its prochild policy and its welfare policy, nobody was saying so.

Those who have worked with the president on welfare say that no one understands the issue and details better than the president does, but Mr. Clinton is pursuing a reelection course that requires him not to be perceived as going back on his promise to end welfare as we know it. He's operating under the so-called triangulation strategy conceived by his political adviser, Richard Morris, under which he runs against

Democrats as well as Republicans, positioning himself in something defined as the center. But running against Democrats is one thing, and running against poor kids is something else. And trying to conceal the evidence while parading your concern for children is something else again.

Today's Media Are Not So Anxious to Argue for the First Amendment

NOVEMBER 14, 1995

Last August, three weeks after being acquired by the Walt Disney Company, ABC settled a multibillion-dollar libel suit by two tobacco companies with a public apology and a payment of legal costs. Last week CBS, on the verge of being acquired by Westinghouse Electric Corporation, killed a *60 Minutes* interview with a disaffected tobacco company executive rather than face the possibility of a lawsuit, and as icing on the tobacco cake, the network-owned Los Angeles station KCBS killed a commercial critical of smoking.

In the media world it seems the bigger they are, the more easily they fall. A generation of money managers who knew not Edward R. Murrow hearken to lawyers more than they hearken to journalists. Lawyers have always been quick to warn of dangers ahead, First Amendment or no. In 1971 the *New York Times* and the *Washington Post* were warned by their lawyers of possible criminal prosecution if they published the Pentagon Papers. Attorney General John Mitchell had asserted that publication would cause irreparable injury to the national interest. After much agonizing, both publishers ignored their high-priced legal talent and the *Times* had to find a new law firm.

Television, fearing reprisals through the regulatory process, has generally been more skittish about standing up to government. In 1976 I urged my employer, CBS, to have one of the two publishing houses it owned print the text of a House Intelligence investigation report that the House had voted to suppress. News executive Richard Salant told me that corporate executives had ruled against it on the advice of lawyers who warned of possible prosecution under the Espionage Law.

There have been other examples of government threats on security grounds. In 1986 CIA director William Casey, threatening espionage prosecution, managed to get the *Washington Post* to delay the publication of a story about the use of submarines to eavesdrop on Soviet communications. But today, generally speaking, pressure for censorship comes less from government than from business. The threat of a libel suit tends to have a chilling effect on smaller newspapers, radio stations, and TV stations because of the ruinous cost of litigation, even if they ultimately win.

The tobacco industry, in its battle for survival, has apparently settled on the threat of lawsuit as a key weapon in its defense against an increasingly unfavorable press. The weapon turns out to be particularly potent in a period of network acquisition when decisions are made under the influence of money managers anxious to dispel any cloud on the financial horizon. The news managers mainly submit, gracefully or less so. The stakes have become too high to argue the public interests and the First Amendment.

Both Sides of the Budget Battle Are Too Entrenched

DECEMBER 20, 1995

If and when a squabble over stopgap spending authority is resolved, it will be Dayton time in the battle of the budget.

That is to say that after the adversaries have inflicted a lot of damage on each other and on the civilian population, the leaders on both sides see nothing to be gained from prolonging the conflict and are ready to seek a combat-weary settlement.

Like Dayton, the Clinton-Dole-Gingrich understanding on the budget starts as an agreement on a negotiating process, and then comes the hard part. That involves coming out of dug-in positions with no Richard Holbrooke or Warren Christopher to knock heads together. President Clinton says there are policy differences on eighty to ninety issues, but the central issue is, On whose back does the burden mainly fall for achieving a budget theoretically balanced over seven years? And at the core of that question is the question of cuts in the growth of health care programs, Medicare, and Medicaid, versus cuts in income taxes.

The president's most entrenched position is that he will protect the health programs from the deep cuts that the Republicans want, but it is almost impossible to do that and cut taxes by $240 billion without virtually gutting most other domestic programs, which mainly serve the middle class and the poor. Mr. Clinton has dug another hole for himself by saying he also favors a tax cut, only $98 billion, but opening the way to being obliged to bargain on a compromise figure.

You may not have noticed that the so-called Blue Dogs, the group of some twenty conservative congressional Democrats, who officially call themselves the Coalition, have come up with a plan proposing compromise figures on Medicare and Medicaid and no tax cuts. The Coalition and some other Democrats have tried to get the administration to drop its tax cut proposal. One of the coalition leaders, Representative Gary Condit of California, says, "We are not against tax cuts, but a tax cut at this time is not in the best interest of setting the priorities for balancing the budget." The administration has so far been unwilling to reverse itself on cutting taxes. Mr. Clinton may by now be sorry he ever proposed it, but he's described as fearful of being perceived as engaging in another of his famous flip-flops. Sometimes it takes courage to flip-flop.

The arithmetic is pretty stern. To get a balanced budget will require relinquishing some firmly held positions. Maybe it can be done with the grace of Ronald Reagan, who signed a tax increase saying, "The sound you hear is the sound of the concrete cracking around my feet."

The State of Peace on Earth in 1995

DECEMBER 24, 1995

As known to my family and a few other exceptionally faithful listeners, each year at this season I look at how peace on Earth has fared in the past year.

And so first the good news, which as usual is shorter than the bad news.

Bosnia, obviously, not because peace will work but because after five years of bloodshed and ethnic cleansing, peace is at least being tried. I think of a Croat soldier who fought in a battle against a Bosnian Serb unit in which his own brother fought and died. And now the young

Croat patriot told a *Washington Post* reporter, "These days I ask myself was it really worth it?" War weariness, perhaps not a great foundation for peace, is about all we have.

The land that was the birthplace of the "peace on Earth" notion ranks next in my peace column. Not that it was all peaceful in the Middle East. There were Arab attacks on Jewish buses and then a Jewish attack that killed Prime Minister Yitzhak Rabin, that warrior who became a latter-day angel of peace. And yet the Palestinian peace process has apparently developed a capacity to survive extremist violence. And now a break in the deadlock between Israel and Syria, a gingerly resumption of talks in Maryland near Washington, and from both sides come murmurs that they think maybe this time something peaceful may come of it.

In the peace column, too, Northern Ireland, where peace moves falteringly but the process has survived another year. And if we count a year of peace surviving, then add Haiti, where there's been an election leading to that rare event—a peaceful transfer of power from President Aristide to his successor.

But then in the long peace debit column, the continuing conflict in Chechnya, which Russia seems unable to subdue and unable to let go. And all those hardy perennials, these civil, religious, and tribal wars in Rwanda, Sudan, Angola, and dozens of Third World places where the television cameras don't go so they hardly register on our consciousness except now and then when there's a particularly brutal event like an execution in Nigeria.

Abroad, bombs are planted in the Paris metro and poison gas in the Tokyo subway. These are the urban equivalents of the guns and machetes of tribal warfare in the deserts and jungles. And at home, what an irony that fertilizer, which is supposed to promote life, is turned into an explosive instrument of death. In the limited terms of which one speaks of peace as absence of military conflict, America remained at peace in 1995. But who in America feels that we can rest merry and undismayed in the face of that kind of war that evidences itself in acts of terror like the Oklahoma City bombing, or violent acts of hate like the killing of two blacks apparently at random by American soldiers, or the killing of eight in the torching of a white-owned and Jewish-owned clothing store in New York's Harlem? Is a nation truly at peace that is still trying to come to terms with Waco and Ruby Ridge? Is a nation truly at peace with itself that divides on racial lines in reacting to the acquittal of O. J. Simpson?

U.S. News & World Report sums up the year—welcome to the divided states of America, dedicated to life, liberty, and the pursuit of anxiety. And so I close, as I closed last year, not a great year peacewise, goodwill-wise—better luck next year.

1996

Stereotypes and Spies

The Budget Issue May Become an Election Referendum

JANUARY 10, 1996

President Clinton says a budget agreement is within reach. Republican leaders say it isn't. Come January 26, if the deadlock persists, the Republicans will face the question of whether to impose a third government shutdown. The indications are they won't. The last one is generally acknowledged to have been a tactical mistake that hurt them with their constituents and raised Mr. Clinton's ratings in the polls. It also caused many people to gain a new appreciation of government.

We face the possibility that the government will limp along indefinitely on highly restrictive, stopgap spending resolutions, setting the stage for an election campaign great debate. That debate may be less about numbers than about concepts, less about a balanced budget than about the role of government in the lives of Americans. You will notice that both sides are already starting to argue on the basis of principle, not dollar signs. The president, vetoing the welfare overhaul bill, says it would make massive structural changes in programs for children and the poor and is contrary to American values, a phrase that may violate a Republican copyright. The Senate's Republican spokesman on the budget, Pete Domenici, rejects the Clinton budget proposal because it merely trims programs without making essential reforms in the way Washington does business.

So the issue that begins to emerge is not how many billions in future growth are cut from Medicare, but how much the federal role is diminished in favor of personal medical accounts. In his welfare veto message, Mr. Clinton spoke of the guarantee of health coverage for poor families. He has yet to speak of welfare as a guarantee.

As the ideological divide comes more clearly into view, candidates begin to position themselves. Senator Robert Dole, who had been exerting himself for a budget deal, now speaks of fundamental differences. President Clinton says the debate is not about abstract numbers, but vital principles. They are both reading the polls that say that Mr. Clinton would beat Senator Dole 53 to 37 percent if the election were held today. The same polls find 57 percent siding with the president on the budget, and 65 percent believing the Republicans are playing politics with the budget.

At a Democratic dinner last night, Mr. Clinton said the right way to address government is not by uncritical condemnation, but by defining in modern terms what we need our government to do. The conventional wisdom after the 1994 election has been that voters are in an antigovernment mood as much they are in a budget-cutting mood, maybe more. The coming campaign may test whether having seen what happens when government stops, they may have changed their minds.

Presidents Spar with Columnists over Attacks on Family

JANUARY 14, 1996

Liane Hansen, host: In this corner, the president of the United States. Although he's often on the ropes, he's known as "the comeback kid." His opponent is mostly a man of words. But he's never shied away from a good fight. Columnist William Safire threw the first punch this past week when he called Hillary Rodham Clinton "a congenital liar" over her statements regarding the Whitewater affair. The first lady countered Safire with a jab of her own during her interview with NPR's Scott Simon.

Hillary Rodham Clinton: I don't take what Mr. Safire says very seriously. As you pointed out, I was working for the committee that impeached President Nixon, for whom Mr. Safire worked and, best I can tell, is still working.

Liane Hansen: Now weighing in, NPR senior news analyst Daniel Schorr puts the bout between the president and the columnist in historical perspective.

"Presidents have feelings, too," said President Clinton. He was talking about his indignation at *New York Times* columnist William Safire for having called the first lady "a congenital liar." Of course, presidents have feelings, especially when the women in their lives are maligned. Interesting is how they express those feelings.

When Nancy Reagan was criticized by the same William Safire—as it happens, for exercising too much influence in the White House—President Reagan said he didn't think much of someone who would attack another man's wife and he left it at that without any threat to inflict bodily harm. Mr. Clinton suggested that he was reverting to an older tradition, to President Truman, who made dire threats to a music critic who had panned his daughter's singing. I'm old enough to remember Truman, and let me say that more interesting than the similarity between the styles of the two presidents is the difference.

Let me recall the Margaret Truman episode, with memory refreshed by David McCullough's marvelous biography. Pursuing her ill-advised soprano career, the Trumans' only child sang a recital in Constitution Hall. That made her fair game for music criticism, and criticism is what she got from *Washington Post* critic Paul Hume. Not mincing words, he wrote: "Miss Truman cannot sing very well. She is flat a good deal of the time. . . . She communicates almost nothing of the music."

President Truman at the time was under great stress. The United States was suffering reverses in the Korean War and the president's aide and best friend, Charlie Ross, had just died suddenly. At 5:30 in the morning, the president opened his *Post* and reached for a White House notepad to write a furious 150-word letter to Paul Hume. Just to give you the flavor: "You are a frustrated old man who wishes he could have been successful. . . . Some day I hope to meet you. When that happens you'll need a new nose, a lot of beefsteak for black eyes, and perhaps a supporter below!"

Mr. Truman sealed the letter, put on a 3-cent stamp, and gave it to a messenger to mail outside the White House. The *Post* decided against publishing it, but it leaked to the rival *Washington Daily News* and thus to history. Margaret Truman eventually retired from the concert stage, married E. C. Daniel of the *New York Times,* and turned to writing novels.

Now, notice how Mr. Clinton did it. Instead of exploding himself, he called in press secretary Mike McCurry and had him explode for him and in heavily qualified language. McCurry said that if Mr. Clinton were not president, he would have delivered a more forceful response to that column on the bridge of Mr. Safire's nose. Safire responded that McCurry sure had an instinct for the jocular.

When Mr. Clinton went before the press himself, the proxy steam had evaporated. He appealed to the American people to listen to Mrs. Clinton's side of the story. He asserted that "if everybody in this country had the character that my wife has, we'd be a better place to live."

Never mind about the syntax of that. Trumanesque it wasn't. One wonders, when Mr. Clinton is angry, why can't he display anger all by himself? P.S.—years later Paul Hume visited Mr. Truman in retirement in Independence, Missouri, and they got along fine. Something tells me it will take less time for Mr. Clinton to make up with Bill Safire.

The Telecommunications Act of 1996

FEBRUARY 11, 1996

To say that I remember a world without television is to define my senior-citizen status. I first saw experimental television demonstrated by RCA at the New York World's Fair in 1939. That prescient writer E. B. White saw it also, and he wrote in *Harper's* magazine, "We shall stand or fall by television, a new and unbearable disturbance of the modern peace, or a saving radiance in the sky."

I was reminded of that when researchers funded by the National Cable Television Association came out with the umpteenth report on the pervasiveness of psychologically harmful programming of violence on television. That gave me that been-there-heard-that sensation that they call déjà vu. My déjà vu goes back to 1952, when a Senate subcommittee on juvenile delinquency, headed by Estes Kefauver, warned about the effects of televised violence on children. In those days, a few kids jumped off the roof emulating Superman. In later years, television would make violence as American as apple pie.

In the 1960s, ABC zoomed out of the ratings cellar with the raw violence of *The Untouchables,* and that did it. The networks found that they could make a killing by portraying killings. As violence on television proliferated, so did the studies of its harmful effects. Controlled experiments by the National Institute of Mental Health show that children who watch a lot of violence tend to be more aggressive than the norm. The 1968 Milton Eisenhower National Advisory Commission on the Causes and Prevention of Violence, created after the assassinations of Robert Kennedy and Martin Luther King Jr., concluded that violence on television encourages violent forms of behavior. And I, if you'll allow an aside, covering that report for CBS Television, found that conclusion censored out of my script for the evening news on orders from upstairs.

Before the Eisenhower Commission, CBS president Frank Stanton testified that the question of a causal connection between TV violence and violence in real life is a question we don't have the answer to. It was like cigarettes and cancer. The industry always argued that a statistical correlation did not prove cause. This, although Surgeon General Jesse Steinfeld in 1972 reported, "The causal connection is clear enough to warrant appropriate remedial action." The research studies went on and television violence went on.

In 1994, the Commission on Violence and Youth of the American Psychological Association reported, "The level of violence on commercial television has remained constant during nearly two decades." In prime time, five to six violent acts an hour, twenty to twenty-five on Saturday morning children's programming. The commission's conclusion sounded familiar: Increased aggressive behavior, harmful lifelong consequences, desensitization to violence.

At the University of Washington in Seattle, Professor Brandon Centerwall calculated that if television had never been invented, violent crime would be about half what it is. Both President Clinton and Senator Dole have made an issue of television violence, and the president wants to talk to network executives about it.

Now the latest report of the NCTA (National Cable and Telecommunications Act) Research Group cites "substantial risks of harmful effects from viewing violence," and some forty years after the first report, here we go again. Or we don't go.

Bosnia War Crimes

FEBRUARY 12, 1996

It seems a long time since last November, when State Department spokesman Nicholas Burns said the United States' position is that indicted war criminals should not be in command positions, and that it would be inconceivable for Radovan Karadzic and General Ratko Mladic—implicated in the deaths of eighteen thousand in Sarajevo and Srebrenica—to remain in positions of authority.

Yesterday, after Karadzic had passed unhindered through four NATO checkpoints, a NATO commander, Canadian brigadier general Bruce Jeffries, said he would not let the "parallel issue" of war crimes interfere with NATO's "primary mission of peacekeeping." And John Shattuck, assistant secretary of state for human rights, took time out from inspecting mass graves to check on the health and well-being of two Bosnian Serb officers held by the Bosnian government on the request of the War Crimes Tribunal in The Hague.

Today, Assistant Secretary of State Richard Holbrooke, that master mechanic, performed a patch-up job that made identification of war criminals mainly a matter between the Hague tribunal and the Bosnian government. Thus, he got the Dayton peace process shakily back on track, to the relief of the Clinton administration, which feared another breakdown on top of Northern Ireland.

Accused war criminal General Mladic still struts around as the unchallenged military power figure among Bosnian Serbs. In Serbia itself, most people believe that ethnic cleansing is a myth, and their media do not tell them otherwise. It is not like after World War II, when the victors made the defeated Germans and Japanese confront their atrocities. In the former Yugoslavia, there was no victory or defeat to make possible a real pursuit of war crimes.

The Clinton administration has found itself unable to stand up vigorously for human rights in China or Chechnya or Burundi. But it singled out the former Yugoslavia as a place where its power was great enough, the devastated people dependent enough, so that it could set an example of international justice and respect for human life. But make no mistake about it, the war criminals are still in charge, and they are exacting their price for keeping the Dayton peace process afloat. And this shining hope of one victory for human rights is fast fading.

Common Thread Binds Hamas and the Irish Republican Army

MARCH 4, 1996

Yesterday, after the bus bombing in Jerusalem, Hamas announced that this was the final act of retaliation for the assassination of one of its leaders and that attacks would cease for three months pending negotiations for a cease-fire. And then came today's explosion in Tel Aviv.

Last month the Irish Republican Army carried out two bombings in London in the face of a seventeen-month cease-fire and emphasized that the attacks were on direct instructions from the army leadership. This suggested that the bombings were planned without the approval, perhaps without the knowledge, of its political arm, Sinn Fein.

What Israel and Northern Ireland appear to have in common is the emergence of die-hard groups within militant movements determined to torpedo peace efforts and becoming more violent the closer peace seems to come.

In Hamas, the military wing is known as the al-Qassam Brigades, named for a martyr in an earlier war against the British. It operated separately from the general protest movement known as the intifada. Its fiercest assaults started after the signing of the first Israeli-Palestinian peace accords in 1993. Since then, it has struck fifteen times, killing more than 130 persons.

Its greatest success is that its terrorism has caused the suspension of the peace process and has forced Prime Minister Shimon Peres to retreat from his ideas of open borders and free movement. He plans now for security separation between Israel and the West Bank. The bombings have also virtually erased Peres's lead over the right-wing opposition in the May election.

The Irish militants known as the "hard men" are centered in the IRA's Army Council, which came into being twenty-five years ago in a split over a cease-fire negotiated by more moderate leaders. Remarkably, the IRA militants developed the suicide bombing technique before Hamas did. In the 1980s it forced civilians, by threatening to kill their families, to drive cars with explosives to British army posts.

In Northern Ireland and in Israel, terrorists find their reward in the disruption of the peace process. It is, as President Clinton says, that they live for division and conflict. The dilemma is that pressing forward with a peace process becomes increasingly difficult in the face of the emotions that terrorism generates.

The Unabomber's Brother Punished for Heroism

APRIL 14, 1996

He did one of the toughest things a person can do. He is an authentic national hero, but when last we checked, he was being pursued and harassed, his telephone was off the hook, he was not answering the doorbell, and he was unable to go to work.

You may guess that I'm talking about David Kaczynski, the social worker who made the agonizing decision to turn in his weird brother in order possibly to save innocent lives. And since then, he's been rewarded by having his privacy shattered in violation of the FBI's promise to protect his identity. Further, he's had to endure suggestions—false, according to his attorney—of having been interested in the million-dollar reward and/or trying to bargain down from the death penalty for his brother.

Like his older brother, David seems to like wilderness solitude, but, unlike Ted, who may have turned his talents and energies inward to plot against the world, David turned them outward toward the unfortunate of the world. Having married his high school sweetheart, he worked at a group home for the disabled and more recently as assistant director of a shelter for runaway and homeless teenagers in Albany, New York.

He also has a strong sense of family loyalty, and so it must have been with mounting dismay that he had to face accumulating indications that his brother had been in places where bombs had been mailed from and that the Unabomber's manifesto read very much like some of the things he knew his brother to have written.

Private investigators confirmed to David his deepening suspicions. And so finally, through a lawyer, he tipped off the FBI about Ted Kaczynski and his location, asking only that his own identity be kept confidential from the public and from his brother. He had to be kidding himself. The FBI, reeling from Waco and Ruby Ridge, eager to trumpet a success for a change, has been leaking details of its investigation like a sieve. Word of the raid on Ted Kaczynski's Montana shack on April 3 was on television before it happened.

Within hours, the name of the agonized brother who had turned him in was generally known. Around David's home in Schenectady, New York, the cameras and the reporters gathered for their stakeout. For having done his duty by society, David found himself surrealistically now the prisoner. It seems that no good deed will go unpunished.

Last Sunday, David called an old friend from his desert days in the Chihuahua Desert of Texas and talked about his brother. "I love him and I can't help but love him, but I can't condone what he did." But David has refused to parade his celebrityhood on the media, and by some lights, that makes him un-American. So, on radio, Gordon Liddy calls him a betrayer, and on television, David Letterman calls him "Unasnitch." And where is the FBI, which spends millions on witness protection and didn't protect its star witness? Spilling out details of the investigation and taking bows, that's where.

How Clinton's Philosophy of Government Has Changed

MAY 2, 1996

The occasion was a White House dinner honoring the memorial to Franklin D. Roosevelt, the protagonist of activist government. At a table where I was seated with President Clinton, conversation turned to his philosophy of government and whether it had changed during his three years in office. The government had just intervened in the market in two ways to buffer its effects. Because of the rapid rise in gasoline prices, it was releasing some of its strategic oil reserves, and it was taking steps to check the fall in cattle prices.

Inevitably, that raised Republican complaints of an election ploy, which Mr. Clinton denied. But he acknowledged that it was difficult to overcome public cynicism about the acts and motivations of the federal government, and he recognized, too, that he was among the politicians who had contributed to this hostility by running against the government in their campaigns.

In three years seeing this from the inside, he had modified his own view of government, he said. He would still, as in his State of the Union message, speak against big government, but he also didn't want to see weak government. He was appalled, he said, when Speaker Newt Gingrich blamed and generalized something called "the welfare state" for acts as reprehensible as Susan Smith drowning her two children, or two men in Louisiana charged with murdering a pregnant woman and her two children and cutting a full-term fetus from her womb.

This was admittedly some rather extreme hyperbole from which Gingrich has since backtracked. But the president said it drew a line between the way the Republicans and the Democrats see government. And after two government shutdowns and government intervention in a series of natural disasters, Mr. Clinton said he himself had a new appreciation of the role of government in the lives of Americans.

And perhaps a new appreciation of what works politically in this year.

Clinton's Stealing the GOP's Show

MAY 7, 1996

Step by step, President Clinton is moving to seize the initiative on family-values issues that Republicans have long considered their intellectual property. He has done it by bully pulpit, as with school uniforms and media violence. He is doing it by executive action and, when necessary, by buying into Republican legislation.

Having given thirty-seven states waivers from federal welfare legislation to develop their own plans, Mr. Clinton has now borrowed an idea from vetoed Republican legislation. He's announced regulations that would deny cash benefits to teenage parents who quit school or don't live with their parents, and he would reward those who do finish school with bonus payments. Senator Dole will have trouble calling that the act of an unreconstructed liberal.

Then, having signed the Multiethnic Placement Act of 1994, Mr. Clinton adopted an idea right out of the Gingrich Contract with America—a $5,000 tax credit for those who adopt a child. He added a punitive twist—a penalty on states whose agencies delay placement waiting for a racial match. By sending letters to Republican leaders in Congress endorsing the adoption tax credit, the president made it look as though he was making it happen.

White House sources say there are more presidential initiatives to come, including programs for job training and job placement for welfare clients. The trouble the congressional Republicans are having getting their legislative act together leaves the president advantageously positioned to upstage them with quick, solo performances. Using some of their material, he reaches for that evanescent place called the center, and borrowing a Dole label, he has amended it to read "doer and talker."

Admiral Boorda Spoke of Suicide in a Speech

MAY 26, 1996

Three weeks before he committed suicide, Admiral Jeremy Michael Boorda talked of suicide.

It was on April 24 at the annual meeting of the Naval Institute at Annapolis, of which he was president. He talked of a laundry list of navy problems that the navy was rooting out and trying to solve. A questioner from the floor raised the issue of the need for a moral compass, not only for sailors, but for society. In a rambling reply, Admiral Boorda agreed, and said that every person in the navy should be accountable to someone higher. Then he said this: "Can a sailor be a member of the Ku Klux Klan under those circumstances and not have the leader know it? No. Can the sailor be committing sexual harassment and not have the leader know it? No. Can the sailor commit suicide and not have the leader know that he or she was in distress? No."

The next day the featured speaker was former navy secretary James Webb, who delivered what was taken by those present as a veiled attack on Admiral Boorda. He denounced those who, after the Tailhook sex harassment scandal, let distinguished officers be hounded out of the navy. He spoke of some as guilty of the ultimate disloyalty of advancing their careers by currying favor with politicians. Webb condemned navy leaders who let politicians interfere with the sacred promotional process. And he continued: "What admiral has had the courage to risk his own career by putting his stars on the table and defending the integrity of the process and of his people?"

Now, I don't know what Boorda's mention of suicide and Webb's scorching denunciation of disloyalty to the old boys' club had to do with the suicide of Admiral Boorda on May 16. My point is that nobody can know beyond the indication in his suicide note that a *Newsweek* inquiry about a decoration may have been the last straw, but it is remarkable how many have rushed to use the suicide to flog their favorite whipping boys.

Former navy secretary John Lehman said Boorda was the victim of a relentless lynch mob that has hounded the U.S. Navy. Navy veteran Richard Grenier, a columnist for the *Washington Times,* said older officers hated Boorda, believing that he bowed to feminist attacks on the navy. And then, of course, the press bashing. On *Larry King Live* Hillary Rodham Clinton said that part of the blame for the Boorda suicide, as for the suicide of Vincent Foster, must lie with the relentless and unforgiving glare of the news media. And retired admiral Leon Edney wrote about character assassination.

How quick they are to read this tragic and complex event in terms of preconceived resentments. Less judgmental was ex-marine Robert McFarlane, a former Reagan national security adviser, who himself attempted suicide nine years ago during the Iran-Contra scandal. In *Time* magazine, McFarlane wrote about what it is like to bottle up one's problems of ethics and honor and fall into a depression, feeling unable to communicate these problems to others. That brought me back to what Boorda had said in Annapolis, about a sailor not committing suicide without letting the leader know about his distress. But Boorda was the leader, the top uniformed person, caught between the old boys and the civilian demands for a rejuvenated, nonsexist navy, and all we know, and may ever know, is that there was no one with one more star on his shoulder for Mike Boorda to go to.

The CIA and Foreign Service Need Better Cooperation

JUNE 2, 1996

There's a lot of talk about reorganizing our intelligence establishment—streamlining, coordinating, centralizing. But one defect in sore need of correction is the relationship between the foreign service and the CIA, which sometimes act as though they're working for different governments. CIA agents frequently operate under diplomatic cover, as it's called. That's to say they have assigned positions in our embassies— labor attaché, economic counselor, whatever. Correspondents who work in major capitals generally know who the spooks are, but we indulge them in their fancies by not confronting them.

One long-standing rule is that all official American activities in a country come under the authority of the ambassador, a rule often evaded or ignored by agents who think they're doing something too secret to share with an ambassador. So that's how it happened that when a Guatemalan army officer on the CIA payroll, Colonel Julio Alberto Alpirez, was involved in the murder of an American and a Guatemalan partisan married to an American in 1991, Ambassador Thomas Stroock was among the last to know. As a result, over a period of two years, the State Department told untruths to Jennifer Harbury about her husband because untruths were all the department knew.

Since then, there's been a shake-up in Guatemala City and Fred Brugger is no longer the station chief. And Director John Deutch has promised that in the future, the ambassador won't be left in the dark. But that promise has been made before.

Then, there's a breakdown that goes the other way, when the diplomats don't tell the spooks what they're doing, and the spooks have to find out on their own. In the summer of 1994, the CIA station chief in Zagreb, Croatia, advised his headquarters in Langley, Virginia, in code, that he had learned that Ambassador Peter Galbraith was involved in a plot to smuggle Iranian arms through Croatia to Bosnia, in violation of the UN embargo.

CIA director James Woolsey demanded to know how come the State Department was conducting a covert operation that the agency didn't know about. Eventually, the explanation came. It wasn't exactly covert action, but more like covert inaction, the State Department explained. On instructions approved by President Clinton, Galbraith had told Croatian president Franjo Tudjman that he had no instructions about the shipping of arms to Bosnia, and that was taken as a green light, as intended. And Ambassador Galbraith thought he had told the CIA station chief, although the station chief said he hadn't.

Hell hath no fury like a spy agency scorned, and the CIA complained to congressional intelligence oversight committees, which have been giving the Clinton administration a hard time on this subject ever since. You sometimes wonder how our far-flung agencies can find out what's happening around the world when they're so busy trying to keep up with each other.

The Dhahran Terrorist Attack Gives Pause on Other Matters

JUNE 26, 1996

When the terrorist bomb killed 241 marines and sailors in Beirut in 1983, President Reagan said, resolutely, "The United States will not be intimidated by terrorists." But soon the remaining marines went aboard a warship offshore, and a few months later sailed away.

Today was President Clinton's turn to be resolute, albeit with an unfortunate slip. Leaving for France, he said, "We will not resist—we will not rest in our efforts."

The ill-defined peacekeeping mission of the marines on unfriendly soil in Lebanon had been controversial within our government from the start. The air force mission in Saudi Arabia is better defined, uncontroversial, and on supposedly friendly soil—but that's the point. The mission of most terrorist groups in the region, many of them Iranian supported, is to make all Islamic soil unfriendly to America. That involves trying to destabilize the ailing King Fahd in Saudi Arabia and President Hosni Mubarak in Egypt, and sabotaging efforts to achieve peace between Israel and the Arabs.

As to the timing of the Dhahran attack, it may be useful to recall what went before. Three weeks ago, when four Saudi men were beheaded for an earlier attack on Americans in Riyadh, there had been the anonymous warnings of retaliation if they were punished. Last week, Congress unanimously passed a bill endorsed by President Clinton imposing sanctions against foreign companies that deal with Iran. The Iranian government denounced the sanctions. Then Mr. Clinton was quoted in an interview with an Arabic newspaper as seeking a dialogue with Iran. A government-run Tehran newspaper commented that the president was "behaving like a drunken bastard shouting in the street."

An event like the Dhahran bomb has a way of making many of our international preoccupations seem suddenly irrelevant. Yesterday candidate Dole was criticizing President Clinton as too soft on Russia; today Dole is supporting him on Saudi Arabia. Today Mr. Clinton was off to Lyon for what was intended to be mainly economic talks. Terrorism has been added to the agenda. Tomorrow in Geneva, governments will try to come to closure on a treaty banning nuclear testing. But then we witness a conventional explosion committed by some unconventional terrorists and realize how fragile is the position of the superpower.

TWA Victims' Families Endure the Pain of Not Knowing

JULY 22, 1996

"People are tired of information," said Corey Snow, whose prospective brother-in-law was on TWA 800. "What they want are answers to let them get on with their lives."

In the case of ValuJet 592, the crash in the Everglades was almost immediately judged to be an accident. In the case of Pan Am 103, which crashed in Scotland with 259 on board, it took six days to determine that it was a terrorist bomb.

In the case of TWA 800, five days after it crashed into the sea there is no hard evidence to go on. The reported discovery of a major part of the fuselage may change that.

Most of those on board have yet to be found and identified. No credible claim of responsibility has come from terrorist groups. President Clinton says he is trying to speed up the agonizing process of the search, but the agony continues, most especially among the relatives housed in a hotel at Kennedy Airport, including one family of forty persons living in what the *New York Times* describes as a swirl of tedium, anger, frustration, and loneliness.

Sudden death is hard enough to bear; not knowing how or why is close to unbearable. Judith Viorst, the author of *Necessary Losses,* says that not knowing what you are dealing with makes it hard to move into the next stage of your own life. It is the pain of not knowing that has given us world war monuments to the unknown—no longer limited to the unknown soldier. The pain of not knowing has been transformed into a potent political force that drives the search for Vietnam POW/MIAs in administration after administration.

The investigators wait in the case of TWA 800 for evidence before announcing a conclusion, but among survivors' families, the conviction is growing that it was sabotage of some sort. In a memorial service in a Catholic church in Tenafly, New Jersey, the parish priest offered a prayer for a world of peace. One mourner, Michelle Krizel, overwhelmed by a sense of futility, began shaking and had to leave the church.

Five days and counting, and not knowing whose work this was and when the shattered bodies can be taken home—this, for America, is an almost unique situation, an agony that goes beyond grief.

Once-Mighty Pravda Dies with Barely a Whimper

AUGUST 4, 1996

Once it printed 11 million copies a day and its word was gospel, or what passed for gospel, in a Communist system. Lately, it was down to three hundred thousand copies, carping feebly at the Yeltsin government, and its editor and reporters were often drunk on the job.

So maybe it was time that *Pravda,* one of the world's most famous newspapers, folded. Yet no one who has worked in Moscow, and started his day trying to decode its pontifical broadsides, could witness the death of *Pravda* without a twinge.

Lenin founded *Pravda* in 1912 as an underground revolutionary paper, the voice of the Communist Party. *Pravda* means "truth," and it was the truth according to Lenin. Later, a government organ was started called *Izvestiya,* which means "news." It was often said by disenchanted Soviet citizens that there was no truth in *Pravda* and no news in *Izvestiya.*

But it was in *Pravda* in 1917 that Lenin first propounded the dictatorship of the proletariat, and in *Pravda* in the thirties that Stalin called for execution of "enemies of the people." It was also in *Pravda* in 1957, while I was stationed in Moscow, that Nikita Khrushchev denounced the "antiparty group," signaling the ouster of Stalinist diehards like Molotov, Malenkov, and Kaganovich, who had plotted to topple him.

I also made it into *Pravda*'s columns in 1972. The editors decided to give their own colorful version of the Nixon-ordered FBI investigation of me. *Pravda* said that I was the victim of an epidemic of snooping bred by a war psychosis, and that after being followed around by the FBI, I decided to compromise and restrain my criticism of the American government. That was simply telling the story in terms that a Soviet citizen would understand.

With the accession of Yeltsin and the collapse of the Soviet system in 1991, *Pravda* lost its raison d'être, but tried to stay in business as an opposition newspaper. It was privatized, and then bought by two Greek businessmen, Yannis and Christos Yannikos. They poured millions into the paper, but *Pravda* continued to decline, several times suspending operation for brief periods, and now, apparently, for good.

The way the once-mighty *Pravda* came to an end must have made Lenin and Stalin turn in their graves. The Greek owners wanted the paper to get off its opposition kick and become more mainstream, and cut down on the vodka drinking. Editor Alexander Ilyin changed the locks to keep the owners out. That was about enough for the Yannikos brothers. They pulled the plug by cutting off the money. The current Communist Party talks of trying to bring the paper back, but it would not be the same old *Pravda*. And so, *dos vidaniya, Pravda*. Good-bye, *Pravda*.

"No reason to mourn," said Aleksandr Prokhanov, editor of the harder-hitting opposition paper *Zaftra*. "Nobody should soak himself in gasoline. It was already dead for years." For the once-mighty *Pravda*, the voice of communism, what a way to go.

America Needs to Deal Responsibly with Terrorism

AUGUST 5, 1996

America has some growing up to do if it is to cope with the sense of vulnerability generated by modern terrorism.

Congress has balked at giving the FBI enhanced wiretapping authority on the grounds, says Speaker Newt Gingrich, that the FBI has been too cozy with the Clinton White House. One suspects that the reaction would have been different if we were dealing with cold war Communist subversion instead of targets like the violence-prone militias.

Suffice it to say that countries like Britain, France, and Israel, more inured to the terrorist threat, have long since overcome their scruples about antiterrorist eavesdropping and peremptory police measures. We will have to learn that solutions to possible terrorist acts do not always come in time for the next news cycle. Three weeks after TWA 800, nine days after the Atlanta pipe bomb, we know essentially nothing about the origin of these events. Yet we are treated daily to stories about the prime and sometimes less-prime suspect in Atlanta. On Long Island the vacuum of knowledge is filled with assumptions and surmisals, the latest being that Iran may have been involved in the bomb explosion aboard TWA 800—that is, if it was a bomb explosion.

Speaking of Iran, rarely have I seen such a search for demons. President Clinton declares economic war against allied nations that deal with Iran and Libya. I do not know what possessed Secretary of Defense William Perry, normally cautious and restrained, to suggest in his NPR interview last Friday that a foreign country, possibly Iran, may have been involved in the Riyadh and Dhahran bombings. That produced the predictable knee-jerk reactions by congressional leaders appearing on Sunday television. Get tough—Senator Orrin Hatch; decisive action—Newt Gingrich; it's an act of war—Senator Joseph Biden.

In fact, there is precious little concrete evidence of widely suspected state sponsorship of recent acts of terrorism. There were military-type detonators on the Dhahran bomb. Iran has shipped some mortar parts and shells to Antwerp en route somewhere. A conference of terrorists was reportedly held in Tehran. Intelligence sources believe there are eleven terrorist training camps in Iran. All of this falls short of the traditional smoking gun that would justify a retaliatory strike.

Counterterrorism is a tough, painstaking business best carried on with a minimum of fist shaking and breast-beating. Terrorism is not a phenomenon of the moment, but a successor to the cold war, the enemy of our generation, as President Clinton put it today. It behooves us and our elected officials not to go off half-cocked.

Politics and Sex—Paid Sex

SEPTEMBER 8, 1996

Indulge me at eighty in a little ruminating about politics and sex, specifically paid sex.

Why Dick Morris paid a reported $200 per session for the favors of Sherry Rowlands I shall never understand. For such access to a powerful White House person, who can let you hear the president and tip you off about possible life on Mars, many a lobbyist in this town would gladly have paid ten times as much.

Indeed, not many years ago Paula Parkinson, registered lobbyist and former *Playboy* model, found sex a useful means of access. Refreshingly candid, as these people often are, Parkinson said, "You usually sleep with the people you meet in this type of business."

But I digress. Henry Kissinger once said, "Power is the ultimate aphrodisiac." As with many facets of his foreign policy, I don't think he had it quite right. What seems to be the greatest aphrodisiac for a powerful person is the excitement of risk. In Britain, in 1963, War Secretary John Profumo not only consorted with a prostitute, but one who was having a concurrent affair with the Soviet naval attaché. It must have been quite a thrill for Gary Hart to challenge reporters to follow him, and then invite Donna Rice to his house on Capitol Hill a few days later.

President Kennedy took unimaginable risks in carrying on with Judith Exner, the mistress of Mafia don Sam Giancana, who was also, at the same time, working on contract with the CIA, trying to assassinate Fidel Castro. That made the president's assignations with Mrs. Exner not only a personal risk but a national security risk and a blackmail risk, as J. Edgar Hoover was happy to point out to him.

Something else about powerful persons who carry on extramarital affairs is how many of them have provided themselves with understanding wives. Mrs. Roosevelt knew, and Jacqueline Kennedy knew, and Hillary Rodham Clinton knew, and all of them seemed willing to come to terms with infidelity and go on being the loyal spouse—but none was like Dick Morris's wife, Eileen McGann, who posed for pictures with her husband and said, "I'm an adult, I accepted Dick's apology." Sherry Rowlands said, "He loves his wife, that's why he would pay me. That makes him feel he's not cheating on his wife. This is business, as long as he's paying for it."

I'll leave you to write the last line of this report. I've run out of snappy summations.

Potential Approval of RU486 Will Change the Abortion Debate

SEPTEMBER 19, 1996

Somewhat to the surprise of retired justice Harry Blackmun himself, his 1973 *Roe v. Wade* decision legalizing abortion still stands.

In recent years, antiabortion groups have turned to a strategy of trying to circumscribe the general right to abortion with specific restrictions such as parental consent, waiting periods, and a ban on a late-term procedure that they call "partial-birth abortion."

But RU486, undoubtedly the most important development in birth control since the pill in the early 1960s, promises now to make moot much of the raging controversy over the surgical termination of pregnancy. The office of a private doctor administering medicines does not offer the visible target that an abortion clinic does, and the right-to-life movement sees this development as jeopardizing everything it has fought for.

By petition and by the threat of boycott against a French-German company that developed RU486, abortion opponents have so far succeeded in keeping off the American market a drug that's been used by more than a quarter million women around the world, but it is losing that fight.

The family-planning organization the Population Council, which is sponsoring RU486 in the United States, now has conditional approval from the Food and Drug Administration to market it. It expects to be able to do so by mid-1997 through a manufacturer whose name it is keeping secret for the time being.

Whether this issue will be injected into the election campaign is not clear. It was President Clinton in the first months of his term who ordered the FDA to look for ways of getting the drug on the American market. But now the White House is declining comment on the latest development. A spokesman for the Dole campaign says that he has long been troubled by RU486, but the spokesman did not repeat Dole's earlier outright opposition to marketing the drug.

Now that the FDA has found RU486 to be safe and effective, it would be difficult for a presidential candidate or even for Congress to intervene. The likelihood is that this country stands on the threshold of a new era of medical abortion instead of surgical abortion that will leave the antiabortion movement with a much harder case to make.

Not Morning in America

NOVEMBER 6, 1996

Senator Dole was gracious in defeat and President Clinton was humble in victory and the pageantry of democratic continuity and renewal was splendid. But behind the hoopla lurked some ominous signs of deepening alienation of Americans from their government. It could be read in the 49 percent turnout, the lowest since the lackluster Coolidge year of 1924. Some 90 million Americans found no reason to go to the polls. And that means that Mr. Clinton, with 49 percent of those who did vote, won a plurality of a plurality.

Those who did go to the polls seemed to go holding their noses. Fifty-three percent told exit pollsters they had reservations about the candidate they were voting for. Fifty-five percent said that Mr. Clinton is not honest. Sixty percent said he had not told the truth about Whitewater. Many voters did not believe either Mr. Clinton or Senator Dole would keep his promises about tax cutting and budget balancing. The gender gap was large, but the angry white male of 1994 seems to have settled down to being the disgusted white male of 1996.

More serious than the gender gap was the huge credibility gap. The voters are coming to believe that with all the special-interest money, especially foreign special-interest money, the government no longer represents the average American. A symbol of this is the White House Lincoln Bedroom for sale for $100,000 a night for a bed-and-breakfast.

In his speech last night, the president once again promised reform of campaign financing. But after Watergate, there was a whole era of reform that collapsed in the frantic rush for the hundreds of millions of dollars needed to pay for television and all those attack ads that served only to turn off Americans even more. It's hard to see what new rules will withstand the political big-bucks imperative.

In a less placid time than this era of relative prosperity and relative peace, Americans might be up in arms about an auctioned-off government. As it is, the voters, those who did vote, voted basically to maintain the status quo of divided government and went back to the mundane things they could do something about.

Stereotypes and Spies

NOVEMBER 19, 1996

At Camp David in 1959, Nikita Khrushchev suggested to President Eisenhower that they pool their payments to double agents to save money. Just a joke, but it underscored awareness of the deadly espionage game going on behind the glad-handing.

A lot of spy cases have flowed over the dam since then, but none quite as unusual as the Harold Nicholson case.

First, for the career path of the suspect. This was no burned-out case like Aldrich Ames or Edward Lee Howard, with a drinking or drug problem, seething with rage at not being promoted. Nicholson was one of the best and brightest types, a model officer, who in sixteen years had risen from trainee to station chief with a bright future ahead. One shudders to think that the future might have held in store a mole as assistant director.

Second, his sheer brazenness—apparently totally unfazed by the conviction of Aldrich Ames, the tightened security, the negative results of his lie detectors, he casually deposited payments in bank accounts he could have known were being monitored. Amid the turmoil about the Ames conviction, he seemed to scorn counterintelligence.

Third, his apparent ordinariness. Like Howard and Ames and almost every spy in the last decade, Nicholson's motive appeared to be money, not ideology. But unlike Howard and Ames, there was no expensive home or car. As a divorced father of three, he spent money on things like a Chevrolet and college tuition for his son, and on his courtship of a woman with whom he appeared to be seriously interested—a study in the banality of betrayal.

In short, this model officer with no known reason to betray his trust defies the profile of the intelligence officer susceptible to hostile recruitment. That means that the procedures put into place in the past four years to preclude another catastrophe like the Ames case have been shown to be less than foolproof. And it may be that when loyalty comes down to a matter of money, there can be no foolproof system.

The Nixon Tapes

NOVEMBER 24, 1996

Did you know that on several occasions President Nixon discussed with Chief Justice Warren Burger matters before the Supreme Court, including school busing?

That Chief of Staff Alexander Haig advised the president that the Internal Revenue Service was investigating his friend Bebe Rebozo?

That Nixon personally ordered the firing of Pentagon whistle-blower Ernest Fitzgerald, saying, "Get rid of that son of a bitch"?

That Nixon used words for Jews and for blacks that I will not repeat here, but at one point talked of blacks as "just out of the trees."

All this on 3,700 hours of tape now being released, 200 to 300 hours at a time, after a twenty-one-year court battle. Remarkable what an eternal source of fascination Nixon remains, and how we keep finding out things about him.

As a result of the most recent tape release, we know a little better how he approached the question of leaving office. On May 1, 1973, having jettisoned Chief of Staff H. R. Haldeman and Domestic Policy Chief John Ehrlichman and fired counsel John Dean, Nixon was still ready for a fight.

He urged House Speaker Gerald Ford to rally Republicans to his support. But some three weeks later, on the telephone after midnight, May 25, with Haig his new chief of staff, Nixon asked whether it wouldn't be better for the country if he "just checked out."

With John Dean talking to the special prosecutor, Nixon said, "I'm not really doing the job because I'm so wound up in this son of a bitching thing."

Nixon apparently allowed Haig then to talk him out of quitting. He continued fighting for another fourteen months, until the "smoking gun" tape cost him most of his Republican support. And facing impeachment, he resigned.

The next 278 hours of tape are scheduled to be released by next April. And I don't promise you not to be talking about them.

Hillary and Eleanor

DECEMBER 8, 1996

In Sydney, Australia, she said the gap between rich and poor grows wider and the marketplace knows the price of everything but the value of nothing.

In Bangkok, Thailand, she met with girls rescued from prostitution.

This past week, at a meeting of hemispheric first ladies in La Paz, Bolivia, she talked of women dying in childbirth in Central and South America because Republicans in the American Congress cut funding for foreign family-planning programs.

Hillary Rodham Clinton speaks with a different voice than the New Democrat president. It's the voice of old Democrat caring and compassion that she's increasingly making heard.

There is speculation about what Mr. Clinton will be like in his second term. Mrs. Clinton leaves little doubt what she will be like. She says she will travel around the country and talk to people about what is happening in their lives.

She used a phrase, "formal role in welfare policy," which was a little misleading, because it'll be nothing like the role she played in formulating a health insurance proposal.

What she appears to have in mind is a role like that of the woman she calls one of her favorite predecessors, Eleanor Roosevelt, who, she says, endured constant criticism for matters great and small.

You think about that for a minute. Mrs. Roosevelt was devastated when she discovered her husband was having an affair with another woman. Divorce was inconceivable to her. She decided to remake her life by becoming a voice in the White House for the disadvantaged, including women.

She toured the Deep South, the dust bowl, Appalachia, where she got her husband to start an aid program. In speeches and a daily newspaper column she gave her own observations, often more liberal than the president's.

In a radio interview she said, "I realized that if I remained in the White House all the time, I would lose touch with the rest of the world."

Does Mrs. Clinton sound a little like that when she asks whether people wanted to put a paper bag over her head? Or when she says, "I want to travel around and talk to people about what is happening on the ground"? Or when she says, "I intend to speak out about it and write about it"?

Mrs. Clinton became the butt of jokes when it was revealed that she had conducted an imaginary conversation with Mrs. Roosevelt with the aid of a New Age psychologist. In Sydney, Mrs. Clinton made fun of herself when she said that she had talked to Mrs. Roosevelt before leaving Washington and "She sends greetings to you all."

So you think about Mrs. Roosevelt and you think about Mrs. Clinton, who also has a mind of her own and intelligence of her own and has had to come to terms with her relationship with her husband.

Or in her words, "Just be who you are and do what you can do and get through it and wait for the first man"—that is, the spouse of the first woman president—"the first man to hold the position."

The State of Peace on Earth in 1996

DECEMBER 22, 1996

Each year, this effort to rate peace on Earth in the past year gets harder. You could say that since the collapse of communism seven years ago, the fear of nuclear Armageddon has dwindled.

But then there is Ruth Leger Sivard, who keeps score on global wars, saying in 1996, there were a record number of twenty-nine smaller wars going on from Chechnya to Peru. And since the end of World War II, more than 23 million people have been killed in 149 internal and across-border conflicts.

Funny about the mention of Chechnya and Peru. I mean "funny curious," not "funny ha-ha." For even in the week before Christmas, we saw in the killing of six Red Cross workers in Chechnya and a hostage episode in Peru, evidence of how fragile peace can be.

And if peace is to be defined as the absence of a big war or the threat thereof, well that, too, is a relative thing. There's no early prospect of an engagement between Russia and America, and our missiles are supposedly no longer targeted on each other.

But it would take about two minutes to retarget them. The START II arms-reduction treaty languishes in the Russian parliament, and few take seriously the call of American and foreign generals to start winding down our nuclear arsenals with the ultimate aim of eliminating them.

Brent Scowcroft, who was national security adviser, laughs at the idea. He tells me that there is no uninventing the nuclear bomb. That the safest and cheapest thing is just to leave them where they are.

You look back over the year; in Bosnia there is no war but no peace either. And the end of 1996 in Belgrade feels like Prague, Berlin, and Bucharest in 1989, the streets alive with protests against a ruthless dictator.

In Israel and the West Bank, peace is a sometime thing, interrupted by suicide bombings and by hardening positions between right-wing prime minister Benjamin Netanyahu and the frustrated Palestinians waiting for the promises of the Oslo agreement to be made good.

Some of the other promises of peace have not been realized. The civil war is on again in Afghanistan. The militantly Islamic Taliban is trying to impose its theocratic rule.

Haiti, American troops gone, seems constantly on the verge of another assassination. The economic noose around Cuba is tightened, but Fidel Castro hangs on. And Northern Ireland, where a cease-fire collapsed in an orgy of bombings, represented a melancholy setback for peace.

It wasn't war, but not peace either, when hundreds of thousands of Rwandans trekked back and forth to Zaire and Tanzania.

Well, that was how it's been this past year. Count your blessings. You're alive to hear this, and I'm alive to talk to you. But I don't think it adds up to what the Prince of Peace had in mind.

1997

Saints and Sinners

Clinton's Hurdles Ahead

JANUARY 6, 1997

Tanned, rested, and ready, lame-duck president Clinton is setting out to soar above Newt Gingrich's and his own ethical problems, and carve out the role of national unifier à la Teddy Roosevelt.

Ahead lie the budget, entitlements, and some modest education initiatives. Behind him lies a first term, the prologue.

Aboard *Air Force One* during his vacation trip, the president was asked by reporters what he considered the three worst mistakes of his first term. In the area of legislation, he mentioned only his failed health reform proposal. He did not mention the welfare overhaul, which split his administration.

At today's prayer breakfast, he acknowledged that "some of you think I made a mistake when I signed the welfare reform bill, and I don't." And he went on to stress the need to create jobs for those leaving the welfare rolls.

But hardly a week after the welfare act went into effect, there are already signs of trouble. State welfare administrators are complaining that they are not being given as much freedom in using block grants as they expected.

The president boasts of a 2.1 million drop in the welfare rolls in four years, but what happens to those leaving welfare is less clear. In California and Massachusetts, where Republican governors were fast off the mark on workfare programs, the results so far have been disappointing.

According to the *Los Angeles Times,* in California, a two-year independent study found that the "Work Pays" program contains faulty assumptions, and that there was little or no change in the behavior of recipients facing cuts in their cash benefits.

In Massachusetts, the *Washington Post* found that although welfare rolls have been reduced, only about half the adults who have gone off welfare have found jobs. And only 15 percent of private-sector jobs designated for them have been filled.

More than 250 teenage parents, who lost benefits because they wouldn't live with their parents or return to school as required, have simply dropped out of sight.

These are only early portents. The major welfare cutoffs lie two years ahead, soon enough for the "unifier president" to think again about the program he still champions.

The Gingrich Ethics Case Will Never Close

JANUARY 21, 1997

"Get on with the people's business" had become the reigning cliché. Democrat and Republican spoke of "crippling partisanship" and of being "bone-tired of partisanship."

And with the lingering aftertaste of inaugural day comity, the House clearly had no appetite for prolonging the two years of Gingrich scandal. So, as expected, the overwhelming vote to accept the Ethics Committee recommendation: reprimand and a $300,000 penalty.

And the Gingrich case is closed, or almost closed. There remains the Speaker's decision whether to pay the penalty from campaign funds and provoke another little firestorm, or from personal funds, which means book royalties.

Ethics Committee chairwoman Nancy Johnson, ever the compromiser, suggested today that some of the money be personal. And then there remains the Internal Revenue Service proceeding in its own deliberate way to determine whether Gingrich broke any tax laws.

In a broader sense, the Gingrich case can never be closed. Gingrich has already shown—as he did at the White House yesterday, joking about cajoling the House to be slightly more favorable—that he is tough-skinned and able to practice denial and come up smiling. But from now on, he presides with a gavel in his hand and an albatross on his shoulder.

He owes too much to too many to be able effectively to crack the whip on Republicans when it may be necessary. He needs too much the good-will of President Clinton, who was kind enough to say last week that he wanted the Gingrich controversy to be over, to be able to stand up to him as vigorously as in the past.

The Speaker must make good now on the new Gingrich he projected to the House after his reelection two weeks ago when he apologized for being "too brash, too self-confident, too pushy," and spoke of "the tragedy of poor children in broken homes and neighborhoods."

The drama of Newt Gingrich isn't over, only act 1. Every day from now on, he will have to fight to recapture the authority he once had. And it remains to be seen whether his manifest talents are equal to the task.

The CIA Torture Handbook

FEBRUARY 16, 1997

Liane Hansen, host: President Clinton's nominee to head the CIA, Anthony Lake, lost some key support on Capitol Hill yesterday. Senate Foreign Relations Committee chairman Jesse Helms said he will vote against Lake when Senate hearings are held next month.

The nomination of President Clinton's former national security adviser has been controversial since revelations about his involvement in campaign financing linked to the White House. Despite his intentions, Senator Helms said he expects Lake will be confirmed.

The former head of the agency's counterintelligence division also was in the news recently.

NPR senior news analyst Daniel Schorr explains.

They haunt our history and keep coming back, at least to me. No, not the ghosts of Watergate this time, but a ghost of the CIA.

I first met James Jesus Angleton, the chief of counterintelligence, on Christmas Eve 1974, when he had just been fired by Director William Colby. He came to the door of his home in response to my knock, and greeted me with: "Mr. Schorr, I never expected to see you trampling on the press."

He pointed to a delivered copy of the *Washington Post,* on which I was standing.

I came to know this singular personality, who raised orchids, had studied poetry at Yale, and could discourse on the finer points of Italian art. But it was only from others that I learned of the destructive side of his personality: his relentless and futile mole hunt that ruined loyal CIA officers and Soviet defectors, and almost brought to a halt the recruitment of spies.

Angleton thought they were almost all double agents. The *Baltimore Sun,* through a Freedom of Information request, recently obtained a copy of Angleton's 1963 secret handbook for dealing with spies, defectors, and suspected double agents. The book is titled *Kubarc Counter-Intelligence Interrogation,* "Kubarc" being an agency code word.

Here are a couple of quotations from this cold-blooded manual.

"The principal coercive techniques are arrest, detention, the deprivation of sensory stimuli, threats and fear, debility, pain, heightened suggestibility and hypnosis and drugs. The interrogatee's defenses crumble, and he becomes more childlike."

A little more:

"Interrogations conducted under compulsion or duress are especially likely to involve illegality. Therefore, prior headquarters approval must be obtained for the interrogation of any source: One, if bodily harm is to be inflicted, two, if medical, chemical, or electrical methods are to be used, three, [deleted]."

Can you imagine what kind of horror that was, to have the CIA excise it even now? I thought back to Jim Angleton, that Renaissance figure of low-key manner and refined tastes, and of what harm can be done by an obsessed person wielding not only power but, most corrupting of all, secret power.

Freedom of the Press

MARCH 16, 1997

Liane Hansen, host: Freedom of the Press Day was observed in many parts of the country Friday.

NPR senior news analyst Daniel Schorr was the keynote speaker for the event at the National Press Club here in Washington. He delivered these remarks.

Indulge me at eighty in some curmudgeonly ruminations about the journalistic craft I have loved, not always wisely, but well.

We are in trouble. It is a natural order of things that we be in trouble with the powerful, whom we try to monitor. But today we are in trouble with the powerless, who identify us more with the powerful than with them. And people are no longer willing to forgive us our press passes.

Antimedia sentiment has been growing by leaps and bounds. In a recent Roper–Freedom Forum poll, fewer than 20 percent rated the ethics of journalists as high. More alarming, 65 percent of respondents said there are times when publication or broadcast should be prevented.

Prevented? That's prior restraint we're talking about there, advance censorship, the heart of the First Amendment. Did we win that fight in the Pentagon Papers case in the Supreme Court, only now to lose it in the court of public opinion?

That is a serious matter. The practice of journalism rests on something called "privilege." The privilege accorded to the press depends on public support, and will wither without public support.

The public today senses an abuse of privilege for profit and self-aggrandizement when a Richard Jewell is falsely named as a prime suspect in the Atlanta bombing case, or when a Dallas newspaper reports a purported confession in the Oklahoma City bombing, which may have been a hoax.

My concern is what we do to ordinary people and to the workings of justice. I am much more worried about the Richard Jewells than about government secrets.

When it comes to government and its millions of pages of mindlessly classified materials, I have no doubt that this nation has suffered more from undue secrecy than from undue disclosure. The government takes good care of itself.

But protecting the ordinary citizen from defamation and invasion of privacy becomes our responsibility. And the public will judge us by how we carry out that responsibility.

I join in the general dismay of the journalistic community about the judgment against ABC for the methods used in its investigation of tainted food being sold by a Food Lion store. ABC was using modern video techniques to do what Upton Sinclair was applauded for doing in penetrating a meatpacking plant in Chicago at the turn of the century.

But given the concentration on video techniques and entertainment values in the remorseless quest for ratings, people can be forgiven if they no longer accept us as dedicated solely to the public weal, even when we perform a public service.

More and more, we're under challenge to show whether we consider the public merely a market, or as part of a community in which we are joined.

I would like to go back sixty years, when I could say to someone who asked that I am a journalist, and not be glared at. For even if the media of today are not admired as the press of yesterday, it is still a great and wonderful thing to work at finding out what the Establishment doesn't want you to know, and tell the people who need to know.

The McVeigh Trial Raises Social Issues

APRIL 28, 1997

Ray Suarez, host: At the Oklahoma City bombing trial in Denver, a highway patrolman testified in detail today about his arrest of Timothy McVeigh. Trooper Charles Hanger explained that he first pulled McVeigh over because his car did not have a rear license plate, then arrested him for carrying a concealed weapon.

Several days later, McVeigh was linked to the Oklahoma City attack.

The McVeigh trial has only just begun, but news analyst Daniel Schorr says it is already assuming its place in history.

The Oklahoma City trial is the latest of those we come to call the "Trial of the Century" because they raise issues bigger than the defendants.

Totalitarian regimes in Germany, the Soviet Union, and China have conducted show trials with trumped-up charges and forced confessions to stigmatize unorthodox ideas and intimidate the public. In our country, the trial as an emblem of conflict occurs more spontaneously, because it encapsulates sharp divisions.

In the Scopes trial in 1925 in Tennessee, teacher John Scopes was fined $100 for teaching evolution—which the state had banned. Scopes became a historic figure as an emblem of the struggle between science and religion—still unresolved.

In the Scottsboro trial in Alabama in 1931, nine young blacks came close to being lynched and on the flimsiest of evidence were then convicted of raping two white women. Scottsboro stands in the history books as a monument to racial injustice.

In 1968, the anti–Vietnam War Chicago Seven were accused of incitement to riot during the Democratic convention. Four years later, the Supreme Court overturned the convictions. The Chicago Seven remain with us as a symbol of justice under wartime tension.

More recently, with the media serving as a megaphone, the national trauma over race was reflected in the names Rodney King, the black man beaten by white police, and Reginald Denny, the white man beaten by black rioters in Los Angeles.

And then, the O. J. Simpson trial, drawing a racial line through America like a San Andreas Fault.

The Oklahoma City bombing trial, not being on television and not being about race, does not rouse the same instant passions, yet it also raises issues beyond guilt and innocence.

In the first place, about the stumblebum FBI crime lab threatening to bring federal law enforcement into disrepute, as has happened with the local police in Los Angeles.

But then the question of what in our society could produce a decorated soldier accused of cold-blooded massacre of innocents. Was President Clinton right when he enraged talk show hosts two years ago—condemning "loud and angry voices trying to make some people as paranoid as possible"?

So now, a trial that raises a question of why our society cannot cope with its lunatic fringe, with its militias, its nativists, and now, in Texas, its secessionists: in its own way, the trial of the century.

Crack and the CIA

MAY 18, 1997

It's not every day that a newspaper prints a correction on its front page, especially a correction on a story in some other paper. But this was no everyday story.

The series in the *San Jose Mercury News* last fall on the rise of crack cocaine in urban America, implying links to the Nicaraguan Contras and the CIA, exploded into a huge controversy, fueling African American suspicions of racial genocide.

CIA director John Deutch was obliged to fly out to Los Angeles to make a denial to a skeptical, mainly African American, audience. Months later, leading African Americans like the Reverend Jesse Jackson, Dick Gregory, and Representative Maxine Waters were keeping the issue alive.

A week ago, the *Mercury*'s executive editor, Jerry Ceppos, published a signed column in his paper saying that some of the more sensational implications in the series were not supported by the facts, and that the articles did not meet his standards.

The *New York Times,* the *Washington Post,* and the *Los Angeles Times* trumpeted the news of the correction on their front pages. Mind you, all three of these papers had done their own exhaustive evaluations and have cast doubt on the *Mercury* series, so it was not as though they had some obligation to apologize to their readers. And yet they treated the *Mercury*'s careful, partial retreat as a major event in the development of the free press in America.

The *New York Times* followed up with an editorial headlined: "The *Mercury News* Comes Clean," lavishly praising the *Mercury*'s editor for candor and self-criticism. Somewhere in the course of praise, the press lost sight of the fact that editor Ceppos had said this story was right on many important points; indeed, its main point—that a Contra leader was involved in cocaine traffic—was based on court evidence.

The odd man out in this controversy is the investigative reporter Gary

Webb, the author of the series. He's left to twist in the wind while the establishment press glorifies an editor having some second thoughts about articles that proved to be explosive. It is as though a lot of papers, battered and bruised from public press bashing, have decided to cleanse themselves of their sins by symbolically transferring them to an editor who has confessed fault.

Is it too early to suggest that a new Pulitzer Prize category be established: the best climbdown of the year under pressure?

McVeigh No Martyr

JUNE 4, 1997

In barring emotional testimony of the sort that could turn the McVeigh penalty hearings into some kind of lynching, Judge Richard Matsch showed great sensitivity to the danger of helping to create a martyr for right-wing extremists. Not that it won't happen anyway.

McVeigh himself exhibits the strange composure of one who's ready to enter some Valhalla of victims of government, peopled by those who died in Waco and Ruby Ridge and perhaps earlier generations of foes of the feds, like white supremacists, neo-Nazis, and the Ku Klux Klan.

For the conspiracy minded, the stage for the McVeigh frame-up conspiracy has already been set. The core of the McVeigh defense as outlined in his petition to the court was that he was being set up to be blamed for a bombing actually carried out by a foreign power, probably Iraq, or maybe by Afghans or Pakistanis.

Remember how many, including news organizations, were ready in the hours after the bombing to assume that this was the work of Islamic terrorists, like the bombing of the World Trade Center in New York. It was embarrassing to realize after McVeigh was caught how easy it is to yield to xenophobia.

But it is also true that America has not had much experience with native terrorism. As President Johnson's national commission on violence reported in 1969, America has a violent history of crime, vigilantism, and rioting. As black militant H. Rap Brown said, "Violence is as American as cherry pie."

But political terrorism was something we associated more with foreigners, bomb-throwing anarchists. And when terrorism was practiced on American soil, it was usually by people from elsewhere: Croatian hijackers of an airplane, Puerto Rican fighters for independence, or a Jordanian assassin of Robert Kennedy.

But now terrorist violence has come home. There is Timothy McVeigh seemingly as typical and American as you can find now on his way to some terrorist pantheon. There is Ted Kaczynski, the suspected Unabomber.

And there was white supremacist Richard Snell, who, the same day as the Oklahoma City bombing, was executed in Arkansas for killing a policeman. His last words were "Governor, look over your shoulder, justice is coming."

Now that site in Oklahoma City serves as a monument to the American way of terrorism.

Reality Takes Second

JUNE 22, 1997

I couldn't believe it when several people told me I'd arrived in cartoon heaven by being mentioned on *The Simpsons*.

But I got the tape and there it was: Homer Simpson, in a conversation with Mo the bartender about an enemies list.

[*Audio clip:* The Simpsons]

Homer Simpson, nuclear power plant technician, city of Springfield: Oh, I can't believe it. I got an enemy. Me, the most beloved man in Springfield.

Mo the bartender, city of Springfield: Ah, it's a weird world, Homer. As hard as it is to believe, some people don't care for me neither.

Simpson: No, I won't accept that.

Mo: No, it's true. I got their names written down right here in what I call my "enemies list."

Barney, bar patron, city of Springfield: Jane Fonda, Daniel Schorr, Jack

Anderson. Hey! This is Richard Nixon's enemies list. You just crossed out his name and put yours!

Mo: Okay. Gimme that.

What struck me was that for many people my being mentioned in a cartoon was more important than a dozen commentaries or documentaries.

Next, I read a release from the U.S. Postal Service saying that its Bugs Bunny stamp was outselling the 1993 Elvis Presley stamp, until now its bestseller. The original order of 265 million Bugs Bunny stamps was being fast exhausted, and another 100 million were being printed.

What is it about cartoons that seems to attract people more than flesh-and-blood characters?

In the *New Yorker* magazine, Kurt Andersen gave other illustrations of how we seem to be entering into the cartoon era. The big musical of 1997 looks like Disney's *Hercules,* a cartoon. The Cartoon Network is the most successful new cable channel.

Who Framed Roger Rabbit is a cartoon movie about an evil genius who wants to destroy cartoon characters and replace them with human beings. Now the opposite seems to be happening in real life.

What's going on here? True, digital animation has given us more lifelike cartoon characters than we have ever known. But more lifelike than life?

And what is the connection between the rage for cartoons and the rage for going online in cyberspace and finding human connections in cartoonlike figures on the screen and enjoying an electronic flirtation in a chat room?

I have long worried about the blurring of the line between reality and fantasy. But if digitally animated figures make better companions than flesh-and-blood figures, maybe reality has been oversold. Or maybe we confuse virtual reality with virtuous reality.

Aliens

JUNE 29, 1997

So the air force issues a 219-page report telling us—no kidding—what really happened near Roswell, New Mexico, fifty years ago.

Those things that look like UFOs? Supersecret balloons to monitor Soviet atomic tests. Those things that look like aliens? Test dummies. The creature with the bulbous head and the slit eyes? A downed human pilot with a bad head injury.

Case closed, the book cover says. But of course, it isn't. Not to thousands upon thousands of people who see no reason to believe what the air force tells them. Remember, this is the same air force that announced in the first place in 1947 that a flying disc had crashed, and next day, that the shiny debris people had seen was from a downed weather balloon.

Now, I don't believe in UFOs and I am not a conspiracy theorist. I'm one of those who believe that President Kennedy was killed with a single bullet, that Watergate was not a CIA plot, and that Oliver Stone's *Nixon* picture was the product of a fevered imagination.

But how is anyone to believe a government that lies so often? The Roswell weather balloon reminded me of the U-2 spy plane downed in 1960 over the Soviet Union, which President Eisenhower announced was a weather plane off course, until Premier Nikita Khrushchev produced a CIA pilot who had survived the crash.

President Johnson lied about the engagement with the North Vietnamese in the Tonkin Gulf, and President Reagan about supplying the Nicaraguan Contras.

A particular form of top-level lie is called "plausible deniability," which is saying you didn't do it, and getting away with it. President Kennedy tried plausible deniability for the Cuban Bay of Pigs invasion. The lie fizzled along with the operation.

I guess there's always been lying in government, but it seems to me that in recent times it has become more frequent. And I'm sure that those who so routinely lie persuade themselves that it is only in the national interest.

And maybe sometimes it is. At Los Alamos, New Mexico, they managed to keep the atom bomb project secret for years, except from the Russians. Now air force colonel John Haynes says of the Roswell Report: "We can't even keep single secrets, so how could we keep secret a cover-up?"

Well, Colonel, you did. And you went on doing it long after the cold war was over. And so if some people believe more in aliens than in you people, are you surprised?

Russians Master Idiomatic American

JULY 20, 1997

American newspapers reported from Moscow that when the commander of the Russian Mir space station, Vasili Tsibliyev, was told by mission control on live television that he was being sidelined because of heart trouble, he responded, according to his simultaneous interpreter, "For crying out loud, this is bad timing."

Well, nothing like "for crying out loud" exists in Russian. It is one of those expressions that William Safire believes serve as sound-like euphemisms for profanity. Thus, "for crying out loud" may serve instead of "for Christ's sake." And "dog gone" may substitute for "God damn."

Interesting, though, was the interpreter's knowledge of the American idiom. I have long been impressed with Russia's corps of interpreters, many of them graduates of Moscow's famous Foreign Languages Institute. They're trained to smooth out the details of their speech.

In my day in Moscow, Nikita Khrushchev's star interpreters, the American-accented Oya Katroyonovsky and the British-accented Viktor Sukhodrev, had a full-time job softening his lusty barnyard epithets and sometimes his menacing language.

Neither of them was present when Khrushchev at a Polish embassy reception bellowed that in the conflict between communism and capitalism, "We will bury you." Had one of his smooth-as-silk interpreters been there, that probably would have come out as "Our system will outlive yours."

Today, the global village created by jet planes and satellite television and the Internet is creating more and more demand for skillful simultaneous interpreters. Secretary of State Madeleine Albright, recently in Prague and herself fluent in Czech, gave her interpreter a hard time, frequently interrupting him to say, "Not exactly," and then giving her own translation.

Russian general Alexander Lebed, on the other hand, on a recent visit to Washington, had an interpreter who could really make Lebed's Russian come out American. For example, when Lebed, in reply to a question, said, *"Nyet,"* the interpreter said, "No way."

The Russians are quite proud of their mastery of idiomatic American. I remember the young Russian who invited me out for a drink in Moscow to show off his English. Raising his glass, he said, "So, Mr. Schorr, here's mud down your hatch."

The CIA and Iraq

AUGUST 10, 1997

The fiftieth anniversary of the Central Intelligence Agency, July 26, when President Truman signed the authorizing legislation, went without much notice.

The $30-billion-a-year agency—that figure is still officially a secret—has not been looking for much attention—beset, beleaguered, and bedeviled as it is over its controversial past and its uncertain future. Leaving aside the recent humiliation of moles like Aldrich Ames, even the agency's greatest covert action successes have led to tragic disappointments.

The governments that it helped to overthrow in Iran, Guatemala, Chile, and Afghanistan were all succeeded by more brutal regimes. Even its assassination plots—most conspicuously with Mafia help against Fidel Castro—all failed. All were aborted.

There is one more failure to record: the effort to mount a coup from northern Iraq in 1991 to topple Saddam Hussein and install a friendlier government. The opposition force was penetrated by Saddam's agents. Eventually, the CIA fled in disarray, leaving its local allies to be captured or submit to Saddam Hussein, who has effectively reoccupied part of the north.

While it usually takes years before some congressional committee digs out the full story of CIA bungling, this time the CIA officer who was in charge, Warren Marik, now retired, went public to tell the story to ABC television and to Jim Hoagland of the *Washington Post*.

He told of arranging flights of unmanned aircraft over Baghdad to drop leaflets, of organizing military training and supplies for Kurdish guerrillas, and millions of dollars' worth of radio and television propaganda denouncing Saddam Hussein's regime.

He told, too, how the plan went sour when it switched from a methodical buildup of an alternate regime in northern Iraq to the effort to mount an armed offensive against Saddam Hussein in 1995. The debacle cost about $110 million.

What has been the outcome of the Marik revelations? You guessed it. The agency says that Marik may have violated his written agreement not to disclose confidential information, and it has referred the matter to the Justice Department for possible prosecution.

Happy fiftieth, CIA.

India Versus Pakistan

AUGUST 16, 1997

Scott Simon, host: After Timothy McVeigh was sentenced to death on Thursday for the Oklahoma City bombing, he limited himself to quoting in court from a 1928 opinion of Justice Louis Brandeis.

It spoke of government "as the potent, the omnipresent teacher, which teaches the people by its example."

Dan Schorr is on vacation, but he left behind these reflections on Timothy McVeigh's enigmatic statement.

Considering the racist culture he came from, it was perhaps ironic that Tim McVeigh should seek validation for his massive crime from the first Jewish justice of the Supreme Court.

Brandeis was writing a dissent against a 5–4 decision upholding the use of illegally obtained wiretap evidence by Prohibition agents against a group of bootleggers. Brandeis went on to say that if the government becomes a lawbreaker, it breeds contempt for the law. It invites every man to become a law unto himself. It invites anarchy.

The speculation is that McVeigh, in quoting Brandeis, was suggesting that the FBI raid on the Branch Davidian compound in Waco, Texas, had delegitimized the government and legitimized his act on the second anniversary of Waco.

When asked about that, the prosecutor in the Oklahoma City case,

Joseph Hartzler, said, "Do me a favor, don't interpret his words as those from a statesman."

Fair enough. The words of a Tim McVeigh are more deserving of psychological than constitutional analysis. Yet it's worthwhile trying to understand the twisted logic that gives the violence-prone a patina of justification.

John Wilkes Booth, who shot President Lincoln, leaped onstage to make his own McVeigh-like statement: *"Sic semper tyrannis."* Leon Czolgosz, the anarchist who killed President McKinley, was presumably striking a blow against government as the oppressor.

Tim McVeigh, when captured, wore a T-shirt inscribed with a line from Jefferson: "The tree of liberty must be refreshed from time to time with the blood of patriots and tyrants."

Our violence-prone society has produced, aside from ordinary criminals, dope-assisted murderers, and random killers, a breed of holy-war fanatics, individuals and militia units seeking license for their conspiracies from the Founding Fathers and the Constitution.

That their fevered thinking about bringing down government should intersect with the pronouncements of respected jurists on liberty is a travesty. Perhaps Tim McVeigh's final act of violence was to the memory of Justice Brandeis, the upholder of individual rights, determined and protected by law.

Censors

AUGUST 17, 1997

Maybe finding out after forty years who your masked torturer was might be something like this. But let me start from the beginning.

As CBS correspondent in Moscow in the mid-1950s, I worked under official censorship, a hangover from Stalin days.

That meant that anything we Western reporters wanted to cable or broadcast had to be brought in three copies to a counter at the central telegraph office. A functionary logged it in and passed it through a slit in the wall to the room where the invisible censor worked.

A copy came back, sooner or later, or not at all. When it did come back, it was usually with words, sentences, or whole paragraphs crossed out in heavy black pencil.

Many were the hours we spent, day and night, waiting for copy and cursing the censor. A radio reporter had the special difficulty of not knowing whether his script would come back in time for a scheduled broadcast, or with excisions that would make it incomprehensible when read into the microphone.

I tried venting my frustration by saying on the air, "Fifteen words deleted here," but the foreign ministry warned me that it would not allow an allusion to the existence of censorship.

You can't imagine the frustration of having a big story, like the secret speech of Nikita Khrushchev denouncing Stalin before the Communist Party Congress, and not being allowed to breathe a word of it to America.

We hated the censor with a consuming passion. We spent hours speculating on what he might look like—a jackbooted thug, a sadistic mastermind.

With this picture in mind for forty years, imagine my feelings when I got a telephone call just the other day from a journalist in Moscow working for a Russian newsmagazine.

She wanted my reminiscences of working in Moscow forty years ago. I asked how she knew about me.

"Well, it was this way," she said. "My grandmother was the censor who worked on your copy, and she would come home and tell us about it."

"Your grandmother? Those heavy black lines were made by a woman?"

"Yes, and sometimes she said she regretted having to butcher your copy, because some of the things you said she agreed with. But she had to follow KGB guidelines."

"Is your grandmother still alive?"

"Yes. And working as a translator. If you come to Moscow sometime, you can meet her. She's a very nice old lady."

Well, I'm not sure I can face that: forty years of pent-up rage at a depersonalized monster. Do I want now to meet this nice old lady to whom killing my best lines was just a job to be done?

I said, "No, just say hello for me. And tell your grandmother the rest of my message is deleted."

Saint of the Media, Saint of India

SEPTEMBER 5, 1997

Linda Wertheimer, host: This has been a week bracketed by the deaths of famous women: Mother Teresa today; Princess Diana on Sunday morning.

Of course it's only time that links the two deaths, thousands of miles apart. Mother Teresa lived a long life. She'd been seriously ill for some time. Princess Diana died suddenly and in her prime.

But for news analyst Daniel Schorr, there is something revealing in the way the world has responded to the lives and deaths of the two women.

Saint of the gutters and saint of the media. The death of Mother Teresa casts a new light on the Princess Diana frenzy sweeping Britain and much of the world. Mother Teresa was celebrated, but was not a celebrity.

She was celebrated for some fifty years of work among the poor. That brought her the Nobel Prize, but not the kind of adulation that attended a death of a princess. You think about it.

Princess Diana, for all her praiseworthy interest in children, land mine victims, and the otherwise disadvantaged, lived a life of the advantaged, a life of yachts and sunny beaches. And when she died, she left an estate estimated at $65 million.

Mother Teresa, according to her order, the Missionaries of Charity, left the world owning only two pairs of sandals, two pairs of eyeglasses, a wooden wash bucket, a well-worn sweater, a well-thumbed Bible, and an olivewood rosary.

President Clinton said today of Mother Teresa, "She was an incredible person. I think I had a chance to be around her a couple of times." He had no trouble remembering Princess Diana, of whom he said, "I will always be glad that I knew the princess."

This is not to diminish Princess Diana, nor to derogate the millions who have identified with her and her surmounting of marital and other troubles. It is only to say that there is a difference between a noble life well lived and a media image of nobility well cultivated.

Media Mistrust

SEPTEMBER 21, 1997

Perhaps enough time has passed since the death of Princess Diana to survey the damage that the episode has done to the press.

The tendency in the media was first to establish distance from the paparazzi, as though the persistent photographers were like some plague of locusts not connected with respectable journalism. And then the huge sigh of relief when it appeared that the security aide driving the Mercedes was under the influence of drugs and alcohol, and the hope that this would let the press off the hook.

But it didn't. Opinion polls continue to report deep resentment among Americans of the Fourth Estate. And any journalist can provide anecdotal evidence of the anger at "you people." What becomes clear was that the violation of Princess Diana's privacy was not the beginning of an antipress trend, but only the climax of a trend long developing.

It displayed itself when a North Carolina jury levied a penalty of $5 million against ABC for using secret cameras in an investigative report in a Food Lion supermarket. It displayed itself when NBC rigged the fiery crash of a General Motors truck, and when security guard Richard Jewell was wrongly singled out as a suspect in the Atlanta bombing.

People sense that the media—being progressively merged into bigger and bigger media—consider them a market more than an audience, and use sensationalism to hold and enlarge that market. Even while spellbound by coverage of O. J. Simpson, Ennis Cosby, Tonya Harding, JonBenet Ramsey, they know they're being manipulated by an increasingly tabloid media.

On February 23, 1973, President Nixon told John Dean, his words recorded on tape: "Well, one hell of a lot of people don't give one damn about the issue of the suppression of the press, et cetera."

And a quarter of a century later, it is coming true. In a Roper–Freedom Forum poll, 65 percent of respondents said there are times when publication or broadcast should be prevented. For those who have fought prior restraint up to the Supreme Court, that's enough to make them shudder.

Some newspeople are forming a Committee of Concerned Journalists.

It reminds me of the Committee of Concerned Scientists worried about the nuclear bomb. The aim here is media disarmament. Lots of luck.

The Script

OCTOBER 29, 1997

Maybe Americans are too distracted by stock market gyrations to pay attention to the man from China with the funny tricornered hat.

Or maybe the drama has been sucked out of the occasion by a sense that a script is being meticulously followed. The twenty-one guns salute, the protesters protest, the exiled dissenters dissent, and constructive engagement is pursued by the leader of the free world and the leader of, er, the biggest country in the world.

As provided in the scenario, there was the unscheduled ice-breaking meeting last night upstairs in the White House. President Jiang Zemin duly read from the Gettysburg Address on the wall of the Lincoln Bedroom.

Their versions of philosophies were duly discussed. Mr. Clinton brought up human rights. Jiang said "duly noted" and trotted out his Einstein theory of "relative" human rights and "relative" democracy.

Today the agreements long ago negotiated were formalized. The two leaders celebrated their common ground and their countries' multifaceted relationship.

This encounter, let's face it, was doomed to succeed. American economic interests in China, from Boeing aircraft to Westinghouse reactors, are too critical to permit the luxury of the conflict over values.

During the cold war, President Reagan supported cooperation with moderate autocrats friendly to American interests. In the post–cold war era, the slogan may well be: "Cooperation with autocrats friendly to American economic interests."

So, after the scripted state dinner toasts, President Jiang resumes his tour of the icons of America's "relative" democracy in Williamsburg and Philadelphia and Boston. An embarrassed White House says that he chose the itinerary. It is as though a visitor to Egypt would ask to see the pyramids.

Constructive engagement marches on. While Chinese antipollution controls are awaited, American industry prepares to sell technology for the cleaner burning of coal. The Disney organization, anxious to build a Shanghai Disneyland, has engaged Henry Kissinger to soothe Beijing's feelings about Disney's Dalai Lama film.

At the summit, Tibet is no big deal. Taiwan is no big deal. The big deal is that America has what China needs, and America needs to sell it. That's how constructive engagements are born.

Demonization

NOVEMBER 19, 1997

At a meeting of the National Security Council, it was agreed that U.S. policy should be the downfall of the dictator. But the CIA warned that this would require a prolonged military occupation. Iraq? No, Cuba— in the 1961 memorandum, one of 1,500 pages of documents newly released by the Assassination Records Review Board.

This reminds us how our presidents have tended to practice a policy of demonization of Third World leaders.

For President Eisenhower, and especially for President Kennedy, the favored demon was Fidel Castro, the target of a long series of murder plots, some in cahoots with the Mafia, some quite zany.

President Reagan's number one demon was Libya's Muammar Qaddafi, whose compound in Benghazi he ordered bombed in retaliation for the bombing of GIs in a Berlin café. Reagan said he would have shed no tears if Qaddafi had been killed. Qaddafi's response, intelligence analysts believe, was the destruction of Pan Am 103.

President Bush's demon of choice after the invasion of Kuwait was Saddam Hussein, whom he likened to Hitler. But in January of 1993, with Iraq defeated in the Gulf War, and under stringent United Nations controls, President-elect Clinton indicated a turning away from demonization. In an interview with the *New York Times,* he said that if Saddam Hussein wanted a different relationship with the United States "all he has to do is change his behavior."

Under criticism, Mr. Clinton backed away from that. And the CIA has tried with dismal success to mount efforts at Saddam Hussein's overthrow.

Secretary of State Albright said last March that sanctions will remain in place "as long as it takes" to remove the Iraqi dictator.

But that goes further than the United Nations resolution, which links sanctions mainly to removal of weapons of mass destruction. If Saddam Hussein sees no chance at getting the oil embargo lifted as long as he is in power, he has little incentive to play ball.

That is what Foreign Minister Yevgeny Primakov means when he says that "Iraq must see light at the end of the tunnel." The Russian peace plan reportedly provides for a phased lifting of sanctions linked to progress in getting rid of weapons.

But to deal on that basis, Mr. Clinton would have to accept a policy of containment rather than overthrow, and return to his preinaugural idea of coexistence with Saddam Hussein if he changes his behavior. The road back from demonization is not easy.

Confidential Sources

NOVEMBER 30, 1997

Is there such a thing as posthumous privilege?

Dr. Frederic Mailliez, the first physician to reach the accident in the Paris tunnel on August 31, told the *Times* of London in a recent interview that Princess Diana kept expressing pain. But when asked just what she said, the French doctor replied he couldn't repeat that because there is a duty between the doctor and the patient.

Even after the patient has died, the question of whether the obligation of confidentiality continues after death is not an easy one for doctors or lawyers or even for journalists. The question of postmortem lawyer-client privilege is now on its way to the Supreme Court.

Nine days before his suicide in July 1993, White House lawyer Vincent Foster consulted another lawyer, James Hamilton, respected veteran of the Watergate investigation. During their two-hour meeting, Hamilton wrote three pages of notes, with check marks and question marks next to some sections, some words underlined.

Two years later, Whitewater independent counsel Kenneth Starr demanded those notes. Hamilton's refusal on the ground of lawyer-client privilege—the oldest privilege known to common law—was upheld by the federal district court but then overruled by the court of appeals.

Hamilton is now taking to the Supreme Court an issue made more delicate by the Foster suicide, the issue of whether a client would speak freely to a lawyer if he thought his confidence would not survive his death.

As a journalist, I have a certain interest in that question. The courts have not given as much weight to protection of the confidentiality of journalistic sources as they have given for lawyer, doctor, and clergy privilege.

In 1976, I faced a possible citation for contempt of Congress and a jail sentence for refusing to reveal where I had gotten a House Intelligence Committee report on the CIA that the House had voted to suppress. Luckily for me, the House Ethics Committee voted 6–5 against a contempt citation.

In my testimony before the committee, I said that to betray a source would dry up future sources for future journalists. And now I have an almost visceral feeling about naming a source, dead or alive.

As long ago as 1948, reporting from Indonesia, I broke the story of a confidential proposal by United Nations mediators aimed at ending the Dutch-Indonesian conflict. As a result, the Dutch broke off the peace negotiations.

Since then, historians interested in knowing who was interested in torpedoing the peace talks have asked me about my source. I don't know whether that source is still alive, and yet so powerful is the grip of journalistic tradition that I cannot bring myself to disclose that ancient source.

The New Global Divide

DECEMBER 12, 1997

Our political lexicon has trouble keeping up with the tides of history. In Kyoto, the advanced countries tried with little success to bring along the Third World in a plan to control global warming.

But there are no three worlds anymore. The Communist Second World has dissolved and there remains the division between developed countries, led by the United States, the European Community, and Japan, and the less-developed countries, led by India, China, and Brazil.

The disappearance of the East-West axis brings into better focus the neglected reality of the North-South axis. It is basically a division between haves and have-nots. Except for the oil-rich haves, and except, at least until recently, for the fast-growing Asian Pacific Rim nations.

During the half century of the cold war, the Third World provided arenas for proxy East-West ideological conflict: from Ethiopia to Nicaragua, from Angola to Vietnam.

Now, Secretary of State Albright barnstorms around Africa, selling human rights to countries, many of which have been left without viable governments to control ethnic slaughter.

In Kyoto, the major polluters, starting with the United States with 4 percent of the world's population and 20 percent of its greenhouse gases, are disappointed at being unable to sell the less-polluting countries on the idea of buying and trading pollution credits, licenses to pollute.

"We have reached a fundamentally new stage in the development of human civilization requiring a better understanding of our connections to God's Earth and to each other." So said Vice President Gore, in his flowery speech in Kyoto.

That kind of language may resonate among American and European environmentalists, but it cannot mean much in the wide expanses of Africa and Asia, where people struggle for a minimal level of subsistence, and pin their hopes on economic development.

If Kyoto has shown anything, it is that the advanced countries have a price to pay for all those years when their East-West fixation left them insufficiently attentive to the gap between North and South.

The State of Peace on Earth in 1997

DECEMBER 21, 1997

It has become something of a tradition for presidents to visit troops overseas during the Christmas season. And President Clinton's trip to Bosnia—where 8,500 Americans are stationed—symbolizes how peace has fared in 1997.

The guns are silent. But hostilities could flare up at any time, were it not for the NATO peacekeepers.

The guns have also been silent in Iraq since the Gulf War ended in 1991. But a huge force of American planes hovers in the vicinity, ready for a contingency, as they call it. Not war, not peace either.

The brighter side of 1997 is that Americans were not engaged in any significant war. And there seemed hopeful portents for the future in the Clinton administration's decision no longer to base nuclear planning on the possibility of an all-out nuclear war with Russia, nor to base the American forces buildup on the possibility of two simultaneous regional wars.

Relative peace for us, perhaps, but not for a large part of the world. Certainly not in large stretches of Africa, like the Democratic Republic of the Congo, where Laurent Kabila fought his way into power and now tries to hide the massacres along the way.

Not in Rwanda, where some three hundred were massacred even while Secretary of State Madeleine Albright was visiting the capital, counseling respect for human rights.

American troops helped to secure peace and democracy in Haiti. But stable rule has not sunk roots, and the corruption and the killing go on.

What is peace, anyway? North Korea poses no imminent threat of war. But can imminent starvation be called peace?

The annual report of UNICEF says 12 million children die in a year in the developing countries, more than half of them because of malnutrition. Surely that cannot be called peace.

Gerald Scully, a University of Texas economist, has studied thirty countries where governments have systematically killed their own people. In this expiring century, 55 million in the Soviet Union, mainly in Stalin's time; in China, more than 35 million, mainly in Mao's time. And then down through Germany, Cambodia, and the rest, for a grand total of 170 million human lives snuffed out by their own governments, four times as many as the 42 million who died in international and civil wars in this century.

I cite these numbers not to dampen yuletide joy, only to say that peace on Earth is not a condition but a process. And as in Northern Ireland and the Middle East, a long and painful process.

And one gets a better understanding of why Saint Luke coupled "on earth peace" with "goodwill toward men." You can't have one without the other.

1998

Lies, Damned Lies, Etc.

The Public Is Focused on Policy over Scandal

JANUARY 28, 1998

Unlike President Nixon, who proclaimed in his 1974 State of the Union address that one year of Watergate was enough, President Clinton chose last night to ignore the aura of scandal threatening his presidency.

It is probably misleading, though, to suggest, as many headlines do today, that Mr. Clinton made an effort to shift the focus to his popular legislative initiatives. Those initiatives have been widely advertised since the year-end. And there is no reason to believe that absent the personal controversy, this speech would have been much different.

Still, the address, drawing rave reviews from the public in overnight polls, falls into place as part of a defense strategy. The strategy appears to be: one, to assume the posture of being absorbed with the nation's business; two, vehement but unspecific denials of wrongdoing pleading some sort of investigative gag rule; three, trying to take the battle to the enemy, namely, independent counsel Kenneth Starr, with the first lady spearheading charges of right-wing conspiracy.

As a stopgap, the strategy is having some success. Volatile public opinion appears to be turning away from personal scandal and turning on a scandal-obsessed media. But the stopgap strategy can succeed only until more is known about the nature of the relationship between the president and "that woman," Monica Lewinsky, for the suspicion of cover-up and obstruction of justice rests on the president's having something guilty to hide.

One waits for that other shoe to drop, that is, for Miss Lewinsky to strike her immunity deal and tell what is expected to be a lurid tale of hanky-panky with a promiscuous president in that national shrine called the White House.

But in this "one-witness case," as lawyer William Ginsburg calls it, next there comes a battle of credibility between a woman who has admitted on tape lying all her life and a man who has on tape in Little Rock counseled Gennifer Flowers to "just deny everything."

It is with a sickening sensation that one can see a protracted contest involving sex and lies between a president and an emotional young woman. It would be a funny New Age drama if it weren't so tragic for the country.

Story Convergence

FEBRUARY 18, 1998

Washington has turned into a two-story town focused on what goes on in presidential mansions.

Perhaps because of overconcentration on the saga of sex and the saga of Saddam Hussein, I sometimes find the two stories beginning to merge in my mind.

One thing they do have in common. Be the adversary Kenneth Starr or Saddam Hussein, the issue becomes a test of President Clinton's credibility. With so much at stake in both cases, there are task forces working strenuously to devise a believable position, be it only a stopgap position.

Mr. Clinton's almost month-old position that he had no sexual relationship with Monica Lewinsky, and would answer all the questions about the matter as soon as he could, is beginning to wear dangerously thin as reports of visits and presents exchanged pile up.

And so it looked like the first harbinger of a switch to a limited hangout when press spokesman Mike McCurry told the *Chicago Tribune* that the Clinton-Lewinsky situation might end up being a "very complicated story as most human relationships are, a story not easy to explain."

McCurry, not hitherto known to shoot from the hip, says the remark was a lapse of sanity and not part of any strategy. But I suspect we will be hearing more about a "complicated human relationship" as the president falls back to a more defensible position.

Now to Iraq, if you don't mind the leap. A few weeks ago, the president was talking about denying Saddam Hussein the use of weapons of mass destruction and coercing him by force, if necessary, into accepting unlimited and unconditional inspection.

That position has not worn well as it became clear that bombing alone would probably not eliminate all hidden stores of biological and chemical weapons, that what was destroyed could be replaced, and that the current inspection regime, incomplete as it may be, would be abolished altogether by Saddam Hussein.

Mr. Clinton's withdrawal to a more credible, if less inspiring position was evident in his carefully couched Pentagon speech yesterday. Weapons would not be eliminated but "seriously diminished." The dictator's capacity to threaten his neighbors would not be ended but "seriously reduced."

And in the end, Saddam Hussein would not be gone but "seriously worse off." Not very ringing words, but this is a hard time for a president, beleaguered at home and abroad, and looking for words that will satisfy the need of the moment.

Sedition

MARCH 1, 1998

"This is the stuff of the Sedition Act," said First Amendment lawyer Floyd Abrams. He was referring to independent counsel Kenneth Starr's use of grand jury subpoenas to ferret out leaks to journalists critical of him and his staff.

Sedition. What a quaint word. Thanks to my friend William Safire, who's been researching the subject for a book, I was able to go back two hundred years to the Sedition Act of 1798 and learn how the government treated irksome journalists then.

The Michael Isikoff of his day—Isikoff is the *Newsweek* reporter who broke the Monica Lewinsky story—was James Callendar, who wrote for the newspaper *Aurora*.

One of Callendar's prize sources was Thomas Jefferson. Thanks to Jefferson's people, Callendar was able to report that an unsavory associate of Treasury Secretary Alexander Hamilton, named James Reynolds, had had late-night meetings at Hamilton's home, getting inside information to speculate in government securities.

Hamilton indignantly denied the charge. His defense was that the reason for the late-night activity at his home was that he was having an affair with Reynolds's wife. Thus, an adulterer, not a speculator.

Out of this, and other such embarrassing reports, came the Sedition Act. It prohibited false, scandalous, and malicious writings, and any writings against the government of the United States, on pain of fines and prison up to two years. That was before the Supreme Court started reviewing laws for constitutionality.

Calendar and thirteen others were convicted of sedition. Luckily, Jefferson was elected president and he pardoned them all. The Sedition Act lapsed and was not reenacted. And a good thing, too, if you will allow a self-serving comment.

Imagine what President Nixon would have done with a Sedition Act! As it was, he had to content himself with an enemies list and an FBI investigation of me.

Even without a Sedition Act, there are ways to send a journalist to jail. In 1976, I was subpoenaed to appear before the House Ethics Committee and threatened with jail for contempt of Congress if I did not disclose the source of a report on the CIA that the House had voted to suppress.

In the end, the committee voted 6–5 not to send me to jail—a little too close for comfort.

Now a new generation of reporters and their sources faces the challenge of an angry independent counsel looking for blood and able to drag people before the grand jury. Just think what Kenneth Starr would do if he had that old Sedition Act!

Fred Friendly Obit

MARCH 4, 1998

Robert Siegel, host: Fred Friendly, who helped invent broadcast journalism, died yesterday at the age of eighty-two. Friendly was a CBS producer who made some of the best TV documentaries ever on the programs See It Now *and* CBS Reports.

In 1964, he became president of CBS News, but quit soon after in a dispute that was a showdown over the direction of network television.

At CBS, our senior news analyst Dan Schorr worked with Fred Friendly.

Don't ask me to write dispassionately of this passionate newsman. He was too important in my life.

Fred Friendly was the other half of Ed Murrow, the one who prodded Murrow to take on Senator Joe McCarthy and who bought a newspaper ad to promote the McCarthy program when CBS wouldn't.

Fred prodded all of us with ideas we often thought zany. When I was in Moscow, he had me ask the Russians to let CBS cover a Soviet space shot live—impossible.

When I was in Berlin, he had me ask the East Germans to let us film a documentary about the land beyond the wall. Impossible, except that it happened and made a bit of television history.

He loved living dangerously. I was in the control room with him when he put on a live program, skipping across the continent to celebrate the completion of the coaxial TV cable. In South Dakota, a herd of buffalo was supposed to run across the screen. It didn't.

"Cue the goddamn buffalo!" Fred shouted.

After our first lunch in 1953, we returned to Fred's office to find a hand grenade on his desk. In mock alarm he rushed out shouting, "If that grenade's a dud, I can think of a dozen people who could have put it there. If it's live, I can think of a hundred."

Fred had his detractors and his admirers. And some of us were ambivalent mixtures of both.

In 1964, as newly named president of CBS News, Friendly had to be talked out of firing me because I had created trouble for him at the San Francisco Republican convention with a broadcast from Germany about Senator Barry Goldwater.

In rage, he said on the telephone, "I've just started this job, and you've given me a club foot." For many months, we were not on speaking terms.

But then there was a Friendly who two years later resigned because, as he put it, "CBS insisted on a fifth re-run of *I Love Lucy*" instead of an important Senate hearing on Vietnam.

"Because television can make so much money doing its worst, it often cannot afford to do its best," he said.

He wrote a book then ironically titled *Due to Circumstances Beyond Our Control* . . . saying the reader would have to decide whether he had lost his head or whether television had lost its way. The book was dedicated to the professionals at CBS News. And in my copy, he wrote: "For Dan Schorr, who could have been a TV producer and is."

Gosh, I don't know about that, Fred. I'd love to argue with you about it.

Leading Us All Down

MARCH 16, 1998

In New Hampshire in 1987, after a well-publicized tryst with a Miami woman, candidate Gary Hart was asked by Paul Taylor of the *Washington Post* whether he had ever committed adultery. Hart refused to answer, but later told his press secretary: "This thing is never going to end, is it? Look, let's just go home."

In 1992, George Bush was asked by Mary Tillotson of CNN whether he had ever committed adultery. The "Big A" Bush called it, and said no, he never had.

Yesterday, Dan Quayle, who in 1992 fended off suggestions of earlier involvement with lobbyist Paula Parkinson during a Florida golf weekend, became the first candidate of the year 2000 presidential season to disclaim adultery. He volunteered his denial on NBC's *Meet the Press,* responding to the question of whether marital fidelity has become a qualification for high office.

Whatever happens in President Clinton's face-off with his women accusers, so dramatized last night by Kathleen Willey on *60 Minutes,* the politics of sex has clearly become a witches' brew likely to poison the political process for a long time to come.

What has happened, as scholar Norman Ornstein points out, is that sex as a political weapon is becoming institutionalized. Ideologically minded foundations that once dealt mainly in policy have developed investigative arms probing for scandal. The laws on sexual discrimination and harassment provide an avenue for a discovery process, enabling the accuser to search for damaging information from the past backed by the threat of perjury.

In the case of President Clinton, a civil suit for sexual misconduct has intersected with an independent counsel's criminal investigation, whose beginnings in an Arkansas land deal are all but forgotten. Gary Hart said in 1987: "What it gets down to is not crime, but sin." But that was before the criminalization of sin.

The presidency has already been substantially diminished and is likely to be further diminished. How many potential candidates will in the future be driven away from electoral politics as a dung heap can only be surmised. It's hard to say when the public will determine that obsession with adultery is not necessarily adult.

Staying Out

MARCH 25, 1998

In his contrition over the massacre in Rwanda, President Clinton reflected his sense of where he thinks America should be, but also a sense of unreality about where America is in the violent world.

Having burned its fingers in Somalia, the Clinton administration in 1994 was not about to lead an international intervention in Rwanda to halt a genocide, refusing even to use that word, because it would have called for action.

America's contribution in Rwanda, in the end, was a short stay of 270 troops. Since then, the appetite for intervention has not increased. And the president, talking of American responsibility as he responds to tumultuous crowds in Africa, is removed from the many trouble spots where America shows reluctance to assume responsibilities.

The Kosovo enclave in Serbia may be on the verge of civil war. But Secretary of State Albright, unable to offer American involvement, could not get European governments even to toughen sanctions.

As Congress prepares to go home on holiday, the $18 billion American contribution to the International Monetary Fund, which could help to avert food riots in Asian countries, is hung up on an antiabortion rider. The billion dollars in back dues to the United Nations, which could help to pay for peacekeeping missions, is hung up on abortion language and other conditions.

Iraq has arrested its biological research mastermind, who might have defected with revelations of a major germ warfare program, but a House committee has unanimously approved an amendment that would require congressional approval for any military action against Iraq.

With that fine sense of occasion which is his hallmark, Mr. Clinton was able to personalize his dismay at the slaughter of more than eight hundred thousand people in Rwanda. He spoke of "people like me sitting in offices who did not fully appreciate the depths and the speed with which you were being engulfed by this unimaginable terror."

But in fact, the outbreak of tribal violence had long been foreseen, and UN ambassador Albright argued for assembling a UN peacekeeping force, but ran into White House and Pentagon opposition.

Will there be a more vigorous response by people sitting in their offices to the next outbreak of violence within sovereign borders? Given the mood of Congress, and perhaps of the American people, probably not. Contrition will come later.

Stephen Glass

MAY 17, 1998

Here are some persons and situations recently described in magazines, and guess what they have in common.

The budget-cutting Concord Coalition has a member named Susan, an eighty-year-old widow who keeps a portrait of the late ex-senator Paul Tsongas on her wall.

Eight young conservatives, in a haze of beer and pot, lured a woman up to a Washington hotel room. One got her to disrobe, whereupon the others appeared from hiding and took her picture while she fled in tears.

There is a Wall Street investment firm whose traders bring out a cake and sing, "Happy birthday, Alan Greenspan!"

An organization in Rockville, Maryland, named the National Memorabilia Convention sells condoms named for Monica Lewinsky.

A fifteen-year-old computer hacker named Ian Restil in Bethesda, Maryland, penetrated the database of a company named Jukt Micronics and so terrorized its executives that they came to his home and offered him a high-paying job.

What these published episodes have in common is that there is not a word of truth in any of them. They are all inventions of the same prolific twenty-five-year-old journalist, Stephen Glass, who has been fired as associate editor of the *New Republic*.

"Merely corroborative detail intended to give artistic verisimilitude to an otherwise bald and unconvincing narrative," *The Mikado*'s Lord High Executioner might say. Well, that's okay for Gilbert and Sullivan, but not for me. I know I reveal myself as an aging curmudgeon when I voice dismay at the way some—thankfully, still only a few—in the current generation of journalists take liberties with what we old-timers used to call the "facts."

It is as though the difference between reality and fantasy has been blurred by too much exposure to various forms of make-believe. It is as though normal restraints are overcome by the urge to produce a sensation, preferably with a sexual angle, that will offer a fast lane to fame and fortune, and multiple appearances on *Larry King Live*.

Ruth Shalit, another *New Republic* writer who herself had some trouble over plagiarism a few years ago, says, "When you're a young reporter, you're a little overzealous, a little unhinged." I know about being overzealous. I don't know about being unhinged.

"There is still a wide chasm between hype and hoax," writes *Washington Post* media critic Howard Kurtz. But that chasm is not as wide as it used to be.

Just the Beginning

JUNE 2, 1998

Robert Siegel, host: There was another surprise move by independent counsel Kenneth Starr today. Yesterday, White House lawyers announced they were dropping the claim of executive privilege they'd invoked to keep White House aides from having to testify before the grand jury.

Today, Starr asked the Supreme Court to expedite consideration of lawyer-client privilege and Secret Service privilege. The White House maintains these issues should be heard first by an appeals court.

News analyst Daniel Schorr says all these legal maneuverings by the president and by the independent counsel are only setting the stage for the main event.

"By testing [executive privilege] on such weak ground—where my own personal vulnerability would inevitably be perceived as having affected my judgment—I probably ensured the defeat of my cause."

That was, let me hasten to say, Richard Nixon in his memoirs. But the lesson could well apply to President Clinton, who's also been losing the battles of the privileges.

Ominous for his cause is the determination of a federal judge with access to sealed grand jury proceedings that White House aides are likely to have relevant evidence bearing on the perjury/obstruction-of-justice investigation of Mr. Clinton.

But the battles over what aides, what lawyers, what Secret Service officers can be compelled to testify are all skirmishes in preparation for the mother of all battles: whether the president himself can be compelled to testify.

It's reliably reported that since February, he has rejected four invitations to appear before the grand jury, citing his busy schedule and his distrust of the independent counsel.

Can Mr. Clinton be subpoenaed to appear? Counsel Starr's position, expressed by spokesman Charles Bakaly, is that this is possible, the Supreme Court having held that the grand jury is entitled to every person's information.

If the president does answer a subpoena, is he then entitled to every person's constitutional protection against self-incrimination? That question leads into some uncharted waters.

The Fifth Amendment presumably could be invoked if he were facing possible indictment, either while in office or afterward. Starr has not taken a formal position on whether a sitting president is indictable in the absence of an impeachment proceeding.

But what if the president were called not as a target, but as a witness against someone else—say Monica Lewinsky?

Merely to raise these questions is to indicate the legal and political nightmare that may lie ahead. This helps to explain why Kenneth Starr is anxious to make an interim report to the House in the hope that the House will exercise its constitutional duty of dealing with any allegations against the president.

But there is no indication that congressional leaders are anxious to have this hot potato dropped in their laps. As long as the House fails to act, Starr has responsibility for fulfilling a mandate that expressly includes the president.

Country and Constitution may face some severe tests in the days and months ahead.

Scandal Lingo

AUGUST 12, 1998

Next Monday when President Clinton faces the grand jury, I'll be away on vacation, far from the investigation tearing at the vitals of the presidency. One judgment can already be made. This scandal has done less than any I can remember to enrich the American lexicon.

Watergate was of course a treasure trove for language lovers. John Dean's "cancer on the presidency," Senator Howard Baker's "what did the president know and when did he know it," spokesman Ron Ziegler's "third-rate burglary," a phrase he later made inoperative, John Ehrlichman's "modified, limited hang-out" and "twist slowly, slowly in the wind."

The Woodward-Bernstein source Deep Throat recycling the title of a movie. The Saturday Night Massacre of Special Prosecutor Archibald Cox. A suffix, -gate, that can make almost any word into a scandal title. And a phrase with special meaning for me, "enemies list."

Iran-Contra didn't compare. It gave us only President Reagan's "mistakes were made," Oliver North's "a cake and a Bible for the Iranian mullahs," and lawyer Brendan Sullivan's "potted plant."

What has the current scandal given us beyond pallid phrases like "talking points," "sexual relationship," and "physical evidence," and of course "mea culpa," which isn't exactly American language?

What is the reason for this paucity of catchy lines? One reason undoubtedly is that we've not yet had televised hearings of the kind that gave Watergate its special cachet. There is, I believe, another reason.

Watergate was about power and this is about sex, which does not lend itself to easy repetition to a mass audience. A whole collection of sex scandal jokes and gag lines is circulating in the Washington underground, none of which I care to repeat here.

So this scandal is discussed mainly in euphemism, leaving not much in memorable usage contributions.

Language-gate, you might call it.

Heroes

SEPTEMBER 13, 1998

It must have been the great impresario who arranged that split screen between the descent of President Clinton and the ascent of Mark McGwire.

The White House spinmeisters were madly spinning in vain, while the home-run hitter without any visible public-relations advice was quite naturally making the gestures to Sammy Sosa and Roger Maris's family, and even to the man upstairs. That paved his way into American hearts as a certified national hero.

Come to think of it, political leaders have seldom been great national heroes, except in wartime, when we looked to a Roosevelt, a Churchill, or a de Gaulle to guard us against a foe and take us to victory. And as Churchill found, victory in war does not guarantee winning the next election.

The first crowning of a national hero that I remember was Colonel Charles Lindbergh. I don't think that at the age of ten I could have named the president of the United States, Calvin Coolidge, but everybody knew and thrilled about Lucky Lindy, the lone eagle, who flew to France in the little airplane all by himself. Never mind that later Lindbergh showed himself to be soft on Hitler's Germany. I remember 1927.

National heroes usually come singly, but space gave us the collective hero, the men with the right stuff, Colonel John Glenn and the men who walked on the moon, like Neil Armstrong. By calling the astronauts with congratulations, President Nixon enhanced himself, as President Clinton enhanced himself by calling Mark McGwire.

One of my earliest national heroes was Gertrude Ederle, who swam the English Channel in 1926. I can still remember that young woman in the modest one-piece bathing suit on black-and-white newsreels. That was before candidates for national hero started disqualifying themselves by acts of violence, by prohibited drugs, by a mania for money that made them look too much like politicians.

But shining like a good deed in a naughty world are those like Cal Ripken and now Mark McGwire, who, when he's not hitting a ball out of the ballpark, is raising a ten-year-old son. Nice to have an unimpeachable figure in a very bad week.

Afghanistan and the Taliban

SEPTEMBER 16, 1998

For a moment last month, America was diverted from the presidential scandal when it became aware that something ominous was happening in western Asia.

Embassy bombings in East Africa were linked to a wealthy Saudi terrorist, Osama bin Laden, holed up in a training camp in Afghanistan. A missile attack was launched on that camp on August 21, with no apparent effect on bin Laden.

Let's bring you up to date. The fanatical Taliban, which controls most of Afghanistan, says bin Laden has been placed under house arrest for violating the terms of his sanctuary. But he's been seen circulating widely and heard threatening new terrorist attacks.

In any event, American scholars recently in the region believe that focusing on one notorious terrorist tends to overpersonalize a much more sweeping problem. The Taliban, once the beneficiary of American support of the anti-Soviet mujahideen, is now fiercely anti-Western, and especially anti-American. Traffic in drugs is its chief source of revenue. Heroin, whose use by Muslims is taboo, is shipped out to corrupt the infidels.

The Taliban also has a working military relationship with Pakistan, with arms and troops flowing freely across their common border.

Pakistani planes are believed to have supported a Taliban attack on an opposition stronghold. Iran, incensed over the murder of nine of its nationals, has been threatening to invade Afghanistan.

Behind the Afghan-Iranian tension lies bitter antagonism between Shiite Iran and mainly Sunni Pakistan for influence in Afghanistan and dominance in the region.

The situation creates a tangled predicament for American policy-makers not anxious to repeat the historic 1980s mistake of backing Iraq against Iran, only to have to fight a war with Iraq.

Pakistan has long been an American ally, a staging area for the CIA's war to oust the Soviets from Afghanistan. Now that Pakistan has tested nuclear weapons and is supporting the anti-American Taliban in Afghanistan, some reconsideration of policy, including the unilateral sanctions against Iran, may be in order.

But dealing with the Taliban problem takes time and maybe a new presidential directive. And who in the White House has time for the Taliban?

Other World Issues

SEPTEMBER 22, 1998

Just thought you might like someone to keep track of the rest of the world while the capital remains transfixed over the deconstruction of the president.

The ovation that Mr. Clinton got yesterday in the United Nations General Assembly, where he may lose his vote at year's end unless Congress pays up its past dues, seemed to reflect relief that he can still speak on foreign policy.

What under present circumstances he can do about several dire situations around the world is another matter. The president presumably heard from Prime Minister Keizo Obuchi today that Japan is nowhere near arresting its financial downhill slide, and that the United States has not been very helpful.

Russia is preparing to print rubles to pay unpaid workers and a spurt of inflation threatens.

Next up for a financial crisis is Brazil. And the International Monetary Fund, without the $18 billion American contribution, is running out of bailout money. And as goes Brazil, probably so goes Latin America.

Kosovo, where the Serbs have driven a couple of hundred thousand people out of their homes, faces a winter of human catastrophe. NATO, which means the United States, has for three months been unable to decide what to do about that.

Iraq has halted inspection of its weapons development, and the United States has been unable to line up a concerted response. The one situation in which the president asserted decisive leadership, the missile attack on Afghanistan and Sudan, may have been a mistake.

The attack on terrorist training camps in Afghanistan apparently did not accomplish very much, and the *New York Times* says: "The administration may have been wrong in concluding that the Sudanese pharmaceutical plant was making chemical weapons."

Afghanistan is threatened with an Iranian invasion that could bring Iran into confrontation with Pakistan, which has tested nuclear weapons. The Clinton administration is trying to get on better terms with Iran, which is still subject to American sanctions.

In the UN Assembly yesterday, Iranian president Mohammad Khatami, who is under strong fundamentalist pressure at home, told the United States to stop trying to rule the world as its only superpower. That is almost ironic.

Right now this superpower doesn't seem to be ruling much of anything. Many of the problems it faces would be intractable under the best of circumstances. But where a solution depends on the president's influence with Congress or his credibility with a Saddam Hussein, his leadership in world affairs is inevitably weakened.

Impeachment History

OCTOBER 4, 1998

"There is no question that an admission of making false statements to government officials and interfering with the FBI and CIA is an impeachable offense."

Who said that?

Law professor Bill Clinton, on August 7, 1974, running for a seat in Congress.

"A president should be removed only for serious misconduct dangerous to the system of government, and not for general misbehavior."

Who said that?

Trent Lott, freshman member of the House Judiciary Committee, around the same time.

Clearly, a lot of shoes are on a lot of different feet. Or, as the French would say, *"Autres temps, autres mœurs,"* "Different times, different customs."

But let me address the question that has come front and center as House Republicans push for an impeachment resolution modeled on the Nixon resolution. It's the question most frequently asked of a journalist who covered the Nixon impeachment. How does the present situation compare to Watergate?

Let me stipulate a possible bias, because I was mentioned in the Nixon bill of impeachment, the FBI investigation of me listed as one example of his abuse of power. But having said that, I have no difficulty determining, at least for myself, that what President Clinton may be charged with, perjury or something close to it, in trying to cover up his relationship with Monica Lewinsky, bears little resemblance to what had already been proved against President Nixon when the impeachment process started.

Before the break-in into Democratic headquarters in the Watergate, Nixon had approved a break-in on the office of a psychiatrist. He had suggested breaking into the Brookings Institution. He approved illegal wiretapping. He planned to bring intelligence agencies into a group that would explicitly carry out illegal surveillance of dissidents. It took G-man J. Edgar Hoover to shoot down that idea.

After the Watergate break-in, trying to cover up higher-level involvement in the Watergate conspiracy, he explicitly talked of using a million dollars for hush money for convicted criminals, and he tried to get the CIA to take the rap for Watergate.

It is conventional wisdom to say that impeachable offenses are whatever the House says they are. But reprocessing the language of the Nixon impeachment resolution will not make bad boy Bill Clinton into co-conspirator Richard Nixon.

Augusto Pinochet

OCTOBER 19, 1998

In recent times, there've been more state-sponsored killings within borders than across borders. In the interest of humanitarian intervention, the international community has found it necessary to place limits on the sanctity of national sovereignty.

Rwanda, Bosnia, Kosovo, and now Chile are examples of reaching across borders to enforce treaties on genocide, terrorism, and human rights.

General Augusto Pinochet came to power in a military coup in 1973, after the CIA had organized a campaign to destabilize the democratically elected but left-leaning Salvador Allende.

Pinochet was a dictator, but at first at least, President Nixon's and Secretary Kissinger's kind of dictator. He privatized social security and introduced free-market reform; and he showed little patience with opponents.

To the professed dismay of his American sponsors, he presided over the execution or disappearance of at least three thousand Chileans. Hundreds of lawsuits have been filed on their behalf, without result. But among the missing were seven Spanish citizens and three British subjects, and that added an international aspect to Pinochet's repression that led to his arrest in London.

Pinochet is part of the leftover legacy of the cold war. Chile, like Guatemala and Nicaragua, was a country where the United States was willing to support, or even install, a dictatorial regime, as long as it was reliably anti-Communist.

In 1970, Secretary Kissinger said of Allende's election: "I don't see why we need to stand by and watch a country go communist due to the irresponsibility of its own people."

The cold war over, the United States today espouses democracy and human rights, and the right to intervene on the treaties against genocide and terrorism to defend these values.

It was under the banner of human rights and democracy that the United States sent troops into Haiti. And as to Chile, the Clinton administration, having disowned Pinochet, offered to provide Spain with documents on human rights violations under the Pinochet regime.

Pinochet, the emblem of an era when America embraced what were called "moderately repressive dictatorships," becomes now an emblem of the era where we must deal with the bitter fruits of "moderate repression."

Thomas Jefferson

NOVEMBER 8, 1998

I had planned a skewed opening for this essay. An investigative reporter broke the story of the president and his sexual liaison. The president denied it, but then DNA evidence proved he was a liar and a hypocrite.

Then I would say this was not President Clinton I was talking about, but Thomas Jefferson, now conclusively revealed to have fathered at least one child by his slave mistress, Sally Hemings, who happened also to be the half sister of his deceased wife.

That, I say, was how I planned it. But then I talked to an African American friend of mine who told me I was missing the real story. Blacks have long known or assumed the long-term affair between the author of the Declaration of Independence and a slave woman who did not share the blessings of life, liberty, and the pursuit of happiness.

And if white historians called it rumor, conjecture, or unproved theory, it was because they find it difficult to come to terms with their racist view of history.

I know now what I did not know before, that Professor Annette Gordon Reed of New York Law School, an African American, has long tried to gain scholarly acceptance for the Jefferson-Hemings liaison, but that the scholars who fashioned Jefferson's image were unwilling or unable to weigh the matter objectively.

Why? Because, says Professor Reed, Americans find it difficult to come to terms with black-white sexuality, and because the dehumanization of blacks, which began with slavery, haunts us to this very day, distorting our historical perspective.

Curiously enough, Jefferson himself wrote in 1791 that "deep-rooted prejudices against blacks will produce convulsions which will probably never end but in the extermination of the one or the other."

A hypocrite, ambivalent, or was his sexual relationship with a woman he owned not a matter of "deep-rooted prejudices"?

Professor Orlando Patterson of Harvard, also African American, writes in the New York Times that today he feels less alienated from Jefferson, and that African Americans will come to see him as part of the family. And, says Professor Reed, perhaps now we can bring a new understanding to slavery and to race, and to our growth as a nation.

Much better story than the story of another presidential scandal that I was going to write.

Credibility

DECEMBER 17, 1998

No single word has gotten more of a workout in recent days than "credibility": America's credibility in the Middle East and President Clinton's credibility with Americans, charged as he is before Congress with multiple lies about his personal life.

Yet Americans were shocked when Senate Republican leader Trent Lott, although briefed in advance about events leading up to the attack on Iraq, questioned its timing, implying an ulterior motive.

Skepticism about presidents' motives in using America's armed might is not new. President Franklin Roosevelt was widely accused of provoking the Japanese attack on Pearl Harbor in order to get America into the war.

President Johnson was believed to have concocted a naval attack in the Gulf of Tonkin to justify the escalation of American involvement in Vietnam.

President Reagan was said to have timed the invasion of Grenada as a diversion from the car-bomb attack on the marines in Beirut. But only one president until now has faced suspicion of employing a military operation in an effort to save his own presidency. That was when President Nixon, facing impeachment, ordered a military alert in the Middle East, warning the Soviets to stay out.

And so the coincidence of an air strike against Iraq on the very eve of House impeachment proceedings made a tempting target for Republicans who already rated Mr. Clinton's credibility very low.

"Never underestimate a desperate president," said Representative Gerald Solomon in a typical comment.

But then the Republican secretary of defense, William Cohen, and a career soldier, Joint Chiefs chairman General Hugh Shelton, got in front of the microphones and staked their own credibility on an operation in the planning stage for a month, and triggered by an official report on Iraq's flagrant noncompliance.

Perhaps Mr. Clinton, having three times in a year backpedaled from threatened attacks on Iraq, had lost credibility with Saddam Hussein. But his very reluctance to resort to force bolstered his credibility at home.

And then this amazing thing happened. The overnight opinion polls registered 74 percent of respondents as approving of the attack. And so the House, which would have been ringing today to impeachment oratory, rang instead to support of the commander in chief and his gallant soldiers.

And for one day, anyway, Mr. Clinton could bask in credibility.

The State of Peace on Earth in 1998

DECEMBER 20, 1998

It's time again to think about peace on Earth and how it has fared this year.

I'd hoped to say that at least there was no major cross-border war this year involving America, but then came the attack on Iraq for flouting inspection for hidden weapons. But that was not all this year that you could call unpeaceful.

Can you call it peace when on a typical recent day, you pick up your newspaper and read, mostly in the column marked "Foreign News in Brief," dispatches such as these: A government plane shot down in Angola. Rebels shelling fleeing refugees. UN secretary-general Kofi Annan says there is war. In Kosovo, thirty rebels killed in renewed fighting. In the Congo, troops loyal to Laurent Kabila have killed forty-five soldiers from Zimbabwe. In Algeria, Prime Minister Ahmed Ouyahia resigned, blamed for his failure to end killings by Islamic radicals.

In Colombia, twenty-seven civilians killed as government troops clash with Marxist rebels. In Iran, a string of slayings of dissident intellectuals by Islamic hard-liners. And I'll spare you Rwanda, Sierra Leone, and Sudan, where civil wars rage.

And there are other kinds of violence. The World Health Organization counts 168 million starving children worldwide. At that, an improvement from 1975, when the figure was 198 million. And the UN

High Commissioner for Refugees counts 22 million people displaced from their homes, down from 27 million in 1995. Count your
blessings.

It occurs to me that war today is not so much between countries as
within countries, and that peace is not so much a condition as a process.
Chalk up one for peace in Northern Ireland, where there is a peace
agreement—shaky, but firm enough to win the Nobel Peace Prize for
David Trimble and John Hume.

And next to Northern Ireland, the oldest established peace process
in the world, between the Israelis and the Palestinians, most recently
kept alive by mouth-to-mouth resuscitation from President Clinton, yet
again on the verge of collapse.

But the peace process is no answer to terrorists, who bomb American
embassies, and governments like Iraq and North Korea, that work on
weapons of mass destruction. This holiday season would feel more
peaceful if travelers in the Gulf area were not on notice from the State
Department to watch out for terrorists. And so, to paraphrase Saint
Luke a little, On Earth, peace process. And maybe someday, goodwill
toward men.

1999

Guns and Children

The Loyalty of Clinton's Friends

JANUARY 17, 1999

Last August 17, when President Clinton, after his grand jury appearance, went on television to confess a not appropriate relationship with Monica Lewinsky, I happened to be attending an Aspen seminar with Senator Dianne Feinstein. She said she'd been in the White House Roosevelt Room in January when the president categorically denied any such involvement. Deeply saddened, she said, "My trust in his credibility has been shattered."

And yet last Monday Senator Feinstein was at a White House state dinner, and she has been vigorous in her defense of Mr. Clinton against impeachment. That came to mind when I read a column by my friend Bill Safire captioned "The Loyalty Mystery." That is, the mystery of how the president manages to retain the loyalty of the public and of his own aides, some of whom have not experienced much loyalty from him.

He has dropped nominees like Zoe Baird and Kimba Wood for attorney general, Lani Guinier for head of the Justice Department's Civil Rights Division, and ex-governor William Weld for ambassador to Mexico when they ran into confirmation trouble. He has fired officials, like Surgeon General Joycelyn Elders, when she ran into criticism for an offhand remark about masturbation. He's not shown great loyalty to aides who got into trouble serving him, like Webster Hubbell, who talked of rolling over one more time for the president, and Harold Ickes, eased out after being passed over for White House chief of staff.

A bemused Safire writes of Mr. Clinton: "There he stands, impeached

178

as a perjurer, certain of censure, roundly denounced even by his political allies for weaknesses that dishonored the office. Yet not one of the aides who called themselves betrayed has turned on him." Safire speculates that it's because of some cultural conflict, cultural war, in which the baby boomers of the sixties stick together against the conservatives of the nineties. Conservative lobbyist Ralph Reed, on *The Newshour with Jim Lehrer,* thought it was because the president is associated with economic good times. Former chief of staff Leon Panetta thinks it's because people who don't believe in him as a person still believe in what he's trying to do for America.

All plausible explanations, but I think there is something else. Many presidents have tended to regard associates and even longtime friends as expendable in the interests of the lofty goals the leaders believe they are pursuing. When President Clinton, like President Franklin Roosevelt, like President Nixon, turns his back on someone who has served him, I'm sure he's convinced it is a sacrifice being made in the national interest. It is when presidents confuse national interest with personal interest that the trouble starts.

Sex in the Media

JANUARY 31, 1999

"She's Back!" the *Washington Post* breathlessly headlined, and if that didn't tell the story, the media mob seen outside the Mayflower Hotel did.

Monica Lewinsky had been summoned under court order to be interviewed by the impeachment managers. She told them she had nothing new to tell them and returned to Los Angeles to escape the paparazzi parade, only to be called back again, now under subpoena from the impeachment prosecutors. What is this obsession with a young woman who has already been questioned twenty-three times? She is the pawn in a high-stakes game seeking to topple a president. It is a game in which politicians, prosecutors, and the media play their assigned roles.

The removal of President Clinton seems headed for defeat for lack of two-thirds of the Senate. If the case is to be rescued, it will take some electrifying event. So on videotape and perhaps in person, Miss Lewinsky's role is to generate a firestorm that could create pressure on the senators to remove the man in the White House who did her wrong. "This is the most investigated sexual relationship in history," says former senator George Mitchell. And Senator Olympia Snowe of Maine has said that if Miss Lewinsky were brought before the Senate, that might turn the proceedings into *Jerry Springer*. Jay Leno may have spoken a profound truth when he told the *Washington Post* that he looks on the impeachment process as entertainment. He said, "It's like the Jerry Springer show, except everyone has a law degree."

In the past year, Monicagate has come to rank with the O. J. Simpson trial and perhaps the death of Princess Diana as a made-for-media drama. Leaks, rumor, and innuendo become weapons of combat in well-orchestrated attempts to manipulate the news industry. Remember 1987, when former senator Gary Hart pulled out of the presidential race after Paul Taylor of the *Washington Post* asked him at a New Hampshire news conference whether he'd ever committed adultery? That was the politics-sex-media nexus in its early days. With Monica Lewinsky, the face that launched a thousand inside stories and a thousand paparazzi pursuits, sex-politics-media has reached its zenith.

U.S. Policy Toward the Kurds

FEBRUARY 17, 1999

Kurdistan is a concept that exists mainly in the minds of the 20 million Kurds, who spill across the borders of Iran, Iraq, Syria, and Turkey. The largest number is concentrated in Turkey, which has tried for eighty years to suppress their culture and aspirations.

Of all the ethnic groups without states—Kosovars, Palestinians, Basques—the Kurds have presented a succession of American administrations with some of their greatest dilemmas and produced some of their most erratic policies.

In 1975, as a favor to the shah of Iran, President Nixon had the CIA organize an uprising of the Iraqi Kurds against Saddam Hussein, with Soviet weapons supplied by Israel, only abruptly to abandon the Kurds to be captured and killed when the shah made a peace agreement with Saddam Hussein.

In 1991, President Bush called for an uprising against Saddam Hussein. And then twelve days later suddenly ceased hostilities, leaving the

Iraqi dictator with enough armor and aircraft to put down Kurdish and Shiite uprisings. After hundreds of Kurds were killed and thousands had fled across the mountains of Turkey, President Bush was forced by American public opinion to send troops back to northern Iraq and declare a no-fly zone to protect the Kurds.

In 1996, under President Clinton, the CIA tried to organize Kurdish resistance. When the operation was penetrated, CIA personnel fled, leaving their Iraqi employees to Saddam Hussein's mercy.

At every point, American policy has been contradictory and opportunistic, and that remains true today. In the great game of Realpolitik, the Kurds don't have much to offer America; Turkey has a lot.

Turkey, the southern anchor of NATO, offers military cooperation with Israel, a moderation in the Cyprus dispute, and an airfield for American planes patrolling the unfriendly skies of Iraq.

And so the rebel PKK is on the American terrorist list for seeking the autonomy that America supports in Kosovo. And while the State Department denies any operational role in the capture of Abdullah Ocalan, Turkish officials say that FBI monitoring of Ocalan's cell phone tipped off the Turkish government to his whereabouts.

In 1975, Kurdish general Mas'ud Barzani, devastated by the American pullout then, wrote Secretary of State Henry Kissinger that "the United States has a moral and political responsibility to our people." That was when Kissinger was quoted as saying that "a covert operation should not be confused with missionary work." That attitude holds true today.

How Did Two Young Men Get Guns?

APRIL 21, 1999

Now attention turns to the other war, the school-yard war. About the two heavily armed young men who shot up the high school and then themselves, we still know painfully little. We hear the familiar descriptions: alienated, isolated, haters of minorities and athletes, maybe admirers of Hitler, whose birthday it was yesterday.

Looking back, the explosion seems to have been inevitable, but seeing ahead remains an elusive problem. For several years, the Justice and Education departments have tried to develop early-warning systems, publish guides, advise about intervening early with students who are at risk for behavioral problems. But as yesterday showed again, identifying young people at risk of committing violent acts remains an inexact science. How many times have we heard, "Gee, he seemed so quiet. Whoever would have thought?"

If the violent act is hard to predict, the wherewithal is not. It can be safely predicted that a school-yard killing spree will almost always involve guns. We've got to get guns out of the hands of young people, says Attorney General Janet Reno. Colorado governor Bill Owens, who talked today of the baneful effects of violence on television and in the movies, said he still supports the bill in the state legislature that would permit citizens to carry concealed weapons. He says that if he knew a law that would stop the killing, he would sign it in a minute, but he's not ready to veto a law that could increase the killing.

It was probably only happenstance that the *Wall Street Journal* featured on its front page today an admiring story about the Ellett Brothers company of South Carolina and the clever telemarketing devices it uses to make it one of the nation's biggest wholesale gun distributors in a $2 billion industry. Telemarketers manning the telephones are divided into teams and pitted against each other in a competition for bonus awards for selling the most guns.

Each time some particularly dramatic act of gun violence occurs, a demand goes up for curbing the gun epidemic. Other than the Brady gun-registration bill, adopted years after the attempt on the life of President Reagan, these efforts generally get nowhere. And so we go back to trying to divine why the young killers do it, never mind about how they do it.

President Clinton's Ability to Empathize

MAY 2, 1999

There is a side of President Clinton difficult to see because it is so visible. It is a side that makes him in public appearances, especially before sympathetic audiences, especially since his impeachment experience, wander off into introspection in which he identifies with the pain of others.

Two days after the Littleton high school massacre, he went out to T. C. Williams High School in Alexandria, Virginia, talking to the students gathered around him about rampant violence among American young people, about how some youths lash out against ridicule and ostracism. And then Mr. Clinton said this curious thing. "They had the wrong reaction to the fact they were dissed. Look, everybody gets dissed sometime in life, even the president; sometimes, especially the president."

A week later at a dinner honoring Rabbi David Saperstein of the Religious Action Center, Mr. Clinton revealed more of himself as he talked of those who reacted to wounds by wounding others. "I can still remember," he said, "when I was in second grade and I was the only kid that wasn't picked to play on the softball team. Nobody wanted me because I was too fat and too slow. I can still remember it like it was yesterday." The president's point was about understanding those who look down on him because they were looked down upon by others. "When I was a kid in the South," he said, "why were the poor whites the worst? Because the rich whites were looking down on them all the time."

From his experience of being a humiliated poor white, the president went on to develop his thesis of humiliated Serbs picking on Kosovars to humiliate. And predicting that the Kosovars would be able to go home, he expressed fear that the cycle of getting even would resume, leading to further violence.

The president was clearly articulating an outlook more than a policy—an outlook that grieved over the way categories of people establish their identities by looking down on other categories. And I found myself being affected by a president willing to look at issues of domestic and international violence from the perspective of poor white trash. Should I mention that I was a poor fat kid, too awkward to go to his senior prom?

Texas Governor George W. Bush to Hit the Campaign Trail

JUNE 9, 1999

On Saturday, Governor George W. Bush flies to Iowa and then to New Hampshire, effectively launching his campaign, and with the election only seventeen months away, the primaries only nine months away, not a minute too soon. The governor's preparing for something like the charge of a light brigade, with rivals to the left of him, rivals to the right of him, ready to volley and thunder at the first misstep of the front-runner with all that money and all those endorsements.

After his saturation briefings, it can be assumed that Bush knows not to say Kosovians for Kosovars or Grecians for Greeks. But no amount of briefing leaves an inexperienced national candidate boo-boo-proof. And Bush or his spokesperson committed one even this week. To a not-surprising question about whether the governor would, like his father, sign a no-new-taxes pledge, communications director Karen Hughes said it was his long-standing policy not to sign pledges from advocacy groups.

Next day, Grover Norquist, the head of the advocacy group Americans for Tax Reform, announced that he had a letter containing the tax pledge signed by the governor. Oops. The instant response: Steve Forbes's campaign said, "Just like a Clinton politician, trying to have it both ways." The more polite Elizabeth Dole campaign said Bush should be given time to figure out where he stands.

And this campaign, which will surely test the Reagan Eleventh Commandment against Republicans attacking other Republicans, has hardly started. One can expect attacks from the right by Dan Quayle, Gary Bauer, Steve Forbes, and Pat Buchanan, on issues like abortion and China trade. And from the left, if there is such a thing as a Republican left, by Senator John McCain and Elizabeth Dole on issues like national experience and gun control.

Bush's plan is apparently to talk to the people over the heads of his tormentors. Iowa will feature fund-raising picnics, and New Hampshire, a visit to a diner and a firehouse.

Governor Bush has a rendezvous with destiny this weekend, and there are plenty of Republicans ready to rain on his rendezvous.

Blaming the Victim

JULY 20, 1999

Noah Adams, host: Federal aviation officials have given new details about the final moments of the flight carrying John F. Kennedy Jr., his wife, and her sister. They say just before the plane disappeared from radar, it went from a right turn into its final fast nosedive. More pieces of the aircraft were recov-

ered from the waters off Martha's Vineyard today. Divers are concentrating their efforts on two sites, but poor visibility in the water and strong currents are hampering their efforts. News analyst Daniel Schorr is among the many pondering the events of the last five days.

On Martha's Vineyard, where I was on Sunday on unrelated business, a man approached me in the airport and asked, "So how come all this hullabaloo over three people lost in a plane crash and so little about ten thousand murdered in Kosovo?" He didn't seem to want an answer. In the *Boston Globe,* columnist Adrian Walker asked, "How come this massive rescue effort, so much more extensive than the search for Patrick Hayes, a fellow African-American whose Learjet went down in New Hampshire in 1996?"

It is as though focusing on the tangential is a relief from focusing on the tragedy itself. Another way to change the subject is to focus on possible culprits. There are many who still speculate on the Cubans, the Russians, the Mafia, the CIA, or all of the above who may have plotted the assassination of President Kennedy in 1963. There are fewer, but some, who believe that Sirhan Sirhan, who killed Robert Kennedy in 1968, may have been part of some Middle East conspiracy.

So whom to blame now? The curse of the Kennedys suggests some divine design. That may work in Greek tragedies, but we mostly think of "curse" as a figurative expression. Few of us think that God has it in for certain families. We have no convenient culprit like the paparazzi, the photographers who pursued Princess Diana. And so in the end, we have no one to blame but John Kennedy himself. Here the word "reckless" comes in handy. What was this inexperienced pilot with a broken ankle doing flying in difficult weather? Versions of reckless crowd the radio talk shows and the Internet. A caller in Salt Lake City: "The Kennedys bring trouble on themselves." Host Paul Harris on KTRS in St. Louis: "Rich people who engage in reckless behavior and end up dying." Someone on America Online: "He was an arrogant brat and killed people."

Let me not exaggerate the dimensions of this Greek chorus chanting, not "Hubris," but "Reckless, reckless, reckless." For most Americans, it is enough to mourn this latest loss in a family for forty years intertwined with America's hopes and fears. "Life is not fair," said President

186 · COME TO THINK OF IT

Kennedy, which means that death is not fair either. And it is surely unfair, without yet knowing the cause of the tragedy, to blame one of the victims.

Criticism of Governor George W. Bush

AUGUST 11, 1999

This may be recorded as a day that began the deconstruction of the candidacy of George W. Bush, Republican front-runner, almost solo runner. This was the day that conservative columnist George Will found the governor to be lacking in taste and seriousness, somewhat adolescent and just not ready for prime time.

In part, that verdict was connected with a profile of Bush written for *Talk* magazine by conservative journalist Tucker Carlson. Carlson quoted Bush as several times using the F word in dismissing his critics. Bush communications director Karen Hughes says she doesn't remember her boss using the F word, but the writer said Bush sounded like Richard Nixon, whose tape transcripts had to be edited with a liberal use of "expletive deleted." It didn't help that the profile was headlined: "George W. Bush Doesn't Give a Damn What You Think of Him."

This was also the day that the *Washington Post* proclaimed drug use as a campaign issue in the making. Bush has so far refused to respond directly to rumors about cocaine use in his earlier days. He could have known that the perception of stonewalling would only whet media appetites. The *New York Daily News* asked twelve candidates if they had ever used cocaine. Eleven replied no; Bush did not answer. The news headline: "Bush Won't Reveal If He's Used Cocaine." That legitimized the subject for television, and the question has been discussed recently on several network talk shows.

This, of course, is cocaine they're talking about, not marijuana, which figured in the Al Gore and Bruce Babbitt campaigns in 1988 and, of course, in the Clinton campaign of 1992, without substantial harm to any of them. Cocaine is a more serious matter. And, as is becoming evident to the Bush campaign, wishing will not make the question go away.

Governor Bush is reportedly preparing to unveil his first major issue initiative, embracing a somewhat more compassionate version of the

Republican tax bill. But earlier than could have been imagined, Bush may be facing a time when the mass media are less interested in his plans for the future than his excesses of the past.

Unrest in Indonesia

SEPTEMBER 13, 1999

General Wiranto, de facto ruler of Indonesia, applied in East Timor the lesson taught by Serbia's Milosevic in Kosovo: Murder, loot, burn, and expel the resistant population, then allow the international community in to police the graveyard. East Timor, unlike Kosovo, is not a break-away province, but a territory invaded after receiving its independence from Portugal in 1975. But never mind the technicalities. Along with Chechnya and Dagestan, whose insurrectionists have apparently carried their war for independence to Moscow with terroristic bombings of apartment houses, East Timor is part of the forces of disintegration that represent the hallmark of the post–cold war world.

It is as William Butler Yeats wrote: "Things fall apart; the centre cannot hold; / Mere anarchy is loosed upon the world." Why can't the tyrants let go of the relatively small slivers of territory and avoid the sanctions and sometimes bombings delivered by an outraged world? In Indonesia, President B. J. Habibie appeared ready to let go of East Timor after a referendum that overwhelmingly favored independence. He was brushed aside by armed forces commander General Wiranto until his army and militia had almost completed their bloody work.

What does East Timor, with its population of 800,000 before the expulsions, mean in a sprawling chain of thirteen thousand islands and more than 200 million people? Indeed, what do Chechnya and Dagestan mean to President Yeltsin's regime at a time when Russia faces overlapping crises of insolvency and corruption? The answer is: fear of the precedent that may be set. From Sumatra to Irian Jaya—formerly West New Guinea—there are ethnic groups dreaming of being freed from the tyranny of the Javanese. In the Russian Federation, there are regional leaders pondering the advantages of getting Moscow off their backs. And Western leaders fumble for answers, or as Yeats said, "The best lack all conviction, while the worst / Are full of passionate intensity."

The U.S. Role in East Timor

SEPTEMBER 26, 1999

Liane Hansen, host: Tomorrow, Indonesia officially hands over control of East Timor to the international peacekeeping force led by Australia. The peacekeepers are trying to assess the damage to the country following East Timor's vote for independence from Indonesia on August 30, which led to widespread violence by pro-Indonesian militias. UN officials now say they have found evidence of torture and murder. As Indonesian troops pull out, East Timor's leaders charge they are burning buildings and destroying evidence of war crimes as they go.

So far, the United States has maintained a supportive but limited role in East Timor. Some 240 U.S. troops are in Darwin, Australia; just 4 are in East Timor's capital, Dili. The Clinton administration has been cautious about U.S. involvement in the current conflict. NPR's senior news analyst Daniel Schorr says given previous U.S. inaction in East Timor, close attention must be paid.

The laying waste of East Timor was twenty-four years in the making, and when it started, it was with a green light from the United States. On a visit to Jakarta, Indonesia, in December 1975, President Ford and Secretary of State Kissinger were informed by General Suharto of plans to start next day the invasion of the little half of an island that had only nine days before won its independence from Portugal.

Kissinger confirmed as much when I asked him about it the other day at a meeting at the Nixon Center. He said Suharto had only brought it up at the airport as they were leaving and Kissinger's reaction was that this was only a stage of decolonization, like India's absorption of the tiny enclave of Goa. But that wasn't the whole story. The Indonesian army, the TNI, was armed with American-supplied weapons as an anti-Communist ally, and the use of these weapons against the Timorese may have violated American law governing the use of American arms. Some of the secret papers from that era have been declassified, and one unearthed by Kissinger biographer Walter Isaacson was a summary of a senior staff meeting that Secretary Kissinger called on his return to Washington.

The assault on East Timor had turned out to be more brutal than expected and the legal office of the State Department, in a cable to the secretary, had raised the issue of whether permission to use American arms had violated American law. Kissinger seemed less concerned about the question than about a possible leak. He reprimanded legal adviser Monroe Leigh for putting the question in a cable that would circulate to other officers. "The only consequence is to put yourself on record," he said. "It's a disgrace to treat the secretary of state this way. What possible explanation is there for it? I told you to stop it"—that is, the arms sales—"quietly." Leigh pointed out, "The Indonesians were violating an agreement with us." Kissinger retorted, "The Israelis, when they go into Lebanon—when's the last time we protested that?"

Arms deliveries to Indonesia were suspended and then quietly resumed. Upwards of one hundred thousand Timorese were killed in the first years of the war. That was almost 20 percent of the population. Many more thousands have been slain since, and Dili, Timor, is little more than a heap of ashes. If Dr. Kissinger had any second thoughts about the green light he gave for this operation, he's not sharing them.

Realpolitik

NOVEMBER 1, 1999

When President Milosevic assaults the people of Kosovo, within the borders of Serbia, NATO ignores sovereignty in the name of human rights and subjects the Serbs to seventy-eight days of bombing. When Russia launches an all-out attack against Chechnya, killing hundreds of civilians, creating a quarter million refugees, and attacking clearly marked Red Cross vehicles, the Clinton administration calls it an internal matter within Russia's sovereign borders.

In Oslo, tomorrow, the president is expected to tell prime minister and presidential candidate Vladimir Putin what the Russians have already heard from Secretary of State Madeleine Albright and Deputy Secretary Strobe Talbott, that it is Russia's duty to defend the state against terrorism but the Russians should try to keep casualties to a minimum and aim at a negotiated solution.

Russia tried a negotiated solution three years ago and seems in no mood to try again soon. After a series of apartment-house bombings attributed to the Chechens, Putin is riding a wave of popularity. The conflict has developed an ugly racial side with people from the Caucasus in danger in Moscow because of their dark skins.

Beyond trying to exercise a moderating influence, President Clinton is expected to offer no hindrance to Putin. This, like human rights sanctions against Cuba but not against China, is what is called Realpolitik. The dictionary defines that as policy based on power rather than ideals. And Russia, as the Clinton administration sees it, has plenty of power, even in its weakness.

The constant worry is nuclear weapons that may go astray. Russia's foundering economy remains a potential threat to the world economy. Russia is exerting pressure on the United States in the United Nations not to try to modify or abrogate the ABM, antiballistic missile, treaty. The Clinton administration has not, so far, gotten much cooperation from the Russian government in investigating massive money laundering. As a result, the congressional leadership has not been much inclined to extend economic aid to Russia.

The Clinton administration has no intention of further exacerbating the situation by coming down hard on the question of Chechnya. Anyway, the Chechens, who have kidnapped several Westerners, including one American, have little international support. That's what you call Realpolitik.

George W. Bush and the Press

NOVEMBER 24, 1999

Noah Adams, host: Earlier this month, a Boston television reporter gave a pop quiz about foreign leaders to Republican presidential candidate George W. Bush. Bush's inability to answer three of the four questions focused attention both on him and on the news media. Some who heard the interview thought the test was unfair. But the relationship between politicians and journalists is often rocky. News analyst Daniel Schorr says the record shows Governor Bush is becoming increasingly adept at handling the press.

Governor George W. Bush has come a long way in techniques of holding the press at bay since last August, which may have marked his low-water point. Having several times said he would not discuss cocaine use, he then kept the subject going by stipulating periods when he had not used cocaine. His interview with *Talk* magazine, using vulgar expletives and appearing to mock a death row inmate, appalled religious conservatives. And his assertion that he thought he'd been talking off the record didn't help a bit.

Since then, Bush has come to realize, or been made to realize, that breezy, Texas-style, off-the-cuff responses to questions can carry deadly perils. It would appear he has developed an arsenal of defenses well honed and ready for all comers. As he showed on his *Meet the Press* interview with Tim Russert, he has the answer to the cocaine question down pat. The technique is to turn the question back on the unpopular media by suggesting harassment that benefits no one but the press. The punch line is "I'm not falling into that trap."

The trap defense also serves for other questions. What does he think of Supreme Court justice David Souter? "I'm not falling into that trap." It's not clear where the trap lies. Another ruse is to deflect a question by enlarging it, thus: Would Bush meet with the homosexual Log Cabin Republicans? "I am someone who is a uniter, not a divider." Should South Carolina pull down the Confederate flag that offends African Americans? "It's up to the people of South Carolina." Would he support condom distribution? "The federal government ought to spend as much on abstinence as it does on other attempts to reduce teenage pregnancies." Would Bush retain the Disadvantaged Business Entrepreneurs program, in which some government agencies reserve 10 percent of contracts for minorities? First, "I think 10 percent is awfully low." Then, apparently sensing danger, "I'm dead-set against quotas."

Bush has clearly learned not to be thrown on the defensive when he doesn't know a fact or a figure. What target would he set for reduction of nuclear weapons? "That's going to depend upon generals helping me to make that decision." When he says that real changes in Russia will come from new leaders, whom does he have in mind? "I don't think we ought to be picking winners in the Russian political system."

Governor Bush has clearly learned a lot about dealing with the press. Next, starting December 2, we learn how he does in debates with other Republican candidates.

The Seattle Protests

DECEMBER I, 1999

Where President Clinton sees trade as a liberating force, the protesters
see it as a force for tyranny. Where he is comfortable with economic glo-
balization, they fear the power of multinational corporations. Already
turned off on their own government, they see the rise of an international
pointy-headed bureaucracy deciding in secret in Geneva what they may
eat and breathe and whether they will work. It is, perhaps, ironic that
UN secretary-general Kofi Annan was kept yesterday from making a
speech in which he wanted to warn of a backlash against globaliza-
tion.

But it may be that, in the end, the tumult on the streets of Seattle will
turn out to have greater significance than the conference, which has had
trouble even agreeing on its agenda. These protesters are not like the
machine-smashing Luddites of nineteenth-century England or the railway saboteurs of France early in this century trying to hold up the wheels
of industrial progress. But here, too, along with all the millennial ner-
vousness, there is an element of fear of change that is out of the control of ordinary people. Like the industrial revolution, trade expansion
will not be stopped. The foreign-trade share of the American economy
has grown from 11 percent in 1970 to 24 percent last year, and it is still
growing.

What makes it hard to enlist popular support for trade expansion is
that short-term losses are usually more tangible than long-term gains.
A worker seeing his or her job migrating to a foreign country is not reassured by being told of more jobs eventually. An environmental group
worried about sea turtles as an endangered species today is not appeased
by being told that the United States will fight for better shrimp nets
tomorrow. Third World countries that see themselves being left further
and further behind by the First World information revolution are not
reassured to be told that they will prosper in the end. "These people
don't understand the benefits of free trade to the developing countries,"
says the German delegate, Arnold Schwez, stuck in his hotel in
Seattle.

Trade may be a powerful force, but so is fear, and it is people's fear of their fate in the hands of technocrats and bureaucrats that drives the battle of Seattle.

Politics, Diplomacy, Law, and a Six-Year-Old Refugee

DECEMBER 12, 1999

Bad cases, they say, make bad law. Add politics, you get worse law. In 1995, the Clinton administration, appalled by the influx of Cuban boat people, some of them criminals, made an agreement with the Castro government. It provided, and I quote, "Cuban migrants intercepted at sea by the United States, and attempting to enter the United States, will be taken to Cuba." Congress enacted an exception for immigrants with extraordinary ability in the sciences, arts, education, and athletics. That opened the door to defecting Cuban baseball stars. For the rest, the law was clear: Cubans who wanted to come to this country would have to apply for visas in Havana.

Then a dilemma arose in the form of a six-year-old boy found clinging to an inner tube off the Florida coast, his mother and stepfather lost with nine others in a powerboat that had sunk. Young Elian Gonzalez was turned over to his great-uncle and great-aunt in Miami, and by extension, to the Cuban American community—a poster boy for America's long-standing feud with Castro's Cuba.

In Cuba, there were huge demonstrations for the return of Elian. The State Department, unmoved, said Elian's custody was a matter for the Florida courts. In the United States, we have laws that we follow and uphold, the spokesman said rather self-righteously; what laws did he have in mind? American laws uniformly recognize the custody rights of a biological parent. And the Cuban-American agreement of 1995 was clear about return of migrants intercepted at sea.

President Clinton, clearly embarrassed about the question at his news conference last Wednesday, sought to distance himself from the dispute with a plea to do what was best for the child. Slowly, the unmovable bureaucracy began to move. Forget about having to argue in the Florida courts; an agent of the Immigration and Naturalization Service would visit the father in Havana and ask him to establish his parenthood by a birth certificate or other document. And then, hold your breath, and then the Clinton administration might face up to the passions of the Cuban American community and send the boy home to his father.

The State of Peace on Earth in 1999

DECEMBER 26, 1999

Each year at this season since 1991, I am asked to reflect on how peace on Earth has fared this year. In doing so, I find myself being not of good cheer.

It is not simply the shooting wars, of which 1999 had its share—Kosovo, where NATO intervened with bombing to stop the Serbs from killing the Albanians, only to be succeeded by a smaller civil war, where Albanians kill Serbs; or East Timor, whose people were punished for voting for independence by an Indonesian invasion that killed at least two hundred and made refugees of at least three hundred thousand; or Chechnya, which the Russians seemed determined to reduce to rubble in order, the Kremlin says, to root out the bandits resisting Russian rule; or Kashmir, where more than twenty-five thousand have died in a decade, as India and Pakistan, both now with the makings of nuclear bombs, dispute with guns whom Kashmir belongs to; or Afghanistan or Angola or Congo or Sri Lanka, where fighting seems to go on endlessly.

But there are other kinds of violence. In Sudan, an estimated 2 million people have died and 4 million have been uprooted in a sixteen-year civil war. But Sudan offers evidence of another kind of calamity. More than $2 billion, half of it from America, has been spent to combat starvation in Sudan. But officials running the program have now concluded that the food aid helps to fuel the war and fails to stop the misery. Something like that is also happening in Rwanda and Congo.

In much of Africa, another kind of war is being lost to an AIDS epidemic. And particularly frustrating at this season is the war on children. UNICEF, in a report on the state of the world's children, says that one in four of the world's children lives with violence that might erupt at any time or with the possibility of becoming a refugee.

One looks for silver linings. Peace has survived in Northern Ireland, peace may be on the horizon between Israel and Syria, peace persists between China and Taiwan, although the Chinese occasionally rattle their missiles. America enjoys peace, but it is a jittery peace with warnings to watch for terrorists.

I guess if we are ever to enjoy real peace on Earth, we will first need a little more goodwill toward men.

2000

Bad for Everyone

McCain and the Christian Right

MARCH 1, 2000

Virginia is about as good as it gets for a candidate fighting off an assault by the Christian right. Exit polls indicate that 80 percent of those committed to the religious right chose Governor Bush over 14 percent for McCain. But this segment represented only 19 percent of all voters, and among the 77 percent not identified with the Christian right, McCain beat Bush 52 to 45 percent. Something like that also happened in South Carolina.

This suggests a schism that is developing in Republican ranks, fostered by McCain, who seems to be trying to lock the front-runner into an intolerant, anti-Catholic box. The message the Arizona senator is trying to get across is that with moderate Republican, plus independent, plus Democratic votes, he's a more likely winner in a general election no matter how far behind he lags in southern primaries.

That conservative Cassandra, columnist Robert Novak, sees an outbreak of religious war in the Republican Party, ominous for its prospects in November. That may be a little stark, but it should be remembered that evangelical Christians were not active in the political arena until Reagan ran for president, and one cannot assume that all of them will stay involved.

In a comprehensive cover story in the *New York Times Magazine,* Margaret Talbot says that some conservative Christians, embittered by President Clinton's survival of the impeachment scandal, despair of politics altogether. Paul Weyrich, a founder of the Christian right, has written, "We need to drop out of this culture." One indication of the waning commitment of the Christian right to political involvement is that most of the fringe candidates who courted its support—Gary Bauer, Steve Forbes, Dan Quayle, John Kasich—were obliged to drop out of the race early, leaving only Alan Keyes carrying on with minimal support.

What McCain is trying to do is to persuade the Republican establishment that those, like Barry Goldwater and George McGovern, who win nomination with core support often do not go on to win elections. What he may succeed in doing is to precipitate the crisis of the Christian right as a political force.

Religion in Politics

MARCH 5, 2000

As he faces Tuesday's crucial primaries and caucuses, Governor Bush doesn't find himself where he'd hoped to be at this juncture, the recognized unifier of disparate Republican factions.

In large part, that's because of the injection of a religious issue into the campaign, which is not what he needed, indeed, perhaps, not what the country needed. Sectarian politics is familiar in Europe, where parties from Germany to Italy, mainly Catholic, have the word "Christian" in their names. But the Christian parties have been suffering reverses as the center of gravity in Europe moves toward the Social Democrats and in Germany the Christian Democrats are enmeshed in a campaign-funding scandal.

In our country, religion has turned up sporadically. John Kennedy, on his way to becoming the first Catholic president, assured southern Protestants that he would not take orders from the pope. Jimmy Carter campaigned as a born-again Christian. But as a significant force in politics, the Christian right entered the arena in 1980 when Ronald Reagan embraced it, saying, "You can't endorse me, but I endorse you." Since then, religious conservatives have been a powerful force almost dictating Republican policy on issues like abortion and school prayer. But now the Christian right has become not only a force but an issue. That is due, in the first place, to Governor Bush's ill-advised visit to reactionary anti-Catholic Bob Jones University and, in the second place, to Senator

McCain's worse-advised attack on Christian Coalition leaders as an evil influence. Both candidates have apologized—Bush to Cardinal O'Connor, McCain through the press. But that is not the end of it.

The Christian right had already been in trouble, with some evangelicals beginning to return to shunning the political arena. The issue of the religious right—columnist Robert Novak speaks of an outbreak of religious war—will not soon go away. Whether the issue will help McCain make inroads among Catholics in northern states, as it may have in Michigan, remains to be seen.

But the Republican schism may well play a more important part in this general election, where Democrats are bound to blast away at the issue of intolerance. Meanwhile, it seems clear that the raising of the religious issue has touched a raw nerve in the Republican Party.

The Economic Road Ahead

MARCH 19, 2000

My friend the stockbroker, who is also something of a philosopher, says the market has metamorphosed.

There is less investment and more trading. You bet not so much on what a company can produce but on whether other people are buying or selling the same security. Traders are attracted by eye-popping mergers. Two years ago the record was $81 billion for ExxonMobil oil; two months ago, America Online–Time Warner set another record at $166 billion. I find these numbers hard to absorb. Money becomes, in a way, not just a medium of exchange but a value in itself, a digit on an electronic screen. In television quiz shows, $64,000 once seemed a fabulous prize. Now anything under a million seems like a consolation prize.

The good side to the cheapening of money is that it becomes easier to give away in good causes—easy come, easy go. The other day high-tech billionaire Michael Sailor gave $100 million as a down payment on something he calls an online university. Small potatoes next to the billionaire's club of Bill Gates, George Soros, and Ted Turner for education, democracy, and the United Nations.

The not-so-great sign of the quick billions is the arrogance it generates. It's great that a Scottish company has created five clone piglets; less great that it wants profitable patents before it tells how. It's great that we may be nearing the human genome formula, opening the way to a cornucopia of new drugs; it is less great that the call by President Clinton and Prime Minister Tony Blair for a sharing of the knowledge triggered a sell-off of biotech stocks.

Do the genetic engineers think they can control the attributes of human beings for fun and profit? My own opinion is that our high-tech world has made it possible to amass too much money too young. Five percent of today's millionaires are under thirty-six. Multimillionaires increased from 67,000 to 350,000 in ten years. I will admit to a certain bias here, but it does seem that whoever is passing out the millions is guilty of age discrimination. You know, you have to be over eighty to really appreciate the value of money.

Privacy and the Internet

APRIL 3, 2000

Who steals my name is bad enough. Who steals my numbers should rot in hell. And when not only government agencies but cyber-age businesses have learned to ferret out my profile and credit history and sell them to the highest bidder, it's time to call a halt.

Americans, unlike Europeans, have always had a thing about preserving their anonymity. They don't carry internal passports, they don't like surveillance. It is a scandal when it comes out that J. Edgar Hoover collected and leaked salacious material about the Reverend Martin Luther King Jr. or that a Bush administration official rummaged in a Bill Clinton passport file in London or that President Clinton disclosed the private letters of Kathleen Willey or that New York's mayor Rudy Giuliani released the records of Patrick Dorismond, slain by the police. Even the long-prevalent state sale of driver's license information was found objectionable by the Supreme Court.

But what we face now is a vast leap ahead of the misuse of public records: the ability of private businesses, with the help of the Internet and without permission of the subjects, to accumulate whole dossiers on individuals, useful to merchandisers but not to merchandisers alone. The Internet's biggest advertising company, DoubleClick by name, is negotiating for a settlement with four states that charge illegal tracking of consumer buying habits. It can do this by planting surveillance files called cookies into computer hard drives, often without the user's knowledge, let alone consent. This cookie monster is a great help to the retailer, but not only to the retailer. It is also an aid to those who want to steal information in order to obtain credit cards, loans, and goods—larceny without a physical presence.

The *New York Times* says that larceny by Internet is one of the signature crimes of the digital era. The Social Security Administration reported more than thirty thousand complaints of misuse of Social Security numbers last year, and Social Security numbers are among the easiest to get, especially with the help of the Internet. One company advertises "Everything you ever wanted to know about friends, family, neighbors, employees, even your boss." A search in cyberspace has acquired a new meaning: a tool for larceny as well as for learning.

Errors in the Death Penalty

JUNE 12, 2000

American public opinion can move in mysterious ways, as politicians can find to their surprise, and sometimes their dismay.

Opinion surveys have generally shown strong American support for the death penalty, running as high as 80 percent in 1994. And so when Governor George Ryan last January suspended executions in Illinois as flawed with error, and the Catholic bishops of Texas appealed to Governor George W. Bush to do likewise, he brushed off the issue. But the issue didn't go away. A Gallup poll this year showed support for capital punishment dipping to 66 percent. Many who are for the death penalty are not for executing innocent people.

Finally, Governor Bush felt compelled to issue his first stay of execution. He's being asked now to act in another case. The facts in this case are most revealing. Gary Graham was convicted of killing Bobby Grant Lambert in a Safeway parking lot, after a two-day trial in which no murder weapon was produced, nor any fingerprint, blood, or DNA match. Only one of five eyewitnesses said she could recognize the killer. She identified Graham in the second of two lineups in which the defendant was the only one who appeared in both. Graham's court-appointed counsel was Ron Mock, four times disciplined for unprofessional conduct in recent years and who has yet to win a murder case.

Now a nine-year Columbia University study has shown that two of three convictions nationally were reversed because of errors by police, prosecution, or defense lawyers. And the *Chicago Tribune,* studying the 131 executions in Texas under Governor Bush, found that in 40, defense attorneys made no real defense and dozens of defendants were compromised by unreliable evidence, including jailhouse informants and untrustworthy psychiatrists.

Professor James Liebman, who led the Columbia study, concludes that America has a broken system fraught with error. In the next five months, Governor Bush and Vice President Gore will undoubtedly have ample opportunity to deal with that indictment.

Children and Presidents

AUGUST 6, 2000

In this interim between conventions, it occurred to me to look back on how presidents past have addressed children. This I was able to do thanks to Stanley and Rodell Weintraub, whose collection of letters of presidents to children is being published this fall under the title *Dear Young Friend.* The early presidents addressed children with the formality of the time. George Washington wrote to his nephew, George Steptoe Washington, urging him "not only to be learned, but virtuous, clothed decently and becoming your station." He counseled his teenage step-granddaughter Nelly to be careful of her suitor. "Is he a man of good character? A man of sense?"

Thomas Jefferson counseled his daughter Martha to be more careful about her spelling. John Quincy Adams was also concerned with style, complaining to his son John Adams II of receiving three letters, all grumbling letters and all badly written. James Polk wrote his nephew Marshall of being mortified at his bad conduct record at West Point.

Abraham Lincoln introduced a more intimate style of letter. His last one, to the daughter of an innkeeper, included a verse: "You are young and I am older; / You are hopeful, I am not— / Enjoy life, ere it grow colder— / Pluck the roses, ere they rot." Woodrow Wilson wrote to

202 · COME TO THINK OF IT

newsboys of Trenton, New Jersey, how glad he was that "you young-sters are starting to take care of yourselves." And Calvin Coolidge wrote his son John at Amherst College to make sure he kept a record of his expenses. Herbert Hoover wrote a ten-year-old boy who asked how to become president: "First," said Hoover, "by being a boy and getting joy out of life."

In 1935, Franklin Roosevelt got a letter from nine-year-old Robert F. Kennedy. He sent him some stamps and invited him to the White House sometime to see FDR's stamp collection. To two school-children in Newport, Rhode Island, asking for an explanation of how the government worked, President Eisenhower replied with a five-page letter starting by saying that elected officials were sometimes puzzled about that.

President Kennedy insisted on seeing one out of every five youthful letters that came in, answering questions about everything from space travel to the little people of Ireland. On the night of the Kennedy assas-sination, President Johnson delayed a cabinet meeting to write in longhand to the Kennedy children.

And finally, in May 1975, ex-president Nixon, in the hospital, received a get-well card from Jonathan Schorr, nearly seven. Nixon wrote expressing appreciation and his hope for a world without war, and he ended, "Perhaps you will choose to follow in your father's footsteps, and if you do, I trust I will live long enough to see you on television."

Yiddish Words and Phrases in American Politics

AUGUST 20, 2000

On August 8, when Vice President Al Gore presented Senator Joe Lieberman in Nashville as his running mate, Lieberman spoke of the naming of the first Jew to a major ticket as a miracle. Then he added as a sort of afterthought, "You know, there are some people who might actually call our selection of me an act of chutzpah." This was not only a milestone in politics but in the language of politics, which now has to make way for the infusion of other Yiddish words and expressions. Chutzpah, for those who don't know it yet, is nerve, audacity. Chutz-pah is when somebody kills his parents and asks the court for mercy as an orphan.

That night on television, Paula Zahn greeted Senator Lieberman with "Mazel tov," meaning congratulations and good luck. Stay tuned as the campaign heats up for more Yiddish expressions to make their appearance: "goniff" or thief, which may be used when discussing campaign financing; "schmuck" for jerk, which originally had another meaning in Yiddish that I can't give on family radio. David Letterman on television called Governor George W. Bush a "putz." That's another version of "schmuck," which I also can't translate literally.

A "schlemiel" is an awkward or unlucky person for whom things never turn out right. A Democrat who lost his way and ended up at a Republican rally could be called a schlemiel. Closely allied to "schlemiel" is "nabech," a nobody, an insignificant person, sometimes played by Woody Allen. For some, "nabech" is a worse insult than "schmuck," who at least has some character. In one interview, Senator Lieberman described his wife, Hadassah, as "bahalten," which means reticent or restrained, not a word you're likely to hear candidates calling each other. A word you may hear more often is "kibitzing," which is being where you're not invited and giving unwanted advice. Lots of political pundits I know are kibitzers. And what you may hear from losing candidates on election night, "oy vey," a general expression of pain and grief.

A Fear of Public Speaking

SEPTEMBER 5, 2000

Linda Wertheimer, host: ABC and CBS Television today rejected any possibility of broadcasting presidential debates carried on other networks' programs. Governor Bush has offered to take part in three debates with Vice President Gore, but Bush wants one of them to be on the NBC Sunday talk show Meet the Press *and another to be on CNN's* Larry King Live. *A bipartisan commission earlier proposed three ninety-minute debates to be held at U.S. universities and broadcast nationwide. News analyst Daniel Schorr says Bush is taking a risk by pushing an alternative plan.*

A rational person is generally considered to intend the logical consequences of his acts. And so in rejecting the proposal of the bipartisan Commission on Presidential Debates for three all-network encounters, it must be assumed that Governor Bush wants to minimize his audience or derail the debates altogether. Question is: Why? Governor Bush has to watch his tongue, as he showed yesterday in Naperville, Illinois, when he was heard on an open microphone labeling Adam Clymer of the *New York Times* with an obscene epithet. This was not his first antipress explosion. In 1986, he approached Al Hunt of the *Wall Street Journal* in a Dallas restaurant and called him a son-of-a-bitch in the presence of Hunt's wife, Judy Woodruff, and their four-year-old son.

But a tendency occasionally to pop off at a reporter cannot be a reason for throwing the whole plan for televised debates into turmoil. Janet Brown, the executive director of the debate commission, will meet with the two sides, but says, "We don't think it's possible to improve on the dates or the sites that we have named as long ago as last January."

Bush's resistance runs up against the tradition that it's usually the challenger who's anxious for debates and incumbents who are reluctant. President Truman would not debate with Thomas Dewey in 1948, nor President Johnson with Senator Goldwater in 1964, nor President Nixon with Senator McGovern in 1972. Nixon did debate with John Kennedy in 1960, and President Ford with Jimmy Carter in 1976, and both had reasons to regret it.

It is hard to say why Governor Bush is interposing obstacles to the bipartisan commission's debate plan, now that he's no longer the front-runner. Gore, since his debate on trade with Ross Perot, has acquired something of a reputation for his forensic skills. Bush, under pressure, sometimes mixes his words. But if he is perceived as fearing to debate with Gore, he's bound to suffer in the eyes of the voters. In the end, Bush will have to consider whether the risk of not debating is greater than the risk of debating.

Evaluating the Presidential Debate

OCTOBER 4, 2000

Those who have dined out over the years on debate wisecracks and gaffes had reason to be disappointed last night.

Vice President Gore and Governor Bush, superbly trained, perhaps overtrained, stayed carefully on message. They also shared a burst of civility. It's a long time since I've heard "my worthy opponent" in

American political discourse. And the issue of character, which allowed Bush to mention the Buddhist fund-raiser, came up only when Jim Lehrer brought it up.

The debate confirmed what observers have noted, that foreign policy plays little role in campaigns in the post–cold war era. What there was on foreign policy, however, revealed a Bush weakness. Both candidates were all out for a strong military, to do what, neither made clear. But when it came to a specific problem, like what to do about the refusal of Yugoslavia's Slobodan Milosevic to accept his election defeat, Governor Bush was on less than solid ground in backing mediation by Russian president Vladimir Putin, who has not even endorsed the outcome of the election.

On domestic issues, the debate was largely a rerun of well-worn stump speeches. But their exchanges on Social Security, Medicare, and prescription drugs brought the candidates' differences into better view. Behind Gore's call for a lockbox for Social Security and a strengthening of Medicare and Bush's insistence on getting something done about these programs lies a philosophical conflict over how big a role for government. Gore thinks that by and large the government has done pretty well on retirement and health care programs. Governor Bush wants to see a greater role for the free market.

Noteworthy was how much time both spent on problems of seniors and those soon to be seniors, and how little on the young. Bush repeated his borrowed mantra "Leave no child behind," but for the most part, children were left behind last night. We heard the ritualistic Gore call for more teachers, better facilities, and the Bush call for testing and education. But education was not much discussed until nearly the end of the debate and only when Lehrer brought it up. It's hardly worth noting that children don't vote.

Missing last night as the two politicians—in the same dark suit, the same red, solid-color tie—sought to establish their leadership credentials was what pundits like to call the defining moment. What we saw, unexciting as it may seem, was two professional politicians acting professionally.

This Year's Presidential Election

NOVEMBER 8, 2000

Our quadrennial election should be a unifying experience. This one was far from that.

Not because of the closeness of the vote, but because of what exit polling revealed about a nation at peace but not with itself, prosperous but not really enjoying that prosperity. Many fissures ran through the voting population. Governor Bush was ahead by 9 percentage points with men, Vice President Gore by 12 points with women. Voters in big cities went three-to-one for Gore; suburban and rural dwellers went for Bush. Gore did better with blacks and Bush with whites; Gore with low-income people, Bush with high-income people; Bush with Christians and Gore with Jews. Gore got 83 percent of those who wanted an experienced president; Bush, 78 percent of those who wanted an honest president.

Some numbers reflect different perceptions of the state of things in America. Gore was favored by 74 percent of those who think that government should do more and Bush by 70 percent of those who think that government should do less. Bush was favored by 71 percent of those who think our military has gotten weaker in the past eight years, Gore by 68 percent of those who think the military is stronger. Gore led by a wide margin among those who consider America on the right track economically. Bush was way ahead among those who think America is on the wrong track morally. From these numbers, one would gather some profound ideological chasm leaving the voting population fractured, like Serbia choosing between freedom and repression or Nigeria between dictatorship and democracy.

In fact, in real terms, the two major American parties tend to cling to the center, where the increasingly important independent voter dwells, and differences over domestic and foreign policy are less sharp than advertised. It was a $3 billion campaign using television to dramatize a sense of faithful choices that left an impression of profound cleavage over health, education, and taxes. And so a free election of the kind people would give and have given their lives for leaves us with a slightly sour taste wishing for a more perfect union.

Bad for Everyone

NOVEMBER 27, 2000

Robert Siegel, host: Twenty days have passed since election day. Several different deadlines have come and gone, and new deadlines are looming. News analyst Daniel Schorr says they, too, may not hold, and he says the protracted election process is taking its toll.

The struggle goes on to choose a president for a nation that couldn't decide on one. The doubt now is centered in the Florida courts in what former attorney general Griffin Bell calls a quagmire of litigation. Vice President Gore's suit to reinstate uncounted ballots will undoubtedly be followed by appeals from the losing side to the state supreme court and to the U.S. Supreme Court.

The U.S. Supreme Court, meanwhile, has scheduled oral argument on Friday on a petition of the Bush camp to override the Florida Supreme Court's suspension of certification pending manual vote counting. That may now be moot with yesterday's certification, although Republican counsel Jim Baker says a favorable decision would serve as insurance.

The judicial phase may not be the final phase of this tumultuous controversy. Waiting in the wings is the Republican-dominated Florida legislature, which has asked to participate in Friday's Supreme Court hearing. Tom Feeney, speaker of the Florida House, has left little doubt that if the choice of Florida's twenty-five electors is still mired in litigation as the official selection date of December 12 approaches, an effort will be made to have the legislature choose a slate of electors. Like almost everything else in this legal maelstrom, that would raise constitutional and statutory questions. Article II of the Constitution says that state electors will be named in such manner as the legislature thereof may direct. A statute says that when a state has failed to make the choice by the deadline, the electors can be subsequently chosen in a manner the legislature may direct.

A Republican move in the legislature to name a slate of electors between December 12 and December 18, the official deadline, will undoubtedly spark a raucous partisan debate, and the Democrats could well come up with their competing slate. Next step, the U.S. Congress and more partisan fireworks. This controversy is fated to leave no branch of government unscarred, not the judiciary, not the legislative, and surely not the presidency.

The Morning After

DECEMBER 13, 2000

In Third World countries such as Pakistan, Chile, and Sierra Leone, a transfer of power is often accomplished by military coup. In an advanced country like ours, it's done by judicial coup. Admitting here to something less than cool dispassion, I marvel at the way the "gang of five," philosophically led by archconservative Antonin Scalia, tried to camouflage their 5–4 operation behind a nominal 7–2 agreement that there was something wrong with the Florida recount. That seemed to leave open a chance of fixing the system. The fix was in all right, but a different fix. It suppressed the recount for good.

Any one of the five who defected could have returned the contest to limbo, but none did. And decades of conservative support of states' rights by overturning federal statutes—from affirmative action to federal review of cases—they all went out the window in an arrogation of authority to judge voting in Florida.

The tactics were adroit. First, the junta on Saturday halted the vote count. That enabled them to say on Tuesday that there was no more time left for vote counting. One thing about Tony Scalia, who once said on a tennis court, "Five-four, I win," he levels with you. Not every justice would say, as he did on Saturday, that the issuance of the voting stay suggested that Bush had a substantial probability of success. Not every justice would own up to partisanship by saying that the recounted votes threatened irreparable harm to petitioner Governor Bush and to the country.

Justice John Paul Stevens, for the embattled minority of himself, Stephen Breyer, Ruth Bader Ginsburg, and David Souter, said on Saturday that halting the vote recount will inevitably cast a cloud on the legitimacy of the election. Last night he said, "We may never know who is the winner of the presidential race, but the identity of the loser is perfectly clear. It is the nation's confidence in the judge as an impartial guardian of the rule of the law." But for five black-robed brethren, including one sister, it was a banner day, the day they named a president.

The State of Peace on Earth in 2000

DECEMBER 24, 2000

I don't know how I got conned nine years ago into doing an annual yuletide assessment of how peace on Earth has fared this year. It has not been a task calculated to lead to a lot of good cheer. And the year 2000 has been no exception.

If there's any consolation to be found in this year, it is that there were no large-scale massacres like Kosovo, Rwanda, and East Timor. There were also no major interstate wars. But the National Defense Council Foundation in Alexandria, Virginia, which keeps tabs on lethal conflicts around the world, figures that this year will end up with a few more than the sixty-five it counted in 1999.

A few samples of the killing fields of this year: Some two hundred guerrillas killed in civil war in the Philippines. Continued fighting in Burundi, where more than two hundred thousand have been killed since 1993. More than three hundred killed in a three-month outbreak of fighting between Israelis and Palestinians. Civil war in Sudan and cross-border skirmishes between Thailand and Burma. Tens of thousands killed in Sierra Leone in fighting that could erupt again after a month-long cease-fire. In Afghanistan, a last-ditch fight against the ruling Taliban with no reliable casualty figures. And Chechnya, that secessionist region of Russia where the war goes on and on and on.

The end of the cold war a decade ago has pretty well eliminated the danger of big-power conflict. But it is a sad fact that small wars and civil wars have proliferated. And the CIA's National Intelligence Council, looking ahead to 2015, sees more trouble on the horizon. It sees interstate wars growing in deadliness because of the availability of more destructive technologies, and internal conflicts, vicious, long-lasting, and difficult to terminate, and weak states with porous borders that will be breeding grounds for terrorism.

And so if there is any reason to be of good cheer this Christmas about peace on Earth, it is because the conflict level is not as bad as it could get.

2001

The World Changes

Echoes of Gulf War

JANUARY 17, 2001

One of the great ironies of family succession is that President Bush the elder left behind him an Iraq defeated in a war that started ten years ago today, and Bush the younger, with two of his father's Gulf War aides, Dick Cheney and General Colin Powell, by his side, comes to town with a challenge of a resurgent Iraq on his doorstep.

Saddam Hussein might have been a little hyperbolic when he bragged on television today of Iraq's triumph in the six-week war that drove his forces out of Kuwait. But it is a fact that he has survived, has rebuilt his conventional forces and developed who knows what weapons of mass destruction. No-fly zones are hardly being enforced, sanctions are widely being ignored, and United Nations secretary-general Kofi Annan plans to meet with Iraqi representatives next month about the lifting of sanctions in return for some kind of weapons inspection acceptable to Saddam Hussein.

The team of Bush the younger may well reflect on this anniversary about why Bush team number one ended the war so precipitately, allowing the Republican Guard to flee to safety and letting Saddam Hussein use his fleet of helicopters to massacre Kurds in the north and Shiites in the south of Iraq. Now the president-elect and his aides have to decide how to deal with Iraq. Candidate Bush talked of taking out any Iraqi weapons of mass destruction that may be discovered. Secretary of State-designate Powell said in his confirmation hearing today that Bush wants sanctions to be reenergized. Paul Wolfowitz, reportedly in line to be deputy secretary of defense, has talked of creating a liberated zone in southern as well as northern Iraq. Security adviser Condoleezza Rice has talked of supporting the Iraqi opposition, which in fact the Clinton administration is already doing.

The prospects for international support are not great. At odds with European and other allies on everything from trade to missile defense to Balkan peacekeeping, Bush will have trouble assembling the broad coalition against Iraq that his father did so spectacularly. It could be expected that one of the new president's first acts will be to order a comprehensive review of policy on Iraq. One can imagine Bush the younger telling his father, "Gee, Dad, I wish you had finished the job."

The Greenspan Effect

FEBRUARY 14, 2001

On Wall Street, they really hang on Alan Greenspan's words.

When the Fed chairman on Capitol Hill yesterday spoke of slower growth, the stock market, smelling another interest rate cut, started up. When later, responding to senators' questions, he talked of not being too aggressive with monetary measures, the market started down again. It took fifty years after Stalin to demolish Russia's cult of personality. Greenspan may be the closest thing that we have to a cult of personality. He can diminish consumer confidence by simply saying that consumer confidence is diminishing. He has become an irrational protuberance on the body politic. And although this may come as a shock to some, he is not omniscient.

On January 25, he reversed position to give his blessing to a tax cut of unspecified size. His main point was that, barring a long recession, the federal debt could be paid off by the end of the decade, leaving money over for tax relief. But his point that seized political attention was that having a tax cut in place would do noticeable good in case of a recession. This seemed to endorse the Bush thesis of a tax cut as a way of jump-starting the economy. That put Democrats on the defensive and jump-started the prospects for the Bush tax cut plan on Capitol Hill.

By yesterday, Greenspan seemed to have changed his mind about the direction of the economy. He testified that the exceptional weakness so evident toward the end of the year apparently did not continue in January. But he did not withdraw his endorsement of a tax cut. This is not the first time that Greenspan has profoundly affected political decisions. In 1993, he gave qualified backing to the Clinton initiative to bring the runaway budget deficit under control. Democrats felt safer voting for a tax increase with the mighty Greenspan running interference for them.

Yesterday Greenspan said that we are not in a recession and that the current slowdown may not last very long. One can sympathize with someone trying to read consumer confidence while the consumer is trying to read him. But given this volatility, was it wise to say three weeks ago that a tax cut was necessary for the economy, or indeed to say anything about matters of political controversy? Advice for the powerful Fed chairman may be "Don't do something, just stand there."

White House, Inc.

MARCH 13, 2001

Our first MBA president apparently wants to be master of a business administration. With Vice President Dick Cheney as CEO, the White House runs pretty well on time. Meetings start and end punctually. The *New York Times* says the president frowned at counselor Karen Hughes for arriving ten minutes late for an Oval Office meeting on Social Security. She had been out briefing the press on Cheney's heart problems.

There's also a sense that the administration, many of its top officers onetime corporate executives, takes a marketing approach to its major initiatives. So when opinion polls showed growing support for a tax cut to boost the economy, the administration struck swiftly for House passage of a major component of the tax program. In another action, the overturning of the Clinton regulation on workplace safety, the administration demonstrated a business approach to a program that would drive up production costs. That point proved more telling than the anticipated increase in health costs from repetitive stress injuries.

But when ideology is tempered by a pragmatic marketing approach, the administration can show surprising flexibility. Thus, for example, the proposal to channel more government money to religious charities

was not testing well among religious groups supposed to be the benefi-
ciaries. The *Washington Post* says the White House showed no hesitation
about recalling the plan for further study. "We're not ready to send up
our own bill," said Don Eberly, deputy director of the Office of Faith-
Based and Community Initiatives.

Even in an area as ideology-laden as the environment, economic con-
siderations are causing the administration to consider the global
warming threat and the need for controls on carbon dioxide and other
air pollutants. The *Wall Street Journal* says that big utility companies
have been talking about controls to head off demands for more drastic
regulation, and pressure for ratification of the Kyoto Protocol with its
tough emissions standards. And so the president, who didn't mention
carbon dioxide in his speech to Congress, is now preparing to call for
limits on major pollutants. He may get some flak from antiregulation
conservatives, but this businesslike administration is going with business.

Kerrey's Confession

APRIL 30, 2001

*Robert Siegel, host: Bob Kerrey's former colleagues from the United States
Senate have been speaking out on his behalf and arguing against the idea of
a Pentagon investigation into a combat mission that Mr. Kerrey led in Vietnam. That mission in 1969 ended with the deaths of more than a dozen
unarmed civilians. NPR news analyst Daniel Schorr has also been thinking
about Bob Kerrey and whether he agrees with the senators, all of them decorated Vietnam veterans, who have leaped to Kerrey's defense.*

John McCain, John Kerry, Max Cleland, and Chuck Hagel have drawn
a defensive line around Robert Kerrey. In multiple media appearances,
they seek to convey that one can hardly understand the awful things that
happened in such a war as Vietnam unless one has experienced them.
The Bush administration busies itself with its hundred-day festivities
and stays a discreet distance away from the Kerrey controversy. It is well
advised to do so. The president, Vice President Dick Cheney, Attorney
General John Ashcroft, and former president Bill Clinton, to name a

few, are political figures from the Vietnam generation who missed the war in which Kerrey served as a navy volunteer.

"What should one think of Bob Kerrey?" is a question he's probably asking himself. Is Thanh Phong in the Mekong Delta, where more than a dozen civilians were killed by a commando unit of navy SEALs, to be considered as another one of those atrocities like My Lai, where civilians were massacred in 1968? I asked that question of my friend Seymour Hersh, who won a Pulitzer Prize for exposing My Lai. "No," he said, "My Lai was a systematic murder by daylight against no resistance. Kerrey's group, if you accept the version of most of them, was a jittery response on a dark night to a perceived attack."

Even after thirty years, there must be Vietnam veterans with uneasy memories of killing civilians, including women and children. It was, they try to tell you, that kind of war. As early as 1967, *New Yorker* correspondent Jonathan Schell wrote of being driven in a jeep by a GI who suddenly turned around and said, "You wouldn't believe the things that go on in this war. No one's ever going to find out about some things." But America has found out about some things—about My Lai, about marines torching thatched huts with Zippo lighters, about the Phoenix assassination program involving the CIA, and now about the navy SEALs who killed a dozen or so innocent people.

War hero and war criminal were not very far apart in that war. Senator McCain said a soldier in Vietnam did inhuman things because his country asked him to do them. "His country" meant Presidents Kennedy, Johnson, and Nixon. And so history leaves us with the Bob Kerreys, good men in a dirty war.

On Leaping, Looking

JUNE 11, 2001

Robert Siegel, host: President Bush pledged today to fight global warming by boosting U.S. spending on research and development, and by working with the United Nations to find an international solution to climate change. The president made the announcement hours before his scheduled departure for Europe, where he has been roundly criticized for abandoning the Kyoto climate treaty. NPR news analyst Daniel Schorr says the new proposals are entirely predictable.

Having denounced the Kyoto global warming treaty, President Bush then asked the National Academy of Sciences to see if there was a global warming problem, and now he takes to Europe a proposal for a multi-million-dollar research effort. This is the latest manifestation of a disconcerting tendency in this administration to act first, propelled by ideological imperatives, and study later.

The Rumsfeld-in-Wonderland Pentagon is working on a crash program to deploy a handful of missile interceptors before the end of the current presidential term even if they have not been fully tested and even if Russian president Vladimir Putin, whom Mr. Bush will see in Slovenia, is still refusing to agree to changes in the Anti-Ballistic Missile Treaty.

There are other examples of "leap before you look." Treasury Secretary Paul O'Neill denounced the Clinton administration for too-frequent bailouts of failing economies. Now the Bush administration has endorsed $17 billion for Turkey and $13 billion for Argentina. Last March President Bush upset the visiting president of South Korea by announcing in the presence of his guest that he didn't trust North Korea and had no plans to resume negotiations. Now the administration has announced new talks with North Korea. Maybe a memo forwarded by his father urging him to resume negotiations helped to change the president's mind.

The administration said it didn't plan to send any special envoy to the Middle East. It has now sent two—CIA director George Tenet and Assistant Secretary of State William Burns.

At home, Attorney General John Ashcroft promised a new study of racial inequities in federal death sentences. But meanwhile, he plans to proceed with the execution of nineteen men on federal death row, only two of whom are white.

But perhaps one should not be surprised at this tendency to act now and think later. This, after all, was the president who decided how much money he wanted to commit for tax relief before he knew how much he would need for defense, education, and prescription drugs.

A Long Line of Summits

JUNE 18, 2001

Robert Siegel, host: After exchanging warm words and even an embrace at their first meeting, President Bush and Russian president Vladimir Putin now face the hard part: putting this weekend's pleasantries into practice. Mr. Bush came away from the talks with a glowing review of the Russian leader, calling him, to the alarm of congressional leaders back in Washington, trustworthy. NPR's news analyst Daniel Schorr recalls that Ronald Reagan's vision of relations with his counterpart was more circumspect: trust but verify. But semantics aside, Schorr says he's not sure the East-West dynamic has changed much.

We are seeing the latest in a history of East-West summit romances that have usually ended badly. The 1955 spirit of Geneva, where President Eisenhower introduced Nikita Khrushchev to the martini cocktail, evaporated with a Soviet crackdown on Hungary a year later. The 1959 spirit of Camp David collapsed with the shooting down of a U-2 spy plane the next year. Khrushchev's flirtation with President Kennedy broke off early with a Berlin crisis followed by the Cuban missile crisis. President Johnson tried to reestablish the East-West bond with Soviet premier Alexei Kosygin at a summit in Glassboro, New Jersey. The spirit of Glassboro did not survive the Soviet invasion of Czechoslovakia in 1968.

An exception was President Nixon, who got along famously with the lackluster Leonid Brezhnev. They signed arms control pacts, and Nixon made a first-ever address on television to the Soviet people. Weeks before Nixon's resignation over Watergate in 1974, he was with Brezhnev in the Crimea scheduling their next summit. Before President Carter could establish a personal relationship with Brezhnev, the Soviet invasion of Afghanistan put relations into deep freeze.

President Reagan became good friends with Mikhail Gorbachev, and side by side with him in Red Square proclaimed that the Soviet Union was no longer an evil empire. President Bush the elder, in Helsinki in 1990, got Gorbachev to join the Gulf War coalition and proclaimed the Soviet Union a partner. After the collapse of the Soviet Union, President Clinton enjoyed a backslapping relationship with Boris Yeltsin, Russia's first president, that chilled with Yeltsin's increasingly authoritarian rule.

So, now love at first sight between Bush and KGB veteran Putin, according him what every Russian leader yearns for, a public display of respect from the superpower. This is, so far, only a matter of atmospherics, which is not to say that it's not important. Putin, for all his Asia and China ploys, signals that Russia's fate lies with the West: European Community, America, NATO. At a joint news conference on Saturday, Putin revealed that the Soviet Union had applied for NATO membership in 1954 and been turned down. Will the Bush-Putin prenuptial agreement survive when they get down to cases on NATO and missile defense? We'll see. But the development of this latest East-West romance will be fascinating to watch.

Terrorist Threats to America

JUNE 24, 2001

Liane Hansen, host: U.S. forces in the Middle East are on high alert this weekend after intelligence warnings of an imminent terrorist attack on Americans. The U.S. Marines have pulled out of joint exercises with Jordan. According to NPR senior news analyst Daniel Schorr, terrorism is a more immediate threat to America than others in the headlines recently.

However seriously one takes the threat of a rogue missile from the sky, it does not seem as imminent as some of the rogue terrorist activities on Earth. A few days ago, FBI agents investigating the bombing of the American destroyer *Cole* off Yemen were themselves withdrawn from Yemen in fear of an attempt to bomb them. And the American embassy was closed to the public for several days. Eight persons, most of them followers of Saudi terrorist Osama bin Laden, were under arrest.

A videotape turned up in Kuwait in which bin Laden is seen boasting of the bombing of the *Cole,* reading a poem about "destroying a destroyer that fearsome people fear." Apparently intended as a recruiting aid, the tape shows bodies of dead Muslims in places from Iraq to Chechnya. This merging of targets in a holy war gives Presidents Putin and Bush a common threat, which they discussed at their meeting in Slovenia.

Since then, Yevgeny Murov, the head of Putin's bodyguard service, has warned of a possible attempt on the life of President Bush during the summit of the G-8 industrial countries in Genoa, Italy, on July 20. Murov told the ITAR-TASS News Agency that the threats are totally serious. Some of Murov's men have flown to Genoa for discussions with protective services of other countries.

According to the Russian news agency, the fear of an assassination attempt is so great that consideration is being given to moving the summit to a military base or a cruise ship. The Italian government says that some meetings may indeed be held on a ship in the port of Genoa.

It is not hard to understand why the Russians are talking up the Islamic terrorist threat. Putin would obviously rather engage Bush on a threat that unites them than on the missile defense issue, which divides them. Still, the menace of Osama bin Laden looks a lot more real than the menace of a North Korean missile.

What Stem Cells Mean for Abortion

JULY 18, 2001

Noah Adams, host: The Senate's only doctor has announced his support for using federal money to fund research on embryonic stem cells. Senator Bill Frist, a Republican from Tennessee, was a heart surgeon before he came to Washington. Today he told a Senate panel he believes stem cell research will save lives. Frist's position on the issue is being closely watched because of the friendly relationship he enjoys with President Bush. News analyst Daniel Schorr says as the president wrestles with whether to approve funding for stem cell research, he's discovering the issue doesn't conform to traditional political fault lines.

President Bush isn't the only American going to England. Dr. Roger Peterson is moving from the University of California at San Francisco to the University of Cambridge, England, to stay. Dr. Peterson is one of the pioneers on the frontiers of embryonic stem cell research, and he's not waiting for the outcome of the tortured controversy over federal funding. In England, funding of this promising research is no problem.

For the Bush administration, this latest confrontation of politics, science, and religion has turned into a nightmare. Little did the president, or his political advisers, realize when they took a position foursquare against funding this research that they would find many of their natural allies in the right-to-life movement parting company with them— Nancy Reagan and Senators Orrin Hatch and Strom Thurmond, and many others with loved ones whom they hope can be healed, and Senator Dr. Bill Frist, and a majority of Catholics, if not the Catholic hierarchy, which leaves the president undoubtedly wondering what to tell the pope next week.

The administration had been hoping to find some way of scrapping the issue by authorizing funding only for research with adult cells or with existing embryonic cells. But now the National Institutes of Health has come out with a report indicating that these might not offer all of the advantages of fresh embryonic stem cells.

To understand how the embryo issue is shaking up the political discourse, you have to listen to antiabortion senator Gordon Smith of Oregon: "This is about giving life to compassionate conservatism. Pro-life means helping the living as well." And House Republican leaders Dick Armey and Tom DeLay found themselves in trouble with Vice President Dick Cheney when they distributed a memo condemning supporters of funding as those who would "rely on an industry of death." Aides to Armey and DeLay said that Cheney asked them to tone down their rhetoric.

This may be a time for lowered rhetoric. A lot of settled assumptions about biology and politics are giving signs of crumbling.

Remembering Katharine Graham

JULY 23, 2001

Most journalists, especially those of the Watergate era, have some particular memory of Katharine Graham. This is mine.

In 1971, when the *New York Times* was temporarily under court injunction against publishing the Pentagon Papers, the *Washington Post* acquired its own copy. *Post* lawyers cautioned against publishing its contents, warning of possible prosecution. A public offering of Post Company stock about to happen was also endangered. *Post* publisher Graham heard the arguments and decided, "Let's go. Let's publish."

By contrast, a copy of the papers was also offered around the same time to CBS News in the person of Walter Cronkite. It was declined by CBS on the advice of its lawyers. My own boss, news division president Richard Salant, later told me that the regulated television medium was less inclined than a newspaper to risk government reprisals.

The timorousness of television showed itself again with Watergate. The Nixon White House threatened Mrs. Graham with dire consequences, including the possible loss of two Florida television licenses, if she didn't back off on Watergate. Mrs. Graham said that whatever the risk to her or her company, there was no going back.

In contrast was the reaction of CBS chairman William Paley when Nixon aide Charles Colson called him to demand the scrapping of the second of a two-part summing-up of Watergate on the *CBS Evening News* a month before the election. Told that it couldn't be killed because it had been widely promoted in advance, Paley had the report cut in half and shorn of its most controversial aspects. Paley also came under White House pressure to abolish instant analysis by CBS correspondents of Nixon appearances. He later reinstated the ad-lib analysis under press and public criticism.

It is certainly true that regulated television stations are more vulnerable to government pressure than a newspaper, but the threat to Mrs. Graham was, in the first place, to her TV licenses. And something tells me that Katharine Graham would have painted a profile in corporate courage in whatever medium she functioned.

The New War

SEPTEMBER 12, 2001

There were two world wars, then the cold war, and September 11 was day one of the new war yet to be named.

America the superpower was rendered, momentarily at least, super powerless by an assault on its financial towers and military vitals. President Bush, who in the first hours was shuttled nervously by the Secret Service from Florida to Louisiana to Nebraska, finally emerged in the White House to assure a stricken nation that the government still functioned, and the president still presided.

September 11 made a mockery of the nation's defense concepts. Missile defense against some rogue state, the Pentagon review of programs of mass destruction, the revamping of the defense structure to fight two—or is it one and a half?—regional wars seemed suddenly like ancient history. Asymmetric warfare, it dawned on us, could be a few zealots eager to die, deploying weapons no more sophisticated than knives, to convert airliners into guided missiles.

The how of the terrorist siege of America may vary from a truck bomb attack on an embassy to an assault on a navy destroyer and now to the exquisitely organized hijacking of airliners. What matters is the who. This day of infamy, unlike Pearl Harbor, had no return address.

President Bush has promised to find those responsible for the terrorist assault and bring them to justice. He has also promised retribution for those who harbor them. We have heard that kind of language before back to President Reagan, who said that terrorists can run, but they can't hide. That kind of language sounds faintly archaic.

We are not simply on the hunt for a gang of thugs, but may be on the threshold of a wider clash centered around, but not limited to, Afghanistan and the Middle East. It is a war without borders, an unconventional war that will test the ingenuity of our military and intelligence resources.

It will also define the Bush presidency. Well-scripted invocations to character and values will not suffice. President Roosevelt rose to the test of Pearl Harbor. Jimmy Carter failed the test of the Tehran hostage crisis. Bush faces a test in many ways more difficult. America wants revenge, yes. America wants to be assured that it is still number one. But more than that, Americans want to feel they are safe in their own country. That is a formidable task for the president.

How to Build a Coalition

SEPTEMBER 20, 2001

Noah Adams, host: President Bush has met with nearly a dozen world leaders since last Tuesday as he continues to build a coalition. Today Saudi Arabia pledged to use all its resources to fight terrorism, and the European Union has agreed to cooperate more closely with the U.S. in a number of areas, including tightening border patrols. But news analyst Daniel Schorr says building a coalition will only get harder.

Events have converted President Bush from unilateralist to instant multilateralist. But after a week of generalized outpouring of worldwide support and sympathy comes the nitty-gritty of coalition building for specific purposes, overcoming a tangle of national and regional pressures.

Pakistan, presumably the principal staging area for a strike against the Taliban, wants not only financial aid to cope with a tide of Afghan refugees, but support in its dispute with India over Kashmir. Russia wants the United States and NATO to keep their hands off Tajikistan and other former Soviet republics in central Asia. President Vladimir Putin also wants acknowledgment of the war in Chechnya as part of the war against Islamic terrorism. China has problems with its Muslim minority that it wants to put on the scale, and it's also taking the opportunity to raise the question of Taiwan.

Dealing with the Arab and Islamic worlds, Mr. Bush is learning not to call his campaign a "crusade." Egypt is using the occasion to urge more pressure against Israel. Iran is being invited into the grand coalition although the State Department lists it as the principal state sponsor of terrorism. Even Castro's Cuba, also listed as a sponsor of terrorism, has been asked for any assistance it can provide.

Europe represents less of a problem in coalition building, NATO having already invoked the alliance treaty to declare the terrorist attack as an attack on all. But beneath the surface of solidarity, European leaders seem concerned about being consulted on decisions involving armed force. French president Jacques Chirac has objected to calling this a war, and Germany has warned against America's going it alone.

In his crash course in coalition building, the president is finding Secretary of State Colin Powell to be a major asset. Powell has managed to convey that the United States will not go off half-cocked, that it is engaged in a long-term campaign against worldwide terrorism that will include legal, political, diplomatic, law enforcement, and intelligence gathering along with military action.

Several hundred citizens of other countries, from Britain to Zimbabwe, were lost in the terrorist attacks, and that makes it easier to internationalize the antiterrorist cause. But as Mr. Bush is learning, building a coalition is a matter of finding partners, not just followers.

Should Rudy Stay?

SEPTEMBER 30, 2001

"He's our Winston Churchill," writes Jonathan Alter in the current *Newsweek,* "walking the rubble, calming and inspiring his heartbroken but defiant people."

But by the time the article appeared, he'd gone back to being Rudy Giuliani, playing political games and making himself the center of a spirited controversy. Giuliani had emerged as possibly the most popular figure in a terrorism crisis. He played host at ground zero to national and international figures, starting with President Bush. He floated on an unbelievable wave of popularity. By refusing to talk politics, he came to transcend politics.

But it didn't last. Barred by the New York term-limit law from seeking a third term as mayor, Giuliani succumbed to the temptation to cash in on his popularity by offering to stay on another few months. Otherwise, he said, he might feel obliged to ask the legislature to change the law and permit him to run for a third term.

In that one political move he expended a good deal of his popularity. For one thing, what he proposed ran against the spirit of the U.S. Constitution. The Twentieth Amendment was enacted precisely because the March 4 presidential inaugural date created an awkward four-month lame-duck administration. But in New York, Giuliani says, a longer transition is needed—five months instead of the current two months. What would the elected mayor be expected to do during those five months? Who would live in Gracie Mansion, to bring up a sore point? Mavens of New York politics tell me it isn't likely to happen, nor is Governor Pataki likely to be willing to sign a law permitting Giuliani to run as a last-minute write-in candidate.

It is understandable that Giuliani, who had to retire from a race for the Senate last year because of health problems, found it difficult to let go of a position in which he now found himself bathed in adulation. A pity. He would surely have been offered a prestigious position, perhaps in the federal government. Now that he is a center of controversy again, the likelihood of that is less.

An Explosion of Joy in Afghanistan

NOVEMBER 15, 2001

Was it only last week that Defense Secretary Donald Rumsfeld was counseling us to settle down for the long haul and not expect miracles? He did not foresee, as perhaps no one could, the explosion of joy of a long-repressed people once they tasted freedom. The scenes in Kabul reminded me a little of the liberation of Paris in 1944 by the Allied-supported French Resistance forces or, in another way, the liberation of Yugoslavia from Nazi occupation, marred by the civil war between Croats under Marshal Tito and Serbs under Draza Mihailovic, whom Tito eventually had executed.

In Kabul, as in Belgrade, indigenous forces were in the saddle, and the best-laid or not-so-well-laid plans of the allies for an orderly entry into the capital were swept aside. The Northern Alliance, having promised to stay out of the city, found itself inexorably drawn into the vacuum as Taliban forces withdrew. Now the Alliance promises not to stay as an occupation force.

The scenes of celebration in Kabul were marred by reports of many killings, and the United States and its allies are aware that some peacekeeping force will have to be inserted quickly if there is not to be a descent into anarchy. At the United Nations, there is talk of assembling a force from countries like Turkey, Bangladesh, Morocco, and Jordan. A peacekeeping contingent made up entirely of troops from Islamic countries would be a historic novelty. But neither the United States nor its European allies seem anxious to shoulder a task that may last for years.

With events moving faster than had been anticipated, hardly a start has been made on assessing, let alone meeting, the vast needs of reconstruction. That needs to be addressed before the next war in Afghanistan.

The Cozy Relationship Between Enron and the Bush Administration

DECEMBER 5, 2001

Robert Siegel, host: Enron shares closed up today, if you can call $1.01 up in any meaningful way. Stock in the Houston-based energy giant was worth more than $80 a year ago. Enron filed for Chapter 11 bankruptcy protection on Sunday. A day later, it laid off four thousand employees. The big question now, says NPR news analyst Daniel Schorr, is how much Enron's troubles will rub off on the Bush administration.

In the wake of the crash of Enron, arguably the biggest bankruptcy in history, federal agencies and Congress will be probing the company's dealings with auditors, bankers, and stockholders. What remains to be investigated is the deeper issue of Enron's close ties with the Bush administration, and how they may have influenced national energy policy to Enron's benefit. It has long been evident that Enron—whose officers and employees gave almost $2 million to the Bush cause since 1993—was close to this administration, and CEO Kenneth Lay personally close to George W. Bush.

Secretary of the Army Thomas White had been an Enron executive. Lawrence Lindsey, the president's economic adviser, had served on an Enron advisory board for pay. Members of the Federal Energy Regulatory Commission were chosen with Lay's endorsement. Several White House officials owned Enron stock, which ironically they disposed of before the house fell in, to avoid a potential conflict of interest.

Seeking favorable regulatory policies, Enron found an open door when Vice President Dick Cheney was named to lead the president's task force on energy policy. Cheney and Lay had an unusual one-on-one meeting, and then the Enron staff stayed in close touch with the commission staff. When Cheney filed his report, the hometown newspaper, the *Houston Chronicle,* said he unveiled a national energy strategy very much to Enron's liking.

What happened in all those close encounters, whether Enron gave any hint of trouble brewing in the company, Cheney will not say. The General Accounting Office, the investigative arm of Congress, has threatened an unprecedented lawsuit to force disclosure, but has put the suit on hold for the duration of the war situation.

Henry Waxman, ranking Democrat on the House Government Reform Committee, has written the vice president saying that continued secrecy from the White House will only compound public concerns. But the Democrats, as a minority, do not have the power to schedule hearings or issue subpoenas. And so what we have yet to learn is whether White House arrangements with a major energy corporation involved a conflict of interest at the public expense.

The State of Peace on Earth in 2001

DECEMBER 23, 2001

A decade ago it seemed a neat idea to chronicle at the yuletide season a progress of peace on Earth. In 1991, it was a mixed bag. Iraq beaten back in the Gulf War, defeated but not vanquished; a grisly massacre in Yugoslavia, but then a hopeful-looking Arab-Israeli peace conference; a cooling-off in Central America; communal warfare ended in Africa; and a big enchilada, the fifty-year cold war ended and with it the fear of nuclear Armageddon.

At Christmastime in 1991, I mentioned briefly Afghanistan, saying, "The Soviet-American proxy war was over. The fighting among rival Afghan factions, not yet." I said, "Peace is a maybe, no better than that." A year ago I mentioned in Afghanistan "a last-ditch fight against the ruling Taliban with no reliable casualty figures."

So now this year, what is there to say about peace on Earth after September 11 that is not profoundly depressing? One can look for consolation in the relative peace in the Balkans, in divided Korea, in divided China, but one has to scrounge for the good news. This year war has become no longer simply a matter of cross-border hostilities or internal feuds. The melancholy fact is that war has taken on an entirely new dimension, transcending borders. It is war by suicide. War today is a young Palestinian with a bomb strapped to his body. On a much vaster scale, it is the meticulously trained hijacker turning our technology against us as his ticket to glory.

There are organizations that annually tally the number of armed conflicts as a way of judging how peaceful the year has been. A year ago the

National Defense Council Foundation in Alexandria, Virginia, counted sixty-eight cross-border and internal conflicts, an increase of three over the previous year. In the age of the war against terrorism, counting conflicts no longer works. There is one great transcendent conflict, a twenty-first-century version of struggling with the barbarians at the gates.

When Saint Luke spoke of peace on Earth, it was not a prediction but a prayer. With it went another prayer, "Goodwill toward men." It was to say you can't have one without the other. This year, sad to say, in much of the world we had neither.

2002

Questionable Connections

A Shipload of Weapons

JANUARY 9, 2002

Last Thursday's interception of a fifty-ton shipload of weapons apparently bound for Gaza is alarming from two points of view.

First, the Palestinian-Israeli standoff. Allowing the shipment to proceed after Yasser Arafat's December 16 speech calling for an end to violence would suggest a cynical cover of plans for an all-out attack on Israel. If, as Arafat claims, he didn't know about the arms shipment in which his own lieutenants were involved, that would suggest the possibility of a plot by militants to seize power from him. In any event, Israeli talks with the Palestinians are probably off for some unspecified time.

Second, the episode is alarming for what it says about the role of Iran. After September 11, Iran denounced acts of terror, and there was a candlelight vigil in Tehran for the victims. The Bush administration welcomed the hope that Iran might be moving toward the antiterrorist camp, but this shipment of weapons, bearing markings in the Farsi language and loaded at an island off the Iranian coast, suggests that the hard-line mullahs are still in control when the chips are down.

So troublesome is this that the Bush administration at first hesitated to credit the story of the interception by Israeli naval commandos, and then finally did. Today, Secretary of State Colin Powell telephoned Arafat and stressed the seriousness of the issue.

For the Bush administration, this represents an unwelcome distraction from the war in Afghanistan and his concentration on destroying the global al Qaeda network. President Bush may consider Osama bin Laden the focus of evil, but Israel's prime minister, Ariel Sharon, said in his speech yesterday that Iran, at the present time, is the center of world terror. It seems clear that the arms episode opens a new phase in both the Israeli-Palestinian confrontation and the broader antiterrorist campaign.

On the Call for Expansion

JANUARY 30, 2002

President Bush ventured into some uncharted waters with a suggestion last night of possible preemptive action against countries like North Korea, Iran, and Iraq, designated as posing threats with weapons of mass destruction. This represents a significant expansion of the Bush antiterrorism doctrine, presumably a response to dangers more immediate than had been realized. In addition, the president suggested that the United States was ready to intervene against organizations in the terrorist underworld, like Hamas in Israel and Hezbollah in Lebanon, if local authorities didn't.

It is hard to account for this sudden assertion of tough-minded unilateralism. In fact, North Korea has suspended the testing of long-range missiles; Iran has been working on nuclear development, but is not believed to be close to having a deliverable weapon. As to Iraq, last November, Mr. Bush warned of consequences if Saddam Hussein did not allow weapons inspectors back into Iraq. But no consequences followed when Iraq defied what it called the "arrogant" demand.

In his interview with NBC's Tom Brokaw last Wednesday, the president did not appear to be overly concerned. He said, "I don't feel the impatience that some might feel." But last night, presidential patience suddenly yielded to this: "I will not wait on events while dangers gather. I will not stand by as peril draws closer and closer." The chilling suggestion of impending action not only against terrorist bands but against constituted governments came as a surprise to observers. It had the effect, if not the purpose, of seizing headlines and diverting attention from more predictable issues, like the budget deficit and the Enron scandal.

But the suggestion of preemptive action against an ill-defined menace has political perils for the president. He may have painted himself into a corner, where his prestige will suffer if he does not deliver.

Getting Away with It

FEBRUARY 3, 2002

There have been some famous confrontations over presidential refusal to yield to congressional demands for information. President Eisenhower asserted executive privilege and prevailed when he turned down Senator Joseph McCarthy's seeking records in order to hound a targeted army officer. President Nixon asserted executive privilege and did not prevail when he fought all the way up to the Supreme Court to withhold his tapes from the Senate Watergate committee. In his memoirs, Nixon wrote wryly, "I was the first President to test the principle of executive privilege in the Supreme Court, and by testing it on such weak ground . . . I probably ensured the defeat of my cause."

The issue that has Congress's General Accounting Office engaged in an unprecedented suit against the White House has a more specific aspect, a 1972 law. The Federal Advisory Committee Act holds that when the executive branch consults outside experts and advisers, it must do so in public in order to avoid a suspicion of favoritism to special interests. A 1988 Supreme Court decision provided for exceptions to that rule. It said the law should not be literally interpreted, which might prevent the president from getting advice from a group of two or more persons.

But First Lady Hillary Rodham Clinton ran into that law in 1993 when she tried to keep confidential the workings of her task force on health care reform that brought together cabinet members, outside experts, and lobbyists. When she was finally forced to go public, some embarrassing facts were revealed, such as $100,000 consulting fees to Clinton cronies. The GAO effort to find out about the energy task force headed by Vice President Dick Cheney started last April, long before the collapse of the Enron Corporation. But clearly the way the task force recommendations on deregulation seemed to track Enron policy was a subject of interest, and so was a recommendation for oil and gas production in India, in which Enron was involved.

But the GAO suit isn't only about Enron. It is about whether well-heeled lobbies can work behind the scenes with official presidential bodies to help fashion federal policy.

Powell Behind the Scenes

FEBRUARY 10, 2002

Colin Powell could have run for president. He would have been a shoo-in for vice president. But Soldier Powell preferred to serve in an appointive office, and so he works at the sometimes thankless job of secretary of state. The bellicose warning by President Bush to North Korea, Iran, and Iraq in his State of the Union address did not go down well in the State Department, but Powell told his subordinates to stick by the letter and spirit of Bush's words. There would be no daylight between him and the White House.

Powell operates mostly out of the spotlight. Reflecting the views of America's allies, he asked President Bush to reconsider a decision to refuse prisoner-of-war status to the captives in Guantánamo. Mr. Bush ruled that the Geneva Conventions would be applied to Taliban prisoners, but not to al Qaeda prisoners.

The secretary's influence behind the scenes can be tracked in the comprehensive eight-part series in the *Washington Post* detailing ten days of deliberations in the White House starting on September 11. At a meeting of a half dozen principal advisers the next day, September 12, Powell laid down the line that the target would be terrorism in its broadest sense. On Thursday, the secretary reported to the National Security Council that Pakistan was on board, and the president said that this was the State Department at its best. On Friday, preparing to speak at the National Cathedral, the president choked up at a meeting with advisers. Powell passed him a note, cautioning against being too emotional. Bush held it up, and told his advisers that it said, "Dear Mr. President, don't break down." Loud laughter all around. On Saturday, Powell opposed the Pentagon, which was proposing an attack on Iraq. He said, "The coalition partners are all with you, every one, but they will go away if you hit Iraq."

Tuesday, September 18, his advisers reviewed a draft of his speech to Congress. Powell suggested that the line serving notice on states that have supported terrorism be amended to read, "States that continue to support terrorism," thus making a distinction between past and future behavior. All this while Powell tries to keep up with Israel and the Palestinians, India and Pakistan, and the other hot spots bubbling up around the world. Last Thursday found him in the Bahamas meeting with Caribbean leaders about the latest crisis in Haiti. Colin Powell reminds me of General George Marshall, the soldier who gave diplomacy a good name.

Bottom-Line Thinking

MARCH 10, 2002

About bumping Ted Koppel's *ABC News Nightline* to make room for the *Late Show with David Letterman*—first, the full disclosure.

I worked in television journalism for thirty years. I'm way at the upper end of the demographic scale that so preoccupies corporate executives. Also, Ted Koppel is a friend of mine. Am I possibly biased? You bet. I thought that Paddy Chayefsky foretold the decline of television journalism twenty-five years ago in his brilliant movie satire *Network*. It had the UBS network, owned by a distant conglomerate, turning over news programming to the entertainment department to raise ratings and profits. The programming chief, played by Faye Dunaway, has her psychotic anchorman shot on camera. She makes a deal with a band of urban guerrillas to tape their crime of the week. Satire, mind you, a little ahead of its time.

What's wrong with bottom-line thinking is that news was not meant to compete for profits. It is what television owes for the free use of the public airwaves. The law says that television will operate in the public interest, convenience, and necessity. But from the Reagan administration to the second Bush administration, that has become a regulatory dead letter. Long gone is the day when Bill Paley of CBS, David Sarnoff of NBC, and Leonard Goldenson of ABC indulged their money-losing news stars to take the curse off the quiz show scandals, and when one-time FCC commissioner Newton Minow called TV the vast wasteland.

As networks get swallowed by conglomerates, which in turn get swallowed by bigger conglomerates, news comes to occupy a small corner of a vast entertainment stage. And so you know what's happening when *Titanic* star Leonardo DiCaprio is assigned by ABC to interview

President Clinton about the environment. Or when the Pentagon invites ABC Entertainment, not News, to produce a thirteen-part series about American forces in action. Or coming back to where we started, when the Mickey Mouse empire wants to install a funny man in Ted Koppel's place, looking for an audience of younger consumers.

Koppel took exception to the anonymous corporate executive who told the *New York Times* that *Nightline* had lost its relevance. "Inappropriate and at worst malicious," said Koppel. And here comes the bias: Look at the world today and the need of Americans to have it all explained. And maybe it is the corporate tycoons of television who are making themselves irrelevant, but profitably so.

The Rise of the Suicide Bomber

APRIL 3, 2002

As though marked on the calendar, seven actual or intended suicide bombings in seven days.

A jittery Israel suffers a damaging blow to its tourism industry as the State Department advises, once again, against travel there. Yasser Arafat deplores the loss of civilian life, but says, "We are marching to Jerusalem as millions of martyrs."

Suicide bombing, it's becoming clear, is not just a phenomenon of youthful resistance but part of a long-term strategy aimed at crushing the Jewish state. The closest thing to a smoking gun, or a bomb, is a document seized in a storming of the Ramallah compound last Friday. It is an invoice from the militant Al Aqsa Martyrs addressed to Fuad Shobaki, the finance officer of the Palestinian Authority. It requests, among other things, about $4,000 in Israeli shekels to pay for electrical and chemical components for a month's supply of about thirty bombs.

Shobaki was also identified by the Israelis as the one who authorized payments for the fifty tons of Iranian-made weapons seized by Israeli commandos in the Red Sea. The invoice helps to explain where the suicide volunteers get the explosives that they wrap around themselves.

The direct link to the Palestinian Authority also helps to explain why Arab leaders have declined to come out forthrightly against suicide bombing. The Arab League summit in Beirut, despite a plea from United Nations secretary-general Kofi Annan, praised the valiant martyrs of the intifada without reference to suicide bombing. A fifty-seven-nation Islamic conference in Kuala Lumpur, Malaysia, refused by a huge majority to define suicide bombing as "terrorism." Of the fifty-seven countries represented, only the delegates from Malaysia and Bosnia were willing to condemn suicide bombings targeting civilians.

Saudi Arabia, in its peace initiative, has proposed returning Israel to its 1967 borders. But the organizers of the suicide bombings seem to have their minds set not on 1967, when Israel occupied the West Bank and Gaza, but 1948, when the Jewish state was created.

Compassionate Conservatism?

MAY 1, 2002

Family-friendly President Bush said of Karen Hughes, his departing adviser, "She has put her family ahead of her service to my government and I'm extremely grateful for that approach and that priority." That's all right for Karen Hughes, but if a welfare recipient decided to adopt that approach and that priority and devote herself to her children, they might all starve under legislation that Mr. Bush supports.

The president was out in California yesterday, talking up his domestic agenda between political fund-raisers. In San Jose he mentioned "compassionate conservatism" about a dozen times in thirty minutes. Under compassionate conservatism he listed the need for stronger work requirements than contained in the 1996 welfare overhaul, which is up for renewal.

Under current rules a welfare recipient must be engaged in work activities, including training, for thirty hours a week. The Republican bill now before the House would raise that to forty hours a week. It would also require states to move 70 percent of their remaining case-loads from welfare to work in the next five years. This would, among other things, turn back the clock on flexibility for the states. The National Governors Association says the states would have to create costly community-service make-work jobs and divert resources now used to train, educate, and move people into private-sector jobs.

What compassionate conservatives still need to address is: Who pays for the child care while the parents are off putting in their forty hours? Who provides the transportation? What of those with low IQs and learning disabilities? A study by the Joyce Foundation found welfare rolls in seven midwestern states reduced by two-thirds over the past eight years, but many of the 2 million former welfare recipients remain in poverty, struggling to pay their bills, as they juggle temporary or part-time jobs.

In San Jose yesterday, President Bush said that by helping people find work, by helping them prepare for work, we practice compassion. But not if it's make-work or forced work creating a new generation of neglected children and discouraged parents.

Keeping Intelligence from Congress

MAY 20, 2002

Liane Hansen, host: Today, FBI director Robert Mueller said that he believes there will be more terrorist attacks on the United States, including suicide bombers like the ones in Israel. And yesterday, Vice President Dick Cheney said that another major attack by al Qaeda is, in his words, "almost certain."

In addition, the vice president said yesterday that he would advise the president not to show a controversial intelligence briefing to Congress. Some say the memo could have been a warning about the September 11 attacks. NPR's senior news analyst Daniel Schorr says that Cheney's reluctance to show the document is par for the course for the Bush administration.

For all of my journalistic bias toward disclosure, I can appreciate Vice President Dick Cheney's position that some information involving sources and methods must be protected. But his argument would carry greater weight were it not for two facts. First, something I learned in my reporting days is that government agencies have a way of leaking classified information when it serves their purpose, especially when that purpose is putting down another agency.

The current uproar about what the president knew and when he knew it originates in leaks concerning two classified documents. One was a memorandum dated July 5 from FBI agent Kenneth Williams in Phoenix, urging his superiors to investigate men from the Middle East training in American flying schools and who might have connections with Osama bin Laden. The memorandum was not acted on. The CIA says it was only belatedly advised of it, and that made the FBI look bad.

The other leak was about the CIA's August 6 briefing memorandum for President Bush titled "Bin Laden Determined to Strike in U.S." That leak was accompanied by word to the *Washington Post* that the White House was disappointed because the analysis lacked focus and provided no new intelligence, and that made the CIA look bad.

It's harder to argue for keeping secrets when these secrets seem to be selectively leaked by those in charge of protecting them. Furthermore, the argument for keeping real secrets is harder to make when an administration has acquired a reputation for being generally obsessed with secrecy. For example, the White House is resisting giving Congress information about Enron contacts with the Cheney energy task force. It is sitting on Reagan-era documents by law scheduled to be released last year. The Justice Department withholds information about witnesses held for interrogation in the 9/11 investigation. Homeland Security director Tom Ridge is not allowed to testify before congressional committees.

The administration would get more support for keeping real secrets if it didn't try to make so much secret, and then if it did a better job of protecting its secrets from interagency feuds.

Civil Liberties After 9/11

MAY 27, 2002

Coleen Rowley's letter bitterly complaining of the roadblocks that hampered the investigation of a leading terrorist suspect is not only a severe embarrassment to the FBI, it reopens the perennial issue of how much liberty to sacrifice in the interest of security.

In the mid-1970s, congressional investigations unearthed years of extensive, illegal FBI wiretappings, surveillance, and break-ins aimed against political dissidents and civil rights activists, including Martin Luther King Jr. The report of a House committee, suppressed by the House, spoke of careers ruined, friendships severed, and in some cases lives endangered.

It was to establish control of FBI activities that Congress, in 1978, passed the Foreign Intelligence Surveillance Act. It created a unique secret court, with judges selected by the Supreme Court's chief justice, to review applications for wiretapping foreign agents. Operating behind walls of secrecy, the bureau became slipshod in writing its applications, with the result that in the fall of the year 2000, according to the *New York Times,* the seven judges called Attorney General Janet Reno to their secret courtroom to complain of misleading affidavits. Backing off, the FBI's counterintelligence unit held back on some new applications. Some requests relating to al Qaeda were held up for review as to whether they met the legal standard.

This was the atmosphere in which Agent Rowley found herself being frustrated in her efforts to get a warrant to search Zacarias Moussaoui's laptop computer, but that was before September 11. In the wake of September 11, the USA Patriot Act gave Attorney General John Ashcroft broader power to circumvent the Fourth Amendment "probable cause" standard and reduce judges' discretion in issuing certain types of warrants.

So are we going back to the days when Henry Kissinger, in the Nixon White House, could write his own list of wiretap targets? Are we faced again with that vexing question of how much privacy to yield in the name of security?

The End of the UN Population Fund

JULY 28, 2002

Colin Powell, secretary of state, has his ear tuned to the world, which includes the United Nations and its humanitarian activities. Karl Rove, White House political mastermind, has his ear tuned to his world, which includes the ideologically conservative community wary of the United Nations and its ways. At Powell's confirmation hearings in January of last year, he praised the UN Population Fund for its invaluable work. The fund spends about $270 million a year providing family planning and reproductive health services. A little of that, $3.5 million, is spent in China for items like a book on healthful practices during pregnancy. The fund is not involved in any way with abortion. Indeed, UN officials say that in the thirty-two counties of China where the fund operates, abortion rates have been falling. Nevertheless, antiabortion groups let Karl Rove know that they ardently oppose giving money to the population fund and demanded that President Bush reverse his decision to allocate $34 million.

The State Department in May sent an investigative team to China and found no evidence that the population fund has promoted abortions. The conservative community was not satisfied. Furthermore, conservatives had lost a battle on another front when the administration retreated from its threat to veto UN peacekeeping operations because of a dispute over the International Criminal Court. They put a lot of heat on Karl Rove to block American funding of the population fund, and Rove, who wields a lot of presidential clout, put a lot of heat on Powell.

And so the Bush administration reversed course and decided to withhold the $34 million already approved. And to make sure it was clear who had won this battle, it was Powell who got to make the announcement. His letter to Congress explained that regardless of the benefits of the population program, any money spent in China could be spent on forced abortion and sterilization.

The National Right to Life Committee expressed great satisfaction with the reversal. For the United Nations, it was one more incomprehensible American flouting of its international obligations.

Efforts to Link Iraq to the 9/11 Terrorist Attacks

AUGUST 5, 2002

John Ydstie, host: Today, Iraq sent an invitation to the United States Congress to visit any site said to be used for weapons of mass destruction. Senate Foreign Relations Committee chairman Joseph Biden rejected the offer as a stalling tactic, saying Iraq should immediately allow unrestricted UN weapons inspections. The White House also dismissed the Iraqi invitation.

News analyst Daniel Schorr says the Bush administration is refocusing on the question of Iraqi support for terrorism in its talk of ousting Saddam Hussein.

Shortly after September 11, a story surfaced attributed to a Czech minister of interior that suicide hijacker Mohamed Atta had met five months earlier in Prague with an undercover Iraqi agent. This was the only alleged link of the al Qaeda terrorists to Saddam Hussein, and it sparked an intensive investigation that failed to produce corroboration. Indeed, intelligence agencies found some indication that during the April period in question, Atta had been in Virginia Beach, Virginia, possibly casing navy facilities.

Now, although the CIA and the FBI remain dubious, the Prague connection is enjoying a revival in the White House. The *Los Angeles Times* reports that the FBI has been reviewing Atta's travel and telephone records with renewed vigor as one of its more urgent priorities. The reason for that is not hard to find. As the Bush administration edges closer to a military engagement with Iraq, it badly needs a casus belli, roughly translated "smoking gun." Pressures are mounting for the administration to seek support in advance from Congress as President Bush Sr. did in the Gulf War. If the president can establish that Iraq was involved in the terrorist conspiracy, there may be a way to bypass a congressional debate.

Within days after September 11, Congress passed a joint resolution authorizing the president to use force against nations he determined had aided the terrorist attacks. The resolution specified that this would fulfill the requirements of the War Powers Act. That puts a premium on establishing an Iraqi connection.

Defense Secretary Donald Rumsfeld told a news conference last Tuesday, without elaboration, that Iraq had a relationship with al Qaeda. Chairman Joseph Biden of the Senate Foreign Relations Committee, which held two days of hearings last week, said on television yesterday that he knows of no evidence that Iraq was connected to the terrorist attacks. But the congressional resolution gives the president wide latitude to determine what countries have aided and harbored the terrorists, and the administration is clearly trying its darnedest to hang the label on Saddam Hussein.

The Civil Rights of Enemy Combatants

AUGUST 11, 2002

In the way that *Miranda* denotes defendants' rights and *Roe* denotes abortion rights, *Hamdi* may come to denote an enemy's rights.

Yaser Esam Hamdi is an American born in Baton Rouge, Louisiana, raised in Saudi Arabia, captured by Northern Alliance forces in Afghanistan while serving with the Taliban. He is now in a navy brig in

Norfolk, Virginia, designated as an enemy combatant, not charged with anything, and denied legal representation. When federal district court judge Robert Doumar ordered unrestricted access to counsel for Hamdi, he was reversed by the appeals court, which told him to hear more arguments and get more facts before ruling. When the judge called for documents, the Justice Department refused to provide them. It asserted that anyone labeled by the administration as an enemy combatant has no rights, and furthermore the courts have no right to interfere.

This asserts a novel separation of power between executive and judiciary that is almost unprecedented. During the Civil War, the Supreme Court prohibited military detention of noncombatant Americans without appeal as long as the courts were functioning. But what if Attorney General Ashcroft says that when it comes to enemy combatants, the Supreme Court has no jurisdiction either? A 1971 law looking back to the detention of Japanese Americans without legal recourse during World War II prohibits the imprisonment of American citizens except pursuant to an act of Congress. The administration says that law does not apply to enemy combatants.

If the administration can decide on its own who has rights and who does not, who can have a lawyer and who cannot, who is an enemy and who is not, and assert that its decisions are not subject to judicial review, then it endangers the very liberties that President Bush says he is trying to defend.

The Bush Administration Continues Its Search for a Justification to Attack Iraq

AUGUST 19, 2002

In the run-up to the promised intervention in Iraq, the Bush administration has been trying hard to establish two kinds of justification. One is the existence of a clear and present danger of weapons of mass destruction that should be preemptively attacked. The administration has not managed so far to demonstrate that. The furthest that National Security Adviser Condoleezza Rice would go in an interview with the BBC last week was to say of Saddam Hussein that if he gets weapons of mass destruction, he will wreak havoc at home and abroad.

The other justification would be Iraqi involvement in anti-American terror. Much attention has been given to a Czech intelligence report of a meeting between hijacker Mohamed Atta and an Iraqi agent in Prague five months before September 11. But that meeting has not been corroborated, nor is the CIA sure how important it was if it did happen. And for what it's worth, Osama bin Laden calls Saddam Hussein a bad Muslim in a videotape unearthed in Afghanistan by CNN.

It is embarrassing that, having designated Iraq as part of an axis of evil, the administration is unable, despite its strenuous efforts, to state definitely that Iraq is involved in anti-American terrorism, or that Iraq has chemical, biological, or nuclear weapons that it's ready to use. While awaiting better intelligence, President Bush is shifting attention from violent regime change to what a changed regime would be like. After one meeting with Iraqi opposition leaders in Washington, the administration is reportedly planning a larger-scale international conference seeking to establish a coalition that could create a new government.

The meeting would be held in The Hague or elsewhere in Europe in the hope of attracting so far absent European support for the enterprise. If an opposition united front can be established, which would be a first, then the invasion of Iraq could be presented as something like the Northern Alliance war with the Taliban, that is, an indigenous movement with American support.

Plans can be made with exiled leaders, but the great unknown is whether there are dissidents in Iraq who have survived Saddam Hussein's tyrannical rule and who will come forward to help liberate their own country. But the administration is still in search of a casus belli, "a cause of war," that will sell armed intervention to the American public.

Political Talk

SEPTEMBER 15, 2002

After an emotion-laden week centered on the 9/11 commemoration, it is probably politically incorrect to be talking politics, but someone has to do it and so here goes.

On Thursday, President Bush made a hard-hitting speech to the United Nations General Assembly, saying, in effect, that the UN had better get rid of Saddam Hussein and his weapons of mass destruction or the United States will. The timing of that speech was interesting. Last January the president's political adviser, Karl Rove, got some criticism for saying that Republicans should view the war on terrorism as an issue to take to the country. The *New York Times* said he was trying to turn the war to partisan advantage, something that Rove denied.

But it was interesting to note how President Bush, during the summer, kept out of the controversy over invading Iraq. White House chief of staff Andrew Card said the administration was working on a strategy, but you don't introduce new products in August. And so the president's media advisers planned for a September 11 speech from Ellis Island with the Statue of Liberty aglow behind him to be followed immediately by that tough UN speech.

Why does that matter politically? Because if the nation's attention is focused on al Qaeda and Saddam Hussein, it is less focused on a shaky economy, stock market gyrations, corporate scandal, and rising costs of health care. Campaign expert Dick Morris wrote in the *Hill* newspaper that Bush has great ratings for fighting terrorism and only mildly positive or negative ratings on anything else. Even before the rollout of his UN offensive, polls showed 65 percent support for military action against Iraq. Now, said Morris, if Bush calls for a congressional vote before the recess, the event will dominate the headlines and sweep all before it. It could be the key issue in dozens of House and Senate races, he said. President Bush has often said that the fight against terrorism is not a partisan matter, but then you go back to Karl Rove and his statement "We can go to the country on this issue"—for whatever reason, Iraq and terrorism are surely before the country as the election campaign gets into full swing.

When Do We Have the Right to Know?

OCTOBER 9, 2002

Robert Siegel, host: More strange twists and turns today in the case of the D.C.-area sniper who has killed six people and wounded two. Today, police spent hours combing a wooded area after a witness reported a suspicious person in that area. But by midday local time, that search was called off; police say they found no trace of the man.

Local media covered the morning's developments in minute detail, a practice about which NPR news analyst Daniel Schorr has mixed feelings.

The frustrating search for a sniper who has carried out eight shootings in the Washington area so far has raised one of those classic cases of press rights versus press responsibilities. Montgomery County, Maryland, police chief Charles Moose has taken vehement exception to the breaking of a story on Channel 9 TV in Washington about the discovery near one of the shooting sites of a fortune-telling tarot card known as the death card, with the scrawled message: "Dear policemen, I am God."

Chief Moose's first problem is with his own investigators, as he acknowledged when he said that someone on his team had done something very inappropriate in releasing the information. But then he broadened his complaint to a denunciation of the news media for interfering with the investigation. "I beg of the media to let us do our job," he said.

I am not a stranger to conflicts over secrecy versus disclosure, having been denounced by a congressional committee in 1976 for the reprehensible act of disclosing an intelligence report that had been suppressed by the House. But these times present a special kind of dilemma for the news media. The violence-prone, in many cases, get their kicks from their coverage, and others are spurred to copycatting. There may be reason on occasion to withhold investigative information.

The news organizations cannot suspend their reporting in the interests of depriving criminals of ego satisfaction. But in this extraordinary time of violence, from Oklahoma City to Columbine High School and now the Washington area, it becomes necessary to balance First Amendment rights with the requirements of community. This may mean a less dramatic presentation than television is capable of; on occasion, it may mean withholding a legitimate story on the plea of law enforcement authorities.

It's unclear to me why Chief Moose was so exercised over the tarot card leak other than his general concern about maintaining control of investigative information. But I can imagine a news director checking with a police chief if there's reason to believe a story might be harmful. I didn't always believe a journalist should ever withhold news, but advancing age and the violent times we live in make me hesitate about absolutes.

Al Gore May Be the Only Democrat to Remain Unscathed After the Elections

NOVEMBER 10, 2002

Several leading Democrats saw their future ambitions shrink in the disaster of last Tuesday's election.

Richard Gephardt gave up the leadership of the House Democrats. Tom Daschle was reduced from majority to minority leader of the Senate. Walter Mondale, defeated in his Senate comeback bid, returns to political retirement. If any Democrat can be said to have benefited from the shambles, it is another former vice president, Al Gore. Gore, who has said he may decide next month whether to run for president again, spent the campaign basically doing two things. He piled up political chits by stumping widely for Democratic candidates from Maine to Florida, and he delivered a couple of major speeches attacking administration policy on Iraq and on the economy in stronger terms than most incumbents were doing.

After his economic speech at the Brookings Institution on October 2, denouncing Bush tax and spending policies, I asked him how he saw his current role in the Democratic Party. He said, "A lot of the most important issues don't seem to be discussed very much and I think that they need to be." This sounded to me like veiled criticism of congressional Democrats for timidity about confronting a popular wartime president.

Postelection analysis indicates that Gore may have had a point. Metooism, like Gephardt's endorsement of the war powers resolution, did not help Democratic candidates very much. Since the election, Gore has taped an interview with Barbara Walters of ABC in which he is more explicit about returning the Democratic Party to its roots. He said, "Democrats have to be the loyal opposition in fact and not just in name. Democrats should not mistake the magnitude of this loss. There has to be a major regrouping." Gore says he hasn't decided yet about seeking a rematch with Bush in 2004. But why would he want to remake the Democratic Party unless he hoped to be its candidate?

Questionable Connections

NOVEMBER 17, 2002

The Bush administration has never been able to make a convincing case for the connection between Iraq and the al Qaeda terrorist network.

Indeed, there were signs pointing to hostility between the Islamic extremists led by Osama bin Laden and the secular regime of Saddam Hussein. Bin Laden was said to have called Saddam "an apostate and an infidel." But there are recent indications that the two have been finding common cause in the conflict with America, at least for propaganda purposes. The bin Laden audiotape, now generally believed to be authentic, was delivered to the Al-Jazeera television network in Islamabad, Pakistan, during the tense week before the Friday deadline for the Iraqi response to the UN inspection resolution.

The speaker likened the suffering of the Iraqis to the plight of the Palestinians and said that the recent terrorist attacks were merely a reciprocal reaction to what Bush, the modern-day Pharaoh, did by murdering children in Iraq. The speaker warned several countries by name against aiding the criminal gang in Washington and denounced Islamic countries allied with the "tyrannical U.S. government"—this possibly a warning to Iraq's neighbors not to support an invasion.

This is as far as al Qaeda has ever gone in embracing the cause of Iraq, making threats of terrorist attacks on the foes of Saddam Hussein. And the Iraqi government seemed to underscore that threat in its letter the next day to the United Nations, agreeing to deal with the UN demand to resume weapons inspection. The letter said that American aggression against Muslims and Arabs was the basic reason why the United States had to close embassies and restrict its interests in many parts of the world while reaping the hatred of the peoples of the world.

There may not have been a link between Iraq and the Islamic fundamentalists before, but at least for tactical purposes, there certainly seems to be one now.

"Information Data" on American Citizens

NOVEMBER 18, 2002

Spying on Americans in America has been a historic no-no that was reconfirmed in the mid-1970s when the CIA, the FBI, and the NSA got into a peck of trouble with Congress and the country for conducting surveillance on Vietnam War dissenters. A no-no, that is, until September 11. Since then, the Bush administration has acted as though in order to protect you, it has to know all about you.

The hastily passed USA Patriot Act reduced some of the barriers to the invasion of privacy. And today, a federal appeals court ruled that the Justice Department has broad discretion in using wiretaps and other surveillance techniques to track suspected terrorists and spies. Last summer, Attorney General John Ashcroft tried to institute a program called TIPS, Terrorism Information and Prevention System, inviting Americans to spy on each other, but Congress refused to endorse that program.

There was some discussion in the White House about whether the United States needed, in addition to a Homeland Security Department, a special internal intelligence agency separate from the FBI, like the British MI5. Homeland Security director Tom Ridge flew to London for a briefing and returned saying he doubted whether such an organization would work in this country. Some senators who are down on the FBI are still interested in the idea.

The most far-reaching plan yet for domestic snooping is being researched in the Pentagon. It is called Total Information Awareness, TIA, and would employ some cutting-edge technologies to establish a centralized grand database on Americans. Into that database would flow every kind of electronic transaction, from telephone bills paid to medical prescriptions filled, from credit card purchases to travel plans, all neatly processed into individual dossiers.

The father of the TIA program is Rear Admiral Retired John Poindexter, who was President Reagan's national security adviser. He is remembered for a perjury conviction, later overturned, in the Iran-Contra conspiracy. That is only one of the reasons to worry about a program that would establish a Big Brother of the computer age.

Iraq's Nuclear Program

DECEMBER 9, 2002

A good rule of thumb in dealing with a Saddam Hussein type is that information freely acknowledged is only intended to steer you away from more damaging information.

And so when senior weapons adviser General Amir Al Saadi confirmed to a news conference yesterday that Iraq may have been close to developing a Nagasaki-strength nuclear bomb until the program was destroyed in an American bombing in January 1991, you had to wonder what weapons development he didn't want to talk about—specifically, the chemical and biological programs, including anthrax and nerve gas, known to have existed, but which Iraq now claims to have eliminated. Iraq's massive declaration gives no compelling evidence of such destruction, but General Al Saadi smoothly explained that all the documentation was destroyed along with the programs. It becomes increasingly clear that the twelve-thousand-page Iraqi declaration will not settle the issue of banned weapons, and surprise inspections are not likely to.

Despite the difficulties involved, America's principal hope rests on inducing Iraqi scientists and technicians to be interviewed outside their country. General Al Saadi said the Iraqi government would not object, but vividly remembered is Saddam's son-in-law, General Hussein Kamel, who defected to Jordan in 1995, talked to the CIA, and was lured back to Iraq, where he and his whole family were slaughtered. Chief UN inspector Hans Blix seems reserved about organizing these out-of-the-country interviews, saying, "We are not going to abduct anyone." But White House spokesman Ari Fleischer says the United States attaches great importance to the interview program. The Bush administration is apparently willing to arrange asylum and a lot more for potential defectors.

Without much concrete proof of existing Iraqi weapons programs, the United States has a lot riding on the defection plan. So does Saddam Hussein. Material breach—the code words for war or peace—may hinge on the success of America's witness protection program.

The State of Peace on Earth in 2002

DECEMBER 22, 2002

About a dozen years ago, the *Weekend Sunday* crew suggested I take a yuletide look at the status of peace on Earth.

It seemed a good idea at the time. The cold war was winding down, and with it the fear of nuclear holocaust. Perhaps, one hoped, peace on Earth might become not simply Saint Luke's prayer but a tangible possibility. And so a tradition was born, the annual peace on Earth wrap-up. I don't know how you measure these things, but peace on Earth seems further away than ever. One can cite a few places where violence has diminished: Bosnia and Kosovo in the Balkans; Afghanistan, if you keep your fingers crossed; Sumatra and Sri Lanka in Southeast Asia; and a few civil wars in Africa. But the hardy perennials of conflict remain with us. Nationalist and religious struggles like Chechnya in Russia; in Kashmir between India and Pakistan; and Palestinian versus Israeli in the region where the words "peace on Earth" were first uttered.

It has become necessary to redefine peace, as it's become necessary to redefine war. War can be a lethal instrument called a suicide bomber, or—we're not sure yet—it could be germs in an envelope, or poison in a reservoir. Peace today is a nervous look at your neighbor, an X-ray of your baggage, a color-coded alert, and a president at war in defense of a place called homeland. Peace has become a sometime thing, a search for enemies without return addresses operating from the shadows. Not a whole lot of goodwill toward men, either. And finally, peace today is waiting for the next war to begin: the war against Iraq that we are promised will make the world safe again.

Sorry about the gloomy note. Maybe there'll be a happier assessment of peace on Earth this time next year. If not, I'm going to beg off doing these wrap-ups.

2003

Earthquake Diplomacy

A Fateful Week for America, Iraq, and the World

JANUARY 27, 2003

This may be a fateful week for America, Iraq, and the world, as the air is sucked out of the diplomacy balloon and all sides brace themselves for what inexorably looks like armed conflict.

The Bush administration dismisses the idea of prolonged inspection as close to being an irrelevancy. It wants Iraq simply to own up and tell what's happened to tens of thousands of liters of biological agents and tens of thousands of missiles known to have existed. The Iraqi government says it's done all it can do or means to do about cooperating with the United Nations and now is resigned to war. A flurry of rumors about a deal with Saddam Hussein for exile and amnesty has subsided. And Secretary of State Colin Powell has about given up his strenuous efforts to achieve a peaceful settlement.

Powell accomplished something of a miracle last August when he induced a skeptical President Bush to try assembling a coalition through the United Nations because unilateral military action simply would not work. In the end, Powell's efforts for consensus were undermined by the defections of France and Germany. Defense Secretary Donald Rumsfeld spoke slightingly of the old Europe, as though placing more reliance on some new Europe of formerly Communist-ruled East European states.

But even the long-patient Colin Powell before the World Economic Forum in Davos, Switzerland, yesterday needled France and Germany with a reminder that America had helped to rescue Europe from the fascist tyranny that led to World War II. Remarkably, the same Powell who last August persuaded President Bush not to try to go it alone in a war against Iraq now spoke as though he'd given up on seeking a diplomatic solution and was ready for military action, alone if need be. He told the assemblage of government and business leaders, "When we feel strongly about something, we will lead, we will act, even if others are not prepared to join us." It was as though the lonely leader of the doves in the Bush administration had resigned that position and joined the hawks, with consequences not only for the Iraq stalemate but for all of America's European alliances.

Nations Respond to Powell's Presentation

FEBRUARY 5, 2003

These ten days between now and February 14 may well be the ten days that shake the world.

Between now and then United Nations inspectors will go to Baghdad and return to tell the Security Council how much it can believe of Secretary Powell's forceful indictment of Saddam Hussein's banned weapons and their banned concealment. Today France, Russia, China, and Germany indicated in the Security Council they were not ready to go all the way with Powell in concluding that Saddam Hussein has blown his last-chance opportunity to come clean and disarm, meaning that a time has come for what are euphemistically called "serious consequences," meaning war.

The Europeans were still talking today of enhanced inspection, of more diplomacy and more discussion in the Security Council. The Bush administration has made a big investment in trying to win over the doubting governments by drawing on intelligence secrets to make its case. Powell pointedly said that Abu Musab al-Zarqawi's terrorists operating from Iraq threatened France, Italy, Germany, and Russia, as well as America.

This is a week of intense transatlantic activity, trying to enlarge President Bush's coalition of the willing—Prime Minister Tony Blair of Britain meets with French president Jacques Chirac; President Bush talks on the phone to Russian president Vladimir Putin; the European Union talks about a special summit meeting; the Turkish parliament meets on Thursday, voting on military plans; Sunday Russia's Putin talks with German chancellor Gerhard Schröder. This becomes a defining moment for America's relations with its allies. If this is a last chance for Iraq, it may also be a sort of last chance for the system of alliances that rests on America's unmatched strength in the world.

For European countries which have been enjoying the popularity they achieved by thumbing their nose at a superpower, it's come time to consider the risks and the costs of letting America go it with the support of only a medley of lesser countries, many of them counting on payoffs from America. In the end, which is about ten days from now, some of the bigger governments may think again of turning their backs on America.

President Bush's Eagerness to Connect the Dots Between Osama bin Laden and Saddam Hussein

FEBRUARY 16, 2003

President Bush likes to talk about tyrants and terrorists as though Saddam Hussein and Osama bin Laden are cut from the same violent cloth.

The president has an interest in that being so. An Iraqi connection with the authors of the September 11 attacks would bolster the argument for invasion and regime change. And so, soon after September 11, administration sources spread word of a meeting weeks before the attack between leading hijacker Mohamed Atta and an Iraqi intelligence officer in Prague. The intelligence community was dubious about such a meeting, so while the president was saying, "There are al Qaeda terrorists inside Iraq," Secretary of State Colin Powell was saying more cautiously, "There are some indications that there were contacts between the Iraqi regime and some al Qaeda members."

By the start of this year, intelligence agencies were in almost open disagreement with the White House and the Pentagon. Some FBI officers let it be known that they were baffled by the administration's insistence on asserting such a connection. The New York Times cited some CIA officers as complaining of exaggerated conclusions from sketchy intelligence reports.

The argument was apparently resolved at a very high level when it came time for Secretary Powell to make his dramatic intelligence report to the United Nations Security Council on February 5. Powell told of a terrorist network headed by Abu Musab al-Zarqawi, described as an associated collaborator of Osama bin Laden operating a training center in poisons and explosives at a camp in northeastern Iraq.

And now Osama bin Laden, or someone sounding a lot like him, has weighed in with an audiotape voicing support for the people of Iraq but denouncing the Saddam Hussein infidels who have lost their legitimacy, which did not keep Secretary Powell from testifying before Congress that the terrorists were in some sort of partnership with Iraq.

If there has been a real operating connection between the tyrant and the terrorists, it remains to be established. For now, it's established to the satisfaction of those planning to bring down the Iraqi regime.

The Brink of War

MARCH 17, 2003

That leaders of democracies have to sneak off to an air base on an Atlantic island free of demonstrating crowds tells its own story. This is not only the end of a diplomatic process, as President Bush says, it marks the erosion of the concept of collective security that has undergirded American policy from Wilson to Clinton. The effort to getting a war-making license from the U.N. Security Council, which the administration said it didn't really need, was defeated by citizen resistance in countries where citizens can exercise influence. Britain's Tony Blair pleaded for a resolution that might help get him out of hot water with his constituents. Mexico and Chile need many forms of American help, but they discovered that they need the consent of their citizens more. France, where you can make a career of America bashing, is another story. So is Russia, which doesn't need voter pressure in order for President Putin to make trouble for Bush.

There is irony here for a president devoted to the spread of democracy, but not always happy with the results. To a group of veterans assembled at the White House last November, Bush said, "We don't seek an empire. Our nation is committed to freedom for ourselves and for others." Yes, but the current *Newsweek* magazine carries a lengthy article entitled "The Arrogant Empire," saying that never will America have waged a war in such isolation as the war with Iraq. Established mainstays of the global order—Western alliance, European unity, United Nations—seem to be cracking under the stress, says *Newsweek*. And most of the countries worried about what they call empire are countries that we call democracies.

Reconciliation Between the Media and the Military

MARCH 24, 2003

The Iraq war and a revolution in communications technology may be opening the way to a historic reconciliation between the American media and the military.

In World War II, correspondents were accredited, not embedded. They wore army and navy uniforms. They ate in mess halls. And they gladly accepted censorship of their dispatches and broadcasts in the interests of the war effort. Since then, the Vietnam War, with its body counts and news management, turned a cooperative into an adversarial relationship. In the 1980s, military leaders, resentful of a perceived press role in eroding support for the Vietnam War, took active measures to keep newspeople away from operations like the invasions of Grenada and Panama. During the first Gulf War, the press operated under onerous restrictions in trying to get where the action was and the soldiers were.

But the development of highly mobile cameras and satellite transmitters foreshadowed a new kind of war coverage. In planning for the Iraq invasion, the Pentagon decided to make the news media an offer they would find it hard to refuse: a front-row seat at the battleground embedded in combat units, frequently live on camera, with a vivid opportunity to become the hero journalists of this war. There are some five hundred newspeople operating in combat units. War makes strange "embed-fellows," you might say. What a live camera shows has a somewhat random quality—"Slices of the war," Defense Secretary Rumsfeld calls it.

The New Age war coverage also creates some New Age problems of professional ethics: what to show and what to withhold. Yesterday a dozen American soldiers were captured near a Euphrates River bridge. The Arab Al-Jazeera network broadcast some grim taped scenes of dead soldiers and others being interrogated. American networks generally acceded to urgent Pentagon requests to withhold using the tape out of regard for relatives not yet aware of what had happened. On his Web site, Matt Drudge raised this question: "If anchormen and others in the media have viewed it, why can't the average citizen?" It's a question bound to arise in many ways in this era of "live from the battlefront." And there is no easy answer.

The Bush Administration Might Have Some Explaining to Do

APRIL 9, 2003

Three weeks into the invasion, the expeditionary force has scored many successes, but one of the biggest has so far eluded it.

Establishing the presence of weapons of mass destruction was the underlying premise for this preemptive war of self-defense. In his State of the Union message last January, President Bush stated as a fact that Saddam Hussein has gone to elaborate lengths, spent enormous sums, and taken great risks to build and keep weapons of mass destruction. In his March 17 statement, setting a forty-eight-hour deadline, he stated again as a fact that Saddam Hussein still has chemical and biological weapons and is increasing his abilities to make more. In planning the invasion, the military went to great lengths to try to find and identify caches of banned weapons as fast as possible. Mobile laboratories and teams of experts were deployed. Division commanders were sensitized to watch out for suspicious substances. There has not been great progress.

The marines have been digging up a school yard some fifty miles southeast of Baghdad on a tip from a war prisoner. Vials of white powder found near the town of Latifiyah turned out to be permitted explosives. The most promising discovery so far, by a patrol of the 101st Airborne, was fourteen drums and barrels that initial tests indicated might contain banned nerve agents or possibly a pesticide. A more definite judgment after mobile laboratory tests is being awaited. If Saddam Hussein's forces do have chemical or biological weapons, it's surprising that they have not yet been used. Assuming, that is, that Saddam can still get his orders obeyed. The bulky protective suits carried by the

American military indicate that the American command had every expectation of having to face unconventional weapons.

One can imagine that President Bush and his staff are sweating this one out. If the war ends without the discovery of any significant stockpile of banned weapons, there'll be some deep embarrassment. The government will have a lot of explaining to do about why it disrupted the United Nations inspection process and split the Western alliance to launch this destructive war.

The Destruction of Ancient Iraqi Artifacts

APRIL 16, 2003

They made exquisite plans to protect Iraq's oil fields, but not Iraq's history. And so for two days last week, with American soldiers standing by and manning checkpoints, the national museums of Baghdad were sacked in a frenzy of looting. Stolen or destroyed were some 170,000 artifacts going back to Nineveh, Babylon, and Ur. Ur, by happenstance, was where Iraqi parties met yesterday to start Iraq down the road to democracy.

Striking was the way American officials reacted when asked how they had let this disaster happen. "As much as anything else, a matter of priority," said General Richard Myers, the chairman of the Joint Chiefs of Staff. "In a transition, there is untidiness," said Defense Secretary Donald Rumsfeld.

Iraqi archaeologist Abdul Ridha Muhammad, who himself had worked on some of Iraq's ten thousand excavation sites, told the *New York Times* that at the height of the looting, he had gotten marines in an Abrams tank to fire over the heads of the looters. That drove some of them away, but then the tank left and the looters returned. "We didn't allow it to happen. It happened," says Secretary Rumsfeld. Since then, American marines have joined Iraqi police in joint patrols, and several looters were reported arrested. But seven thousand years of history, told in such things as stone carvings and a golden harp of the Sumerian era, are gone. "A wound inflicted on all humankind," says United Nations secretary-general Kofi Annan.

President Bush says that our victory in Iraq is certain, but is not complete. He's referring not to the sacking of Baghdad's museums, but to pockets of resistance elsewhere. When, in the future, America is remembered for the liberation of Iraq, it will also be remembered for how it exerted military mastery over Baghdad and then let the country's past civilization go down the drain.

Unexpected Mobilization of Shiite Muslims in Iraq

APRIL 27, 2003

Jacki Lyden, host: When Islam was still in its infancy in the seventh century, a dispute over who would succeed Muhammad as the faith's spiritual leader touched off a split that endures to the present day. Followers of Muhammad's son-in-law, Ali, felt he and his descendants were the rightful heirs of Islam. Known as Shia Ali, "followers of Ali," they were eventually called Shiites. But a group whose name, Sunni, meant "orthodox" or "traditional" had more followers. They did not recognize the heirs of Ali as having any automatic rights and preferred to elect a leader.

Thus was born a rift that saw the assassination of Ali and a grandson of Muhammad's, and centuries of friction between Sunni and Shiite Muslims. Sunni Muslims in the region gained dominance during the four hundred years of the Ottoman Empire, and stepped into leadership roles in Iraq after independence in 1932. As NPR's senior news analyst Daniel Schorr notes, after decades of repression, the depth of feeling among Shiites came as a surprise to Americans in Iraq.

The Pentagon planners had planned for a lot of contingencies in the Iraq invasion. What they didn't anticipate was the hundreds of thousands of chanting, self-flagellating Shiite Muslims who marched to the holy city of Karbala carrying as many anti-American as anti–Saddam Hussein placards. Karbala was where the prophet Imam Hussein, the grandson of Muhammad, was killed and decapitated in battle in the year 680, his martyrdom becoming the symbol of the branch of Islam called Shia.

This was not the first time the American government had reason to study up on Shia. Vividly remembered is the uprising in Iran in 1979, led by Ayatollah Khomeini, which toppled the shah and seized the American embassy with its staff for 444 days. The Shiites are 60 percent of Iraq's population. As in Iran, the mullahs who lead this fundamentalist multitude seem ready to reach for power. They denounce the American occupation. They demand that administration of Iraq be turned over to a national and independent government. There is talk among the mullahs of establishing an Islamic republic, based on the Koran, like the one in Iran.

The Bush administration has warned Iran to keep its hands off Iraq. According to the *New York Times,* the administration is promoting an Islamic democracy, which may be a little hard to define, except that it is less authoritarian than an Islamic republic.

To that end, special forces and intelligence agents are working at the community level, trying to identify moderates and secular figures. This is a delicate operation, if the impression is not to be given of America trying to install handpicked officials.

Lies and Deception in Journalism

MAY 11, 2003

"I lied to the people who were my coworkers and cared about me, I lied to my family, I lied to my editors, I lied to all of the readers, and I lied to the people I was writing about."

That was Stephen Glass in an interview for CBS News' *60 Minutes,* telling how he'd fed lies for years as a writer for the *New Republic* until he was fired in 1998. He invented characters like a teenage computer hacker, and in a freelance piece for *George* magazine, Glass falsely alleged that lawyer Vernon Jordan behaved lecherously with young women—all kinds of lies. And now, writing a book about it, he's cashing in on his lies one more time.

As full disclosure, if that's needed, I have a bias against journalists who lie. In some sixty years in journalism, I've always thought of the reporter as a guardian of reality. Lies come in all sizes and shapes. There was the famous episode of the *New Yorker*'s Janet Malcolm, who in an article about a psychoanalyst in 1981 put words in his mouth that he did not say and then waved off criticism by saying that "every journalist is a confidence man." And there was a 1981 episode of the talented *Washington Post* reporter Janet Cook, who won a Pulitzer Prize for a series of articles on a ghetto child hooked on drugs, a child that she had invented. And now there's Jayson Blair, recently forced out of the *New York Times* for a story about the family of a soldier missing in Iraq, a story apparently borrowed from another newspaper, the *San Antonio Express-News*.

Misleading on television is a more complicated matter because the medium lends itself so readily to deception, such as promotion videos for health products by Walter Cronkite, Morley Safer, and Aaron Brown, made to look like news reports, and to outright falsehood, like the unlabeled reenactment on ABC of an espionage meeting between American diplomat Felix Bloch and his Soviet handler in 1989.

Indeed, the word "reality" has a special meaning on television, as in reality-type *Survivor* episodes on distant islands. I don't know about you, but when I read about Stephen Glass, who lied about everything and now seeks to peddle a book rewarding himself for having done so, I wince.

The Occupation of Iraq

MAY 12, 2003

Having enjoyed the fruits of victory in Iraq, the Bush administration is learning the hard way about the burdens of occupation. The administration has clearly botched the first month of the postwar era. It acted as though endless gas lines and looted hospitals and museums were part of the untidiness of war. Without clear authority or adequate military power in an atmosphere of pervasive fear, General Jay Garner's staff of eight hundred functioned from inside a walled palace. It didn't have much contact with people suffering from unbelievable privation and rapidly coming to blame their liberators.

Many of Saddam Hussein's Baath Party minions continued in their old jobs for lack of more trustworthy Iraqis. The Garner team has now been recalled, including Ambassador Barbara Bodine, one of the most fluent Arabic speakers of the lot. And today, phase two started. Paul Bremer, a Reagan counterterrorism expert, is being given a mission and the authority to try to avert a looming breakdown in civil order that would make a mockery of liberation.

The Bush administration, generally not very high on international

treaties, has advised the United Nations Security Council that it is forming with Britain a unified command called the Authority. The draft
resolution filed last Friday cited The Hague regulations of 1907 and the
Geneva Convention of 1949, which spell out the powers and the obligations of an occupying power after a successful invasion. That means that
Bremer will be able to deploy American and British forces to guard the
streets and pursue the looters. He will also presumably have authority
to dispose of existing and future oil revenues. He will certainly have a
say on when authority should be transferred to an Iraqi body.

Under the pressure of threatening chaos, the United States is being
forced into an unaccustomed role: virtually full responsibility as an occupying power for a country and its 23 million people.

Insufficient Evidence

JUNE 9, 2003

*Melissa Block, host: Today, President Bush again argued the U.S. effort to
find weapons of mass destruction in Iraq will be fruitful.*

*President George W. Bush: Iraq had a weapons program; intelligence
throughout the decade showed they had a weapons program. I am absolutely
convinced with time we'll find out that they did have a weapons program.*

*And, look, the credibility of this country is based upon our strong desire to
make the world more peaceful, and the world is now more peaceful after our
decision; the strong desire to make sure free nations are more secure, and free
nations are now more secure; and the strong desire to spread freedom, and the
Iraqi people are now free and they're learning to have bits of freedom and
the responsibilities that come with freedom. I read a report that somehow,
you know, that there's no al Qaeda presence in Baghdad. I guess the people
who wrote that article forgot about al-Zarqawi's network inside of Baghdad
that ordered the killing of a U.S. citizen named Foley. And history will
show — history, in time, will prove that the United States made the absolute
right decision.*

*Block: Over the weekend, National Security Adviser Condoleezza Rice
and Secretary of State Colin Powell made television appearances to defend
the administration's case. News analyst Daniel Schorr says their efforts attest
to the importance of proving Iraq had illegal weapons.*

America's going to war on false pretenses is not without historic precedent. President McKinley and Congress declared war on Spain in 1898 after an explosion aboard the battleship *Maine* that was probably an accident. President Johnson, in 1964, escalated the war against North Vietnam on the strength of a resolution wrongly charging unprovoked attacks on two American destroyers in the Gulf of Tonkin. That was when the phrase "credibility gap" was born.

President Reagan, in 1983, ordered the invasion of the Caribbean island of Grenada on the dubious ground that American medical students were menaced by a left-wing government. So now Iraq and the question agitating Congress of whether America was in imminent enough danger from weapons of mass destruction to justify a preemptive invasion, and if so, why has so little evidence of that turned up in a country now under American military control?

All that's been found is two trailers suitable for housing biological laboratories, but with no sign that they ever did. Yet the president said in an interview with Polish television on May 29, "We found the weapons of mass destruction, and those who said otherwise were wrong." He has not since then repeated that obvious misstatement.

It has not helped the administration's case that intelligence reports released by British prime minister Tony Blair, who worked closely with the White House, turned out to contain at least one forged document and some material downloaded from the Internet that included an American student's thesis. Former foreign secretary Robin Cook said his government used intelligence to support a conclusion it had already come to, which is that it was going to war.

President Bush's lieutenants, Condoleezza Rice and Secretary Powell, made the tour of TV talk shows yesterday with emphatic assurances that their administration had relied on intelligence and not prejudged the issue of war with Iraq. On such questions hangs that fragile thing called "credibility," which the administration will need for future confrontations.

The CIA and the White House

JUNE 15, 2003

What did the president know and when did he know it?

Thirty years ago, Republican Howard Baker was raising that question in the Senate Watergate Committee, hoping to shield President Nixon from responsibility for the break-in and wiretapping of Democratic headquarters. It turned out that Nixon knew plenty, more than Baker had bargained for. The question arises again because of a bitter dispute in part between the CIA and the White House about how President Bush came to make a representation about an Iraqi nuclear program that was known in the intelligence community to be based on forged documents.

In the State of the Union address on January 28, the president spoke of an advanced Iraqi nuclear weapons program in the nineties, and he added, "The British government has learned that Saddam Hussein recently sought significant quantities of uranium from Africa." If true, that would have been the first solid indication of a current Iraqi nuclear weapons program, but it apparently was not true.

Eleven months earlier, according to the *New York Times,* the CIA, at the behest of Vice President Dick Cheney, had sent to Niger a knowledgeable retired ambassador whose name is being withheld. He was told to investigate reports that Iraq was trying to buy uranium from Niger. The diplomat brought back word that the government of Niger denied any such dealings with Iraq and that the documents on which the allegation was based were patent forgeries.

How under the circumstances the president could give credence to the uranium canard in a speech almost a year later is hard to imagine. National Security Adviser Condoleezza Rice said, "It had not been realized in the White House that the report was not credible until after the president had spoken." That would suggest that the CIA had kept the White House in ignorance, which CIA officials deny.

In any event, there was no further reference to an African uranium deal when Secretary of State Colin Powell gave his extensive briefing to the United Nations Security Council on February 5. Since then, the International Atomic Energy Agency has conducted its own investigation and reported to the Security Council that the uranium documents were "not authentic," in a word, fakes. By whom and for what purpose?

It is hard to believe that a president would lie to the American people about a nuclear threat in order to promote a war. And so the question remains: When did the president know and how did he deal with the information?

Sandra Day O'Connor

JUNE 25, 2003

Almost presciently, the conservative weekly *National Review* put Justice Sandra Day O'Connor on its cover last weekend with the caption: "How Justice O'Connor Has Ruled the Court." The article painted her as moderate on abortion rights and several other issues. On Monday she did it again big-time, emerging as the leader of a 5–4 majority that endorsed a sort of "don't ask, don't tell" policy on affirmative action. In essence, it is okay for a university to seek diversity but not to set up a formal scoring system for admission.

The most strident dissent came from Clarence Thomas, himself an affirmative action graduate of Yale Law School. He appeared to reflect the views of some conservative blacks that students who get a leg up from affirmative action are automatically stigmatized as losers: "the cruel farce of racial discrimination," he called it.

Justice O'Connor's centrist position went back to the opinion of the late Justice Lewis Powell in the 1978 *Bakke* case. He supported affirmative action, not to remedy earlier discrimination, but to achieve diversity, "a compelling state interest," he called it.

That is where most Americans seem to be on affirmative action. President Bush, whose administration has submitted briefs opposing the University of Michigan affirmative action programs, yesterday applauded the Court's decision as a "careful balance between diversity and equal treatment." A recent poll by the Pew Research Center showed Americans two to one in approving programs designed to increase the number of minority students, although three to one against giving them preferential treatment. My friend the late Harry Blackmun wrote in the *Bakke* case, "In order to get beyond racism, we must first take account of race. There is no other way."

By taking a position anathema to many conservatives, Justice O'Connor may have hurt her chances of succeeding William Rehnquist as chief justice. But she is widely regarded as having struck a blow for common sense.

Howard Dean's Fund-raising Abilities

JULY 6, 2003

Who first said "Money talks," I do not know. But it was a veteran California politico, Jesse Unruh, who said, "Money is the mother's milk of politics." Among Democrats, money raising has become a sort of invisible preprimary primary. Money is raised not only for what it buys but because it is a key test of a candidate's viability. And history teaches that, more often than not, the candidate who has amassed the most hard money before the primaries ends up winning the nomination. So it was no small matter when in the first quarter of the year North Carolina senator John Edwards reported $7.4 million in contributions, edging out Massachusetts senator John Kerry with $7 million. That made Edwards instantly a serious contender to many pundits.

Official tallies for the second quarter are due from the Federal Election Commission in mid-July. But the unofficial count shows Senator Kerry still in second place with $6 million and Senator Edwards in third place with $5 million–plus. And in first place, with $7.5 million—are you ready for this?—the former governor of Vermont, Howard Dean, who is making his first bid for national office. He still runs third in cumulative totals for the two quarters, but few professionals any longer are asking "Howard who?"

What accounts for this amazing showing by a maverick who has taken some maverick positions: strong opposition to the Iraq war, strong support for gay partnership, strong opposition to the Bush tax cut, his own assessment that only he represents the Democratic wing of the Democratic Party, and his intensive use of the Internet to raise money? In politics, money talks, all right. But now the experts are trying to figure out what it says.

Mounting Questions About Manipulated Intelligence

JULY 7, 2003

Former foreign secretary Robin Cook, who resigned from the British cabinet over the Iraq war, told the House of Commons on June 17, "We used intelligence as the basis on which to justify a policy on which we had already settled." Evidence is mounting that something of that sort happened in the Bush White House. A retired diplomat, Joseph Wilson, has come forward to say that the CIA sent him to Niger in February 2002 to investigate a reported uranium deal with Iraq, but ignored his finding that the story was a hoax.

In his State of the Union address eleven months later, the president was still talking of an African uranium deal and ignoring the evidence to the contrary. On television yesterday, Chairman John Warner and ranking Democrat Carl Levin of the Senate Armed Services Committee clashed over whether the Wilson revelation justified an investigation of whether intelligence was manipulated to make the case for invading Iraq.

Recently released documents indicate that the invasion of Iraq was long in the planning. A 1992 defense policy guidance paper drafted by Paul Wolfowitz, undersecretary of defense for policy under President Bush Sr., called for a preemptive strike against Iraq. The stated reason: to avert the spread of destructive weapons and to ensure "access to vital raw materials, primarily Persian Gulf oil." Nothing about an imminent threat from an Iraq that was defeated and disarmed in the Gulf War only a year earlier.

September 11 provided momentum for an attack on Iraq, although no connection between the terrorist acts and the Saddam Hussein government has ever been convincingly established. According to Bob Woodward's book *Bush at War,* at a meeting of the war cabinet four days after 9/11, Wolfowitz pushed for an assault on Iraq rather than Afghanistan because it would be easier; but it has not been as easy as Wolfowitz hoped. And now the continuing and escalating guerrilla war against American troops has raised the question of whether the Bush administration took America into the war under false pretenses with selective use of ambiguous intelligence.

The question of whether the president got congressional approval for a war against Iraq on false pretenses comes at a delicate time. The White House may soon be asking to send troops to Liberia, and that is bound to reopen for Congress the whole issue of the administration's credibility.

Where the Buck Stops (and Where It Doesn't)

JULY 14, 2003

How does a president act when things go wrong or responsibility has to be assigned? Like President Reagan, who used a passive "Mistakes were made" to explain the Iran-Contra affair, or like the few presidents I can remember in my lifetime who refused to shift responsibility?

In 1960, President Eisenhower was advised by several—including his own brother, Milton—to blame the CIA for the U-2 spy plane shot down over the Soviet Union, its pilot captured. As described in Michael Beschloss's book *Mayday,* the president barked back at his brother that if he blamed a subordinate he would have to fire him and that would be hypocrisy. President Eisenhower took full responsibility for the spy plane, and refused to apologize for it, with the result that Soviet leader Nikita Khrushchev stormed out of the Paris summit.

President Truman had that famous painted glass sign on his desk, "The buck stops here." And in his farewell address in January 1953, Mr. Truman said, "The president, whoever he is, has to decide. He can't pass the buck to anybody."

In 1961, President Kennedy was advised by Vice President Johnson, among others, to blame the CIA for the debacle of the Cuban Bay of Pigs invasion. According to then–White House staffer Arthur Schlesinger, Kennedy had the White House issue a statement saying that as president, he bore sole responsibility and he opposed any attempt to shift that responsibility. That was also the time Mr. Kennedy said, "Victory has a hundred fathers and defeat is an orphan."

So now President Bush, facing an unexpected firestorm set off by a now-famous sixteen words in his State of the Union address last January: "The British government has learned that Saddam Hussein recently sought significant quantities of uranium from Africa." Mr. Bush, peppered with questions on his African trip, said tersely, "I gave a speech to a nation that was cleared by the intelligence services," and he left it to others to explain more fully. CIA director George Tenet loyally stated, "The CIA approved the president's State of the Union address before it was delivered." It appears that "mistakes were made."

Time to Come Clean

JULY 23, 2003

As the poet Sir Walter Scott wrote, "Oh what a tangled web we weave, / When first we practise to deceive!"

One after another, officials impale themselves on that crowded sword assuming responsibility for those sixteen "radioactive" words in the State of the Union address last January about Iraq and African uranium. First, CIA director George Tenet, who was not consulted on the final draft, accepted responsibility for the process. Next, Alan Foley of the CIA confessed that he had let Bob Joseph, of the National Security Council, talk him into a formulation that attributed the uranium story to the British. Then, although National Security Adviser Condoleezza Rice has said that no one in the White House knew of any CIA objections, her own deputy, Stephen Hadley, has now apologized for letting the words stay in the speech despite a CIA warning. "The process failed," said White House communications director Dan Bartlett.

But the process didn't fail at all; it simply responded to the determination of the president and like-minded officials to orchestrate congressional and public support for an invasion of Iraq. For that purpose, nothing was better than the prospect of a nuclear-armed Iraq. In a speech in Cincinnati in October, the president said that Saddam Hussein was moving ever closer to developing a nuclear weapon. On the advice of the CIA, the dubious African uranium deal was deleted from that speech.

By January, the invasion lobby in the White House clearly perceived the need for stronger medicine. The officials who negotiated the sixteen words for the CIA had every reason to believe they were pursuing the policy of President Bush and Vice President Dick Cheney, who had made some strong speeches of his own. Who could know that the uranium deal would blow up in their faces after retired ambassador Joseph Wilson went to Niger on assignment for the CIA and reported back that there was no Niger-Iraqi deal?

As President Kennedy said in the Cuban Bay of Pigs invasion debacle, "Victory has a hundred fathers and defeat is an orphan." Perhaps in the end it didn't matter. Mr. Bush got his war anyway.

The California Recall Bonanza

SEPTEMBER 15, 2003

The postponement of the California recall election plus votes on matters like school and road funding creates a situation full of exquisite ironies.

How does one explain to a dubious world that this most technologically advanced nation can organize an election system for Afghanistan and Iraq but not for itself?

How does one explain that the richest nation in the world cannot ensure that precincts in underprivileged areas have the same ability as those in affluent suburbs to have their ballots counted?

How does one explain that the people's will expressed directly in ballot initiatives can still not prevail if the courts rule otherwise?

And what is the likelihood that the Supreme Court, which effectively chose a president of the United States in the year 2000, will now effectively decide who is to be the governor of California for the next six months?

Who came out ahead in today's order of the Ninth Circuit Court of Appeals in San Francisco? By all indications, Governor Gray Davis, who believes that time is on his side as he rallies senior Democrats to his side. Former president Bill Clinton, traveling with his Secret Service convoy, which denotes presidential charisma, has been getting some resonance telling cheering crowds that they should not let their state become a laughingstock. But it already is.

Today's court injunction sends the opinion pollsters back to the drawing board. The latest *Los Angeles Times* poll last Friday showed 50 percent ready to vote for the governor's recall, 47 percent against. To succeed him, a plurality of 30 percent favored Lieutenant Governor

Cruz Bustamante, 25 percent favored Arnold Schwarzenegger, and 18 percent were for conservative state senator Tom McClintock.

With the probable postponement of the election, those margins are bound to change. What will not change is the image of disarray that America presents to the world.

A War Without a Rationale

SEPTEMBER 21, 2003

Six months since the invasion of Iraq, this remains a war in search of a rationale.

A massive search and a series of interrogations have yet to produce the weapons of mass destruction that were supposed to put the United States in imminent danger. Now the theory of a Saddam Hussein–9/11 link is being deemphasized. This despite a *Washington Post* poll last month that showed 69 percent of Americans believing it likely that Saddam Hussein had some role in the attacks.

In his May 1 victory speech, President Bush said that the battle of Iraq is one victory in a war on terror that began on September 11, 2001. On NBC last Sunday, Vice President Dick Cheney said Iraq was the geographic base of the terrorists who have had us under assault now for many years, but most especially on 9/11. Then something remarkable happened. Last Tuesday, Defense Secretary Donald Rumsfeld said he had no reason to believe that Saddam Hussein had a hand in the September 11 attacks. And more remarkable, the next day, President Bush said we have no evidence that Saddam Hussein was involved with September 11. What occasioned the public put-down of the vice president by the president can only be imagined.

Then there was the bizarre new justification for the war offered by Secretary of State Colin Powell. In a visit to the Kurdish region in northern Iraq, Powell said that a 1988 poison gas attack that killed some five thousand Kurds was justification enough for bringing down the Saddam Hussein regime. What makes Powell's statement so bizarre was that at the time of the poison gas attack, he was President Reagan's national security adviser, and in those days the American administration was backing Iraq in its war with Iran. And while the Reagan administration condemned the use of chemical weapons as a grave violation of international law, no sanctions were imposed on the Bagh-dad regime. "The world should have acted sooner," said Powell to Kurdish families at a mass grave site. As a justification for the invasion of Iraq fifteen years later, that is almost embarrassing.

On Not Naming Sources

OCTOBER 5, 2003

As a CBS correspondent in 1976, I obtained a draft of a report of the House Intelligence Committee on CIA errors and misdeeds. I quoted from the report on the air and even showed a copy on television. Then the House, under pressure from the CIA and the Ford administration, voted to suppress the report and put all the printed copies under lock and key. That left me with what might be called the only copy in the Free World. I consented to let the *Village Voice* weekly in New York print the entire text of the report. The House Ethics Committee was commissioned to find out who had given me the report. And when several months of interviews and investigation failed to turn up the leaker, the committee subpoenaed me to appear in open session. I testified that I could not betray a news source, and committee chairman John Flynt of Georgia three times warned me that refusing to reply could subject me to being cited for contempt of Congress, carrying a jail sentence and a fine. In the end, the committee voted 6–5 to denounce me but not to cite me for contempt. You can imagine that I was relieved.

Now the Justice Department wants to know who told Bob Novak that the wife of Joseph Wilson is an undercover CIA officer. Wilson is the former ambassador who went to Niger for the CIA to investigate reports that Iraq had tried to acquire uranium for a nuclear bomb. To the irritation of the White House, he came back with word that the report was malarkey. To the greater irritation of the White House, Wilson went public with an article in the *New York Times* headlined: "What I Didn't Find in Africa."

No one has yet stepped forward to admit being the leaker. At some point Novak, as happened to me, may be called under subpoena and asked to name his source. Can they do that? Well, a 1982 statute makes it a felony for a government official to identify an undercover officer. That applies to officials, not journalists. But if an official committed a crime, then Novak was a witness to that crime. And he could be asked under subpoena to name his source on penalty of a citation for contempt or obstruction of justice. I once discussed that possibility with the late William Colby, the former CIA director, and we agreed that we hoped that this untested weapon against the press would never be tested.

The Thinning Line Between Show Business and Politics

OCTOBER 12, 2003

The nexus between show business and politics took a leap forward with Ronald Reagan. Asked by biographer Lou Cannon what had been his greatest movie role, Reagan responded, "President. That was the role of a lifetime."

Now the link between real life and celluloid life moves a step further with Governor-elect Arnold Schwarzenegger, who inaugurated his campaign on *The Tonight Show with Jay Leno* and ended it on *Entertainment Tonight*.

Announcing his candidacy on television, even while an aide was preparing to hand out a news release announcing his decision not to run, was what the French call a coup de théâtre, a theatrical masterstroke. At one of the final rallies before the election, Schwarzenegger had a wrecking ball dropped on an old car. "That," he said, "was to show you exactly what we're going to do with the car tax." Nothing like a good visual to make your point.

What will it be like being governor? Schwarzenegger said he had explained to one of his four children concerned about not seeing much of their father, "It's like being on a movie location, that sometimes I'm home and sometimes I'm not home." All right, as long as he understands the difference between acting and governing, between the statehouse and a movie set.

So far, he has talked of California's crushing debt burden as something that can be fixed without a tax increase by just digging through the books and finding where the waste is. John Burton, the Democratic president pro tem of the state senate, says he will try to educate the governor-elect to some harsh realities. "He'll learn that this isn't make-believe," Burton says. "They're firing real bullets." Schwarzenegger took Burton's call while working out on his exercise bicycle. He said he promised to see Burton, one of the most senior Democrats, as many times as possible.

One way the new governor plans to go about easing the burden of debt on California is to capitalize on his relationship with President Bush, quote, "working with him and asking him for a lot of favors." If Schwarzenegger expects a lot of aid from a federal government itself up to its armpits in debt, I suspect that pretty soon he'll get a dose of reality to rouse him from his dreams of iron-pumping power.

"The Leak"

NOVEMBER 2, 2003

It is now commonly referred to in Washington as "the leak."

That is to say the disclosure to columnist Robert Novak, and perhaps other journalists, of the sensitive fact that Valerie Plame was an undercover CIA operative. It appears on the surface that someone in the Bush administration had chosen this way to retaliate against her husband, former ambassador Joseph Wilson. He incurred the wrath of the White House by throwing cold water on the idea, backed by forged documents, that Saddam Hussein in pursuit of a nuclear weapon had tried to buy uranium in the African country of Niger.

Who was responsible for the lethal leak of highly classified information about the identity of an undercover officer is something that the Justice Department says it is investigating. But don't hold your breath waiting for the answer. Administrations have rarely been very good about investigating themselves. And history suggests that a congressional investigation with the power of subpoena would be a more promising route to take. I can recall several White House self-investigations that I have covered. There was, first of all, Watergate. Not many remember that President Nixon first designated his counsel, John Dean, to find out who had ordered the break-in into Democratic headquarters. Dean never did write that report. Instead, he jumped ship and negotiated a plea bargain with the prosecutor.

The first real investigation was conducted by a special Senate committee headed by Sam Ervin of North Carolina. That led to a House impeachment investigation and that forced Nixon to resign. President Ford named a commission headed by Vice President Nelson Rockefeller to investigate CIA surveillance of antiwar dissidents and other misdeeds by the agency. The tougher investigations that led to the disclosure of CIA assassination plots against Fidel Castro and others were conducted by Senate and House special committees.

President Reagan named former senator John Tower as head of a panel investigating what became known as the Iran-Contra scandal, that is, the illegal transfer of missiles to Iran in return for money to finance the illegal Contra insurgency in Nicaragua. There followed a lengthy investigation by a joint congressional committee best remembered as the launching platform for White House staffer Oliver North. North, along with his superior, Admiral John Poindexter, was eventually convicted of perjury; the convictions, however, were overturned on a technicality.

Will there be a congressional investigation of "the leak"? Less likely than the others because of the Republican majorities in both chambers of Congress. But if there is one, maybe it could recycle Senator Howard Baker's famous question in the Watergate investigation: "What did the president know and when did he know it?"

Jessica Lynch and the Military-Media Complex

NOVEMBER 10, 2003

The marketing of young Jessica Lynch in book, docudrama, and television interview is a parable for the marketing of the Iraq war.

It started with the extravagantly hyped Pentagon account of the Rambo-like soldier that she herself disowned. In fact, she was not shot, but injured when her vehicle broke down. She was captured without firing a shot, because her gun jammed. Then the rescue from an Iraqi hospital was caught on a conveniently available military tape. Earlier claims to the contrary notwithstanding, the raid encountered virtually no resistance.

Once back in this country, PFC Lynch became a hot-ticket item for the media. Every news executive sought to become embedded in her adventure. It seemed natural, given all the hype, that the inventive *New York Times* man Jayson Blair would write of visiting the Lynch family in their home overlooking a nonexistent tobacco field. It would seem natural, too, that PFC Lynch's own story should be written by that other inventive former *Times* man Rick Bragg. Anointing the young soldier as an icon of heroism is an enterprise in which military and media have a shared interest.

Early on, CBS made a stab at getting the big get, the exclusive first interview, offering a package deal that included a book and a television show. No dice, and CBS retired from the competition. Over the next six months, NBC took a different route, coming up with a docudrama aired last night, based on the account of Muhammad al-Rehaief, the lawyer who led the rescuers to the injured soldier's hospital room. Al-Rehaief, welcomed to America, also has a book, of course. Jessica Lynch will be all over the media in coming weeks, interviewed by Diane Sawyer on ABC, Katie Couric on NBC, and David Letterman on CBS, and much, much more, as they say in the television business.

In her ABC interview, PFC Lynch says the military used her capture and rescue to sway public support for the Iraq war. With mounting casualties in Iraq and mounting doubts about the war, the creation of a heroic icon could not have come at a better time for the military. PFC Lynch is making a great contribution to the military-media complex.

How Saddam's Trial Could Help Mend Fences

DECEMBER 15, 2003

Hailing the end of a dark and painful era in Iraq, President Bush said that Saddam Hussein would face the justice he denied to millions. How that justice is to be carried out presents the Bush administration with a dilemma and an opportunity.

The dilemma arises because of confusion and disagreement about who should try the captured dictator. Last week the American-appointed Iraqi Governing Council issued regulations providing for the naming of a five-member tribunal empowered to try war crimes and crimes against humanity. This was done with American encouragement, but the United Nations has not recognized the Governing Council as a government and therefore questions its ability to create a tribunal. There are associated disputes over whether the trial would be held in Iraq, vulnerable to insurgent attack, or whether it could impose a death penalty, banned in most countries.

In what must have been a slip of the tongue, Defense Secretary Donald

Rumsfeld said on CBS's *60 Minutes* last night that Saddam Hussein would be treated according to the Geneva Conventions and given the protection of a prisoner of war. Well, if that is so, then Saddam's rights have already been violated by the circulation of humiliating pictures of him.

Today, leading members of the Governing Council altered their position on the tribunal and said there should be some form of international involvement in the judicial process. The president, at a news conference, also talked of developing a system to try Saddam that will stand international scrutiny. This presents the Bush administration with an opportunity to start patching up relations with countries like France, Germany, and Russia, who were offended by being barred from bidding on reconstruction contracts in Iraq.

Human rights organizations point to the so-called hybrid courts created under UN auspices for countries like Sierra Leone and Cambodia, in which international judges sit side by side with indigenous judges. Iraqi judges sitting side by side with, say, an American, a French, and a German judge would be a promising start in restoring a measure of American cooperation with its onetime friends and allies.

The State of Peace on Earth in 2003

DECEMBER 31, 2003

In these times, "Happy New Year" sounds more like a hope than a forecast. The revels in Times Square go on under the watchful eye of police snipers on rooftops. The government wants more armed marshals on airplanes as it considers the color code of the day. We are told to worry about everything from mad cows to mad diet supplements. In Iraq, casualties have mounted into the hundreds from the insurgency. In Iran, the earthquake on Friday leaves deaths in the many thousands.

An encouraging note is struck in a not very encouraging year by the American earthquake relief effort, what an Iranian professor calls earthquake diplomacy. The axis of evil is laid aside as the Bush administration rushes in the first American planes to land in Iran since the ill-fated hostage rescue effort in 1980. Where once American flags were burned in demonstrations against the Great Satan, an American flag now flies over the relief team's headquarters tent. Iranian relief workers ask to have their pictures taken with the Americans. This is an application of what Harvard dean Joseph Nye would call "soft power," using America's vast peaceful resources to gain influence around the world.

Cautious after all these years of hostility, President Mohammad Khatami tells a news conference that American help is welcome but does not in itself denote better relations. That, he says, requires a change in tone and behavior. An equally cautious State Department finds it encouraging that Iran is accepting American aid, but this does not in itself establish a new relationship. A Shiite cleric, Sheikh Ahmed Faiz, says all Iranians appreciate what America is doing.

There are still questions about Iran's nuclear program, and one earthquake doesn't make a spring. But in Washington, one of those senior officials without a name tells the Reuters news agency that President Bush is considering opening a new dialogue with Iran. The humanitarian invasion of earthquake-stricken Iran is as good a reason as any to say "Happy New Year."

2004

Swift Boats and Tsunamis

A New Humility

JANUARY 19, 2004

It is with a certain air of controlled desperation that the Bush administration is asking for a bailout in Iraq from the United Nations that it has
long scorned.

Having invaded Iraq without a UN mandate last March, the administration didn't think to mention any role for the world organization
when it reached an agreement with the American-created Governing
Council in November for a transfer of sovereignty less than six months
from now.

The idea was that assemblies of notables, something like caucuses,
would select a parliament with a safe number of delegates friendly to
America. The parliament would, in turn, elect an interim government
to which power would be handed over with great ceremony on June 30.
But, incomprehensibly, the plan did not reckon with the feelings of the
long-persecuted Shiites forming 60 percent of the population. They have
bitter memories of having been twice summoned to rebellion by the
Nixon and by the first Bush administrations and twice left to the mercy
of Saddam Hussein when the chips were down.

Eight days ago, apparently to the surprise of administrator Paul
Bremer, the election plan was rejected by Grand Ayatollah Ali al-
Sistani, the charismatic leader of the Shiites. He demanded popular
elections, which would give his people a dominant voice, and they turned
out in the streets by the tens of thousands to support him.

Now Ambassador Bremer, having felt the pulse of the White House, has gone figuratively hat in hand to ask Secretary-General Kofi Annan to broker some kind of compromise. That, presumably, would include a role for the UN in the governing process that the administration has long refused.

The Bush administration has a lot at stake. Disruption of the time-table for the creation of an Iraqi government could delay the rotation of American troops and could conceivably become an issue in the American election campaign. And so the administration approaches the UN with something it hasn't displayed for a long time: humility.

What President Bush Chose Not to Say in Last Night's State of the Union Address

JANUARY 21, 2004

President Bush's speech was effectively the kickoff for his reelection campaign couched in the lofty, above-politics language of a constitution-ally mandated message to Congress. The word "Democrat" never crossed his lips last night. The targets for his criticism were "some" and "those who."

He spoke of the "dangerous illusion" that terrorists are not plotting against us without saying who suffers under such an illusion. He admon-ished "some people" who question whether America is in a war. What people? Discussing weapons of mass destruction, a particularly delicate matter for the president, he cited the report of inspector David Kay as having "identified dozens of weapons of mass destruction–related pro-gram activities." "Program activities" can be anything down to calcu-lations on paper. Mr. Bush did not say that last October's report of Kay's 1,200-person team found no actual weapons and little evidence of a nuclear program.

Without mentioning countries like France, Germany, and Russia that have opposed the war, the president gave them the back of his hand by saying, "America will never seek a permission slip to defend the secu-rity of our country."

Educators and Democrats who have criticized the testing provision and the underfunding of the No Child Left Behind education act became an unspecified "some who want to undermine the act."

But possibly the trickiest passage of the speech was the president's

bow to the Christian right on opposition to gay marriage. Without saying the word "gay," he said that "if judges insist on forcing their arbitrary
will upon the people, the only alternative left to the people would be the
constitutional process": he made no specific reference to a constitutional
amendment. And as though to soften the impact of his statement, he
went on to say that "each individual has dignity and value in God's
sight."

I detected only one ad-lib in a speech many weeks in the making. The
closing words in the text were "God bless America." He said, "May God
continue to bless America." I'm not sure what to make of that.

The U.S.-Led War in Iraq May Have Brought About What It Was Intended to Thwart

FEBRUARY 11, 2004

In his State of the Union address, President Bush cited the invasion of
Iraq as part of the offensive against terror. In his NBC interview last
Sunday, the president said his decision to go to war was made in the
context of the war against terror. But there are growing indications that
Mr. Bush may have created some self-fulfilling prophecy with occupied
Iraq serving, like Soviet-occupied Afghanistan, as a magnet for holy
warriors and suicide bombers from all over the region.

The most concrete evidence that terrorists in Iraq are reaching out to
al Qaeda is a seventeen-page document on a computer disk captured by
American forces who intercepted a courier. It was written by Abu
Musab al-Zarqawi, a thirty-seven-year-old Jordanian terrorist operat-
ing from northern Iraq. He is implicated in more than a score of
bombings, including the attack on United Nations headquarters in
Baghdad last August and the killing of an important Shiite leader.
According to the *New York Times,* the electronic document asks senior
leaders of al Qaeda for help in waging war against the Shiites in the next
six months. This appears to be part of a plan, along with attacks on the
Americans, to foment civil war that would make Iraq ungovernable.
There is little sign of any prewar connection between al-Zarqawi and
the Osama bin Laden leadership.

Jessica Stern, a Harvard scholar, has written that America has taken
a country that was not a terrorist threat and turned it into one. She said

that the United States had created a weak state unable to control its borders, a breeding ground for terrorism. Last July, General Ricardo Sanchez, the U.S. commander in Iraq, was one of the first to warn that Iraq was in danger of becoming a terrorist magnet for young jihadis swarming to take on the occupier. If weapons of mass destruction was the first wrong reason for fighting the war, then rooting out terrorism may be the second.

In Memory of Daniel Pearl

FEBRUARY 22, 2004

Liane Hansen, host: For more than four decades after World War II, American foreign policy was defined by the cold war. Simple slogans — "East-West," "evil empire," "Free World" — symbolized the clash of cultures and ideologies. Last week, NPR senior news analyst Daniel Schorr visited UCLA to deliver the Daniel Pearl Memorial Address in honor of the Wall Street Journal *correspondent murdered two years ago in a new kind of war, a war without clear front lines. This is an excerpt from Dan Schorr's speech.*

When the cold war ended, America was left facing a very different kind of war. That war did not begin on September 11, 2001, but at least a quarter century earlier, when young Khomeini zealots in Iran seized the American embassy and its staff. Then, a series of bombings directed against the U.S. Marines in Beirut, Lebanon; an air force installation in Saudi Arabia; a U.S. destroyer off Yemen; against American embassies in Africa; and, climactically, against the World Trade Center in New York and the Pentagon. The signature on most of these terrorist acts was suicide. Willingness to die confers great power.

I remember asking Israeli prime minister Yitzhak Rabin on his last visit to Washington whether he had an answer to suicide bombing. He shook his head and said, "There is no answer to suicide bombing."

America was not prepared for this kind of war that lurks in the shadows. When Hezbollah terrorists abducted several Americans in Lebanon, President Reagan responded by illegally selling missiles to Iran in return for the release of two American hostages, who were promptly replaced by the abduction of two more Americans.

Today, America fights a war against what are called "enemy

combatants," a loose term that permits the compromising of civil liberties. It is hard to apply American military power when one doesn't know where to apply it. A generally successful operation in Afghanistan rooted out al Qaeda training camps. Looking for somewhere else to apply force of arms, the Bush administration chose Iraq on the questionable assumption that Saddam Hussein was cooperating with the al Qaeda terrorists.

Iraq became not a unifying principle but a disorganizing principle. Fought without United Nations support or any major European support, it has left a system of alliances and collective security built over half a century in tatters. It was ironic when the United States, which has scorned the United Nations, sought the UN's aid in extricating itself from Iraq by helping to organize the transfer of power to the Iraqis.

America has yet to find a unifying principle for this age of terror. It will have to repair alliances and relations with the UN. It will have to overcome the widespread feeling that we are all involved in some clash of civilizations. America will have to find itself before it can lead this new kind of war against this new kind of enemy.

The Same-Sex Marriage Ban

FEBRUARY 25, 2004

The constitutional amendment has generally been used to expand rather than to contract individual rights, with the significant exception of Prohibition, which was repealed after fourteen years of widespread violation. Some proposed amendments with strong backing have failed, like a flag burning ban, school prayer, and equal rights for women.

Presidents can afford to play politics with proposed amendments because they play no constitutional role in a process that is a matter between Congress and the states. And so when President Bush found himself in trouble with his right-wing base over matters like immigration and Medicare, he decided to support a constitutional ban on gay marriage that religious groups have been demanding for months. But it was without the careful gearing-up that precedes the rollout of a measure that he's intent on getting passed.

Popular demand for such an amendment seems less than overwhelming. A poll taken by the University of Pennsylvania's Annenberg Center

shows 64 percent opposed to same-sex marriage, but only 41 percent in
favor of changing the Constitution, which is why Republicans in Congress reacted with studied caution. Senate leader Bill Frist said,
"Amending the Constitution is a huge issue," and House Republican
leader Tom DeLay said, "We're not going to take a knee-jerk reaction
to this."

It's hard to know how the issue will play in the election campaign.
Senator John Kerry has carefully voiced opposition to gay marriage, but
has also opposed amending the Constitution. But he's not gone as far as
noncandidates like Senator Edward Kennedy, who said that "President
Bush will go down in history as the first president to try to write bias
back into the Constitution."

If the president wanted to make a gesture to the religious right, he
has undoubtedly succeeded. At what political cost remains to be seen.

John Kerry's Victories

MARCH 3, 2004

Welcome to day one of the eight-month campaign for the presidency.

Not in forty years of observing elections have I seen a nonincumbent
contestant chosen so early and on such unspecific grounds. Daniel
Boorstin, the late historian, used to talk about people well known for
their well-knownness.

Senator John Kerry appears to have won basically for his winnabil-
ity, as voters made clear to exit pollers. A third of the voters cited the
ability to beat President Bush as the most important of six qualities they
were asked to choose from. About eight in ten voters said they would
be satisfied with Kerry as the nominee. In Ohio and Georgia, 71 and 68
percent, respectively, named Kerry as the candidate who could beat the
incumbent. And although Senator John Edwards made jobs and trade
a centerpiece of the final stage of his campaign, people worried about
the economy voted two to one for Kerry.

This choice, based more on perceived electability than specific issues,
was happening on a day when more than 270 Shiites were being killed
in Iraq, when Haiti was plunging toward anarchy, when another corporate CEO was being indicted for fraud, and when Alan Greenspan
said interest rates are too low. All this suggests that yesterday's holiday

from issues, as voters concentrated on style over substance, is not likely
to last very long as the attack ads begin to sprout on television.

Eight months is a long time in an unstable world, plenty of time for
unpremeditated events that will impinge on the campaign, testing both
incumbent and challenger. Super Tuesday and President Bush's con-
gratulatory phone call to Kerry may be remembered as the good old
days when appearances were what mattered.

The Terrorist Bombings

MARCH 15, 2004

It may not be too great an oversimplification to say that the al Qaeda
terrorists won the Spanish election and President Bush lost it.

As Madrileños by the million vented their anguish in anger over last
Thursday's multiple-railway bombing, the party of President Bush's
great and good friend, Prime Minister José Maria Aznar, went down
to a crushing upset defeat at the hands of the opposition Socialists,
who had opposed the Iraq war. As an immediate consequence, Prime
Minister–elect José Luis Rodríguez Zapatero has advised that he will
pull out the 1,300 Spanish troops in Iraq except in the unlikely event
that the United Nations takes over the occupation. For the Bush administration to seek UN endorsement would counter President Bush's
statement in his State of the Union message last January that America
will never seek a permission slip to defend the security of our country.

Even before last Thursday's bombing, Spaniards were overwhelmingly opposed to the invasion of Iraq. But unlike German chancellor
Gerhard Schröder, who won reelection last September by campaigning
against Mr. Bush, Prime Minister Aznar chose to buck the tide of Spanish public opinion in the hope that American friendship would help
Spain win a greater role in Europe.

It would have served the interest of Aznar's center-right party and
President Bush if the railway bombing could have been attributed to the
Basque separatists. But after some delay, the government confirmed that
al Qaeda was probably responsible, and a shudder of apprehension ran
through Europe, which has felt relatively immune to Islamic-centered
terrorism. Now European ministers are planning to meet to consider
beefed-up security measures. Countries like Britain, Italy, and the Neth-

erlands, which have been supportive of the United States, feel especially vulnerable. The effects on tourism are nervously awaited.

The Bush administration has the problem of overcoming the fear that it is dangerous to support the United States. It is too early to say whether the Madrid bombing will drive European countries closer to or away from the United States, but it seems evident that there will be a profound reassessment of relations with America.

Why Colin Powell Supported a War That He Did Not Believe In

APRIL 28, 2004

In an address last November at his and my alma mater, the City College of New York, Secretary of State Colin Powell gave his recipe for happiness. "Happiness cannot be achieved solely by amassing possessions or power. Real happiness is a by-product of serving others." You find there a clue to how Powell could bring himself to support a war he didn't believe in.

According to Bob Woodward's book *Plan of Attack,* Powell warned President Bush that if he invaded Iraq, he would own this country of 25 million people. Powell was not advised of the president's final decision to go to war until two days after Prince Bandar of Saudi Arabia was briefed in January 2003. As late as mid-January, Powell was telling British foreign secretary Jack Straw, "I have a war to stop." And yet on January 13, 2003, the president, not asking for his opinion, told Secretary Powell he had decided to go to war and asked: "Are you with me on this?" Powell replied, "Yes, sir, I will support you. I'm with you, Mr. President."

At a symposium last night at Georgetown University, with David Sanger and Steven Weisman of the *New York Times,* we generally agreed that if Powell had refused to support the war and offered his resignation, the war might have been averted.

Powell followed the soldier's credo: "Happiness is serving others." But what goes for a military officer may not necessarily go for a civilian official entrusted with serving the public interest. Britain's foreign secretary Robin Cook resigned from Tony Blair's cabinet to announce his opposition to the war. But America doesn't have that British tradition of resignation on principle. If Colin Powell found happiness in supporting a war he had long resisted, he certainly doesn't look that way as he surveys the Iraq that his president owns.

American Torture of Iraqi Detainees

MAY 3, 2004

Abu Ghraib, Saddam Hussein's prison that became a torture chamber for American military intelligence, will undoubtedly take its place with the My Lai massacre in Vietnam as a dismaying symbol of sadism . . . this time with pictures, which are now being flashed around the Islamic world. In Baghdad, a tabloid newspaper enjoying Iraq's newly minted freedom of the press spreads across its front page the pictures of brutalized prisoners and smiling Americans. The caption reads, "This is the democracy and freedom that Bush promised us."

For President Bush, who has voiced his deep disgust, this scandal could not have come at a worse time. It is bound to complicate the negotiations for a turnover of some form of sovereignty to the Iraqis on June 30. The army has gone into a familiar defensive crouch. "An aberration," says Joint Chiefs chairman Richard Myers. He said he had not seen, as of yesterday, the fifty-three-page internal report completed in late February by Major General Antonio Taguba. That report detailed the sadistic, blatant, and wanton abuse of prisoners. Nor had Defense Secretary Donald Rumsfeld seen the report. Nor was Brigadier General Janis Karpinski aware of what was going on in a prison for which she bore command responsibility.

They and the world know now, thanks to the reporting of the *New Yorker*'s Seymour Hersh and the CBS *60 Minutes* program. The leak of the internal report suggests that some constructive whistle-blowing was going on in the military. Now a plethora of investigations is being planned by the army and the CIA into the actions of the soldiers and the civilians to whom some of the interrogation work had been outsourced. Courts-martial will undoubtedly follow. But like My Lai, this episode leaves a stain that will last.

Possible Terrorism May Be a Political Boon

MAY 26, 2004

Robert Siegel, host: Attorney General John Ashcroft and the director of the FBI, Robert Mueller, warned today that they have good reason to believe that al Qaeda is planning to attack the United States this summer. The announcement came at a news conference today in Washington. Attorney General Ashcroft showed photographs of seven suspects who pose, in his words, "a clear and present danger to America."

Melissa Block, host: Senior news analyst Daniel Schorr says there's a disconnect between today's announcement and recent comments by President Bush.

On television Monday night, President Bush asserted, as he has many times, that Iraq is the central front in the war on terror. But not if you listen today to his attorney general and FBI director, who called an unusual news conference to issue a dire warning of credible intelligence indicating advanced terrorist plans to hit the United States hard this summer or fall, perhaps during a summit meeting, perhaps during the Democratic or Republican convention, perhaps, as with Spain in March, a massive bombing connected with a national election.

And so what happened to the terrorist threat from Iraq? An ideological fixation dies hard, and the failure so far to discover weapons of mass destruction has left the president with terrorism as the next best rationale for invading Iraq. Today, most observers believe that Iraq played little or no role in 9/11 or other terrorist episodes. But since the invasion, Iraq has become a magnet for jihadists—that is, holy warriors—infiltrating Iraq to join the insurrection and avenge the assault on Arab soil.

Raising the threat level on terrorist plans in America can serve as a political asset for the president. Americans care about terror more than they care about nation building in Iraq. According to the latest *Washington Post*–ABC poll, approval of the president's handling of the Iraq conflict has dropped to 40 percent, a new low. And disapproval of his handling of the prisoner abuse scandal stands at a dramatic 57 percent. But when it comes to dealing with terrorism, Mr. Bush leads Senator

Kerry 52–39 percent. Thus, intended or not, raising the alarm about a terrorist threat in this country tends to play to the president's political strength as protector of the nation.

Use of Presidential Authority to Override the Law

JUNE 27, 2004

It's called the imperial presidency.

The notion that the president has inherent powers conferred by the people that permit him to issue orders as good as law, or maybe better— we may have just seen the imperial presidency at work in the bitter dispute over the permissible limits of pressure on foreign prisoners. Now that several hundred pages of memos have been released, we learn that in February 2002 President Bush asserted in a memo that he believed he had the authority under the Constitution to deny a prisoner the protection of the Geneva Conventions, but that he would decline to exercise that authority at this time.

Justice Department official Jay Bybee, since then named to the federal appeals court, carried that a step further with a memo in August 2002 stating that "torturing prisoners might be legally defensible in some circumstances." The White House has now repudiated that opinion.

Where did the president get the power to defy a solemn treaty, signed and ratified? Where other presidents have assumed powers not written down in any law or Constitution: Presidents before him have done so. Presidents Franklin Roosevelt and Harry Truman asserted wartime powers to end crippling strikes. Former President Nixon held that when a president broke the law in the interest of national security, it wasn't illegal. President Reagan, who illegally sold missiles to Iran and sent arms to Nicaraguan rebels, noted that President Lincoln acted outside the Constitution when he freed the slaves, when he drafted troops, when he blockaded Southern ports.

So now the theory is that if, in the conduct of the war on terrorism, the president has to violate a treaty in order to put the squeeze on prisoners, he has the inherent right to do so. But the administration has now backed away from any idea of introducing tougher interrogation methods. There is another inherent power that the president has to answer to: the power of public opinion.

The 9/11 Report

JULY 19, 2004

Coming reports cast their shadow before.

There has been enough advance word of the contents of the bipartisan 9/11 Commission report due out Thursday to get a fix on some of the controversies it is likely to generate. The proposal for a White House–based national intelligence director has already been opposed by acting CIA director John McLaughlin, who said that an additional layer of bureaucracy is not needed. The controversy over the Iraq–al Qaeda connection is advanced with a statement that there were meetings between them but no sign of a collaborative relationship. In fact, Osama bin Laden at one point sponsored Islamic radical guerrillas fighting to overthrow Saddam Hussein's regime and establish an Islamic religious government.

It is the relationship not with Iraq but with Iran that appears to have played an important role in the terrorists' plans. Based on electronic intercepts and interrogation of al Qaeda detainees, the report says that Iran arranged safe passage for members of the hijack group coming from Afghanistan. Guards at border stations were under orders not to stamp their passports, which might have alerted immigration authorities when they arrived in the United States. This is not to say that Iran had specific knowledge of the 9/11 hijacking plan, but it will fuel the argument about whether the Bush administration focused on the wrong antagonist. Why Iraq? Why not Iran?

Upheaval in the Gaza Strip Is a Crisis Within a Crisis

JULY 21, 2004

The streets of Gaza are awash in rioting that the police seem unable to control.

There are attacks on the headquarters of the Palestinian Authority. Prime Minister Ahmed Qureia tries to resign, and President Yasser Arafat won't let him. But Arafat gives up on trying to make his cousin the security chief. Legislator Nabil Amr, who has called for democratic reforms in the Palestinian Authority, is shot in the leg returning from a television interview. This is a crisis within a crisis. The prospect of Israel's moving out of Gaza is intensifying the largely generational struggle of young militants in the Fatah Party to wrest the leadership from a group regarded as corrupt and unrepresentative of the Palestinian people.

Many militants in Gaza support Muhammad Dahlan, a former security official who is forty-two years old, against Arafat, who is seventy-four. This is emblematic of the rising opposition to Arafat, who has ruled basically with a group of cronies who came with him from exile ten years ago. The *New York Times* quotes a resident of a camp in central Gaza, saying, "All of them are thieves. Arafat is just looking out for these thieves." Two years ago I heard Khalil Shikaki, a leading Palestinian demographer, give the results of a poll he had taken among Palestinians. Arafat's approval rating was 35 percent. Eighty-three percent believed there was corruption in his regime. Shikaki said that conditions were ripe for an Arab secession struggle, perhaps even a civil war. That was two years ago, and not much has improved for the Palestinians since.

If Arafat has not been forced out by young militants, it is probably because of Israeli pressures on him, isolating him in his Ramallah headquarters with threats from Israeli prime minister Ariel Sharon of exile, perhaps even assassination. But now the prospect of an Israeli pullout from Gaza, giving the Palestinians a piece of land to administer, appears to have spurred the young militants to more vigorous action against a tired, corrupt Arafat old guard. The secession struggles that Dr. Shikaki foresaw two years ago may be under way.

Flip-flopping in Politics

AUGUST 8, 2004

I'm going on vacation this week, leaving behind my flip-flop indicator.

Truth to tell, I've become a little weary of the flip-flop accusation, which is a political form of "Gotcha," and just about as meaningful. Senator Kerry, before he was a presidential candidate, voted with most everybody in Congress to authorize the president to use force against Iraq. One could hardly do otherwise when the president said he had information about a threat. I am reminded of 1964, when only two senators, Ernest Gruening of Alaska and Wayne Morse of Oregon, voted against the Tonkin Gulf Resolution, which took America into the Vietnam War, and they were called traitors by many at the time.

President Bush accused Senator Kerry of flip-flopping when he voted against the funding bill for the war that he voted to authorize. Sure. But how about Mr. Bush nation building in Afghanistan and Iraq, having campaigned against nation building; or praising the report of the 9/11 Commission, whose formation he opposed; or negotiating with North Korea, which he promised not to do?

Let's face it: every politician, at one time of another, will have to change his announced position to meet a changed situation. My favorite flip-flopper was Franklin D. Roosevelt, who campaigned for a balanced budget, and then launched a series of budget-busting New Deal programs, trying to spend his way out of the Great Depression. Full disclosure? I benefited from one program, the National Youth Administration, which helped me through college with 50 cents an hour for sorting library slips.

The answer to the flip-flop accusation is: Consistency is the hobgoblin of little minds. Show me a politician who has stuck to his position through thick and thin, and I will show you a politician who cannot be trusted to represent our interests in a changing world.

Putin and the Massacre Versus Bush and 9/11

SEPTEMBER 13, 2004

On the surface, President Vladimir Putin's reaction to 9/01, the schoolhouse massacre, resembles President Bush's reaction to 9/11. There is increasing surveillance of citizens; he's creating a centralized homeland security organization; he asserts the right to take preemptive action against hostile groups. The difference is that in Russia, democratic institutions had not had time to establish themselves before the retreat to authoritarian rule began. Putin apparently assumes that Russians will sacrifice some freedom for more safety, and Putin told a group of Western scholars last week that he observes some nostalgia for Soviet days.

And so the Kremlin tightens control over the news media, reduces parliament to a rubber stamp, and asserts authority over regional governments. The nervous-twitch reaction is in some ways understandable. Russia has its own one thousand milestone to observe: approximately the number killed in terrorist assaults starting with the apartment house bombing in 1999, continuing through airplane and metro station bombings, until Beslan Middle School no. 1 this September.

Putin's move to tighten control on power creates a dilemma for the Bush administration. Suggestions from Washington that he seek a political solution with the Chechen separatists fall now on very stony soil. Putin told the group of Western academics that his answer to Bush is "Why don't you meet with Osama bin Laden, invite him to Brussels or the White House and engage in talks, ask him what he wants and give it to him?"

That day on the ranch three years ago, when President Bush said he looked into Putin's soul and liked what he saw—that's a dim memory. An authoritarian ruler sees his regime trembling on the brink of destabilization and is running scared. "Running scared" for a KGB alumnus means cracking down on dissent. And what he wants from America is what he says he gave America after 9/11: complete support.

The Vietnam War as a Campaign Issue

SEPTEMBER 15, 2004

Russia may be headed back to dictatorship. In Iraq, the casualty toll keeps increasing. At home, the National Guard has expressed concern about the largest call-up of part-time soldiers since World War II. But watch the media, especially television and most especially cable television, and you'll get the idea that what the current campaign is about is what the candidates did in the Vietnam War.

With close to $7 million of the many millions that slipped through the Article 527 loophole in the law, an organization calling itself Swift Boat Veterans for Truth placed TV ads casting doubt on whether Senator John Kerry earned the Bronze Star he won rescuing an imperiled Green Beret aboard his Swift boat.

President Bush's wartime record came into play when CBS News surfaced documents purporting to show that Bush got his place in the Texas Air National Guard through political pull and was grounded after failing to take a required physical exam. The authenticity of the documents has developed into a battle of the microscopes. What seems beyond dispute is the belated statement of Ben Barnes, who was then speaker of the Texas House, that he interceded at the request of a family friend of Representative George Bush to get his son into the Guard, saving him from the draft.

Bush was not the only draft-age American to take refuge from Vietnam in the National Guard. What remains mysterious is why Bush would have refused to take a routine physical examination, as the documents indicate he did. But more mysterious is the way America's presidential election campaign, once involved with grave matters of war and peace, prosperity and recession, has degenerated into something close to personal gossip with attached documents about who did what in that war that remains an open wound.

The Possible Link Between Greenhouse Gases and the Severity of Hurricanes

OCTOBER 3, 2004

You read of more than a thousand American troops killed in the war in Iraq, never mind the number of Iraqis; in Sudan, 50,000 dead and 1.6 million people uprooted; and more than 330 children and teachers slain in an assault on a school in southern Russia; and dozens of killings of Palestinians and Israelis. And what these have in common is that they are all examples of man's inhumanity to man.

And then vying for newspaper space or time on the tube is the violence committed by forces of nature—the hurricanes sweeping through Florida and the helpless Caribbean islands like Haiti and Grenada—and you have to stop for a minute to distinguish between the violence committed by human hands and the violence committed by the raging elements beyond the control of the human hand.

Or is the separation so clear anymore? I'm looking at a report in Thursday's *New York Times* on an extensive computer analysis of hurricanes and global warming published by the *Journal of Climate*. It says that by 2080, hurricanes will grow stronger and wetter as a result of global warming. That's because hurricanes draw their intensity from the warming of ocean waters. Dr. Kerry Emanuel, a hurricane expert at the Massachusetts Institute of Technology, says of the report, "This clinches the issue."

The Bush administration has adamantly refused to sign the Kyoto Accord, a treaty aimed at diminishing the threat of global warming. Russia has now agreed to support that treaty. At the United Nations last week, leaders of small island nations pleaded for more attention to the potential for devastation from tidal surges. Dr. James Elsner, a hurricane expert at Florida State University, was among the first to predict the recent increase in Atlantic storm activity.

Now with the increase in greenhouse gases, the hurricane danger is bound to get worse and worse in the next forty years, but like the ballooning budget deficit, that's something for another generation to worry about.

Long-Lasting Divisions

NOVEMBER 3, 2004

Divided we stand is the way it's apparently going to be for a while.

On this program four years ago, I said the election had revealed a nation at peace but not with itself; prosperous, but not enjoying that prosperity. Four years later, the exit polls taken yesterday of voters who had just cast their ballots revealed an America with more and deeper fissures.

Geographically, the country seemed to be divided between a Republican solid South plus the Plains states, and a Democratic fortress in the Northeast. Voters were divided by age, by race, by belief. The president was favored by 90 percent of those who had voted for him last time; Senator Kerry did well among those voting for the first time.

Mr. Bush captured the evangelical Christians and the Catholics who opposed abortion, gay marriage, and stem cell research; Senator Kerry, himself a Catholic, got the other half of Catholic voters. Of voters who cited terrorism as a top issue, 85 percent supported Mr. Bush. Kerry was apparently less than successful in siphoning off Bush voters on this issue.

Mr. Bush was favored by married voters with children, by gun owners, by those concerned with terrorism and those who said they were concerned with moral values. Character seemed to emerge as a more important motivator for Bush voters than foreign policy, including the war in Iraq. White voters voted predominantly for Mr. Bush, while Hispanics favored Senator Kerry and blacks voted for Senator Kerry by a ten-to-one margin. Somewhere in this welter of angry and passionate voters voting their anger, you may be able to find a second-term mandate; I can't.

Powell's Resignation

NOVEMBER 15, 2004

Melissa Block, host: One Bush administration official who won wide respect abroad announced today that he's stepping down: Secretary of State Colin Powell. Powell has often been described as a voice within the Bush administration pressing to moderate hawkish policies. He plans to stay on until his successor is named and he quickly returned to official business today, meeting with the Israeli foreign minister. News analyst Daniel Schorr says Powell played the good soldier but was at odds with the Pentagon to the end.

One of the last unpleasant chores that Secretary Powell performed was a twenty-four-hour trip to Beijing last month to reassure the Chinese government that the United States was not supporting independence for Taiwan no matter what the Pentagon might be saying. But in the end, what left Powell bitter and frustrated, as he was described by some close to him, was Iraq, the war that he thought shouldn't have been fought without America's traditional allies, and most especially the assignment to tell what turned out to be an untruth to the United Nations Security Council about weapons of mass destruction. It was like Colin Powell, having enlisted for a four-year hitch, to serve out that hitch and then to allow his resignation to be disclosed along with other cabinet departures. "Casualty of war" was the way Powell's position was described last June by Wil Hylton, who had interviewed him at great length for an article in *GQ* magazine.

But frustration over Iraq was not all there was. Since President

Reagan first brought Powell into the White House as national security adviser, Powell had played a basically nonpartisan role. He could have run for office, even for president, maybe even won. But he remained the soldier, serving country, not party. The first to be named to the Bush cabinet, Powell found he had joined an intensely partisan administration that didn't leave much room for nonpartisan service.

It is hard to guess when Powell decided to quit, but it was not recently. Powell said he had discussed it at various times with the president, but that he had never planned to stay longer than one term. And one of the reasons he stayed was to get the administration to focus on the atrocities in Sudan. But serving as secretary of state was clearly not a happy experience for Colin Powell, and whatever he does next, it is likely to be in the private sector.

The Year of the Suicide Bomber

DECEMBER 26, 2004

Dedicated listeners to this program may recall that, since 1991, I have attempted an annual assessment of how peace on Earth has fared in the year gone by.

Nineteen ninety-one, with the end of the Gulf War and the war in Afghanistan, got high marks. The succeeding years have been mixed. And this year peace on Earth sounds like a sardonic joke. So we have decided to skip the evaluation.

If I were asked what typified this year, I would say that it's been the year of the suicide bomber, that unstoppable weapon. The latest example was the bombing of the American mess hall in Mosul last Tuesday, for which a radical Muslim group has claimed credit, calling it a "suicide operation." The last time I saw Israeli prime minister Yitzhak Rabin at breakfast in Washington, in September 1995, he said, "The greatest menace to peace are the crazies willing to sacrifice themselves to blow up a bus." But in their terms, they are not crazy but martyrs willingly giving their lives so that they can be admitted to paradise. In one of his videotapes, Osama bin Laden praised the martyrs who gave their lives for the sake of Islam. On occasion Yasser Arafat also praised the martyrs.

The principal terrorist attacks aimed against America have been suicide attacks: the bombing of the marine barracks in Beirut in 1983; the attack on the destroyer in Yemen; the assault on the air force barracks in Saudi Arabia. The suicide tradition among some Islamic groups goes back a long way. The word "assassin" is derived from a fanatical Persian sect of a thousand years ago called Hashishin, or "hashish users," who considered murdering their enemies to be a sacred duty. Back in 1995, Prime Minister Rabin said, "No answer has yet been found for the phenomenon of the suicide bomber." That could be repeated today.

The Tsunami Disaster

DECEMBER 30, 2004

The tsunami is a uniquely nonpartisan event. The monitoring system for nuclear test explosions might conceivably have detected the tectonic collision that produced that surge of waters. But the general consensus is that, unlike global warming or air pollution, the tsunami cannot be blamed on any group or party. So there are no political points to be scored over the Asian catastrophe, and that presents a rare opportunity to rise above politics, above ideology, above denomination, to show a doubting world what America is really made of.

The early signals are mixed. If it took President Bush seven minutes in a Florida schoolroom to respond to 9/11, it took him three days on his ranch in Texas to respond publicly to 12/26. But it is only fair to note that the magnitude of this disaster engulfing faraway places was even harder to grasp. It would take time before the tough-guy lexicon of shock and awe would yield to the new Bush lexicon of loss and grief to the world. So it was that the administration's initial gesture of $15 million in aid, criticized by a UN official as stingy, was quickly revised to $35 million. For hurricane relief mainly in Florida, Congress allotted $13 billion. But then, Sri Lankans don't vote in Florida.

The measure of America's capacity for nonpartisan response will not be known before the new Congress convenes in January. Senator Patrick Leahy, ranking Democrat on the Foreign Operations Subcommittee, said from his home in Vermont that the $35 million pledge was laughable. He said, "We spend thirty-five million before breakfast in Iraq." But that sounds like old-style partisan reflex. It remains to be seen whether politicians can respond to this rare opportunity to rise above politics.

President Bush says he has spoken to the leaders of Sri Lanka, India, Indonesia, and Thailand and told them that "we are only at the beginning of our help." He and the whole political structure of this country will have ample opportunity to deliver on that promise and give the world a new image of America.

2005

The Year of the Flood

The U.S. Interrogation Policy

JANUARY 3, 2005

When Alberto Gonzales appears before the Senate Judiciary Committee on Thursday for confirmation as attorney general, the ghosts of Abu Ghraib will figuratively be seated alongside him. It was White House counsel Gonzales who, in the first flush of rage and fear generated by 9/11, advised President Bush in a January 2002 memo that the war on terrorism renders obsolete the Geneva Conventions prohibiting coercive interrogations. He described the conventions as quaint and said that terrorists are not legally entitled to humane treatment. That was updated in an August 2002 memo prepared by the John Ashcroft Justice Department with help from the White House counsel's office. It did not retreat from the January memo, and it added a narrow definition of torture saying that mistreatment reached the level of torture only if it produced severe pain equivalent to organ failure or death. It was a document that prison guards in Abu Ghraib, Guantánamo, and Afghanistan could cite in their defense.

But then, on November 10, President Bush nominated his old friend from Texas, Alberto Gonzales, as attorney general. And with Gonzales coming up before the Senate, there came word of a new policy paper. The new memo was prepared by Daniel Levin, acting assistant attorney general in charge of the Office of Legal Counsel. There was no news conference, no effort to call public attention to it. The seventeen-page document could be found last week on a Web site by diligent search. It repudiated the previous memos as wrong in stating that only excruciating and agonizing treatment constituted torture. Such treatment, it said, is wrong, even if the aim is to protect national security.

The White House now says that all torture is abhorrent. The Geneva Conventions are not quaint after all. It took a long time for the administration to reach that conclusion, and then the hope of avoiding painful interrogation for the attorney general–designate before the Senate Judiciary Committee.

A Hard Sell

JANUARY 19, 2005

President Bush has called Social Security overhaul his highest domestic priority. But even before a concrete plan has been rolled out, it appears to be in serious trouble, and not just with Democrats. "The president proposes and the Congress disposes," says Bill Thomas, chairman of the House Ways and Means Committee. And in a speech two days before the inaugural, he warned that partisan warfare could quickly render an administration plan a dead horse.

As supporters and opponents of the president's ideas gear up for the heaviest ad campaign since the struggle over the Clinton health care plan, the administration appears to be trying to avoid a collision, the White House saying that it has a lot of respect for Thomas and hopes to work with him. But it may be difficult to find common ground if the Bush proposal turns out to call for a future cut in benefits, as a recent White House memo has suggested, or an increase in payroll taxes to help finance private investment accounts for younger workers.

In his speech yesterday before an audience assembled by the *National Journal,* Congressman Thomas suggested broadening the issue of Social Security overhaul, possibly replacing payroll taxes as the Social Security financing mechanism. Congressman Thomas's ideas—which could link the financing of Social Security with Medicare—are far from clear. What does seem clear is that he is anxious to avoid a partisan battle that might produce some Republican defections and wants to kick the can down the road for more study.

As chairman of the committee that originates tax legislation and oversees Social Security, Congressman Thomas has a lot of clout. If he says that an administration proposal for overhauling Social Security could become a dead horse, he's in a position to make that happen.

President George W. Bush's Second Inauguration

JANUARY 23, 2005

President Bush embarks on his second term with more approval from Americans for himself than for his policies.

That's the thrust of two opinion polls completed before the inauguration on Thursday. In a *New York Times*–CBS survey, most Americans said they do not expect the economy to improve or American troops to come home from Iraq by the time Mr. Bush leaves the White House. A *Wall Street Journal*–NBC poll says that fewer than half of Americans are optimistic about the next four years or confident that Mr. Bush has the right policies for the presidency. But Mr. Bush is apparently still enjoying the popularity he achieved as a wartime president after the 9/11 assault.

In one area, ability to handle a crisis, Mr. Bush has risen sharply in public esteem since his first inauguration. The *Journal* survey reports that ability to handle a crisis is the strongest asset the president brings to his job. But the *Times* poll reports that as he enters his second term, Mr. Bush has a job approval rating of only 49 percent, and 56 percent say the country has gone off on the wrong track.

On specific issues, 50 percent in the *Times* poll think that individual Social Security accounts are a bad idea. And in the *Journal* poll, just 14 percent accept the president's characterization of a crisis in Social Security.

Unsettling for the administration is the *Journal* finding that a 52 percent majority now believe that the war to remove Saddam Hussein in Iraq wasn't worth its financial and human cost. And in the *Times* poll, 75 percent say the president has no clear plan for getting out of Iraq. As economic conditions improve, the president gets a slightly improved 47 percent in the *Journal* poll for his handling of the economy. The *Times* poll, by contrast, reported nearly two-thirds believing Mr. Bush would leave the country with a greater deficit. Yet the *Journal* reported that the singular strength enjoyed by the president is a continued regard he gets for his personal traits. Fifty-seven percent rate him highly as being easy-going and likable.

Recalling Observations of Auschwitz

JANUARY 30, 2005

In 1959, not many from the West had visited Auschwitz, and I was not prepared for what I would see and try to capture on film. I have always tried to separate my Jewish heritage from my reporting. But keeping emotion under control in Auschwitz, where members of my family may have died, was not easy. I had to leave parts of my script several times, trying to control a catch in my throat, and sound detached as I reported.

Here was the greatest death factory ever devised, where a million died, pushed through these gas chambers at a rate of sixty thousand a day, their bodies efficiently moved out and lifted mechanically into brick ovens after their clothes and hair and gold teeth had been removed. For many, there was no room in the ovens, and they were buried in open pits, now these stagnant ponds. If you run your hand along the bottom, you will pick up human ashes and fragments of bone.

I interviewed a guide, Tadeusz Zimanski, who had Auschwitz number 200314 tattooed on his forearm. Asked whether he found it painful to be working there, he said, "When some of my friends were carried off to be executed, they shouted, 'Remember us and avenge us.' So I am here to see that they are remembered." As we talked, a group of young Poles passed, ushered along by a woman who also had an Auschwitz tattoo. She sounded so remarkably matter-of-fact: "Here stood a crematorium. Here was where people were pushed into a room, and then the doors were sealed and the gas, so-called Zyklon B, was released. In most cases they died in ten minutes." A young Polish girl gulped. Mostly they just stood and stared. And no one asked any questions.

Security Versus Reporters

FEBRUARY 16, 2005

On the issue of protecting a reporter's sources, I can hardly claim to be a disinterested party. I came close to being cited for contempt of Congress in 1976 for refusing to say where I had gotten a classified House report on intelligence failures. It strikes me now, as it struck me then, that the courts and the public are generally disinclined to side with the press in an issue involving national security.

The courts, over the years, have come to recognize doctor-patient privilege, priest-penitent privilege, husband-wife privilege, and lawyer-client privilege, but there is no generally recognized reporter-source privilege derived from the First Amendment. This puts whistle-blowing sources at risk along with the reporters who try to keep their promises of confidentiality to their sources.

Special prosecutor Patrick Fitzgerald maintained that Judith Miller of the *New York Times* and Matthew Cooper of *Time* magazine may have witnessed a crime, the leaking of the identity of a covert CIA officer. Judge David Tatel, the most liberal of the three-judge appeals court panel, said that the case involves a clash between two truth-seeking institutions: the grand jury and the press. But the press seeks truth at its own risk, a risk to those who want to make the truth known.

There still appear to be secrets to keep. The unanimous decision was based in part on secret evidence submitted by the prosecutor. Judge Tatel's concurring opinion includes eight blank pages with a notation that they have been redacted. Judge Tatel may have come close to the heart of the case when he wrote that the purpose of the leak of the CIA officer's identity appeared to be to smear someone who had cast doubt on the reasons for going to war against Iraq.

The Trouble with Guantánamo

MARCH 14, 2005

The American military has been operating on the quaint premise that the piece of Cuba called Guantánamo Bay, fully American controlled since the Spanish-American War, is somehow foreign territory, outside the reach of American justice. On that premise, so-called suspected enemy combatants, 750 of them at one point, have been held under rigorous conditions without access to a court.

On another quaint premise, the American government assumes a right to send suspects anywhere it chooses, country of origin or other. On this supposition, the CIA has been operating a program called "rendition," which has nothing to do with music. It means transferring an inmate in great secrecy to a country like Yemen or Egypt, where interrogation can be pretty rough. The Bush administration's suppositions have not been faring well in the courts. The Supreme Court ruled last June that the United States has exclusive control over Guantánamo Bay, and therefore prisoners are entitled to access to American courts.

And now the federal District Court for the District of Columbia has issued an emergency order blocking the transfer of thirteen Yemenis to Yemen pending a hearing to determine if they are in danger of being mistreated there. The CIA's "rendition" program apparently goes far beyond Guantánamo Bay. Italian, Swedish, and German authorities have reported kidnappings on their streets of targets who are then flown to other countries on planes that have been chartered by CIA front companies.

Now that President Bush says he forbids torture at the hand of Americans, it looks as though part of the "rendition" program has been outsourced.

Terri Schiavo and John Paul II

MARCH 28, 2005

I'm reminded of 1997, when Princess Diana and Mother Teresa died in the same week—as different as two persons could be, yet both sealed in the public mind by their incessant exposure on television. So now with Pope John Paul II and Terri Schiavo, the melancholy presence in the Vatican window and the brain-damaged woman in the Florida hospice.

He has become part of our lives, believers and unbelievers alike, because television has brought into our homes the gallant priest who struggles to speak. She has become part of our lives because of the hundreds of times we have seen the four-year-old videotape of the vacantly smiling woman. The power of the image led the president and Congress into the colossal blunder of trying to manipulate her condition to make political points. They misread the mind of the public, which by and large wants death with dignity without the benefit of political interference.

The Vatican made its judgment in the Schiavo case. Its organ *L'Osservatore Romano* said the feeding tube should be restored, adding,

"Who can decide to pull the plug as if he were talking about a broken or out-of-order appliance?"

But in the case of the pope, suffering from advanced Parkinson's disease, the Vatican may face its own dilemma. According to the *New York Times,* the pope himself said in 1998 that keeping patients alive by extraordinary or disproportionate means and artificial hastening of death are both at odds with Catholic principles. He may not have dreamed seven years ago that he might face this dilemma himself. According to the newspaper *La Repubblica,* the Vatican has set up a hospital room in the pope's quarters, complete with electronic ventilator, suction devices, and a resuscitation team.

In the end, we are held spellbound by the dramas of two human beings whom television has made familiar to all of us, two human beings whose lives are in the hands of the gods.

The Beginning of the End

APRIL 6, 2005

A politician can withstand, perhaps even revel in, the attacks of his opponents. Often his troubles start when he embarrasses his own party.

So it was that the beginning of the end for red-baiting senator Joe McCarthy came when Republican senator Margaret Chase Smith denounced him in a declaration of conscience and Ralph Flanders of Vermont introduced a motion of censure. President Nixon's decision to resign, so he wrote in his memoirs, came when conservative senator Barry Goldwater led a delegation of colleagues to the Oval Office and said that he himself was leaning toward voting for impeachment.

So now the aggressive House majority leader, Tom DeLay—in trouble with colleagues, many of them beholden to him for money raising and a few for gerrymandering of their districts—his trouble is of two sorts: first, alleged ethical lapses in money raising and accepting favors and foreign trips from lobbyists for foreign countries, including Russia and South Korea; second—and perhaps more damaging—his intervention in the Schiavo controversy, an effort to divert attention from his own problems with ethics and the law.

After Mrs. Schiavo's death, DeLay denounced what he called an "out-of-control judiciary" and vowed that the judges would have to answer for their behavior, suggesting the possibility of impeachment. That was apparently too much for Senate majority leader Bill Frist, who had joined DeLay in driving home the resolution calling on the courts to review the case. Frist stated that he believed the courts had acted in a fair and independent way.

DeLay is also in some trouble with his own constituents. In a *Houston Chronicle* poll, 45 percent said they would vote for somebody else if the congressional election were held today, and only 38 percent said they would stick with DeLay.

Representative Roy Blunt, the number three Republican in the House, said today he saw no wavering in support for the leader. But the tough majority leader appears to be in that troublesome zone, where some colleagues and some constituents are shaking their heads about him.

Eavesdropping on Americans

APRIL 17, 2005

It was like a whiff of old times when the issue of eavesdropping on Americans by the National Security Agency bubbled up in Senate confirmation hearings for two Bush nominees.

The existence of the NSA, America's big ear in the sky, was known to only a few when it was laid bare in the congressional investigation of intelligence agencies in the midseventies. It was revealed that the NSA maintained a watch list of some 1,700 Americans, mostly antiwar dissidents, whose phone calls were intercepted on behalf of the Nixon White House. The resulting outrage led to rules forbidding targeted electronic eavesdropping on Americans. But as we have now learned, there were exceptions.

Lieutenant General Michael Hayden, director of the NSA for the past six years, is up for confirmation as deputy to prospective intelligence chief John Negroponte. He told the Senate Intelligence Committee on Thursday that his agency was conscious of protecting Americans' privacy, but on occasion, and with his approval, the names of Americans in reports of intercepts had been shared with other agencies.

That dovetailed neatly with the testimony the day before of John Bolton, former undersecretary of state, now nominated as United Nations ambassador. Questioned by Democratic senator Christopher

Dodd before the Foreign Relations Committee, Bolton admitted that on a couple of occasions, maybe a few more, he had asked the NSA to identify American government officials whose telephone conversations had been intercepted. Why would Bolton, whose field was arms control policy, need to know what other officials were discussing on the phone? Did these intercepts have anything to do with Bolton's feud with State Department intelligence officers, who rejected his assertion that Castro's Cuba was running a biological weapons program? That is not clear.

But I am reminded of 1975, when Senator Frank Church, who led the searching investigation of the NSA, said the agency had an enormous capability that could be turned against the American people.

"The Periscope Item"

MAY 18, 2005

Newsweek seems to consign interesting items not fully authenticated to its Periscope column. The report of a copy of the Koran being flushed down a toilet at Guantánamo Bay may well be the gossip item heard 'round the world. It triggered a wave of violence in which at least fifteen persons were killed, hundreds were injured, and anti-Americanism received a huge boost, even in an American client country like Afghanistan.

I write this critique of valued colleagues without pleasure. No one could have known the extent of the reaction. But *Newsweek* went with a single source that was perhaps unwitting, perhaps mischievous, and then stood back appalled at what it had wrought. It sent a shocking message like Abu Ghraib, this time without the pictures.

Actually this was not the first report of Koran desecration as a way of breaking the spirit of detainees. John Sifton of Human Rights Watch in New York told me today that his organization has been receiving reports from released detainees since 2003 of the defiling of a Koran by interrogators, who would routinely kick the book across the floor with the detainee watching. This was apparently in violation of military orders barring the showing of disrespect for the Islamic holy book.

Why did this latest incident touch off such a profound reaction from Gaza to Indonesia? In part because the citing of an unnamed American official made the report seem official, but perhaps in larger part because

306 · COME TO THINK OF IT

of a communications revolution in the Islamic world. From satellite newscasts to the Internet, the new media have facilitated the work of the anti-American agitator.

Newsweek's formal retraction is not likely to change much, nor is the promised letter to the staff from the magazine's chairman, Richard Smith, discussing the handling of information from anonymous sources. *Newsweek* and the world will have to live with the consequences of that little Periscope item.

The Iraq War Memo

MAY 22, 2005

This must rank as the undercovered story of the year.

Secret documents leaked to the British press indicate that President Bush was set on invading Iraq at least as early as July 2002. White House press secretary Scott McClellan has denounced this as "flat-out wrong" and said the invasion decision was made only after Iraq refused to comply with international obligations. He did not, however, deny the existence of the British documents, which he said he had not seen.

According to one memo, which has not been disavowed by the British government, Richard Dearlove, head of MI6, Britain's intelligence service, visited Washington in July 2002 to ascertain American intentions. A memo dated July 23 summarized a meeting of Prime Minister Tony Blair and his top security advisers. The memo quoted Dearlove as reporting what he had learned from American officials who were not named. His report said, "There was a perceptible shift in attitude. Military action was now seen as inevitable. Bush wanted to remove Saddam through military action justified by the conjunction of terrorism and weapons of mass destruction. But the intelligence and the facts were being fixed around the policy," he said.

This at a time when the White House was saying, "There are no plans to attack Iraq on the president's desk." The memo was marked: "Secret" and "Strictly personal. UK eyes only."

Another briefing paper for the Downing Street meeting referred back to the prime minister's visit with President Bush the previous April in Crawford, Texas. Blair was quoted as having told the president then,

"The UK would support military action to bring about regime change."

This, although a British legal memo said, "Regime change, per se, is not a proper basis for military action under international law." These memos, first reported in the London *Sunday Times* on May 1, created a great stir in Britain, perhaps because, at the height of the British election campaign, they appear to support attacks on the prime minister as a lap dog for President Bush.

In the United States, perhaps because there have been so many stories suggesting a cynical White House decision, there was much less reaction. The *New York Times* did not get around to reporting it until last week and on an inside page, apparently no big deal.

Views of Deep Throat

JUNE 1, 2005

It's the day after "D Day," Deep Throat Day, and slowly the capital begins to adjust itself to life without its longest-running mystery. Former Nixon counsel Len Garment, who had speculated incorrectly about the identity of Deep Throat, said, "Every good secret is entitled to a decent burial. It's about time." A lot of speculative Deep Throats—John Dean, Al Haig, Henry Kissinger, to name a few—will have to be content with other forms of notoriety.

Some of the former president's men are finding it difficult to reach closure over the Trojan horse in the Nixon administration who helped to do them in. Mark Felt is no hero to them. On the talk shows, their deep resentments come through. Patrick Buchanan, who used to write speeches for Nixon, called Felt a dishonorable man who behaved treacherously. Charles Colson, Nixon's special counsel, who runs a religious prison fellowship, said he was really shocked that the consummate professional should have acted that way. Gordon Liddy, who masterminded—if that's the right word—the Watergate break-in, said Felt was honor-bound to report to a grand jury rather than leaking to a selective news source. And David Gergen, who served four presidents, including Nixon, thought that a question of what the whistle-blowing role of a government official should be was a really hard one.

The identification of Deep Throat bids fair to reignite the controversy over the role of the confidential source. No other source in history has had the effect of helping to bring down a president. But whatever they may say in journalism class about the ethics of insiders spilling secrets, the Nixon-era officials who saw their careers derailed mostly seem to have their minds made up. To them, Felt was a traitor to Nixon and to them.

Guantánamo Bay's Shameful Place in American History

JUNE 6, 2005

The controversy over abuses in the Guantánamo detention camp has reached that uneasy bipartisan stage where Judiciary Committee chairman Arlen Specter plans hearings this month, and Joseph Biden, ranking Democrat on the Foreign Relations Committee, demands an independent inquiry and the closing of the camp.

Amnesty International undoubtedly committed a tactical error in speaking of the "Gulag of our time," a reference to Stalin's murderous system of forced labor camps. "That charge was reprehensible," said Defense Secretary Donald Rumsfeld, without dwelling on details of mistreatment in the 308-page report, which concluded that the United States was one of the biggest disappointments in the human rights arena. William Schulz, the director of Amnesty International USA, later acknowledged that the Gulag reference was not meant as a literal analogy.

As some of the about 540 detainees at Guantánamo are gradually released, we are likely to hear more stories of ill-treatment by interrogators and desecration of the Koran. The army has so far acknowledged only five cases involving Korans. The New York Times yesterday devoted two columns to the story of one nineteen-year-old Muslim from Germany picked up in Pakistan, held as a terror suspect, first in Afghanistan, later at Guantánamo, where he's been for three years, although no evidence against him was ever found.

The wave of anger, sometimes violent, that coursed through the Muslim world after one item appeared in Newsweek magazine about Koran desecration is an indication of what can be expected if there are open Senate hearings. Senator Biden said that Guantánamo has become the greatest propaganda tool that exists for recruiting terrorists around the world. Senator Robert Byrd has proposed deleting funds for Guantánamo from the defense budget.

What can be called a close-Guantánamo lobby has begun to form in the press. *New York Times* columnist Tom Friedman, calling Guantánamo a national shame and a gift to America's enemies, has called for shutting down the facility. CBS's Bob Schieffer wondered if the greater danger is the impact Guantánamo is having inside the United States. Talking of torture, he said, "Do we want our children to believe this is how we are?" By present appearances, Guantánamo is likely to take a shameful place in American history, alongside the internment of Japanese Americans in World War II.

The Case Against Matthew Cooper and Judith Miller

JULY 6, 2005

"Journalists are not entitled to promise complete confidentiality. No one in America is," special counsel Patrick Fitzgerald told the court. That is debatable.

Confidentiality is observed in doctor-patient relations, in priest-penitent relations, and, yes, in lawyer-client relations. If reporters do not in equal measure enjoy a First Amendment privilege to protect their sources, it is because the public does not in equal measure value their services. That is not to say that reporter-source relations are completely unprotected. A 1972 decision of the Supreme Court held, in effect, that journalists do have a qualified First Amendment protection. The government can demand to have a source identified only after demonstrating that there is no other way to obtain information needed in a criminal investigation.

Over the years subpoenas for reporters have been increasing without arousing any great outcry from a public largely turned off on the news media symbolized by Jayson Blair and Dan Rather. Fitzgerald's pursuit of Judith Miller and Matt Cooper seems less designed to find out who leaked the identity of an undercover CIA officer, which the prosecutor probably knows by now, than to discourage future leaks regarded as threatening.

Confidential sources have played a vital role in exposing wrongdoing in government, from Deep Throat in the Nixon era to Iran-Contra in the Reagan era to Monica Lewinsky in the Clinton era. Reagan once complained of being "up to my keister in leaks."

As one who came close to being jailed for contempt of Congress in 1976 for refusing to reveal a confidential source, I have an obvious interest in this case. Today's decision to jail Judith Miller for refusing to testify about her source, while Matt Cooper said he would testify with the permission of his source, can be regarded as part of a frontal attack on the press. One can expect many a future investigation to be dropped for fear of subpoenas to journalists to expose their sources. One can expect many a whistle-blower to think twice before blowing that whistle to a reporter. Think for a moment of what the situation would have been if the Nixon administration had found a way to subpoena Bob Woodward and Carl Bernstein, threatening them on pain of jail to identify Deep Throat.

The Real Issue in the Karl Rove Controversy

JULY 13, 2005

Robert Siegel, host: Today President Bush steered clear of questions about his chief political adviser, Karl Rove. Rove is under investigation for his role in the naming of CIA agent Valerie Plame. The president spoke with reporters this morning in the Cabinet Room at the White House. Rove was seated behind him.

President George W. Bush: I have instructed every member of my staff to fully cooperate in this investigation. I also will not prejudge the investigation based on media reports. We're in the midst of an ongoing investigation, and I will be more than happy to comment further once the investigation is completed.

Siegel: NPR senior news analyst Daniel Schorr is keeping an eye on the Rove affair, and he has this admonition.

Let me remind you that the underlying issue in the Karl Rove controversy is not a leak but a war and how America was misled into that war. In 2002, President Bush, having decided to invade Iraq, was casting about for a casus belli. The weapons-of-mass-destruction theme was not yielding very much, until a dubious Italian intelligence report, partly based on forged documents, it later turned out, provided reason to speculate that Iraq might be trying to buy so-called yellowcake uranium from the African country of Niger. It didn't seem to matter that the CIA advised that the Italian information was fragmentary and lacked detail.

Prodded by Vice President Dick Cheney and in the hope of getting more conclusive information, the CIA sent Joseph Wilson, an old Africa hand, to Niger to investigate. Wilson spent eight days talking to everybody in Niger possibly involved and came back to report no sign of an Iraqi bid for uranium in any way. Niger's uranium was committed to other countries for many years to come.

No news is bad news for an administration gearing up for war. Ignoring Wilson's report, Cheney talked on television about Iraq's nuclear potential. And the president himself, in his 2003 State of the Union address no less, pronounced those fateful sixteen words, "The British government has learned that Saddam Hussein recently sought significant quantities of uranium from Africa."

Wilson declined to maintain a discreet silence. He told various people that the president was at least mistaken; at most, telling an untruth. And, finally, Wilson directly challenged the administration with a *New York Times* op-ed article on July 6 headlined "What I Didn't Find in Africa"— and making clear his belief that the president deliberately manipulated intelligence in order to justify an invasion.

Well, one can imagine the fury in the White House. Five days after the appearance of the *Times* op-ed, we now know from the e-mail traffic of *Time* correspondent Matt Cooper, the reporter advised his bureau chief of a supersecret conversation with Karl Rove, who alerted him to the fact that Wilson's wife worked for the CIA and may have recommended him for the Niger assignment. Three days later Bob Novak's column appeared, giving the name of Wilson's wife, Valerie Plame, and the fact that she was an undercover officer in the CIA. Novak has yet to say, at least in public, whether Rove was his source.

But enough is known to surmise that the leaks of Rove and others deputized by him amounted to an angry act of retaliation against someone who had the temerity to challenge the president of the United States when he was striving to find some plausible reason for invading Iraq.

The role of Rove and associates added up to a small incident in a very large scandal: the effort to delude America into thinking it faced a threat dire enough to justify a war.

"Intelligent Design" and Hard Times

AUGUST 31, 2005

On my eighty-ninth birthday I ask indulgence to depart from customary journalistic detachment.

Into the long-running argument about creationism versus evolution, there's lately been added a new catchphrase, a version of creationism called "intelligent design." President Bush has staked out a nonposition on the subject, which is that both sides ought to be properly taught in the schools of America in case there are some who haven't made up their minds. But as the president cut short his vacation by two days to deal with the catastrophic effects of Hurricane Katrina, he might well have reflected that if this was the result of intelligent design, then the designer has something to answer for.

Rarely in my lifetime can I remember—aside from world wars, the Holocaust, and plague epidemics—so much grievous pain visited upon the human species by human beings or by forces beyond their control. Drought, flood, and famine; a deadly tsunami, war, and insurrection; and the United States, while engaged in conflict in Iraq and Afghanistan, leads the way in sales of arms to developing countries. Death and destruction seem not to be equal opportunity scourges. Hurricanes strike with greater force at well-heeled occupants of beach homes than inland residents. On the other hand, as the *Wall Street Journal* noted, the evacuation of New Orleans was a model of efficiency for those with cars, leaving the others to seek shelter in the Superdome.

Are hurricanes part of some mysterious design? The *New York Times* explains that the severity of hurricane seasons varies with the cycles of natural change in temperature over the Atlantic over several decades. Did you say natural? But where does natural come from? Oh, here we go again.

After Katrina, an Atmosphere of Finger-Pointing

SEPTEMBER 7, 2005

How different the atmosphere from 9/11, almost four years ago, when Americans flew their flags and rallied to a president speaking through a bullhorn at New York's ground zero. Now, as Dick Cheney is dispatched to the flood-stricken area to ride herd over the belated federal effort, the president defensively asks Americans to put off the blame game, promising his own investigation of what went wrong in the federal response to Katrina. I hope he won't be too hard on himself.

Now even tried-and-true conservatives are turning away from Mr. Bush. William Kristol, editor of the *Weekly Standard,* tells the *Washington Post,* "Almost every Republican I have spoken with is disappointed." Congress will undoubtedly examine not only the chaotic initial reaction to the flood, but why the White House cut back sharply on funding for levees and infrastructure in favor of tax cuts and the war in Iraq.

It will undoubtedly reassure you to know that the president, tanned and ready after his long Texas vacation, retains his flair for lighthearted jokes. At the end of a cabinet session yesterday, he noted that the list of replacements for Supreme Court justice Sandra Day O'Connor is wide open. And he added, "Make sure you notice when I said that, I looked right at Al Gonzales, who can really create speculation." Attorney General Gonzales is opposed by many right-wing Bush supporters because of his ambiguous stand on abortion. Kristol said that nominating him would utterly demoralize many of the president's supporters.

There'll be controversy over the Supreme Court, but Katrina is not likely to go away. Liberals and conservatives alike want to know not only how Michael Brown, director of the Federal Emergency Management Agency, and Michael Chertoff, head of the Homeland Security Department, could have been among the last to know about the chaos in the convention center. But they will also want answers to the larger question of whether it was a good idea to lump the emergency agency into a massive Homeland Security Department to be administered by political cronies.

The Insidiousness of Cronyism

SEPTEMBER 28, 2005

Former emergency manager Michael Brown—somehow still on the federal payroll as a consultant after leaving his job, accused of mishandling the Katrina disaster—played an inning of "the blame game" with a largely Republican House committee yesterday. The bottom line is that the former horse show administrator still thinks he did a heck of a job on the storm and the flood, and criticism, if any, should be leveled at dysfunctional state and municipal officials in Louisiana and maybe the White House, which diverted funds for natural emergencies to anti-terrorism needs.

Let us not linger too long over the Michael Brown embarrassment. He's only one example of cronyism in high places. Another example is David Safavian, the lobbyist with no auditing experience who oversaw $300 billion in federal procurement until he resigned and was arrested, alleged to have lied to investigators about his dealings with superlobbyist Jack Abramoff. The larger story is the deep corruption that occurs when leaders contemptuous of the government they lead use federal positions to reward friends and money raisers.

A long time ago, in the era of Andrew Jackson, it was called the spoils system: "To the victor belong the spoils." It was also called patronage. Starting in 1883, there came a series of reforms culminating in the Pendleton Act, which established civil service and a merit system for persons competing for jobs.

But in time, presidents found a way to evade the merit system. At the start of every administration, the Office of Personnel Management publishes the Plumb Book, listing some three thousand jobs that the president can fill without regard to civil service merit rules. That's how you get a horse show commissioner entrusted with the lives of millions of Americans facing emergencies, and that's how you get a former lobbyist overseeing billions in federal contracts. In 1980, when a series of scandals rocked the Reagan administration, the *Washington Post* coined a phrase for it: "a big bowl of sleaze." That characterization could be dug up today.

The Plague of the Middle East

OCTOBER 2, 2005

In the wake of the Israeli withdrawal from the Gaza Strip, completed on September 12, there have been sporadic exchanges of rocket fire between Palestinian militants and the Israeli army.

In the hope of getting American pressure for a cessation of hostilities, Palestinian president Mahmoud Abbas is journeying to Washington later this month to see President Bush, for in the coming months, the future of the Israeli-Palestinian relationship may be influenced more by power struggles in the two camps than developments between the two camps.

On the Israeli side, former prime minister Benjamin Netanyahu is bent on the ouster of Prime Minister Ariel Sharon as the leader of the governing Likud Party. Netanyahu narrowly failed to win a vote in the Likud Central Committee to hold a new election for party leader next April, but he continues to be a thorn in Sharon's side. If Netanyahu eventually succeeds in deposing Sharon from the leadership of the right-wing party, the incumbent prime minister would probably try to stay in office, assembling a new coalition of supportive Likudniks along with Labor and perhaps one or more of the fringe parties, but Sharon will probably be weakened in negotiations with the Palestinians.

The Palestinian leadership also faces an early trial by ballot. President Abbas has renounced violence in the quest for a Palestinian state, but has so far not managed to win over the militant Hamas and Islamic Jihad. An election next January 25, for the Palestinian Legislative Council, the Palestinian parliament, will determine how much support he has among the population. In recent municipal elections, Fatah, Abbas's party, and Hamas emerged as the major players. Even while Hamas has been gaining ground against Fatah, Abbas continues to enjoy popular support, and significantly, in opinion polls, 57 percent of Palestinians oppose armed attacks on Israel.

On both sides, Israeli and Palestinian, there appears to be a struggle for legitimacy. On each side, there are hard-liners seeking to wrest control of policy and return to confrontational opposition. That this drama is being played out, at least for now, by ballot rather than bullet may

316 • COME TO THINK OF IT

itself be a hopeful sign. But as we have so often seen, that could change in a minute.

The Miers Nomination Blurs the Party Lines

OCTOBER 19, 2005

Melissa Block, host: On Capitol Hill today, the Senate Judiciary Committee set the date for Harriet Miers's confirmation hearings. They'll start on November 7. But as they set the calendar, leaders of the committee said the questionnaire that Miers filled out was incomplete, and they asked for more information. Here's what the committee's chairman, Arlen Specter, had to say.

Senator Arlen Specter (Republican, Pennsylvania): Senator Leahy and I took a look at it and agreed that it was insufficient and are sending back a detailed letter asking for amplification on many, many of the items.

Block: NPR senior news analyst Daniel Schorr is keeping track of the Miers nomination and trying to tally who's winning and losing.

Judiciary chairman Arlen Specter says that the confirmation process so far has been chaotic, and no wonder. It's becoming increasingly difficult to tell the score even with a scorecard. A good number of conservative Republicans continue to oppose Harriet Miers, despite her revelation that in 1989 she supported a constitutional amendment to ban almost all abortions. On the other hand, some Democrats support her; a recent Gallup poll said it was 24 percent of Democrats. Democratic senator Tom Harkin said all the trashing is coming from the right wing of the Republican Party. That may not be strictly true, but it is true that opposition among Republican conservatives remains strong. Senator Trent Lott, for example, says, "The question remains whether she is qualified, whether she is competent."

President Bush has reached out to evangelicals by saying that religion is part of Harriet Miers's life. That could conceivably run up against Article VI of the Constitution, which says that no religious tests shall ever be required for any public office. But more to the point, it has backfired among some conservatives. Concerned Women for America, the largest women's antiabortion organization, says that focusing on evangelical Christianity is both patronizing and hypocritical.

The latest conservative to enter the ring against Ms. Miers is Robert Bork, who himself failed to be confirmed to the Supreme Court in 1987. In the *Wall Street Journal,* he says that Ms. Miers is not qualified to sit on the Court, and her nomination as a kind of stealth candidate has damaged the prospects for Court reform.

As strange a disclosure as any in this process has been Ms. Miers's revelation, in documents furnished to the Senate, that she originally declined to be considered for nomination and that, for a time, she was being considered by White House officials without her knowledge. Perhaps that's meant to indicate humility, which served Chief Justice John Roberts in good stead in his confirmation battle. What can be said is that the Miers situation is fluid.

Hitting the Neediest Hard

NOVEMBER 2, 2005

America finds itself facing billions of dollars in expenditures unanticipated when President Bush was reelected a year ago today: the Iraq war, Hurricane Katrina, and now $7 billion to help prepare for a possible flu pandemic. Where is all that money supposed to come from? A lot is borrowed, of course, but Congress is busy making cuts in planned expenditures, and those cuts bear disproportionately on the Americans who can least afford them, the poor. They are officially numbered as 37 million people, up 1 million in a year.

So think of all those numbers as you learn that a House committee has voted to cut the food stamp program, lopping 300,000 recipients off the rolls, or that another committee has voted to cut Medicaid by $9.3 billion over five years, or that similar cuts are proposed in housing assistance, or that some 225,000 persons, including 40,000 children, could lose their help from the program called Temporary Assistance to Needy Families.

Are there other ways to deal with the ballooning deficit? One way obviously would be to postpone tax cuts. Another way would be to repeal some of the nonurgent projects in the highway bill, like that famous Alaska bridge to nowhere. Senate Budget Committee chairman Judd Gregg has come up with the novel idea of taxing windfall oil company profits to help the poor with their winter heating bills. But oil companies have effective lobbies in Washington and poor people don't. And so when House Republican leaders talk of cutting entitlement programs by $50 billion, they're not talking about oil companies.

Nixon's Vietnam Versus Bush's Iraq

NOVEMBER 20, 2005

Worried about flagging support for the war? The president tells his aides in a secret memo, "Publicly we say one thing; actually, we do another."

That was not President Bush on Iraq, but President Nixon on Vietnam and Cambodia. It's only one line in some fifty thousand pages of newly declassified documents in the National Archives. It's not surprising, but still a little unsettling, to learn how often a president will not level with the people. The revelation of the abuse of detainees in the Abu Ghraib prison near Baghdad was bad news for the Bush administration, much like the 1968 massacre of more than 350 South Vietnamese civilians in the village of My Lai. My Lai was treated by the Nixon White House as a public relations problem more than a moral problem. Defense Secretary Melvin Laird warned Nixon that My Lai could prove acutely embarrassing to the United States and could affect the Paris peace talks with North Vietnam. Laird added that My Lai would provide grist for the mill of antiwar activists and could be ruinous to our image.

Nixon said that an image could be changed, and Secretary of State Henry Kissinger weighed in with the observation that the trial of Lieutenant William Calley, implicated in the My Lai massacre, would alleviate press concerns about a cover-up. Some of the discussions about the future of Vietnam read eerily like memos on Iraq. In May 1969, a Nixon White House document said the United States wanted to establish in Vietnam procedures for political choice that give each significant group a real opportunity to participate in the political life of a nation. Sound a little like Iraq? And to bring this up to date, former secretary Laird has an article in the current *Foreign Affairs* magazine. Its title: "Iraq: Learning the Lessons of Vietnam."

Arguing for de-Americanizing the Iraq war, Laird says that our presence is what feeds the insurgency. Laird says he's the one who invented the term "Vietnamization." And maybe the word today should be "Iraqization."

Bush's "Charming" Diplomats

DECEMBER 11, 2005

President Bush's secretaries of state have a good deal of charm.

But as Colin Powell and Condoleezza Rice have discovered, charm doesn't help much when you're in a dispute with the president's inner circle. In a march to war, they walked all over Colin Powell and saddled him with the ultimate humiliation of having to read to the UN Security Council a mendacious speech about Saddam Hussein's alleged weapons of mass destruction.

On the eve of war, according to Hendrik Hertzberg in the *New Yorker,* a foreign diplomat told Powell at a social event that he heard that Mr. Bush was sleeping like a baby. The secretary replied, "I'm sleeping like a baby, too. Every two hours I wake up screaming."

And so, few were surprised when, after Mr. Bush's reelection, Powell resigned, and characteristic of the camaraderie in the White House, a source said that no one had asked him to stay. So now, Condoleezza Rice, jetting around the world, putting out fires, some of which others in the administration have helped to fuel; the most vexing of the fires, which set the chancelleries of Europe ablaze, came from the impression that the Bush administration was not categorical enough about forbidding cruel and inhumane techniques in interrogating terrorist suspects. That issue dogged the secretary's footsteps from Berlin to Kiev and into Brussels, and her job wasn't made easier by the way that the White House sometimes undercut her assurances to foreign ministers.

White House spokesman Scott McClellan, on whose instructions I do not know, defended the practice of rendition, that is, secretly moving suspects to other countries, as a vital tool in the war against terror. And that led foreign ministers and American reporters to ask, "Who speaks for the president?" The visiting Austrian chancellor, Wolfgang Schüssel, after a meeting in the Oval Office, said, "I'm quite happy that Condoleezza Rice went to Europe. She took the heat." She did, indeed, just as Colin Powell did before her.

The State of Peace on Earth in 2005

DECEMBER 26, 2005

This is my last contribution of the year to *All Things Considered,* and so allow me to say good-bye 2005 and good riddance. Even allowing for a journalist's innate pessimism, it has been a year of almost unprecedented disasters natural and tragedies human.

The tsunami struck the Indian Ocean countries a week before the new year, and through the year the death toll kept rising as more bodies were found. Hurricane Katrina brought disaster to our shores. The death toll to date? More than thirteen hundred. Disaster compounded by evidence of human failure: the disclosure of a race and class fault line running through New Orleans, and the early abdication of government in dealing with the crisis. The Iraq war was a tragedy in danger of becoming a disaster, as the Bush administration pressed its efforts to assemble a parliament and a government and avert a sectarian war. The devastating earthquake in Pakistan: seventy-four thousand dead and counting—the only consolation being the great response of international governments and organizations, their resources almost overwhelmed.

Perhaps more tragic than what nature does to humans is what humans do to humans. In the Darfur region of Sudan, an estimated 180,000 with the wrong ethnic background were being slaughtered. And in Africa and elsewhere, 85 million human beings were going hungry.

In our well-fed democracy, there were other kinds of tragedy: the routine peddling of influence by members of Congress, the revolving door between Capitol Hill and the lobbyist hangout on K Street, the unusual fact that the majority leaders of the Senate and the House were both in legal trouble.

Also, not a good year for civil liberties: the disclosure of wiretapping of Americans without warrants, the secret prisons for terror suspects, and the mistreatment of prisoners under interrogation.

And finally, not a very good year for journalism, under increasing pressure to cooperate with the authorities and stop asking for special privilege.

Better luck next year.

2006

Old Fights, New Scandals

The Abramoff Scandal

JANUARY 4, 2006

What a relief to be able to lay aside reading about the investigations of national security leaks and turn to the well-trampled ground of congressional sleaze.

I have warm memories of corruption past. In the late eighties and early nineties, there were the Keating Five, five senators accused of helping Charles Keating, chairman of a collapsed savings and loan institution, avoid a searching investigation. The five senators had received a total of $1.3 million in campaign contributions from Keating.

There was ABSCAM in 1980, when the FBI set up a sting operation that caught on videotape a senator and five representatives receiving cash payments from a fictitious Middle Eastern businessman in return for political influence. That was the first major FBI operation against a member of Congress.

And now the biggest of the lot, superlobbyist Jack Abramoff and company, one after another copping a plea and probably more to come. A contrite Abramoff has reportedly said he is ready to name as many as sixty members of Congress and staffers who have benefited from his largesse, no doubt for value received. What is especially cheering about the Abramoff case is that it's being conducted by a Bush appointee, Alice Fisher, head of the Justice Department's criminal division. "The corruption scheme with Mr. Abramoff is very extensive," she said yesterday. "We're going to continue to follow it wherever it leads." You can imagine the shudders on Capitol Hill.

Amid all the corruption in government, it's also cheering to find public servants who are willing to pursue their ethical standards even when their superiors may be involved. I'm reminded of Watergate, where President Nixon did not succeed in corrupting the FBI, and Attorney General Richard Kleindienst ended up with a perjury conviction.

But as with Watergate, it is not only our prosecutors who deserve credit, but the much-maligned press. The story of Abramoff and company was brought to national attention in February 2004 by the *Washington Post;* the government investigation followed. Between them, the prosecutor and the press may make a contribution to clean government.

The Sago Mine Disaster

JANUARY 9, 2006

The West Virginia legislature has announced an investigation of the Sago Mine disaster. And the U.S. Congress will undoubtedly soon follow.

What can be noted at this stage is that the accident that took the lives of the twelve miners occurred against a background of deregulatory zeal fostered by the Bush administration and especially by the no longer House majority leader Tom DeLay. DeLay has called the Environmental Protection Agency a government gestapo, and he's been called "Congressman Dereg." Colleagues have said he has embarked on a jihad against regulation. The *National Journal* said his zest for deregulation dated back to his encounters with federal inspectors when he ran a pest control business in Houston.

Direct connections between lax regulation and accidents may be hard to establish, but the *Charleston (WV) Gazette* and the *Washington Post* are among the newspapers that have reported a record of lenient enforcement at the Sago Mine, which last year was cited two hundred times for a variety of safety violations. The U.S. Mine Safety and Health Administration has gone very easy on the International Coal Group, the owners of the Sago Mine. The biggest fine it's had to pay is $440. The deregulatory attitude of the government was evident in the drop in referrals in all coal mines for possible criminal action from thirty-eight to twelve last year. The Bush administration pursued a policy of forging a cooperative relationship between the mine operators and the safety administration. Most of the regulations proposed during the Clinton administration were dropped by President Bush soon after coming into office.

The federal and state investigations may take months, perhaps years to complete. Today one can only raise the question of whether the Bush-DeLay passion for deregulation and lax treatment of violators had any connection with the disaster.

Hamas Victory at the Polls

JANUARY 25, 2006

The astute Palestinian demographer Khalil Shikaki had it doped out four years ago. Palestinians were getting fed up with the corrupt old-guard Fatah movement of Yasser Arafat, which was increasingly being challenged by militant groups led by Hamas, the Islamic resistance movement. Hamas has made its entrance onto the national electoral stage, calling itself the Change and Reform Party. The relative success of Hamas, a philanthropic as well as political organization, in the election is likely to represent a major headache for both Israel and the Bush administration, both of which have banned any dealings with Hamas as a terrorist organization. The White House said today that nothing has changed.

The Bush administration sank $1.9 million of aid money into the Fatah-led government during the campaign. Israel's acting prime minister, Ehud Olmert, in a speech yesterday that seemed to be addressed to Palestinian voters, backed the creation of a Palestinian state as outlined in the so-called "Road Map" plan, and said that Israel was willing to yield part of the West Bank if only to retain a Jewish majority in the Jewish state.

Assuming that Hamas with a strong showing will be given a place in the Palestinian Authority government, one can see an intense period of negotiation, including some demand that Hamas renounce violence. The situation raises the question: Democratic elections are fine, but what do you do when the wrong guys win? If no way is found out of the stalemate, then Israel may do what Sharon did with Gaza, unilaterally withdraw from parts of the West Bank and announce Israel's final borders.

Whatever happens, it seems clear that the Israel-Palestinian conflict is entering a new phase with Hamas as a player. It could be called the post-Arafat, post-Sharon era.

Cheney's Hunting Accident

FEBRUARY 16, 2006

Finally, after four days in an undisclosed location, one of his favorite places, Vice President Cheney emerged to appear on the Bush-friendly Fox News Channel and accept full blame for the shooting of fellow quail hunter Harry Whittington.

"One of the worst days of my life," Cheney said. But the accident that for a time shook the country would not soon be forgotten. It had its bizarre aspects. On Sunday Sheriff Ramone Salinas was dispatched to talk to the vice president and establish that the shooting had been an accident. I guess the police are trained not to assume anything. Today they announced that they had decided not to press any charges.

Equally bizarre was that the shooting first became known through what might be called a high-level leak. While the vice president's party and the White House maintained their silence, the proprietor of the ranch, Katherine Armstrong, was dispatched on Sunday morning to tip off her local newspaper, the *Corpus Christi Caller-Times*.

The paper then posted the story on its Web site, and thus a serious incident involving the man a heartbeat away from the presidency became known to a bemused public.

Cheney could've learned a lesson from the president about leveling with the public. In his 1999 memoir as governor, Mr. Bush tells of accidentally killing a protected songbird while hunting with his friend Karen Hughes. They agreed immediately to go public and confess. Bush wrote, "People watch the way you handle things. They get a feeling they like and trust you, or they don't."

Cheney would have been well advised to do as Mr. Bush had done, go public immediately rather than spend four days figuring out how to handle this problem. As it was, he was already facing declining popularity. The CBS News polls showed an approval rating of 35 percent and a disapproval rating of 46 percent.

Perhaps even worse news for Cheney was an article in the *Wall Street Journal* today by conservative speechwriter and columnist Peggy Noonan. She said her hunch is that people in the White House are thinking that if Cheney wasn't vice president, who would be a good vice president?

In his Fox News interview yesterday, Cheney said that he would never get out of his memory the image of Whittington falling. The chances are he's going to have a lot of help remembering.

Congress Drops the Ball

MARCH 29, 2006

The day of sentencing of superlobbyist Jack Abramoff may be as good a day as any to review progress toward ethics reform in Congress.

Briefly, not much.

The bipartisan congressional Ethics Committees are virtually missing in action, and the proposal in the Senate to establish an outside Office of Public Integrity was rejected by a substantial margin.

The Senate today, by a lopsided 90–8 vote, passed a bill that emphasizes disclosure rather than new prohibitions on lobbyist contacts. In the House, there have been some halfway gestures toward reining in lobbyist-paid meals, trips, and sports tickets, but the restriction on travel has a sunset provision, expiring at the end of this session of Congress.

Thanks to some vigorous lobbying by the National Restaurant Association, lobbyist-paid meals would not be banned, but they would be capped at $50 per meal. Gifts from lobbyists would not be banned, but they would be subject to disclosure.

One irony in the current flurry of quasi reform is that the Senate appears ready to enact restrictions on Internet gambling, provisions that Abramoff was paid by his casino clients to oppose.

One interesting change: the Senate has voted to end a practice by which a single signature acting in secret could block a piece of pending legislation, a potent weapon in the hands of a legislator exercising his veto on behalf of a well-heeled lobbyist.

Will these halfway changes change the picture that the public has of Congress as a corrupt institution whose name is Jack Abramoff and Randy "Duke" Cunningham? The answer to that may come in next November's election.

Rumsfeld and the Grumbling Generals

APRIL 16, 2006

"Old soldiers never die; they just fade away."

That famous quotation from General Douglas MacArthur may have to be amended in light of an amazing uprising of retired generals against their civilian boss, Defense Secretary Donald Rumsfeld. The generals challenged the conduct of the war in Iraq and in some cases the rationale for the war. In *Time* magazine, retired lieutenant general Gregory Newbold decried an unnecessary war fought on a zealous rationale that made no sense.

On NPR, retired army general John Riggs called for Rumsfeld's resignation as one who only listens to the military when it serves his purpose. Retired army general Eric Shinseki, while still in service, warned that the expeditionary force in Iraq was spread too thin, and thereafter he was marginalized by the Bush administration. Retired army general John Batiste said that civilian leadership was needed that respected the military. And retired major general Charles Swannack, who commanded the Eighty-second Airborne Division, spoke of Rumsfeld's absolute failures in managing the war.

To all of this, President Bush responds by praising Rumsfeld's energetic and steady leadership. But this flap is not likely to end there. It's bound to escalate when Congress returns from its Easter recess, and the pressure on Rumsfeld is likely to grow, raising an uncomfortable issue of civilian control over the military.

Petropolitics Play into Fall Elections

APRIL 26, 2006

"Petropolitics" is a word coined by Tom Friedman in *Foreign Policy* magazine to describe the way nations with oil tend to be less democratic than nations without oil. I borrow the term to denote the impact of oil on politics, national and international.

One reason for the spike in oil prices, the experts say, is the fear that menacing American moves toward Iran may affect exports and petroleum futures. At home Exxon rolled up a record $36 billion in profits last year, and its retired chairman Lee Raymond rolled up $400 million as a fond farewell. The industry is contemplating a multimillion-dollar educational outreach campaign. Translated: Don't blame us.

The administration and Congress are striving to position themselves as sharing the pain at the pump. The pressure is greater on the Republicans simply because it happened on their watch, and people are demanding that they don't just stand there. They are trying to persuade the public that they aren't just standing there, but that there is no short-term way of getting prices down. President Bush yesterday announced some small steps, like suspending purchases for the strategic reserve and encouraging the purchase of hybrid cars.

The usually industry-friendly leaders in Congress, Speaker Dennis Hastert and Senator Bill Frist, have asked the White House for an investigation into possible price gouging. The *Hill* newspaper says that a bill with bipartisan support in the Senate Judiciary Committee would direct antitrust enforcement agencies to take a closer look at proposed mergers in the petroleum industry. If gas prices this summer are as painful as foreseen, the Democrats have the potential for a zinger issue in the November election. The Democratic Congressional Campaign Committee is encouraging candidates to go beyond talk of price gouging and windfall profits and to talk about reform that would reduce dependence on foreign oil. None of this is likely to bring down gas prices anytime soon. But that's the way the great game of petropolitics is played.

Remembering Journalist Abe Rosenthal

MAY 14, 2006

Permit a personal aside about my friend Abe Rosenthal, A. M. Rosenthal to readers of the *New York Times*.

His funeral is today in Central Synagogue in New York. We shared a neighborhood, the Bronx; a high school, De Witt Clinton; and a college, City College of New York. Also, we shared some interesting cold war assignments.

In 1959, we were together in Poland, Abe more skeptical than I was about signs of liberalization in Communist rule. He wrote with glee about the tumultuous reception that Vice President Richard Nixon received on a visit to Poland, and the chilly reception for Soviet Communist boss Nikita Khrushchev.

Abe knew that he was risking expulsion when he wrote about Polish Communist chief Wladyslaw Gomulka as being moody and irascible and spurned by Polish workers. And indeed, the Polish government sent Abe packing with a statement saying candidly that the government could not tolerate such probing reporting.

But such probing reporting won Abe a Pulitzer Prize for international reporting, and as it happened, we were together in Geneva when word came of the award.

In 1963, when Abe was offered an executive position on the *Times,* I advised him not to take it. I said that managers were a dime a dozen, but gifted reporters and writers were rare. He said that having been offered the promotion, he had to accept it or he would have to leave the paper. And so he climbed the ladder to executive editor, but he retained some reportorial instincts.

In 1975, he was one of a group of *Times* editors to be invited to the White House for lunch with President Ford. Ford had just named a commission headed by Vice President Nelson Rockefeller to investigate CIA misdeeds. Rosenthal noted to the president that the members of the commission seemed too conservative to have much credibility. President Ford replied that he had to be careful because the commission members would have complete access to CIA files and would run into something much worse than what they thought they were investigating.

"Like what?" Abe asked. "Like assassinations," Ford shot back. And then he asked that this be kept off the record.

The *Times* did not pursue the lead to CIA conspiracies to assassinate Fidel Castro and others, and so I was able to break the story on the *CBS Evening News.* It was one time I imagined that Abe would rather have been a reporter than an executive.

Let's Not Make English the National Language

MAY 28, 2006

Back in 1913, my parents came to the United States from Russia speaking fluent Yiddish and fairly good Russian. They swiftly began to learn English in the way that most of that wave of immigrants did.

I mention this because I just may be predisposed in the recent controversy over giving English some special status, whether it is the official language, the common language, the unifying language, or most recently, the national language, in the bill that the Senate passed on Thursday.

This may seem a harmless addition to the immigration bill, but we have learned that language-proficiency requirements can be used as a weapon in political campaigns. After the Civil War, when the Fifteenth Amendment to the Constitution banned deprivation of the vote, some states responded by instituting especially tough literacy tests.

It is not pleasant to recall that when William Rehnquist came up for confirmation to the Supreme Court in 1971, he had to respond to a series of questions about his actions on behalf of the Republican campaign in 1964. Bill Rehnquist, as he was called then, headed a squad of campaign workers in Phoenix, Arizona, who challenged minority voters to read the U.S. Constitution in English before they could vote.

The result, according to one witness, was a line half a block long, four abreast, and some just gave up and left. The test was administered only to blacks and Hispanics.

So what is the purpose of giving the English language some special status? It is not a flag to be waved. It is not an oath of allegiance to be taken on becoming an American.

Attorney General Alberto Gonzales, who had three grandparents come to the United States from Mexico, must have had an uncomfortable moment when he was asked about his position on English. He said it is very, very important for people to speak English. It is the path to opportunity.

Yes, but wouldn't that still be true without needing some special designation for English in an immigration bill?

Haditha

MAY 29, 2006

At the West Point commencement on Saturday, President Bush said that each loss is heartbreaking.

In that context, Mr. Bush was talking about the thirty-four academy graduates killed in Iraq and Afghanistan over the last four years, not the dozens of Iraqi civilians apparently killed in their homes by U.S. marines last November 19.

The massacre was first reported by *Time* magazine in March, and since then the grisly details have begun to emerge, mainly from survivors. It seems clear now that in Haditha, north of Baghdad, a marine lance corporal was killed by a roadside bomb. And his enraged buddies swept through three nearby houses shooting point-blank at residents, men, women, children, old, young. It didn't seem to matter.

Only when he came home to Hanford, California, did Lance Corporal Roel Briones tell the *Los Angeles Times* of feeling tormented. He didn't take part in the killings, he said, but he did take pictures of the carnage and he helped to carry bodies out of their homes.

At his joint news conference with British prime minister Tony Blair last Thursday, President Bush listed as America's biggest mistake the Abu Ghraib scandal, in which prisoners were photographed while being tormented. We've been paying for that for a long time, he said. The president didn't mention the Haditha massacre, which has been under investigation for months.

Although on a much smaller scale, Haditha brings back My Lai, 1968, the massacre of hundreds of Vietnamese villagers which came to symbolize American disregard for human life. In this case, the victims were citizens of a country whose sovereignty the United States has hailed. It is not likely, though, that any marines will be turned over to the Iraqi justice ministry for trial.

There will undoubtedly be congressional hearings. Senator John Warner, chairman of the Armed Services Committee, says he plans to look into whether the military chain of command acted properly and legally, that is to say, whether there was a cover-up. And undoubtedly Haditha will add to the pressures for withdrawal from Iraq from Americans, many of whom are already dubious about the assertion that their mission is liberation.

Control or Closure at Guantánamo

JUNE 12, 2006

From Guantánamo to Haditha, the administration's war against terrorism occasionally reveals some stark contradictions.

I am still trying to understand how a squad of U.S. marines could kill up to twenty-four civilians in Haditha, including women and children, and then claim they were following normal rules of military engagement. One wonders what kind of rules of engagement cover house-to-house shooting and hand grenades?

I am also having trouble understanding how the American command, having launched two 500-pound bombs at Abu Musab al-Zarqawi, bristled at the notion that he was killed by gunfire. We are told that American soldiers made every effort to administer medical assistance to keep him alive and he actually died while being transported on a stretcher.

Finally, and almost incomprehensible to me, the reaction to the hanging suicides of three inmates of the military prison at Guantánamo Bay. Others have tried suicide by hanging and by hunger strike, but these were the first to succeed.

The camp commander, Rear Admiral Harry Harris, took it as a personal offense. He said the suicides were not an act of desperation, but an act of asymmetrical warfare waged against us. The inmates, he said, have no regard for life, either ours or their own.

What a peculiar reaction considering that some 460 inmates have been incarcerated for up to four years without trial, without hope, and when some went on hunger strikes, they were strapped into restraint chairs and force-fed, and yet Admiral Harris has a point about asymmetrical warfare. A suicide with or without a bomb is the weapon that confers power on the powerless. These three suicides may accomplish what an international outcry has failed to accomplish, some changes and maybe the closing of Guantánamo.

As the struggle against terrorism drags on, it becomes clear that this is not a war in any customary sense, but a series of engagements that makes up its rules as it goes along.

Hillary Clinton's Polarizing Force as a Candidate

JULY 16, 2006

Listeners may have noticed that I don't comment much about domestic politics.

That's because in the volatile climate of today, no judgment about potential candidates is likely to stand up for very long. I make an exception for Hillary Clinton, who strikes me as the great political paradox of our time. I've admired her since the first time I heard her speak extemporaneously for three-quarters of an hour on a favorite subject, children, and since then, she has shown a grasp of many subjects. So where's the paradox?

Well, you talk to people and they generally express admiration for her, but then comes the "yes, but" factor. A *Washington Post*–ABC poll indicates that as of now, about six in ten Americans would consider supporting her for president and four in ten have ruled her out. Does that make her the Democratic front-runner? Well, yes. But in the Gallup poll last summer, 53 percent of respondents thought she would divide rather than unite the country.

Personal interviews show ambivalent feelings about Senator Clinton. A veteran Democratic voter in Iowa City says, "I hope she won't run and I don't know whether I would support her." Another active Democrat says, "I don't quite understand why she is such a polarizing figure, but she is." And still another Iowa Democrat: "I don't think she could win. It would just keep the country split." In effect, many Democrats seem to be saying, "I would vote for her, but I think a lot of other people wouldn't."

That's what you call the "yes, but" factor. Iowa Democrat Lloyd Jones may have said it all when he said, "Those of us who think she would be a great president are fearful of the viciousness of the attacks we anticipate the opposition would level against her." And what do I think? Well, you're not going to get me to stick my neck out about the chances of this first-class politician with a social conscience.

Political Gaffes? Welcome to America

AUGUST 27, 2006

Once again we learn the danger of the ill-considered word in politics.

Especially in a day when opposition cameras are there to record it and the Internet is there to send it coursing around the country.

The latest verbal misstep in politics was committed by Republican senator George Allen of Virginia, who is seeking a second term in the Senate and possibly the presidency. At a fund-raiser in southwest Virginia, he referred to a man in his audience as a macaca. Macaca is literally a genus of primate; the word is used in some circles as a pejorative reference to any dark-skinned person. The twenty-year-old man is of Indian descent, and it was his camera that caught the slur. So Senator Allen offered apologies, but the word "macaca" is now an indelible part of the campaign.

I looked back to other verbal transgressions. Senator John McCain, running for president in 2000, referred to his prison guards in North Vietnam as gooks. "I hate the gooks," he said. "I will hate them as long as I live." But "gook" is also a more general pejorative word for Asians. Senator McCain caught some flak but he stuck to his verbal guns.

Then there was the Reverend Jesse Jackson running for president in 1984. He referred to New York City as Hymietown and to Jews as Hymies. He said it in what could be construed as a private conversation with a *Washington Post* reporter, but it ended up in the *Post* under the byline of a different reporter. In the end, Jackson admitted guilt and asked for forgiveness.

And then Earl Butz, secretary of agriculture in the Nixon and Ford cabinets, was forced to resign for making remarks about blacks. "I'll tell you what the coloreds want," he told reporters on a Ford campaign plane. What followed was too obscene to repeat on the air.

And finally, Senator Trent Lott, the former majority leader. He sought to pay a compliment to Senator Strom Thurmond on his 100th birthday by saying the country would have been better off if the presidential bid by Thurmond had been successful. That was 1948, a time when Thurmond openly supported segregation. Senator Lott is majority leader no longer.

Why do they do it? In most cases because they don't grasp the effect of their bigoted words on others. But a tin ear is no great qualification for high office.

Dividing the "Moral Vote" After New Scandals

OCTOBER 25, 2006

Speaker Dennis Hastert went yesterday where a Speaker rarely goes, to testify before the House Ethics Committee. There have been more lobbying and corruption scandals in the House than at any time in a generation. Randy "Duke" Cunningham, Robert Ney, Tom DeLay, William Jefferson, et cetera.

But a so-called congressional page scandal, and questions of who failed to act before ABC broke the story, have gripped the American public in a way that money corruption has not. The scandal surrounding the disgraced Mark Foley and his suggestive e-mail communications with House pages hit Americans where it hurts—the vulnerability of teenage boys to men of power who are predators. Republican leaders have been heading for the hills; there have been failures of memory and contradictions with the recollections of staff members.

We do not know what Speaker Hastert and Tom Reynolds, the chairman of the National Republican House Congressional Committee, testified. The Ethics Committee is not known for speedy investigations, nor is it likely to have a report before the election thirteen days from today. But the page scandal and the suspected cover-up have already had their effects on the electorate.

In a *Newsweek* poll earlier this month, 27 percent of registered voters said the scandal and how the leadership handled it made them less likely to vote for a Republican congressional candidate. A *Time* magazine poll said that two-thirds of those aware of the scandal believe that Republican leaders attempted a cover-up.

This is the first time in recent years, says *Newsweek,* that more Americans trust the Democrats than Republicans on moral values. One can only speculate on how the election will be affected. How many disaffected evangelicals will change their vote? How many will just stay home? But one way or another, the case of one errant congressman may have a profound impact on the voting pattern.

The Legacy of Supreme Court Justice Brandeis

NOVEMBER 20, 2006

Indulge me in a little sesquicentennial sentiment about my favorite jurist.

A hundred and fifty years ago this month, Supreme Court justice Louis D. Brandeis was born in Louisville, Kentucky, the son of immigrants from Czechoslovakia. He was graduated from Harvard Law School with some of the highest grades ever received there. He was named to the Supreme Court by President Woodrow Wilson as its first Jewish and its most liberal member.

If he is remembered for nothing else, he is remembered for discovering a constitutional right to privacy, which became the underpinning of the right to abortion. But there is more.

Brandeis upheld your right as an individual to think as you will and to speak as you think, even against the government. He enunciated a right to be left alone by the government as the right most valued by civilized men. He held that decency, security, and liberty require that government officials be subjected to the same rules of conduct that are commands to the citizen. He asserted that a doctrine of separation of powers was adopted not to promote efficiency, but to preclude the exercise of arbitrary power.

And on an issue hotly debated during the Roosevelt New Deal days, he held that there must be power in the states and in the nation to remold through experimentation our economic practices and institutions.

And a few other lines from Brandeis. "Sunshine is the best disinfectant." "The most important political office is that of the private citizen." And finally, "Those who won our independence . . . did not fear political change. They did not exalt order at the cost of liberty." And as full disclosure—I hold an honorary degree from Brandeis University.

A Melancholy Milestone in Iraq

NOVEMBER 26, 2006

This is an occasion of sorts, a melancholy one. On this Sunday, the war with Iraq has lasted longer than America's involvement in World

War II. And unlike VE Day and VJ Day, there is no VI Day in sight in a deepening insurrectionist war and a spreading sectarian war. Many thousands of Iraqis have been killed. Up to 2 million have fled, and there are signs of a society in a process of disintegration.

A telling sign is the Iraqis who work as police by day and sectarian militias by night, wearing police uniforms that facilitate kidnapping— almost routinely Sunnis are kidnapped by Shiites and Shiites by Sunnis, stuffed into car trunks and taken away to be tortured and murdered.

President Bush is going to see Iraqi prime minister Nouri al-Maliki, not in Baghdad, where even the heavily fortified Green Zone is no longer considered safe, but in Amman, Jordan. Nothing better illustrates the Bush administration's air of helplessness than this latest idea of involving Syria and Iran in efforts to bring some stability to Iraq.

Syria? Isn't that the country implicated in the assassination of Lebanese officials? And Iran? Isn't that the country trying to dominate the Middle East and inviting Iraq and Syria to a summit conference in Tehran? Not to mention the Iranian nuclear program and threats to annihilate the state of Israel. So where do we go from here?

White House counselor Dan Bartlett says to reporters, the president will assure the prime minister—that is, al-Maliki—that he's the one who sets foreign policy for the country. Well, that's nice. But meanwhile, the killing goes on.

My Brush with Russian Drugging

DECEMBER 10, 2006

In the beginning, there was the strange case of Alexander Litvinenko, the onetime Russian spy who had denounced Vladimir Putin, himself a former spymaster.

On November 1, Litvinenko, who was living in London, began to feel not well. Three weeks later, he died in a hospital, diagnosed with radioactive poisoning from a substance called polonium 210. From his deathbed, he dictated a statement accusing Putin of organizing his murder.

Now Scotland Yard is treating Litvinenko's death as a homicide. And it's sent a group of investigators to Moscow with a hope for Russian cooperation. So far, radioactive traces have turned up in places as disparate as British Airways' Moscow-to-London flights and a hotel bar where seven bartenders have tested positive for radioactive contamination.

I have a particular interest in Russian intelligence and its way with chemicals stemming from my own experience a half century ago. In 1956, as Moscow correspondent for CBS, I was covering a visit to the Soviet Union by Yugoslav president Tito, a guest of Khrushchev. When we reached Yalta on the Black Sea, a Soviet press officer told the several foreign correspondents to turn back. The rest of the trip was off the record. I said I had no intention of turning back. Next morning, I had breakfast on the hotel balcony and had hardly finished before I began to feel giddy and then blacked out.

When I regained consciousness, I found myself on an Aeroflot airliner nearing Moscow. Eventually an American embassy physician told me I had been given knockout drops, what some call a Mickey Finn. At that, I got off easier than Litvinenko or the several others who have shown traces of toxic poisoning.

Yegor Gaidar, a former Russian prime minister and another critic of Putin, turned violently ill during a conference in Ireland. He said he was certain he had been poisoned. And last week we learned that Dimitri Kovtun, who met with Litvinenko at that London hotel bar, has been hospitalized with signs of polonium contamination.

Now the Kremlin is no longer dismissing suspicions about the painful death of Alexander Litvinenko as nonsense. It's announced its own investigation. I wish them a lot of luck. Never did find out who fed me those knockout drops a half century ago.

Bush Gives Few Clues to the Next Steps for Iraq

DECEMBER 20, 2006

President Bush's year-end news conference was almost painful to watch. His state of denial appears finally to have been punctured.

While he still sees merit in his decision to unseat Saddam Hussein, he ruefully acknowledges that the war in Iraq is not being won and that a greater commitment of manpower will be necessary to sustain the military. He admitted that it was his decision that caused young men to lose their lives, and the loss of good men and women he counted as the most painful aspect of his presidency.

Beyond a show of emotion about the sanguinary state of the war that he launched, Mr. Bush gave no indication of what comes next. His delayed new-way-forward speech is apparently still being negotiated with the Joint Chiefs of Staff, which has reportedly expressed reservations about demanding even more from the overstressed army and marines.

The president denied any clash with the Joint Chiefs. But officially, the military doesn't clash with the commander in chief. He just lets his opinions become known. One plan reportedly being considered involves a surge, that is, a temporary deployment of reinforcements to stabilize Baghdad. A decision is needed in the next few weeks, not only because of the president's speech, but because Congress will have to act soon to continue to fund the war effort. The president has apparently sought to buy some time by sending his new defense secretary, Robert Gates, to Baghdad for a fresh look at the situation.

Meanwhile, Secretary of State Condoleezza Rice is going to the Middle East early in the new year to drum up support from the so-called mainstream states—Jordan, Egypt, and Saudi Arabia—for stability in Iraq, Lebanon, and the Palestinian Territories. Her mission apparently is to assure them that the American military will not pull out precipitately.

Caught between these contending forces, that's what you call a quagmire.

Remembering President Ford

DECEMBER 31, 2006

Gerry Ford never sought to be vice president.

He never sought to be president. These offices fell to him because of the misdeeds of others. Ford told me once how it started. In October 1973, the House minority leader, Ford, was summoned to the Oval Office. President Nixon got right to the point. Vice President Spiro Agnew was about to resign in disgrace. Nixon had to designate a new vice president. He would have liked to have had former treasury secretary John Connally, but for quick confirmation he needed someone from Congress. And so he was offering the position to Ford. But Ford had to know that when Nixon completed his second term, he intended to back not the vice president but Connally as the 1976 Republican standard-bearer. Ford said he had no ambition for higher office.

At this early stage of Watergate investigations, Nixon apparently didn't dream that he would not get to complete his presidency or to designate his successor. Nixon said that Ford would be hearing from him soon, and that evening the president telephoned Ford: "Gerry, I want you to be my vice president." By the end of July 1974, Nixon was in serious trouble over the Oval Office tapes that he was refusing to release. He summoned his vice president to hear an angry denunciation of Congress and the press. The House Judiciary Committee was well along in its impeachment inquiry. Nixon gave no indication that he might be driven from office.

But on August 1, Chief of Staff Alexander Haig came to see the vice president in great secrecy, told him that Nixon was in serious shape emotionally and might take some desperate step like pardoning himself. Ford asked about the presidential pardon powers. He was later to insist that there was no pardon-for-presidency deal. And so the accidental vice president became the accidental president as first Agnew, then Nixon were driven from office.

2007

The Truth Is Hard to Come By

The Policy and Politics of Extraordinary Rendition

FEBRUARY 4, 2007

Shocking. So shocking that it was a lead story on the front page of the *New York Times*.

The headline, "German Court Challenges CIA over Abduction." Say what? Well, it seems that a German citizen named Khaled al-Masri was kidnapped while visiting Macedonia and flown to Afghanistan for five months of abusive interrogation before being told it was all a mistake and dumped on a hilltop in Albania. Something similar happened in Italy, where a former intelligence chief is alleged to have been involved with the CIA in kidnapping an Egyptian cleric. This is the extraordinary-rendition program at work, a CIA program that permits the CIA to seize people anywhere and fly them to, say, Afghanistan, to be grilled for months at a time about what they know, if anything, about terrorism.

But European governments don't take kindly to kidnapping. Warrants have been issued in Germany for thirteen CIA agents, and five intelligence agents face indictment in Italy. There is a paradox in all of this. When the Bush administration complains to the German government, it is reminded by the minister of justice that the German courts are independent, that not even Chancellor Angela Merkel can suppress a legal proceeding.

Permit me a personal word. For six years after World War II, I worked in Germany. I was impressed by the way the Germans, with American help, tried to live down their Nazi past and learn the arts of democracy. I had ample occasion to witness German democracy at work. I witnessed German trials of German war criminals. I reported on the denazification of the German system of justice. And so now August Stern, the prosecutor in Munich, says of the warrant that he's issued for thirteen CIA agents that this is a very consequential step before filing criminal charges. The CIA agents will probably never face trial, but they would be well advised to stay out of Germany, where, as we taught, no one's above the law.

The War Lexicon Shifts in Approach

FEBRUARY 12, 2007

If the Iraq war has done nothing else for us, it has enriched the lexicon of conflict, investing old words with new meanings.

Take "surge," for example. To me and to Webster, "surge" is a sudden wave that a surfer might encounter. Now, it's a temporary deployment of troops that you might also call "escalation." The dictionary doesn't tell you how long is temporary.

"Nonbinding" means morally binding, but without the guts to say so. It means getting the credit for wanting the troops to come home without running up against that other slogan, "Support the troops." "Extraordinary rendition"? I would've thought that that refers to Itzhak Perlman playing Beethoven, but no, now it refers to abducting and transporting a terrorism suspect across borders to some other country for some rough interrogation.

Currently, my favorite expression is "alternative intelligence assessment." The first time I heard of that was when it became known that the CIA had not come up with the information that the administration wanted in 2003 as it prepared for the invasion of Iraq. The fuddy-duddy CIA and its associates didn't come up with strong enough intelligence, no smoking guns to be found or weapons of mass destruction or a rumored link between Iraq and the 9/11 hijackers. The undersecretary of defense, Douglas Feith, turned to the Pentagon's own intelligence office.

In the end, there was an investigation by the Pentagon's inspector general. It concluded that Feith's office produced reports not fully substantiated by available intelligence. The inspector general also concluded that the Feith team acted inappropriately but did not violate the law.

On February 2, the National Intelligence Estimate on Iraq was released. It is unfailingly pessimistic, explaining that the term "civil war" does not adequately capture the complexity of the conflict in Iraq, which includes extensive, widespread, criminally motivated violence, according to the estimate. And this time around, no one is talking about an alternative assessment.

Intelligence Questioned in Talks with North Korea and Iran

MARCH 4, 2007

I don't know why they call it intelligence, because it's responsible for some of the most disastrous stupidities in our history.

In 1976, I covered congressional investigations of intelligence mishaps like failing to see the launch of an Egyptian invasion of Israel, even when the tanks were already deployed in a desert. But the nuclear age presents an intelligence challenge of a wholly different order. And when President Bush designated Iran, Iraq, and North Korea as an axis of evil, it was with the nuclear threat in mind.

The invasion of Iraq can be said to have been the result of a failure of intelligence, or perhaps, as a British memorandum put it, the fixing of intelligence to serve the buildup for invasion. Some thousands of lives, some billions of dollars later, the weapons of mass destruction have not yet been found.

So next stop, North Korea: supposed to have a half dozen or maybe it was ten nuclear bombs, or so the intelligence community said. The story was that North Korea had gotten centrifuge technology from Pakistan, enabling it to enrich uranium and make bombs. So now comes the intelligence community on second thought, according to the *New York Times,* and says that come to think of it, maybe North Korea hasn't made as much progress as originally thought.

So now the Bush administration has invited a North Korean delegation to come to Washington and talk the whole thing over. Now there are questions about the Bush decision to confront North Korea in 2002 in the first place.

Next Iran, which says it is enriching uranium but only for peaceful purposes. Until now, the Bush administration has refused to believe that. The United Nations sanctions, not very drastic ones, are in place, and Vice President Cheney says that there are no plans to invade Iran but all options are still on the table. Of course the CIA will be looking at the latest National Intelligence Estimate before making any drastic moves.

The Independence of U.S. Federal Attorneys

MARCH 5, 2007

The scandal of the shoddy treatment of American war heroes at the Walter Reed Army Medical Center, intensely embarrassing to a support-our-troops administration, is being addressed by the army, and heads are rolling. Time to move on to the next festering scandal: the firing of eight U.S. attorneys for reasons that will be explored on Capitol Hill starting tomorrow.

Members of Congress want to know if the attorneys were fired purely for political reasons. David Iglesias in New Mexico, a Republican, believes he was discharged for failing to deliver indictments in a Democratic kickback investigation in time to influence last November's election.

Senator Pete Domenici admitted having queried him about the status of the investigation. The eight discharged prosecutors had all been confirmed by the Senate. I don't recall any confirmation hearings for their replacements. It seems there weren't any. Under a little-noticed amendment to the reauthorized USA Patriot Act, the attorney general can name a U.S. attorney to fill a vacancy who can serve indefinitely without confirmation. I'm reminded of 1974, when the House Judiciary Committee drafted a bill of impeachment against President Nixon.

Article 2 accused him of abuse of presidential powers. One item was the firing of Watergate special prosecutor Archibald Cox in what became known as the Saturday Night Massacre. Another item in the abuse of powers was the unwarranted FBI investigation of me, but that's another story. And so, starting tomorrow, these former U.S. attorneys will tell their stories on Capitol Hill.

Their latest performance reviews found them to be well regarded, capable, or very competent. All of them are Republicans. One of them, H. E. Cummins of Arkansas, was fired to make room for J. Timothy Griffin, a deputy to White House adviser Karl Rove.

The unmaking of the Bush administration marches on.

In Washington, the Hard Truth Is Hard to Come By

MARCH 26, 2007

The front-page story tells of Attorney General Alberto Gonzales being contradicted by e-mail messages on what he says was his level of involvement in the firing of U.S. attorneys. And now several senators are calling for him to step down.

Another front-page story tells of former deputy interior secretary Steven Griles being contradicted by e-mails on his link to superlobbyist Jack Abramoff.

It seems almost exceptional when John Edwards tells the simple truth about his wife's cancer. It may be that electronic recordkeeping has raised a new peril for officials who seek to conceal unpleasant facts. But the urge to avoid unpleasant truths is not new. One doesn't have to go further back than President Reagan in the Iran-Contra scandal to remember "mistakes were made," or President Clinton, "I did not have sexual relations with that woman," to be reminded of the urge to obfuscate at the very top. President Nixon hardly needs to be mentioned.

High-level prevarication has been the subject of academic study. Dr. Sissela Bok, in the 1978 book called *Lying: Moral Choice in Public and Private Life,* wrote that lying cannot be wiped out, but it can be counteracted.

Lynne Cheney, in the 1995 book *Telling the Truth,* wrote that thanks to untrustworthy officials, our culture and our country have stopped making sense.

And Princeton professor Harry Frankfurt, in a 2005 book titled— let's see how I say this—*On Bull* . . . writes about deceptive misrepresentation short of outright lying.

Griles has now pleaded guilty, thus acknowledging that he tried to get away with a lie. The attorney general still insists in the face of evidence to the contrary that he was not involved in the firing of the attorneys. That drama remains to be played out.

Haditha and Abu Ghraib Are Two Shameful Episodes in U.S. History

SEPTEMBER 2, 2007

Liane Hansen, host: Michael Gordon has witnessed and written about the valor of America's troops in Iraq. But two very dark episodes have sullied the reputation of the U.S. military there. NPR's senior news analyst Daniel Schorr offers these reflections.

Haditha, Abu Ghraib, the very words make one wince. They are the titles of two shameful episodes in the history of American war making.

In the Iraqi town of Haditha in 2005, four marine infantrymen killed twenty-four Iraqi civilians including women and children in a rampage through their homes. The Marines were apparently avenging the killing of a comrade.

There were many expressions of outrage in this country, right up to the Pentagon. Secretary Donald Rumsfeld promised a thorough investigation and punishment, but only now is the Haditha investigation nearing its close.

A hearing is currently under way at Marine headquarters in Camp Pendleton, California, to determine whether Staff Sergeant Frank Wuterich, the alleged ringleader of the marauding Marines, should face a court-martial. This from an editorial in the *New York Times:* One court-martial after another asks, what is war? In other words, is war a defense against war crimes?

And there is still the matter of Abu Ghraib. Three years ago, CBS's *60 Minutes* and the *New Yorker*'s Seymour Hersh exposed the abuse, sexual assault, and torture of terrorist suspects under American control at Abu Ghraib prison and elsewhere.

Then too, Rumsfeld was quick to promise a crackdown that would spare no one. But Lieutenant Colonel Steven Jordan was the only officer charged, and he was merely reprimanded. It is interesting to note that the court-martial convicted Colonel Jordan not for what happened at Abu Ghraib, but for disobeying an order to keep quiet about it.

This is not the first time or the last, I'm afraid, that disclosing a crime is deemed greater than the crime itself. Someday, Americans will look back at this decade, at Haditha and Abu Ghraib, and they'll ask, was that us?

Craig Affair Makes for Strange Bedfellows

SEPTEMBER 9, 2007

It's been said that politics make strange bedfellows. But then, bedfellows can make for strange politics.

Liane Hansen, host: NPR senior news analyst, Daniel Schorr.

Consider now the strange case of Idaho Senator Larry Craig. He got caught in an airport men's room sting operation and then announced his intention to resign on September thirtieth.

This past week, Craig hinted that he might instead try to finish his term. That now appears unlikely, but for a moment, Senate Republican leaders were sweating bullets. Their anxiety increased further when Craig retained lawyer Billy Martin to challenge his conviction for disorderly conduct. Martin's clients have included Monica Lewinsky.

Remember Monica Lewinsky? Well, Bill Clinton does. Her experience stood figuratively in the wings on Wednesday night, when the former president appeared on *Larry King Live.* Clinton said to Senator Craig, I don't like to see a person suffering from a self-inflicted wound that comes from some conflict in his other life.

As for his impeachment by the Republicans, Clinton told King, every serious student of the constitution knew that the whole thing was bogus and that they were jumping on a terrible personal mistake I made.

Mr. Clinton, meet Mr. Craig, who apparently wishes to be forgiven for one terrible mistake he made. Craig wants to clear his name in the Minnesota courts and if he doesn't, resign in the Senate ethics committee.

What the Republicans need like a hole in the head is a legal process that drags on into the campaign and casts a lurid light on Republican claims of being the family values party. The Senate investigation will proceed whether or not the GOP wants it to.

Article I of the Constitution states that the Senate may punish its members for disorderly conduct and expel a member via two-thirds majority. It doesn't say that a punishable behavior has to be in the cause of doing Senate business.

So settle down. It's going to be a long fall and, it appears, a long fall from grace.

Bill Not Hillary Was Responsible for Health Care Debacle of '90s

SEPTEMBER 19, 2007

Melissa Block, host: Democratic presidential candidate Hillary Clinton has made health care one of the top political issues this week. And NPR's senior news analyst Daniel Schorr says she's been able to set the record straight about her history with the issue.

In Iowa on Monday, unveiling her proposal for universal employer-based health insurance, Senator Clinton said she had learned the hard way how not to get such a program enacted. All these thirteen years, Mrs. Clinton has worn Hillary care as an albatross around her neck— the chair of President Clinton's task force on health insurance, responsible for the disaster, had opened the way for the insurance companies to sink their plan as too involved with government controls.

Now, it appears that the First Lady suffered a bum rap. In the current issue of a liberal magazine, *American Prospect,* Paul Starr, who was a senior policy adviser to the task force, says the basic decisions that led to the debacle were President Clinton's. According to Starr, Mrs. Clinton was not involved when her husband, campaigning for president in 1992, settled on a proposal for universal health insurance based on competing health plans and consumer choice from private health plans.

By the time the First Lady was designated as chair of the task force five days after the inauguration, the plan was pretty well set. From then on, says Starr, President Clinton maintained control of the policy-making process. Mrs. Clinton was an active force, but there never was any doubt that it was the president who was in charge. In a meeting with Starr, she referred to: my husband's plan. When an effort to include the plan in the budget failed, Mr. Clinton said, this is entirely my mistake and no one else's, conceding that, I set up the Congress for failure.

The liberal editor of *Atlantic* magazine, Jim Fallows, wrote that the plan hatched in secret was delivered too late and got bogged down. Mr. Clinton's idea was to submit an ambitious plan to Congress and then reach compromises with the Republicans. Mrs. Clinton said, every time we moved toward them, they moved away. Now, running for president, Senator Clinton lets it be known that she didn't screw up. Her husband did. And the myth of Hillary care is just that. A myth.

Recalling Reaction to Sputnik Fifty Years Later

SEPTEMBER 30, 2007

I was reporting for CBS News from Moscow when the Russians launched their Sputnik.

James Hattori, host: NPR senior news analyst Daniel Schorr.

It's hard to imagine but most people alive today had not been born when the Russians put their little vehicle into orbit and startled the world.

Things were quiet in Moscow in early October in 1957. Nikita Khrushchev and most of the Polit Bureau were on vacation. And then, at 6 a.m. on October fifth, Radio Moscow proclaimed that the first ever artificial satellite had been launched the day before, it was visible to the naked eye on a clear night, and that it was emitting a beeping signal that you could hear on a radio.

The Soviet news agency TASS stressed that Sputnik was crossing over America seven times a day. The Soviet press portrayed Sputnik as a peaceful scientific venture. But it didn't take much imagination to conjure up a Russian military satellite that could carry a lethal payload down from space.

Pravda said that Sputnik should impress upon the United States— that's the Eisenhower administration—the need for peaceful coexistence ending the cold war and stopping the arms race.

I recall being struck by how average Russians reacted. Many lined up at newspaper bulletin boards to get the latest word on the satellite. They spoke in terms of pride in their government, which was rare for Soviet citizens. Their communist government went all out to exploit its propaganda advantage over capitalist America.

Pravda proclaimed Sputnik a victory of a Soviet man with his Bolshevik boldness and clearness of purpose, determination, and energy. A confident Nikita Khrushchev told me that the Soviets were willing to put satellites and missiles under international control but only as part of a comprehensive arms control agreement.

One personal note, I had met Khrushchev at many receptions and on foreign trips. In fact, I had to interview him earlier that year for CBS's *Face the Nation*, where I circulated among his entourage on the trip to Austria. He pointed to me and said, "There is correspondent Schorr— my Sputnik!"

Tradition of Lying Politicians

OCTOBER 8, 2007

Michele Norris, host: Thanks to a recent ruling by the Washington State Supreme Court, politicians can lie about their opponents. Our senior news analyst, Daniel Schorr, isn't sure a court ruling is needed for politicians to shave the truth.

If a politician can't lie, what's left? Washington was one of more than a dozen states with laws making it illegal to say false things about a candidate for office. Last week, the Washington State Supreme Court, by a 5–4 vote, held the law unconstitutional.

Justice James Johnson wrote for the majority that the notion of the government as the final arbiter of truth was fundamentally at odds with the First Amendment. Hurray for Justice Johnson. It seems to me, and to Justice Johnson, that the First Amendment guarantee of free speech includes the freedom to lie. Veracity becomes an issue on a broader plane than political campaigning.

Many of the current political controversies have to do with a question of who's lying. The president can shield secrets through executive power. So it's sometimes hard to tell when the president is less than truthful.

President Clinton is still remembered for his impeachable lie: I did not have sexual relations with that woman. The current president finds his truth telling challenged on legislative and national security issues.

Was it accurate of President Bush to say this government does not torture people when secret memos reported by the *New York Times* seem to authorize some pretty harsh methods of interrogation? Was it accurate of him to say that Congress's SCHIP child health bill would provide federal coverage for families earning up to $83,000 a year when senators from both parties said that simply wasn't true? Or to step just outside the charmed circle of government, was it truthful of Erik Prince—the head of Blackwater Security—to testify that his mercenaries acted appropriately when the Iraqi government said they committed deliberate murder of civilians?

Very little is taken at face value anymore. Who was it who said that in times of war, truth is the first casualty?

Mukasey Torture Testimony Weak

OCTOBER 21, 2007

It was pretty smooth sailing for Michael Mukasey in his confirmation hearing except on one point—torture.

Democratic whip Dick Durbin pressed Mukasey on the issue and the nominee seemed unable to come up with a coherent answer to the question of where he stood on the issue of torture as a tool of interrogation. At one point, Mukasey said, incomprehensibly, that if it is torture as defined by the Constitution or defined by constitutional standards, it can't be authorized. Torture defined by the Constitution?

It seems to me that Mukasey's confusion reflects the tension in the administration over torture versus terror. President Bush has said this government doesn't torture people. But Mr. Bush has also said that rigorous questioning of a suspect has provided information that has helped to stop a terrorist attack.

The Bush administration seems unwilling or unable to face the issue squarely. So it makes public statements that are contradicted by secret memos. One such memo from the Justice Department in 2002 advised that torturing suspected al-Qaida members may be justified. Another said that laws and treaties that outlaw torture do not bind the president because of his constitutional authority to conduct military operations.

The solution that the Justice Department came up with was to define torture narrowly enough to permit almost any method of interrogation. A 2005 legal opinion said that such techniques as head slaps, freezing temperatures, and waterboarding—that is, simulated drowning—do not fall under the definition of torture. That permitted

White House Press Secretary Dana Perino to say that—deadpan—U.S. policy is not to torture and we do not. The Congress did not include waterboarding as a permitted tactic in a law it passed on the treatment of detainees.

Under the circumstances, one can understand Mukasey's quandary. After all, how do you speak for an administration that publicly abhors torture and secretly uses it?

Presidential Candidates Gang Up on Frontrunner

OCTOBER 31, 2007

Presidential candidates of both parties may well consider whether they benefit from televised debates.

Melissa Block, host: News analyst Daniel Schorr.

On both sides, the strategy seems to be to gang up on the frontrunner, which diminishes one candidate without necessarily enhancing the others. On the Republican side, frontrunner Rudy Giuliani has engaged in an exchange with Mitt Romney over whether President Bush would need congressional authorization to attack Iran.

On the Democratic side, Senator Hillary Clinton found herself in a no-win position in the Philadelphia debate last night, when Tim Russert raised the sensitive question of New York governor Eliot Spitzer's proposal to give driver's licenses to illegal immigrants. Sensitive, because what Governor Spitzer sees as a way to reduce traffic accidents is taken by some as coddling of illegal immigrants.

An aide to Homeland Security Secretary Michael Chertoff conveyed his concern to Spitzer. In a recent newspaper interview, Senator Clinton said that driver's licenses for illegal immigrants make a lot of sense, given the danger of accidents caused by unlicensed drivers.

Last night, Senator Chris Dodd bore in on Senator Clinton, asserting that a driver's license is a privilege, not a right, that should not be extended to illegal immigrants. Senator Clinton declined to endorse or oppose the Spitzer proposal, but driven into a corner, she said the governor is dealing with a serious problem.

Mrs. Clinton was trying to navigate between her friend, the governor of New York, and the increasingly strident anti-immigrant ranks. She left it by saying that Governor Spitzer is desperate to act where the Bush administration has failed.

What gets lost in this emotional one-upmanship is the simple fact that requiring immigrants to qualify for licenses is not a favor to them, but a public safety measure to reduce road accidents, just as admitting immigrants to hospital emergency rooms is not a favor to them, but a public health measure. But there is a determined anti-immigrant lobby that votes and Senator Clinton must look ahead past the nomination battle to the pockets of voters she must confront.

So Senator Dodd may have scored a point against the frontrunner, but it's doubtful that he did himself or the public any good.

Our Post-9/11 Fear of Foreigners Is Depressing

NOVEMBER 21, 2007

At this Thanksgiving season, the mood in Washington is heavy.

Melissa Block, host: NPR's senior news analyst Daniel Schorr.

The business of running the government has become increasingly combative with threats of vetoes, veto overrides, and filibusters. The nation's presidential campaign concentrates increasingly on searching for chinks in the opponent's armor. Six years since 9/11, the nation runs scared, with yellow and orange homeland security alerts and stepped up surveillance.

The millions going home for the holidays face longer lines at the airport and more expensive gasoline on the road. One can no longer say that getting there is half the fun. But for me, the most depressing aspect of our national life on this Thanksgiving is our post 9/11 fear of foreigners.

Entering the United States has become such a nightmare that tourist trips to this country have declined 17 percent, with a loss of $94 billion in tourist revenues. And that's not all that's been lost. The lesson of Thanksgiving that I learned in grade school was tolerance, tolerance toward strangers.

If the pilgrims landed on America's shore today without valid visas, I wonder if they would be arrested and deported as illegal aliens. Not very funny perhaps. But then I read about how some aliens are treated. A German woman overstays her visa by a couple of days and applies for an extension so she can spend more time with her fiancée, a Dartmouth College athletic coach. She is arrested and for a time faces deportation. Or a case from the front page of the *New York Times:* Immigration agents raid a home in Toledo, Ohio, find an undocumented Honduran woman breastfeeding her baby. She is arrested for deportation. The child, a native-born American, is turned over to social services. America, America, God shed his grace on thee and crown thy good with brotherhood.

What's in a Nickname?

DECEMBER 9, 2007

What's with this Jimmy Carter, Bill Clinton, and Dick Cheney business?

Liane Hansen, host: NPR's senior news analyst Daniel Schorr.

I mean, when did public figures start referring to themselves by nicknames?

It's well known that President Bush has a penchant for nicknames like Boy Genius for Karl Rove and Fredo for Alberto Gonzales. And who can forget former FEMA director Michael "Brownie" Brown?

Time magazine reported that the president went into Moscow for a summit, referred to Russia's president Vladimir Putin as Pootie Poot—whether to his face is not clear. Senator Dole is officially Elizabeth. Yet her husband refers to her in public as Liddy.

But that's not what bothers me. It's the growing practice of referring to oneself by a nickname, as though that would endear one to the masses as a regular fellow. You go down the U.S. Senate's official roster and it's amazing how many have listed their nicknames as their official names.

It is Chuck Schumer, Chuck Grassley, and Chuck Hagel. It is Norm Coleman and Larry Craig, although it's still Joseph Biden and Joseph

Lieberman. It's Mel Martinez and Ted Stevens. Senator Kennedy is known to his admirers as Ted, but he's officially listed as Edward.

And then there is Newt Gingrich. I had a look after I discovered that the name his parents gave him was Newton. There is Lewis "Scooter" Libby who worked for Dick Cheney, oops, I mean, Richard Cheney.

You may wonder why I make such a point to this. It undoubtedly has to do with my age and memories of a time when we expected public affairs to be conducted with a certain degree of dignity. Eisenhower was universally known as Ike, but as far as I know, he never called himself Ike.

And so here is my request. All you Chucks, Bobs, and Eddies, on your letterhead and when you're invited to speak, please make it Charles, Robert, and Edward.

Bush Administration and Raison d'être in the Post-9/11 Era

DECEMBER 10, 2007

The English gave us the ancient principle of habeas corpus (loosely translated, show us the body). A Roman constitution gave us the ban on unreasonable searches and seizures.

Michelle Norris, host: NPR's senior news analyst, Daniel Schorr.

The French gave us raison d'être in the state's or the national interest. In the wake of 9/11, the Bush administration cited the national interest in combating terrorism to justify restraints on civil liberties. The judiciary, up to the Supreme Court, has been wrestling with the detention of so-called terrorism suspects without trial, without even formal accusation. When challenged, the administration has asserted the right to harsh interrogation in the interest of averting planned attacks.

That has given us the Guantánamo Bay controversy, and now, the stunning revelation of the destruction of hundreds of hours of videotaped CIA interrogations, presumably involving torture. There will be investigations. But Jose Rodriguez, the former head of CIA Clandestine Services, reportedly told colleagues he thinks he acted lawfully and had the authority to destroy the tapes.

Raison d'être, you might say. You might also call a raison d'être when national intelligence director Mike McConnell writes in the *New York*

Times under the catchy headline, "Help Me Spy on al-Qaida," that the so-called Protect America Act should be renewed by Congress. That's the law that permits massive monitoring of communications.

McConnell says the intelligence community should spend its time protecting the nation, not protecting the liberties of foreign terrorists. That's raison d'être in the post-9/11 era.

Candidates Run for President or Church Deacon?

DECEMBER 23, 2007

With the television show writers on strike and the season of candidate debates over for now, it's hard to know where to turn for stimulation. Actually, that's a joke.

Liane Hansen, host: NPR's senior news analyst Daniel Schorr.

The truth is that I was getting not to like the debates which tended to become not so much debates as taking potshots at rivals without elevating the discussion very much. There was also this not very subtle business of who had the better religion—Mormon or Evangelical. And because a campaign has elements of a spectator sport, they developed a tendency to manipulate visual symbols.

I speak here specifically of ordained Baptist Minister Mike Huckabee who started his upward climb in the polls with a television ad displaying the words "Christian leader." Later, he appeared on camera with what looked like a big white cross behind him.

There's nothing subtle or subliminal about it, the former Arkansas governor told people in a shopping mall. Then there was a picture also, not very subliminal, of Huckabee standing in front of a Christmas tree and saying, God doesn't just love the land of Iowa. He loves the people of Iowa.

Mitt Romney, the Mormon ex-governor of Massachusetts, also makes some claims to intimacy with the divine. I believe, he said in a much anticipated speech, I believe that Jesus Christ is a son of God and a savior of mankind.

After a while, you begin to wonder whether they are running for president or for church deacon. Sometimes, it gets even a little bit nasty.

Huckabee was quoted in the *New York Times Magazine* as saying: Don't Mormons believe that Jesus and the devil are brothers? A little below the belt—the Bible belt, you might say. At that point, you might expect someone to issue a fatwa. Huckabee apologized for the remark, which had, by now, served its purpose.

And in a crowded Christmas party in Iowa, when Huckabee was greeted by someone who said his wife was a lifelong Democrat, he replied: We'll pray for her.

Well, be of good cheer. I can't wait for the TV writers' strike to end.

President George W. Bush's Legacy

DECEMBER 30, 2007

Liane Hansen, host: This is Weekend Edition *from NPR News. I'm Liane Hansen.*

Daniel Schorr: When a president enters his last year in office, he may begin to think of his legacy and change some longstanding position.

Hansen: NPR's senior news analyst Daniel Schorr.

Schorr: The soldier-president Dwight Eisenhower left office with a blast against what he called the military industrial complex.

Lyndon Johnson, announcing he would not run again, spent some of his last months in office trying to find a way out of the Vietnam War.

Cold warrior Ronald Reagan, encouraged by his wife, abandoned his evil empire rhetoric and clasped hands with Mikhail Gorbachev at one point, proposing that both sides scrap their nuclear weapons.

So now, President Bush embarks on his last year in office, and the question arises: What may he change as he contemplates his place in history? We know he's planning a lot of foreign travel, starting on January eighth with an eight-day trip to Israel, the West Bank, Egypt, Saudi Arabia, and the Gulf Emirates.

He will presumably try to breathe some life into the faltering post-Annapolis effort for an Arab-Israeli peace agreement. If he fails, he can at least claim credit for trying.

Brokering a peace treaty would make a handsome legacy trophy for any president. But not since President Carter and the Camp David treaty between Israel and Egypt has any president actually succeeded in bridging the gap between two warring parties.

For the rest, I cannot sense any policy changes in the wind. On the Iraq war, President Bush seems to live in a bubble of isolation that divides the world into patriots and nonbelievers. He seems at peace with himself on this less and compassionate, deficit-induced restraints on social spending.

On a variety of issues, from waterboarding to stem cell research, he shows no sign of any big shift.

Perhaps, we won't know what's happening until it suddenly happens. But it will be interesting to see what Mr. Bush will do as the word legacy looms over him.

2008

Presidential Candidates and Lying Politicians

Fact-Checking the Politics of Truth and Celebrity

JANUARY 2, 2008

Melissa Block, host: Whether overseas or in this country, politicians have a reputation for bending the truth every now and then. NPR senior news analyst Daniel Schorr has witnessed his share of it. He and others are not impressed.

Princeton professor Sean Wilentz calls it the delusional style in politics and in media. And he calls an unnamed senior White House official as predicting the downfall of reality-based politics.

The new reality, Wilentz says in a *New Republic* article, is the reality of touchy-feely politics in the media, relying heavily on the regard for character and instinct and sometimes taking liberties with the literal truth. Still, vividly remembered in pundit circles is Senator Joseph Biden. In 1987, Biden cribbed from a speech by British labor leader, Neil Kinnock, saying he was the first in his family to go to college. He later called a news conference to acknowledge his mistake.

More recently, there have been several lapses from the truth in this bitterly fought primary campaign. Rudy Giuliani relies heavily on rapid-fire statistics that often turn out to be wrong, like his claim that New York is the only city that reduced crime rate every year since 1994, when he became mayor.

Mitt Romney said incorrectly that he saw his father march with Martin Luther King, Jr. Barack Obama said incorrectly that there are more young black males in prison than in college.

Newspapers have noted that Obama's autobiography, *Dreams from My Father,* includes some events that never happened.

Mike Huckabee tried to link the crises in Pakistan to the issue of illegal immigration in the United States with the assertion that we have more illegal Pakistani immigrants coming across our borders than all other nationalities, except those immediately south of the border. Wrong. And Senator Hillary Rodham Clinton criticized the Bush administration for cutting funds for the National Institutes of Health. In fact, funding has increased under Mr. Bush.

The Annenberg School at the University of Pennsylvania and various other such organizations have established a full-time political fact-checker to check candidates' misstatements. Does it matter when fast-talking candidates talk questionable facts to burnish their images? As Professor Wilentz suggests, it may be that truth has been overwhelmed by celebrity worship.

The Rise of Barack Obama

JANUARY 7, 2008

Not everybody was surprised by the emergence of a Barack Obama coalition of the young and the independent rallying around the magical word "change."

Robert Siegel, host: NPR senior news analyst, Daniel Schorr.

As long ago as last February, a Harvard sociologist, William Julius Wilson, wrote in the student newspaper, *The Crimson*, that Democrats and some Republicans would respond to Obama's political message that he had the great potential to unify this divided nation. Obama doesn't have a lock on the word change; "it's time for a change" is a staple of political campaigns.

And Senator Hillary Clinton has responded to Obama by citing her thirty-five years of fighting for change. But that was still looking backward. The 70 percent of Americans who tell pollsters that America's on the wrong track seem to be demanding a break with the corrupt and partisan past and a new set of names, faces, and ideas.

It may or may not be relevant that Senator Obama, at forty-six, is the youngest of the candidates on both sides. It's commonplace to say that

Iowa is oddball and atypical. It tells you nothing about what will happen in subsequent contests, starting with New Hampshire. But if that was ever true, it is no longer true. The networks, which have been giving unprecedented time to this political spectator sport, have helped to nationalize these state-by-state primaries.

And there seems to be no doubt about a spillover effect from Iowa in New Hampshire and beyond. Obama is probably justified in saying, as he did in his Iowa victory speech, that this is a defining moment in history. He's reaching for the high ground with a unifying theme of moving on from the bitterness and pettiness and anger that have consumed Washington. This campaign, as few would have foreseen, may be turning into a transforming event.

Bill Clinton's Campaigning for Wife May Boomerang

JANUARY 23, 2008

Michele Norris, host: NPR senior news analyst Daniel Schorr is following the Democratic presidential contest closely. And he has these thoughts on the most famous spouse on the campaign trail.

In a moment of introspection on the campaign trail in South Carolina, Bill Clinton said, "Think what being president is like. They play a song every time you walk into the room. After I left the White House, nobody played a song anymore. I didn't know where I was."

Clinton may not understand where he is these days as his campaign support of his wife adopts an increasingly striking tone. The man who was once described by Toni Morrison as "America's first black president" wages a personal war for the defeat of the candidate who would indeed be the first black president.

Clinton says that he's not standing in the way of Barack Obama's becoming the first black president—just not this year. I think Hillary would be a better president at this point in history, he says. But Bill Clinton's sharp criticism of Senator Obama with phrases like "fairy tale" and "rolling the dice on the presidency" may have alarmed some in the Democratic camp. They fear it may boomerang against Senator Clinton in the crucial primary next Saturday in South Carolina with its large African American Democratic electorate.

Former Senate majority leader Tom Daschle says that Bill Clinton's conduct is not in keeping with the image of a former president. I think it destroys the party, Daschle said. And indeed, the tone of Bill Clinton's stump speeches does not seem to be in keeping with the ex-president who has written a book on giving and has joined high-minded bipartisan ventures with former President George Bush.

Many think that Clinton's current position as his wife's attack dog is a departure from his image as a philosopher philanthropist. He has provided an opening for Obama to say—as he did on ABC on Monday—that the ex-president has taken his advocacy on behalf of his wife to a level that I think is pretty troubling.

Bill Clinton has become more than a surrogate for his wife. Asked about the prospects for his wife in South Carolina, he said, this is a state I won in 1992. And I like it here and love being here. Some people are asking what's gotten into Bill. Whether Clinton yearns for the sound of "Hail to the Chief," well, that's something it'll take more than a journalist to analyze.

Latest Political Buzzword Is "Post-Racial"

JANUARY 28, 2008

Robert Siegel, host: Senator Barack Obama received several high-profile endorsements today including one from a Nobel Laureate, writer Toni Morrison. It was Morrison who famously dubbed Bill Clinton America's first black president.

In a letter to Obama, she wrote this: In addition to keen intelligence, integrity, and a rare authenticity, you exhibit something that has nothing to do with age, experience, race, or gender. And something I don't see in other candidates. That something is a creative imagination, which coupled with brilliance equals wisdom.

Well, senior news analyst Daniel Schorr agrees with Morrison in part. He says Senator Obama's appeal seems to transcend race.

Welcome to the latest buzzword in the political lexicon: "post-racial." It is what Senator Barack Obama signals in his victory speech in South Carolina when he tells of the woman who used to work for segregationist Strom Thurmond and now knocks on doors for the Obama campaign.

It is what makes Bill Clinton seemed disconnected when he compares

Obama's campaign to the campaigns of Jesse Jackson in 1984 and '88. The post-racial era, as embodied by Obama, is the era where civil rights veterans of the past century are consigned to history and Americans begin to make race-free judgments on who should lead them.

Post-racial began to come into vogue after Obama won the Iowa caucuses and fared well in the New Hampshire primary.

The *Economist* called it a post-racial triumph and wrote that Obama seemed to embody the hope that America could transcend its divisions. The *New Yorker* wrote of a post-racial generation and indeed, the battle-scarred veterans of the civil rights conflict of forty years ago seemed less enchanted with Obama than those who were not yet alive then. Ambassador Andrew Young, a one-time aide to Martin Luther King, Jr., argued that former president Bill Clinton was every bit as black as Senator Obama.

The nation may have a way to go yet to reach color blindness. Exit poll data in South Carolina indicates that Senator Obama won 78 percent of the black vote, but only 24 percent of the white vote. But perhaps equally significant, Obama won 67 percent of voters in the 18–29 age group. The post-Selma generation, you might say.

The wish for a post-racial politics is a powerful force and it rewards those who seem to carry its promise, says Peter Boyer in the *New Yorker*. It may still be too early to speak of a generation of color-blind voters, but maybe color blurred?

Another Journalist Subpoenaed to Reveal Sources (DP)

FEBRUARY 5, 2008

Melissa Block, host: The cases of CIA worker Valerie Plame Wilson, nuclear scientist Jeng-Hung Lee, and the Balco steroids scandal have one thing in common: reporters who refuse to give up their confidential sources.

This week, news analyst Daniel Schorr says, you can add another case to that list.

Two years ago, Pulitzer Prize–winning *New York Times* reporter James Risen wrote a devastating book about the CIA and the Bush administration. It was called *State of War.* The most devastating of all, a chapter about the CIA and Iran titled "A Rogue Operation."

In stunning detail, he reported the story of how a CIA officer had sent a high-tech message to the wrong agent in Iran with the result that a double agent was able to identify every spy the CIA had in Iran. The CIA had to advise the White House that it had no idea whether Iran was on the way to becoming a nuclear power.

The book told also of Operation Merlin, a failed attempt to send Iran down the wrong path by having a defector deliver the wrong design for a nuclear weapon. And then, an aborted plan to detonate a device that would knock out the power grid of Iran's nuclear complex.

One can imagine that the CIA was enraged at this enormous leak. There was a referral to the Justice Department which has been investigating for two years, apparently without result. And so finally in frustration, the effort to make the reporter tell who it was that exposed the agency's colossal failure.

And so James Risen has been subpoenaed to appear before a grand jury in Alexandria, Virginia, on this Thursday. Risen's lawyer David Kelly says that Risen is going to stand by his commitment of confidentiality to his sources.

Whether he will refuse to appear or will appear and refuse to testify about his sources is not clear. But it begins to look like one more in the increasing number of cases of officials using a threat of a contempt citation to force reporters to divulge their sources.

Another *Times* reporter, Judith Miller, spent eighty-five days in jail in 2005 until she said her source agreed to waive confidentiality.

Some thirty years ago, a congressional committee threatened me with a citation for contempt which, happily, was not pursued. So I cannot pretend to be neutral on this issue. But let me simply express my conviction. That when a reporter cannot protect his or her sources, then investigative reporting dries up and the public is the first casualty.

Will you rather not know about the catastrophic failures of our spymasters?

Imagining a Letter from McCain to Bush

FEBRUARY 13, 2008

Melissa Block, host: This week, President Bush had some favorable words for John McCain.

President George W. Bush: I know his convictions. I know the principles that drive him. And no doubt in my mind, he's a true conservative.

Block: The president made those comments on Fox News. It's not an endorsement, the president said, but it was enough to spur the imagination of NPR senior news analyst Daniel Schorr.

A letter that Senator McCain might have—I repeat, might have—sent to President Bush.

Dear Mr. President,

That was quite a surprise. Your praise of me as a true conservative in your interview with Chris Wallace on Fox News. It was especially surprising after you said you would take no position on the candidates in the presidential race.

You know, I had to smile. It took me back eight years to another primary fight, when we were saying some unfriendly things about each other. Remember how I denounced you for spreading a negative message of fear and running on an empty slogan of reform? When your campaign people were circulating rumors that I was a liar and a fraud? When I was condemning your Christian right supporters as agents of intolerance?

A lot of water has passed under the bridge since then, and here you are now praising my sound and solid conservative principles. But at the same time saying that I have some convincing to do of other conservatives.

This was all a nice gesture on your part, and don't think I don't appreciate it. So don't misunderstand me when I ask you to return to your previous position of staying out of the primary fight. It's not that I'm not grateful for your kind words about me, but my campaign advisers have been telling me that being linked to you might not necessarily help me with some groups. As you yourself told Chris Wallace, some animosity is probably directed against you.

To put it bluntly, Mr. President, a lot of people right of you and left of you don't think well of you. And so, your praise might be counter-productive. Negative coattails, you might say. I consider you a good friend. I hardly ever think anymore of the things that got me so mad at you eight years ago in South Carolina, when you deployed the Christian Coalition against me.

I hope to see you at my inauguration on January twentieth. But for now, could I ask you to cool it on publicly supporting me? Yours, John.

And to repeat, this is a totally imaginary letter.

Campaigns Need to Clean Up Their Language

MARCH 9, 2008

Liane Hansen, host: As for election news in this country, Barack Obama won the Wyoming Democratic caucuses yesterday, beating Hillary Clinton by a wide margin. In another closely watched election in the Chicago suburbs, former GOP House speaker Dennis Hastert's Congressional seat was won by a Democrat.

Bill Foster captured 53 percent of the votes against GOP opponent Jim Oberweis in a district that has long been held by Republicans. Democrats say it's a sign of things to come on the national scene, while Republicans say they're not worried.

And NPR's senior news analyst Daniel Schorr says now is the time for the candidates and the media to concentrate on the linguistics of their politics.

Call it fuddy-duddy if you like, but indulge me in a few pet peeves about language usage by politicians, and yes, the media. This, with a bow to my friend Bill Safire, the reigning usage maven.

First, about the recent squabble between the Obama and Clinton camps over the ad showing a hypothetical 3:00 a.m. phone call to the White House. Who do you want answering the phone, they say. Whatever the crisis, I would like them to say, *whom* do you want answering the phone? Grammar 101. You know, Ernest Hemingway did not write *For Who the Bell Tolls.*

Then the word "nation." The media reports that President Bush has landed in the nation of Liberia. No, he has landed not in a nation, which is a social concept, but in a country, which is a geographical concept. The nation may also have organized itself into a state. But you land in a country, not in a nation.

Then a phrase, which is on its way to becoming a cliché: "up for grabs." In its original meaning, "up for grabs" was meant to denote some disorganized situation in which there was just no way of telling who might end up with a majority of votes or supporters, whatever.

But "up for grabs" has evolved into a catchall phrase for "in contention." So now it's customary to hear that so many convention delegates are "up for grabs" in the primary contest. They are not up for grabs. It is known who the contenders are. There may be so many delegates at stake, but they are not up for grabs.

One last word: the commonly used protest of some action. Wrong. To protest is to proclaim or announce, as methinks thou dost protest too much. What you mean is to protest against.

I'm not sure how many people care about language usage in the political arena. But I would like to see a little elegance in the words of the politicians and the media.

Politicians and Infidelity: Why They Do It

MARCH 13, 2008

Melissa Block, host: As David Paterson prepares to take over, the scandal of Governor Spitzer's involvement in the prostitution ring is still dominating public attention. Pictures of the call girl that Spitzer allegedly met at Washington's Mayflower Hotel were splashed across many front pages today. She had previously been known as Kristen. Now she's identified as a twenty-two-year-old singer with a MySpace page, Ashley Alexandra Dupre. Her mother told the New York Times *she obviously got involved in something much larger than her.*

NPR's senior news analyst Daniel Schorr has seen quite a few scandals like this one come along and he has been thinking less about how it all happened than why.

Why do they do it? The question hangs in the air after Governor Eliot Spitzer's latest contribution through the annals of indiscretion in high places. If there is anything that runs through these sex scandals involving Nelson Rockefeller, Gary Hart, President Bill Clinton, and now Governor Spitzer, it is the risks that they took of being exposed.

John Kennedy's mistress, Judith Campbell Exner, said that Kennedy would meet her in public places unworried about being exposed. She said he thought he was above it all and that arrogance typified him. Students of behavior have tried to understand what drives celebrities to go beyond (unintelligible) lusting in his heart.

Judith Viorst is the author of a book titled *Imperfect Control*. After the Clinton scandal, she wrote of the illusion of invulnerability that possesses one who is surrounded by Secret Service, spin doctors, and advancement—the belief is they can't lay a glove on me.

Social psychology professor Martin Monto of the University of Portland said on this program that putting on a public face—being President Clinton or a Governor Spitzer—requires a great deal of effort, and illicit sex may represent an escape from having to be on all the time.

Dina Matos McGreevey, who is in the process of divorcing the disgraced former governor of New Jersey, writes in the *New York Times* that powerful men are motivated by arrogance and the search for a thrill, and they seem blindly unaware of the lives they will destroy.

So there is the phenomenon of the stand-by-your-man wife appearing ashen faced with her two-timing husband as he confesses on camera. In these scenes which have become all too commonplace, there is the contrite official and the loyal wife—what we don't see are the shattered children.

My Lai Anniversary at Time to Reconsider Iraq

MARCH 16, 2008

Forty years ago today, an atrocious event changed the course of the Vietnam War. The My Lai Massacre shocked Americans and marked a turning point in how the public perceived the conflict.

NPR's senior analyst Daniel Schorr wonders about the similarities between My Lai and Iraq.

It's a melancholy anniversary. Anybody out there remember March 16, 1968? A bad year anyway, with the assassination of Martin Luther King, Jr., and Robert Kennedy, and on that day, the men of Charlie Company,

Eleventh Brigade, Americal Division, was sent out on a search-and-destroy mission to an area where Vietcong were believed to be dug in. They attacked the village and killed some five hundred inhabitants, some of them children, all of them unarmed.

My friend Seymour Hersh won a Pulitzer Prize for exposing the massacre that officers tried to cover up. Lieutenant William Calley, who helped to round up villagers and shoot them, testified at his court-martial that he acted under orders from above. He was sentenced to life in prison, was released in 1974, and went into the insurance business.

Just think, My Lai was forty years ago, and the Marines fighting in Haditha in Iraq weren't even born yet. I wonder whether Lieutenant Calley would regard Haditha as today's My Lai. Three years ago in Haditha, after a Marine was killed by a roadside bomb, Marines stormed into the nearby houses and killed twenty-four civilians.

As with My Lai, the military command didn't disclose the massacre; it was exposed by *Time* magazine. Eight Marines were charged with murder, but those charges were later dropped. Four still face trial on lesser charges.

I asked Seymour Hersh what Haditha had in common with My Lai. He said that both are examples of what can happen when American soldiers are surrounded by a culture they don't understand. They come to see everything and everyone around them as threatening.

Lessons from the Great Depression

MARCH 23, 2008

This commentary will undoubtedly stamp me as an unreconstructed liberal, but here goes.

Liane Hansen, host: NPR's senior news analyst Daniel Schorr.

I am old enough to remember vividly the stock market crash of 1929 followed by the Great Depression. I remember the suicides on Wall Street, and I remember men on street corners selling apples for a nickel each, if memory serves.

Out of that crisis came one word: regulation. To restore confidence in the banks, the federal government would set up a system to insure them against going bust, but in return, the banks would have to operate under a federal regulatory system to keep them from taking undue risks.

Regulation is a term that true-blue conservatives abhor, yet it is needed more than ever in this complex world. A crane topples over in Manhattan and it turns out there was not adequate inspection. And Southwest Airlines is found to have flown dozens of older planes without adequate FAA inspection.

With the credit crisis of today, we don't see runs on banks such as we saw in 1930 and '31. Instead, what we see are unregulated investment banks like Bear Stearns that dabbled in the mortgage market and set off a chain reaction.

Franklin Delano Roosevelt responded to the credit crisis of his time by closing the banks temporarily and calling on Congress to set up a regulatory system. It is not likely that this regulation-averse Bush administration will seek supervision of financial markets.

As the Sherman Antitrust Act shows, the key to a free market is necessary regulation. After all, we don't want to see the return of apple peddlers on street corners or songs like "Brother, Can You Spare a Dime?"

Tibet Crisis Impacts China's Olympics

MARCH 30, 2008

Liane Hansen, host: As China gets ready to receive the Olympic torch in Beijing tomorrow, there was more unrest in Tibet as police apparently tried to carry out security checks. In Nepal, Tibetan exiles and monks attempted to storm the Chinese embassy and were stopped by police.

China's human rights record remains under scrutiny as the country prepares to host the summer's Olympics. NPR's senior news analyst Daniel Schorr recalls the controversies surrounding previous Olympic games.

The Olympic truce it's called. Two warring kings in the area of Greece called Olympia agreed to suspend fighting that would interfere with athletes and pilgrims traveling to the games. But in modern times the Olympic truce has been honored in the breach.

I remember 1936 when Chancellor Adolf Hitler left the Olympic stadium in Berlin to avoid having to honor a very non-Aryan black

American Jesse Owens who had won four gold medals that year. Some may remember 1968 when the games were held in Mexico City despite a campus riot in which many students were killed, and two African American competitors flashed a black power salute through the national anthem to protest against racism in America.

Many may remember 1972 in Munich when Arab commandos killed two Israeli athletes. Then there was 1980 when President Jimmy Carter declared a boycott of the Moscow Olympics to protest against the Soviet invasion of Afghanistan. So next August, Beijing. What will China's violent crackdown on Tibetans and Chinese dissidents bring?

We may get a taste of that on April 9 when the Olympic torch, winding its way from Greece to Beijing, arrives in San Francisco. That is likely to become an occasion for anti-Chinese demonstrations. But not many governments are willing to incur the wrath of the Chinese economic powerhouse.

President Bush has confirmed that he'll be in Beijing for the games. He said he's going for sports, not politics. French President Nicolas Sarkozy talks of maybe boycotting the opening ceremonies. But Foreign Minister Bernard Kouchner has made it clear that France is not looking for trouble with the economic giant that China has become.

As the Chinese continue sweeping up dissidents in preparation for the August games, these timorous governments may come under pressure from their people to voice some protests. It looks as though the day of the Olympic truce, when fighting was put on hold for athletes and spectators alike, that's over.

NATO's Mission, Sense of Unity Is Flagging

APRIL 1, 2008

Robert Siegel, host: NATO is fifty-nine years old this week. And NPR news analyst Daniel Schorr is taking the occasion of this NATO meeting to size up how the organization has evolved. He says the issue of which new members to accept is not the only source of discord within NATO.

Old alliances, like old soldiers, never die. They just fade away. And in the case of NATO, The North Atlantic Treaty Organization, they may even expand as they fade.

372 · COME TO THINK OF IT

In 1949, twelve nations—the United States, Canada, and Western Europe—united under the American nuclear umbrella. Its mission was simple: Deter a Stalin Soviet Union from aggression.

Nearing its sixtieth birthday, NATO meets in Bucharest Romania— once a communist enemy—and has expanded to twenty-six countries, several of them former Soviet Republics. And two more from Soviet Republics, Ukraine and Georgia, are knocking at the door seeking admission.

But NATO no longer snaps to attention when the United States whistles. Its members are mostly critical of the war in Iraq, and members, like Germany, have resisted sending more troops to Afghanistan. Defense Secretary Robert Gates says that NATO risks becoming a two-tier alliance: those willing to share the load and the free riders.

All three candidates in the U.S. election have called for larger contributions from other NATO countries. Senator Barack Obama has promised to rally our NATO allies for our common defense. Senator Hillary Clinton has said that Europe and the United States must work together. And Senator John McCain says that our commitment to Afghanistan must include increasing NATO forces.

It's been a long time, fifty-nine years, since twelve governments signed a treaty to create a fighting force. Its mission was described to me as keeping the Americans in, keeping the Russians out, and keeping the Germans down.

In those days, our allies would standardize their weapons to be better able to operate with the United States. That is no longer true. NATO was one of the more successful alliances once when its member perceived a common enemy. Today with America, unpopular in many of the NATO countries, NATO goes on expanding its membership, but no longer has a clear mission or a sense of unity.

August 31, 2006

Ninety Years in a Newsworthy Life

Robert Siegel, host: We do not typically observe the birthdays of our colleagues on All Things Considered. *But there are birthdays and then there are birthdays. When someone works at his trade every week at age seventy-five or eighty, we say that's admirable. When he does it at the age of ninety, we say that's our senior news analyst, Daniel Schorr.*

Dan Schorr was born in New York City on August 31, 1916.

Schorr: I was the son of immigrants who had come from Belarus somewhere about 1913 to 1914. My father died when I was five years old. Also, I was a very fat kid and I have no doubt that the insecurity that I felt then had a very important effect on my journalistic career later, because I used to be so intent on getting the story. I had to have the story. I had to have it in the paper when I was working for a paper. I had to have it for television when I was working for television.

I was aware that a lot of people thought I was a little impolite in the way I constantly strove to get the scoop, the story. Even if I was fat, they couldn't ignore me because I had a big story.

Siegel: Today Dan turns ninety. Over the past few weeks we've sat down together and recorded interviews about his career in postwar Holland, in Khrushchev's Moscow, in divided Germany, and in Richard Nixon's Washington.

I've heard Dan Schorr's stories many times, and I confess my favorites are the oldest ones. Here is the story of Daniel Schorr's first scoop. He was twelve.

Schorr: It was in the Bronx. Ground-floor apartment. I heard a big plop outside the window, put my head out the window, and there was a man lying dead on the ground. And I stood there, waited for the police to come, tried to find out from them what they were finding out, and then eventually I called our local newspaper, the *Bronx Home News,* which offered $5 for original news stories.

I dictated an original news story about a suicide and earned my first $5 in journalism. I often think back to that and say why did I stand there taking notes on what he wore and waiting for the cops? It was the first time I'd ever seen a dead person in my life. Why didn't I react more emotionally to that? It was the essential journalist who manages to absent himself from the situation and simply report it without feeling it.

Siegel: And then there's the story of how Dan Schorr became a news reporter instead of a music critic. He loves music and in the 1930s at the City College of New York he had written about the composer Ernest Bloch. His article drew the attention of Olin Downes, renowned music critic of the *New York Times,* who invited the young music writer to come brief him. Dan went to the Times Building to meet the great critic.

Schorr: And in the subway on the way down there, I was reading the *Times* and there was a review by the famous Olin Downes of a concert the previous night. The New York Philharmonic had played. The soloist was Joseph Szigeti. And I read the review and it said at one point, Szigeti's tone was as usual impeccable but the profile of the tone left something to be desired. And I said, "What the hell does that mean?"

[*Laughter from Robert Siegel*]

I mean, this guy has a level of music that I'll never reach. And so I got there, we talked about Ernest Bloch, and when we finished, I said, "Mr. Downes, could I ask you a question?" "Sure, my boy, anything." "In this review here, where you talk about Szigeti and you say that you liked his tone but you didn't like the profile of the tone, what does that mean?" He put his hand on my shoulder and said, "Boy, don't let that kind of thing worry you. That's bull—— that you write when you're on deadline."

[*Laughter from Robert Siegel*]

I decided that music criticism was not a respectable career.

[*music*]

Siegel: And for more than twenty years Dan has been writing for us, analyzing world events, drawing on a wealth of experience, asking good questions, and leaving out that ingredient that you write when you're on deadline.

On this, his ninetieth, we'd like to wish a happy birthday to our colleague, Daniel Schorr.

Index of Essays

Index

Abbas, Mahmoud, 315
ABC, vii, 101, 109, 137, 150, 232, 233, 258, 273, 335
Abdel-Rahman, Omar, 43, 44, 46
ABM treaty, 190, 215
abortion, 18, 219, 237–38
  Blackmun decision, 68, 125
  opponents, 32, 197, 292, 316
  privacy right, 336
  restrictions, 125
  RU486, 125–26
Abouhalima, Mahmoud, 43, 46
Abramoff, Jack, 314, 322, 323, 326, 327, 345
Abrams, Floyd, 159
ABSCAM scandal, 322
Abu Ghraib prison, 284, 285, 297, 318, 346
  photographs of, 331
Adams, John Quincy, 201
adoption tax credits, 115–16
adultery. See sex scandals
affirmative action, 262–63
Afghanistan, 24, 38, 43, 45–46, 179, 216, 239–40, 305, 372
  bin Laden hideout, 169
  CIA involvement, 145
  peace status, 15–16, 194, 209, 226, 248
  as terrorist center, 46–47, 221, 287
  U.S. liberation, 224, 241, 280
  U.S. missile attack, 171
  See also Taliban
Africa
  AIDS, 194
  conflicts, 82, 104, 156, 176, 194, 248
  starvation, 320
  See also specific countries
African Americans. See race
African National Congress, 97
Agnew, Spiro, 26, 339
Aidid, Mohamed, 51, 75
AIDS, 194
Al Aqsa Martyrs, 233
Alaska bridge to nowhere, 317
Albanians (ethnic), 24, 194

Albright, Madeleine, 144–45, 152–53, 155, 156, 163, 164, 189
Algeria, 17, 176
aliens (outer-space), 143–44
Al-Jazeera network, 253
Allen, George, 334
Allende, Salvador, 173
Alpirez, Julio Alberto, 118
al-Qaeda. See Qaeda, al
Al Saadi, Amir, 247
Alter, Jonathan, 223
Altman, Roger, 72
American Prospect, 348
Ames, Aldrich, 76, 127, 145
Amnesty International, 308
Amr, Nabil, 287–88
Andersen, Kurt, 142
Angleton, James Jesus, 134–35
Angola, 45, 46, 82, 104, 176, 194
Annan, Kofi, 176, 192, 210, 233, 255, 277
Annenberg School, 360
Ansberry, Clare, 88–89
anthrax, 247
Anti-Ballistic Missile Treaty, 190, 215
anti-Semitism, 28
apartheid, 16, 61
Arab League, 233–34
Arafat, Yasser, 6, 50–51, 68, 69, 81, 228, 287, 288, 324
  on suicide bombers, 233, 294
Argentina, 43, 215
Aristide, Jean-Bertrand, 51, 53, 75, 81–82, 104
Armey, Dick, 219
Armstrong, Katherine, 325
Armstrong, Neil, 168
Ashcroft, John, 213, 215, 237, 240, 246, 285, 297
Aspin, Les, 40, 62–63, 76
astronauts, 168
Atlanta, 21, 123, 136, 150
Atlantic, 348
Atta, Mohamed, 238, 239, 241, 251
Auschwitz, 300